Ducks and Men

by W.G. Leitch

YEARS OF CO-OPERATION IN CONSERVATION

Ducks Unlimited (Canada)

Not long ago the writer was interviewed by a young lady obviously of completely urban background who struggled desperately to rationalize the concept of Ducks Unlimited. Her question "Really, who needs all these ducks?" revealed her dilemma.

Any wildfowler who has heard the whisper of mallard wings over the stubble before light, or watched the last of the bluebills speed across a freezing marsh, climbing swiftly and surely southward against the red and yellow of a clear, cold, late November sunset, would not ask the question. The answer would lie deep and strong in his very soul.

But it is unlikely he would be able to express himself as eloquently as Frederik Peterson:

Dark flying rune against the western glow —
It tells the sweep and loneliness of things.
Symbol of Autumns vanished long ago.
Symbol of coming Springs!

One feels a deep sorrow for those who do not know.

Photo by B. N. Virbiwski

DEDICATION

Dedicated to the wildfowlers of North America who have demonstrated through Ducks Unlimited their sincere concern for the resource they cherish, and to the Kee-Men, landowners, and governments without whose co-operation that concern could never have been translated into action.

ACKNOWLEDGEMENTS

Many people contributed to this history, by interview, letter, and word of mouth. The writer was fortunate to be able to tape interviews with Arthur Bartley, Tom Main (since deceased), Ed Russenholt, George Fanset, Lloyd Bunting, and Rennie Harley — all important personalities in the early days of Ducks Unlimited. Their help was further sought on many occasions to clarify specific items. Angus Shortt provided a written account of his early days with the company.

A special tribute is due the late E. B. Pitblado for carefully preserving the records of the earliest beginnings of the organization, and for his availability and helpful reading of an early draft of the era in which he was particularly involved.

Thanks are also due to Isabel Curwain who cheerfully tolerated repeated interruptions of her busy day to supply personnel statistics. Elsie Breland retained her interest and good humour through the many typed drafts of the manuscript. Special thanks are due to Clifford Schultz for his editing assistance, and to Patrick Lang for proofreading.

The writer is particularly grateful to D. S. Morrison, Executive Vice-President of Ducks Unlimited (Canada), for his continued encouragement and strong support for the project.

All photographs are by Ducks Unlimited (Canada) employees, past or present, unless otherwise noted.

ISBN 0-919213-78-2

Printed and bound by Friesen Printers,
A division of D. W. Friesen and Sons Ltd.
Altona, Manitoba, Canada

Published by Ducks Unlimited (Canada), 1978.
1190 Waverley Street
Winnipeg, Manitoba   R3T 2E2

Table of Contents

Poem   *2*

Dedication   *3*

Acknowledgement   *4*

Foreword   *6*

Prelude   *7*

1
Ducks Unlimited, Inc.   *13*

2
Ducks Unlimited (Canada) is born   *23*

3
Getting Underway   *27*

4
The First Year   *39*

5
Into The North   *75*

6
Public Relations   *93*

7
The War Years   *105*

8
Postwar   *123*

9
The Wet Fifties   *139*

10
Reorganization and Expansion   *159*

11
The Directors   *199*

12
Canadian Co-operation   *209*

13
Broadening Horizons   *215*

Appendices

I
Speeches by John C. Huntington, Judge W. G. Ross and E. B. Pitblado at the Annual Banquet of the Manitoba Game and Fish Association March 25th, 1937 launching Ducks Unlimited (Canada).   *217*

II
Radio Broadcasts — "Rebuilding The West" 1938 and 1939.   *223*

III
Radio Broadcasts — 1950 and 1951.   *232*

IV
Ducks Unlimited (Canada) Directors, Officers and Committees 1938 to 1977.   *235*

V
Duckological   *249*

VI
Summary of Waterfowl Breeding Seasons 1939 to 1977. Condensed from Duckologicals.   *250*

VII
Active Kee-Men as of December 31, 1977.   *254*

VIII
Co-operating Landowners.   *256*

FOREWORD

The story of Ducks Unlimited, Incorporated, the American genesis of Ducks Unlimited (Canada), has been told in *"A Singleness of Purpose"*, the history of their forty years of operation published in 1977.

This in turn is the 40-year story of Ducks Unlimited (Canada) whose active history began in 1938, a year later than the parent company. It is the story of how the money donated by American duck hunters was spent in Canada to preserve and develop waterfowl habitat.

It is, in particular, the story of the people who with dedication, experiment, and innovation applied the theoretical concepts of game management to a practical problem. Their success reflects the time given generously by an unpaid directorate, the co-operation of Kee-Men, and the free use of land given by both private individuals and governments.

It is a success story only because so many people believed in its goals, and were willing to give as much of themselves as success demanded, and because so many others were willing to co-operate to bring a magnificent experiment to practical fruition.

The name *Ducks and Men* was first proposed by E. S. Russenholt in 1941 for a similar book which was never written although the idea remained active until 1943. It was also the title given by T. C. Main to his unfinished and unpublished memoirs.

This history covers the period to December 31, 1977.

Prelude

As early as the beginning of the century, American sportsmen were already expressing concern for a dwindling waterfowl population in their various journals and periodicals. If they were concerned then, considering the relatively large numbers which still existed, one may have some idea of the original abundance, though waterfowl populations must always have fluctuated in harmony with water conditions on the breeding grounds.

In both the United States and Canada, sportsmen saw the necessity of preserving game birds and restoring their numbers. However, Western Canada was only beginning to develop its agricultural resources, habitat was still plentiful, and the reduction in waterfowl was probably not as noticeable or considered as important as in the United States. Nevertheless, the Canadian Federal Government in 1887 did set aside several areas in Western Canada as Game Bird Sanctuaries and Public Shooting Areas primarily to preserve waterfowl habitat, the first areas so designated in North America. These sanctuaries were not refuges in the modern sense, as shooting was permitted. Although naturalist and sportsmen groups existed, most lacked the financial resources and political clout to be as effective as their American counterparts. In addition, Canadians always seem inclined to wait for the government to act rather than attempt to solve their problem themselves.

In the United States the attitude was different and while this is not meant to be a complete account of naturalist and sportsmen's organizations in the United States, it is important to be aware of the influence of such groups, and of individuals, on United States wildlife policy.

The National Association of Audubon Societies, for instance, began work in 1902 on the study and protection of wild birds and animals. No doubt local organizations existed long before the national group was formed. Within a year, it had been responsible, under the aegis of President Theodore Roosevelt, for establishing the first federal bird sanctuary, and by the time Roosevelt went out of office in 1909, thirty-eight bird sanctuaries, extending all across the United States, had been established through the initiative of the National Audubon Society.

The companies manufacturing sporting arms and ammunition organized and funded the American Game Protective and Propagation Association in 1911. Its chartered objectives were:

(a) To preserve and propagate game and fish.
(b) To urge enactment of proper laws to that end and to obtain uniformity of such throughout the country.
(c) To co-operate with and assist the proper authorities, clubs, associations, and individuals in enforcing these laws.
(d) To establish and maintain preserves and reserves where game may be protected.
(e) To awaken public interest in the work of protecting and propagating wildlife and to demonstrate that propagation is a practical means of increasing the general food supply and can be made commercially successful.

This group assisted in drafting important legislation relating to the protection of migratory game birds: the Federal Migratory Bird Law, bringing all migratory birds under federal rather than state jurisdiction in 1913 and the Weekes-McLean Migratory Bird Law, culminating in the Migratory Bird Convention (with Great Britain acting on behalf of Canada) which became law in Canada in 1917 and in the United States in 1918. The organization changed its name in 1935 to the American Wildlife Institute and in 1946 to the Wildlife Management Institute. It remains a powerful voice in conservation in the United States today.

Numerous smaller organizations and even individuals also did some interesting and, considering the times, rather unexpected things. As early as 1912, "two public spirited citizens" established a sanctuary in Connecticut and sent an "expert" to

Lake Winnipegosis in Manitoba "to study the habits of the ducks that nest and breed in that area . . . and to bring back young ducklings to form a nucleus for the propagating work. . ." About thirteen different species, including a considerable number of canvasbacks were obtained. Another organization, "Wildfowlers," sent two investigators to Alberta in 1928 to study nest depredations by crows "on the duck breeding grounds." This may well have been the first investigation into crow-waterfowl relationships in Canada.

It was from this background of private initiative and funding, and belief that sound business methods could restore gamebird populations, that The More Game Birds in America Foundation, and finally, Ducks Unlimited, Incorporated evolved.

Even at this time it was realized that habitat preservation and development were the keys to increased waterfowl populations. Restrictions on hunting, which seemed severe at the time, but would now be considered generous, were accepted as an emergency measure which would be eased when populations were restored to normal by management.

It is strange that in the decade prior to the devastating drought of the 1930's, private citizens and organizations in the United States seemed more concerned about bag limits, and the waterfowl kill, than the government officials responsible for the resource. Perhaps the government was more aware of the real impact of the loss of habitat. Thus we see in 1926, Edward W. Nelson, Chief of the U.S. Bureau of Biological Survey (forerunner of the United States Fish and Wildlife Service) rightly or wrongly, defending a Federal bag limit of 25 birds a day and stating that "the bag limit question has had publicity out of all proportion to its relative importance in the problem of maintaining our wildfowl. The overwhelming importance of saving the water areas so that the birds may have food and resting places should take precedence over everything else".[1] From a long range point of view, he was right.

But it took the shock of a near catastrophe to bring all agencies and organizations to the realization that the waterfowl resource was in really serious difficulty. This shock was supplied by the drought of the thirties.

Drought swept the prairies (D.R.E.E. Photo).

1"Our Migratory Waterfowl and Present Conditions Affecting Their Abundance" Special Report, Bureau of Biological Survey, March 26, 1926.

Sloughs disappeared.

Although waterfowl populations had been noticeably and gradually decreasing through the early decades of the century, there had been nothing comparable to the drastic decline of the early 1930's. It was remarkably sudden. Thus, while the 1926 waterfowl report by the U.S. Bureau of Biological Survey was one of confident abundance, by 1934 there was grave concern for the future of the resource.

From a waterfowl standpoint, 1929 was said to be the last normal year before the coming decade of drought. Conditions were very bad in 1931 with some improvement in 1932. Water conditions in the spring of 1933 gave promise of better things but this hope was squashed by summer drought and heat, and the year was a disaster for waterfowl, as was 1934, when the waterfowl population fell to its low point of an estimated 27 million ducks. In 1935, water conditions on the prairies were much improved, the best in the past six years, but the prairies were dry again in 1936, though the hatch was said to be better than the previous year. Conditions were drier in 1937 as compared to a year earlier and "drought made staggering inroads into the bush country". After this point, although 1938 showed little real improvement, the worst of the drought appears to have been over, and from 1939 through to 1944 water conditions were relatively good through the prairies.

Even marshes were dry.

Ducklings huddled in the last of the water and then wandered across the prairie in search of a new home.

There have been individual dry years since 1939 when waterfowl populations have declined, but drought has never been as widespread as it was in the '30's. Nor have there been the consecutive years of poor water conditions, which were so devastating to waterfowl populations during the decade of drought.

The reaction of the U.S. Bureau of Biological Survey to the decimation of the waterfowl resource was twofold: what was thought to be a short term solution at the time — reduction of the kill through lower bag limits, abolition of baiting and live decoys, and plugging of repeating firearms to three shells — and a long term program to provide dependable waterfowl habitat by establishing refuges to produce waterfowl as well as provide staging areas during migration.

By this time, More Game Birds in America and other private organizations, and the U.S. Biological Survey itself, knew that any program to increase waterfowl by improving habitat would have to be extended to Canada, if it were to be successful. Since there was no mechanism by which United States public funds could be spent in Canada, the ball was clearly in the court of private enterprise. To their everlasting credit, they had the courage and faith in themselves to accept the challenge.

The concept.

Ducks Unlimited, Inc.   1

Asked who was most responsible for the creation of Ducks Unlimited, Arthur Bartley, senior executive officer of the organization from its inception until 1962, replied without hesitation, "Dwight C. Huntington and Joseph P. Knapp". Dwight Huntington had the vision — Joseph Knapp the wealth and power to make dreams come true.

Huntington's basic philosophy was that game birds constituted a crop, which by good management could be produced like wheat or corn. This led directly to the realization that adequate habitat was the key to game bird abundance and gave positive and constructive focus to the policies of both More Game Birds in America and Ducks Unlimited, Inc., when they evolved. "The coming generation . . . must be taught to think in terms of restoration and management rather than restriction and protection." This aggressive attitude was typical of these organizations and in sharp contrast to resigned acceptance of progressively restrictive hunting regulations except as temporary emergency measures. They were prepared to *do* something about the problem!

Bartley's association with Dwight Huntington came through his son, John, with whom Bartley served during World War I. As early as 1912, the senior Huntington had founded the Game Conservation Society and both Huntington and Bartley came to work for the Society soon after the war ended. The Huntingtons also established the Game Conservation Institute at Clinton, New Jersey, in 1928 and Bartley became the Director. The Institute was initially financed by the firearms and ammunition companies and offered a free two-year course in game management to interested students.

Joseph Knapp helped support the school after the arms industry withdrew. But it was finally forced to close due to lack of funding at the end of February, 1935.

The successful, politically powerful businessmen led by Joe

Joseph P. Knapp.

Arthur M. Bartley.

Knapp who formed "The More Game Birds in America Foundation" (the progenitor of Ducks Unlimited) on October 6, 1930, were convinced that, by applying to the production of game birds the same business methods that had made them successful, they could restore their former abundance. Emphasis was not on passively conserving what was left, but on aggresssively carrying out whatever was required to increase game bird populations.

The Foundation first proposed a 10-year program for the restoration of game birds on the North American continent. Then, in true business-like fashion, they accumulated and analyzed the available data on game birds. From these data the first publication of the Foundation appeared in August, 1931, titled *More Waterfowl by Assisting Nature*. In its preparation, the cooperation and input of Canadian authorities was sought and utilized. This was probably the first contact between Canada and the United States for the purpose of discussing the current status of the waterfowl resource, the destruction of habitat, and the remedial action which might be taken.

The recommendations of this publication were as follows:

An International Agency to be created to increase migratory waterfowl production and to disburse,

Ample funds, to be raised by a cent-a-shell tax, supplemented by such governmental appropriations as may be obtained, to promote production expeditiously and with the highest efficiency by acquiring,

Breeding grounds, preferably by purchase, wherever they exist or can be restored in the United States and Canada — hundreds of thousands of acres — to be efficiently supervised by,

Game bird management forces to (1) control water levels and provide ample supply of food and cover, (2) control natural enemies where necessary, (3) prevent fires, stop unauthorized grazing and suppress shooting on these breeding grounds.

Refuges to be established by the Agency for use of wildfowl on northern and southern flights, coordinated with a system of, Concentration areas for winter use.

That the Foundation, and its members, were held in high esteem is apparent from the choice of Thomas R. Beck of the Executive as Chairman of President Roosevelt's Committee on Wildlife Restoration, established January 2, 1934, in response to a memorandum from the Foundation. The Committee included two distinguished conservationists and scientists, Jay N. (Ding) Darling and Aldo Leopold. John Huntington and Arthur Bartley, both now employed by the Foundation, were assigned to assist.

The report was published February 8, 1934. Pressure from, and generated by, the Foundation was also responsible for the allocation of funds to carry out the recommendations of the Committee, at least in part, by the use of emergency relief funds and relief workers for the restoration of habitat and for the refuge program.

The Foundation sponsored the cent-a-shell tax but the bill was defeated in Congress. It then lent its support to the Federal Duck Stamp Law which was approved March 16, 1934. Thereby, at least some of the money requested by the President's Committee on Wildlife Restoration was made available.

But there was nothing for a program in Canada, since United States law prohibited the use of money for such purposes in a foreign country. There was no source of funds, private or public, in Canada, and thus no way to restore the breeding grounds, where most of the continent's waterfowl were known to nest.

The Foundation's concern with the Canadian problem however impelled them to continue investigations in Canada.

Arthur Bartley says that from 1929 to 1936, he made annual trips to Canada during the waterfowl breeding season. As

Arthur recalls, the original contact with interested Canadians, established by way of a broker in Minneapolis, was through James Richardson of James Richardson and Sons of Winnipeg. It was a result of this contact that Arthur Bartley first met E. B. Pitblado, and then B. W. Cartwright who later became Chief Naturalist when Ducks Unlimited (Canada) was formed.

Edward B. (Ed) Pitblado was to Ducks Unlimited (Canada), in its formative years, what Joe Knapp had been to The More Game Birds in America Foundation and later to Ducks Unlimited, Inc. His credentials were impressive, his concern for waterfowl sincere, and his efforts on their behalf untiring. Not only was he a member of the prestigious Winnipeg law firm of Pitblado, Hoskin, & Co., but he had, with his father, a long wildfowling tradition. He had been an active member of the Executive of the Manitoba Game and Fish Association since 1917 and its President from 1934 to 1936. He was also President of the Interprovincial Council of Western Fish and Game Leagues and a member from 1917 of the Natural Resources Committee of the Young Men's Section of the Winnipeg Board of Trade.

Bartley could hardly have made a better contact. Not only was Ed the effective link between the sportsmen and sportsmen's organizations of Western Canada and the American group during their activities prior to the formation of Ducks Unlimited (Canada), but he did the legal work necessary to incorporate the Company and remained its legal counsel until his death on December 2nd, 1977. He was also the Secretary, except for the War years, when he was on active service with the Royal Canadian Air Force, and was replaced by W. S. McEwen, another member of his firm. He became both an Honorary Director and Honorary Secretary on June 16, 1973, when his secretarial duties were assumed by Sterling R. Lyon and subsequently by D. C. Groff.

What was probably the result of several of Bartley's trips to

Edward B. Pitblado, 1936.

Western Canada but pertains specifically to that of the first half of July, 1933, was a booklet published by More Game Birds in America, titled *The Duck Decline in the Northwest*. Pitblado made available all the material on waterfowl in the Manitoba Game and Fish Association office. While no author is given, it was probably the combined effort of Arthur Bartley, John Huntington and Alexander C. Camerle, who are listed in 1935 as Vice-Presidents. Camerle is important since it may be that he was the first to suggest carrying out a waterfowl census by aircraft. Whether this was a technique he brought with him from Hungary, we will never know.

The Duck Decline in the Northwest is a remarkable publication and demonstrates amazing understanding of the problems facing the waterfowl resource. Since 1933 was a year of severe drought, some of the statements made were proven incorrect during the wet years which followed, but for the long-term, the basic concepts are sound.

It suggested that waterfowl counts are best made on the breeding grounds, where, for a short time in their restless lives, the birds are immobilized. It states that the relative abundance of waterfowl cannot be determined by surveys during migration or on the wintering grounds. It recommended that seasons and bag limits should be established on the basis of inventories carried out on the breeding grounds, and the kill limited to production less a percentage to provide an increase in breeding stock. Such breeding ground surveys became a part of the regulations procedure of the U.S. Fish and Wildlife Service and the Canadian Wildlife Service following World War II.

The report emphasized the obvious effect of severe drought and agriculture activities on waterfowl habitat and noted a lack of nesting cover and elimination of emergent plants by overgrazing. It commented on the great value to waterfowl of the area north of the agricultural zone in years of drought, and in the face of increasing agricultural pressure on the prairies. But it also confirmed the inherent productivity of true prairie wetlands, and the need to develop and preserve this habitat wherever possible. What we would now call a wetland inventory was also suggested.

It is remarkable that nothing we have learned in the last 43 years has invalidated these basic concepts.

During his trips to Canada in 1933 and 1934, Arthur Bartley was searching for more economical ways of amassing data on waterfowl populations. This led to the idea of utilizing aircraft as Camerle had promoted. In 1934, Pitblado, Huntington, Bartley, and Camerle made experimental flights over the Lake Winnipeg Marshes to develop techniques and evaluate aerial surveys of waterfowl. Tom Lamb, a pioneer bush pilot from The Pas, in what was then considered northern Manitoba, took Bartley and Camerle on a flight over the Saskatchewan River Delta, which convinced them that waterfowl numbers could be estimated from the air.

The groundwork for *The Duck Decline in the Northwest* and the experimental aerial surveys of 1934, were preparatory to the almost unbelievable effort and organization which went into *The 1935 International Waterfowl Census*. It was carried out by the Foundation, with some financial assistance by the arms and ammunition companies, and the Chrysler Corporation who supplied Dodge cars for the survey in the United States.

This was the first attempt to census North American waterfowl on the breeding grounds. The organizational skills required to accomplish it boggles the mind. Particularly when the report states that the decision to conduct the census was only made in mid-July, without prior preparation, and it was completed by the end of August. One can only assume that the organizers were very familiar with the Canadian situation, and had made the necessary contacts in previous years.

Ground surveys were carried out in Minnesota, North and South Dakota, and the three Prairie Provinces of Canada. In the United States, these were organized on a county basis, and in Canada on a municipal basis. A co-ordinator was appointed in each area. In Western Canada it was the Municipal Secretary-Treasurer, who then appointed a volunteer in each township of the municipality to collect the data and forward them to the provincial committee, composed of executives of the respective fish and game associations, natural history associations, and government personnel. It is particularly interesting that even the Manitoba Division of the Canadian Bankers Association was involved in that province and that the rural branch bank managers helped in the survey.

By use of prepared forms and township plats, (blank charts except for the outlines of sections and quarters), the following data were collected and compiled:

1. Counts of ducks, by species wherever ascertainable.
2. Counts and sizes of broods, by species if possible.
3. An estimate of ducks present in addition to those actually counted.
4. The main causes of losses of ducks and nests.
5. Information on duck breeding places which might be improved or restored by building dams or dykes.
6. Recommendations for improving duck breeding conditions.
7. Exact location of area investigated, and name, occupation, and address of investigator.

BEGIN AIRPLANE CENSUS OF WILD DUCKS IN NORTH

Observers Cover District Between Mouth of Red River to Ontario Boundary

Airplane surveys in the 1935 international wild duck census started Friday afternoon from Winnipeg with a five-hour flight over the Red river, Netley marshes, Winnipeg river and eastward into Ontario.

The survey party, consisting of John C. Huntington, New York, vice-president, More Game Birds in America; Edward B. Pitblado, president Manitoba Fish and Game association; and A. C. Camerle, director of water fowl activities for the More Game Birds Foundation, were flown by K. Johannesson.

Found Many at Netley

The flight, Mr. Huntington said, disclosed an exceptionally good duck crop on the Netley marshes, with water and food conditions excellent and approximately normal after several dry years. Eastward of Lac du Bonnet practically no ducks were observed, confirming the known facts regarding the eastern limit of duck breeding.

On Saturday shortly after lunch, Mr. Huntington, Mr. Camerle, and William Vogt, unofficial observer of the duck census for the National Association of Audobon societies, left by airplane for northern Manitoba, piloted by Mr. Yuill, for Thomas Lamb, Moose Lake, owner of the plane.

Their route lay by way of Oak Point, Clandeboye and Delta marshes, along the west shore of Lake Manitoba, north along the Waterhen river to Waterhen lake, and then southwest to Lake Winnipegosis.

It is proposed to spend a day or two in around Long island and West Waterhen river. After that the party will go to Moose and Cedar lakes, and then to The Pas, covering Cormorant lake and the several smaller water areas in the locality. From The Pas, Mr. Huntington and Mr. Camerle will fly westward as far as the Peace river delta, a famous waterfowl breeding ground.

Winnipeg Free Press, August 13, 1935.

Overall co-ordination was supplied in the three States by individuals hired for that purpose. In Canada, Huntington worked in Manitoba, Camerle in Saskatchewan, and Arthur Bartley in Alberta.

Aerial surveys were made of the important waterfowl areas north of the agricultural fringe as far as the edge of the Pre-Cambrian Shield and extending down the valley of the Slave River as far as Great Slave Lake. The observers were four members of the Foundation staff, the three mentioned above and William Vogt of the National Audubon Society. Estimates were made of the number of ducks per acre for individual marshes and lakes. Records were also kept of the general nature of the terrain and the character of waters, marshes, and streams along the route. The report summarizes the census as follows:

In the entire census area there were at least 42,700,000 ducks during August, 1935, distributed as follows —

1. Alberta — Southern section	1,600,000
2. Saskatchewan — Southern section	2,400,000
3. Manitoba — Southern section	1,400,000
4. Alberta-Saskatchewan, Central Lake Area	10,900,000
5. Saskatchewan, between Central Lake Area and edge of the Canadian Shield	1,800,000
6. Manitoba-Saskatchewan, The Pas Area	3,500,000
7. Manitoba, Winnipegosis-Winnipeg Lakes Area	2,200,000
8. Alberta — Northern section (north of 53rd parallel and Central Lake Area, exclusive of 9 and 10)	5,500,000
9. Alberta — Lake Claire Area	900,000
10. Alberta — MacKenzie, Slave River Area	7,300,000
11. The Canadian Shield in Saskatchewan and all areas in Manitoba, exclusive of 3, 6 and 7	3,000,000
Total	40,500,000
North Dakota, South Dakota and Minnesota	2,200,000
Grand Total	42,700,000

Totals by provinces:

Alberta	16,400,000	
Saskatchewan	12,000,000	
Manitoba	7,500,000	
Portion of MacKenzie District	4,600,000	40,500,000

Total by states:

North Dakota	1,200,000		
South Dakota	350,000		
Minnesota	650,000	2,200,000	42,700,000

The report is an outstanding document. It is difficult to believe that such a complete and accurate understanding of waterfowl habitat in Canada could have been obtained in such a short time. Regrettably the author is unacknowledged and remains unknown, although Ed Pitblado helped edit the original draft. It emphasizes the importance of the relatively narrow strip of habitat (only a quarter of the area under investigation) between the northern edge of agriculture and the Pre-Cambrian Shield, where three-quarters of the waterfowl population was found. Subsequent experience suggests that this was likely a response to drought on the prairies at that time. It points out the value of this area to the resource, temporarily in times of drought, and on a long term basis, as agriculture intensifies on the prairies. These points had already been made in *The Duck Decline in the Northwest*.

The results and experiences of the 1935 census confirmed to The More Game Birds in America Foundation the belief expressed in their two previous publications, *More Waterfowl by Assisting Nature*, 1931, and *The Duck Decline in the Northwest*, 1933, that the future of waterfowl lay in preserving the breeding grounds in Canada.

The first official announcement of the Ducks Unlimited program comes in the sixth Annual Report of the Foundation for the period October 1, 1935 — September 30, 1936.

It quotes first from *More Waterfowl by Assisting Nature* as follows:

While many former breeding grounds in the United States can be restored and existing areas made more productive, it is to

Canada largely that we must turn for more waterfowl. About seventy-five per cent of the waterfowl on the North American continent are Canada bred.

It would be unreasonable and unjust to expect Canada to carry the load unassisted, particularly in view of the fact that the bulk of the 'crop' is bagged each year in the United States. Therefore is seems eminently fair that the sportsmen of the States, far outnumbering the Canadians, should largely bear the cost of maintaining the waterfowl supply, the Dominion and its game officials being asked to cooperate.

It then goes on to describe the plan:

The Canadian waterfowl restoration plan, in brief, calls for the creation of a non-profit Canadian foundation to be governed by a board composed of four Canadian and four American businessmen and sportsmen. The new organization would proceed with the preservation of unspoiled northern breeding grounds through cooperation with provincial and Dominion officials. Restoration of southern areas would be accomplished by selection and development of local projects after careful choice of the most suitable sites. Funds with which to support the work are to be obtained entirely through contributions from sportsmen in the United States — those who are the beneficiaries of the wild duck crops produced in Canada.

"Ducks Unlimited" will be the name of the new Canadian foundation. A tentative draft of the plan of operation has been presented to the Premiers of Alberta, Saskatchewan, and Manitoba, fish and game officials, and leading businessmen and sportsmen of the provinces. Most complimentary letters of endorsement and approval have been received from all concerned — along with promises of complete co-operation.

All of the development and organization work is being financed by More Game Birds in America so that every dollar subscribed for "Ducks Unlimited" will be spent solely to produce more ducks in Canada — where at least five times as many ducks can be produced for each dollar of expenditure as in the United States.

Arthur Bartley gives an interesting account of the origin of the name "Ducks Unlimited". A group, including several contributors to The More Game Birds Foundation, were at Joe Knapp's fishing camp on the Beaverkill River. After fishing, they were sitting around talking and primarily discussing the poor waterfowl hunting season. The suggestion was made that an organization be formed called "Ducks Limited", since it was to be a Canadian corporation, and Canadian corporations were known as limited companies. The idea was apparently that of Arthur Bartley; and Joe Knapp, who reportedly had a quick trigger, (Arthur says one didn't argue very much with Joe Knapp!) bawled him out for even suggesting limited ducks. Joe said, "Dammit, we don't want limited ducks." Arthur came back with "Ducks *Un*limited, then". And so the name was born.

Late fall mallards and whistling swans. Goodman Project, Manitoba.
(Photo by R. Dodds.)

In their next annual report, October 1, 1936 — September 30, 1937, the Foundation was able to announce the official incorporation of Ducks Unlimited, Inc., on January 29, 1937, and the incorporation of Ducks Unlimited (Canada) on March 10 of the same year.

The Ducks Unlimited plan was prepared and the organizational expenses of approximately $50,000 paid by the Foundation. The plan called for raising $600,000 a year in membership contributions for the next five years. Three million dollars was considered sufficient to re-establish a million or more acres of waterfowl nesting grounds in Western Canada.

The first meeting of the Trustees of Ducks Unlimited, Inc. was held in Chicago on March 11, 1938, though two organizational meetings had been held previously in New York. During the inaugural year of 1937, Dr. John A. Hartwell had been President. He resigned due to ill health just before the Chicago meeting and Louis H. Eagan of St. Louis was elected President.

In the first year of operation, $90,447 had been raised and, according to Arthur Bartley, even with the help of the Foundation — some $30,000 — which had been given to Ducks Unlimited, Inc., the Trustees believed that it was insufficient to carry out the coming year's program. Certainly it fell far below the annual objective of $600,000 and there was considerable pessimism about the future of the organization. Arthur Bartley says that Lou Barkhausen of Chicago, who had originally supported More Game Birds, and who was an enthusiastic supporter of the new Ducks Unlimited, Inc., made an additional contribution to keep the organization going, and to get the first year of operations underway. An initial appropriation of $100,000 was finally sent to Ducks Unlimited (Canada) for 1938.

Canada

By the Honourable FERNAND RINFRET,

Secretary of State of Canada.

To all to whom these presents shall come, or whom the same may in anywise concern,

GREETING:

Whereas, in and by Part II of The Companies Act, 1934, it is, amongst other things, in effect enacted that the Secretary of State of Canada may, by Letters Patent, under his Seal of Office, grant a Charter to any number of persons, not less than three, who having complied with the requirements of the Act, apply therefor, constituting such persons, and others who thereafter become members of the Corporation thereby created, a Body Corporate and Politic without share capital, for the purpose of carrying on in more than one province of Canada, without pecuniary gain to its members, objects of a national, patriotic, religious, philanthropic, charitable, scientific, artistic, social, professional or sporting character, or the like, upon the applicants therefor establishing to the satisfaction of the Secretary of State of Canada, due compliance with the several conditions and terms in and by the said Act set forth and thereby made conditions precedent to the granting of such Charter.

And Whereas, HENRY PLATT GRUNDY, OSCAR SAMUEL ALSAKER, WILFRID STANLEY McEWEN, FREDERICK JAMES TURNER and EDWARD BRUCE PITBLADO, Barristers-at-law, FRANCIS EDWARD LANGDALE, RICHARD BYRNES PATTINSON and ALEXANDER JAMES MILLIGAN, Solicitors, all of the City of Winnipeg, in the Province of Manitoba,---

have made application for a Charter under the said Act, constituting them, and such others as may become members in the Corporation thereby created, a Body Corporate and Politic, under the name of

DUCKS UNLIMITED (Canada)

for the purposes hereinafter mentioned, and have satisfactorily established the sufficiency of all proceedings required by the said Act to be taken, and the truth and sufficiency of all facts required to be established previous to the granting of such Letters Patent, and have filed in the Department of the Secretary of State a duplicate of the Memorandum of Agreement executed by the said applicants in conformity with the provisions of the said Act.

Now know ye, that I, the said FERNAND RINFRET,------------------ Secretary of State of Canada, under the authority of the hereinbefore in part recited Act, do, by these Letters Patent, constitute the said --

HENRY PLATT GRUNDY, OSCAR SAMUEL ALSAKER, WILFRID STANLEY McEWEN, FREDERICK JAMES TURNER, EDWARD BRUCE PITBLADO, FRANCIS EDWARD LANGDALE, RICHARD BYRNES PATTINSON and ALEXANDER JAMES MILLIGAN,------------------

and all others who may become members in the said Corporation, a Body Corporate and Politic without share capital, by the name of

DUCKS UNLIMITED (Canada)

with all the rights and powers given by the said Act and for the following purposes and objects, namely:---

The operations of the Corporation to be carried on throughout the Dominion of Canada and elsewhere.

The head office of the said corporation will be situate at the City of Winnipeg, in the Province of Manitoba.

And it is -- hereby -- ordained and declared that, if authorized by by-law, duly passed by the directors and sanctioned by at least two-thirds of the votes cast at a special general meeting of the members, duly called for considering the by-law, the directors may from time to time:

(a) borrow money upon the credit of the corporation;

(b) limit or increase the amount to be borrowed;

(c) issue debentures or other securities of the corporation;

(d) pledge or sell such debentures or other securities for such sums and at such prices as may be deemed expedient;

(e) mortgage, hypothecate, charge or pledge all or any of the real and personal property, undertaking and rights of the corporation to secure any such debentures or other securities or any money borrowed or any other liability of the corporation.

Nothing in this clause contained shall limit or restrict the borrowing of money by the corporation on bills of exchange or promissory notes made, drawn, accepted or endorsed, by or on behalf of the corporation.

And it is further ordained and declared that the business of the said Corporation shall be carried on without the purposes of gain for its members and that any profits or other accretions to the Corporation shall be used in promoting its objects.

That the said HENRY PLATT GRUNDY, OSCAR SAMUEL ALSAKER, WILFRID STANLEY McEWEN, FREDERICK JAMES TURNER, EDWARD BRUCE PITBLADO, FRANCIS EDWARD LANGDALE, RICHARD BYRNES PATTINSON and ALEXANDER JAMES MILLIGAN,------------------

are to be the first directors of the said Corporation.

Given under my hand and Seal of Office, at Ottawa, this -- Tenth -- day of March, 1937.

Under Secretary of State.

Ducks Unlimited (Canada) charter.

Ducks Unlimited (Canada) is Born 2

Ducks Unlimited (Canada) evolved concurrently with Ducks Unlimited, Inc. In fact their official incorporation dates were only a few months apart.

Ed Pitblado believes that as early as 1934, while Huntington and Bartley continued their work quietly in the western provinces, the officers of More Game Birds in America had already decided to proceed with a program in Canada. Moreover, in spite of the agonizing drought and unemployment, which well might have engaged all their sympathy, the Fish & Game Associations of Manitoba, Saskatchewan, and Alberta were deeply concerned about the drought-induced plight of waterfowl, particularly after taking part in the 1935 census. Ed says that they pleaded with the various sportsmen's organizations in the United States to send money to Canada to preserve the marsh lands. So the proposal for an organization such as Ducks Unlimited (Canada) had, for the most part, a cordial reception from Western Canadian sportsmen.

There were, of course, those who opposed the intrusion of an American-financed company into Western Canada. This opposition was based on the fear that its real objective was to buy all the worthwhile shooting properties for the exclusive use of Americans, or to control the harvest of waterfowl for the benefit of American hunters. It was long after the incorporation of Ducks Unlimited (Canada) that these apprehensions were completely laid to rest.

By 1936, representatives of More Game Birds, while in Canada, had contacted some of the top influential people to see if they would head an organization like the proposed Ducks Unlimited (Canada). In particular, they had spoken with James A. Richardson of Winnipeg and Senator William Paterson of Fort William, Ontario. One can only assume they received all the encouragement they needed, since they proceeded with the plans for incorporation.

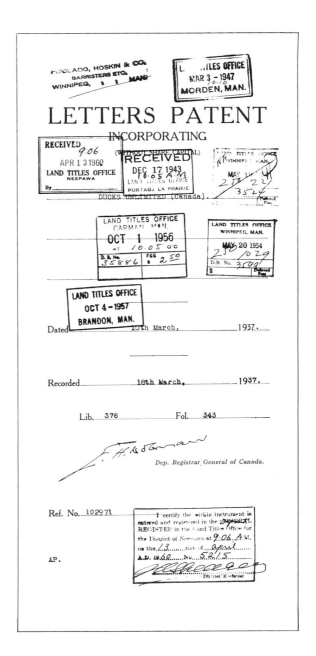

In April, 1936, telephone calls between John C. Huntington, now President of More Game Birds in America, and Ed Pitblado, initiated the first moves toward the formal incorporation of Ducks Unlimited (Canada). A long letter of May 26, 1936, addressed to Ed Pitblado, as President of the Manitoba Game and Fish Association, contained some legal questions regarding incorporation procedures.

Pitblado's reply outlined the charter requirements. On December 31, a letter addressed to Pitblado as lawyer, instructed him to take out a charter at the Federal level — in Ottawa — as quickly as possible. Copies of the Certificate of Incorporation for More Game Birds in America and their by-laws were sent as a guide.

Early in 1937, Pitblado, Hoskin, & Co. drafted an application for the Ducks Unlimited (Canada) charter and sent it to More Game Birds for review. In January of the same year, Ed Pitblado received a letter from them requesting him to see if James A. Richardson would act as a director, and advising him that Judge W. G. (Bill) Ross, recently retired President of the Saskatchewan Fish and Game League and member of the Saskatchewan Legislature, had agreed to participate as had S. S. Holden of Ottawa. On January 26, 1937, Pitblado saw James Richardson, who expressed himself as most pleased to act on the Board and do anything else he could.

A few days later, Ed Pitblado met James Richardson again,

advised him that he had been in touch with Bill Ross and some of the other potential directors, and would now appreciate some guidance as to how the organization might get started.

The first thing Richardson asked was whether they had anyone in mind for a General Manager. There had been some discussions with people in the fish and game leagues, but there seemed to be only one man who had the essential knowledge of surface water in Western Canada — Thomas C. Main, Surface Water Engineer for the three Prairie Provinces for the Canadian National Railways.

Richardson said "If he's your man, we'll get him". So he phoned a Mr. Warren of the Canadian National Railways and made arrangements for the transfer of Tom Main on leave of absence to Ducks Unlimited, and asked the matter to be kept secret pending confirmation. Richardson then told Warren, in glowing terms, that this new organization would be the salvation of the ducks in Canada.

At this stage, information was gradually leaking out about the new organization that was coming to Canada, and, since the name of Ed Pitblado and his firm were associated with it, they were deluged with applications for involvement. Farmers wrote to offer their marginal land for sale; university professors, tired of the classroom, applied to try their hand in the field of practical application; and some people just applied for work. In any event, Ed Pitblado says that the best brains in Western Canada seemed anxious to get into this particular type of work.

On the 17th of March, 1937, Pitblado was advised that the charter had been issued under date of March 10, and that the Secretary of State was pleased to waive all incorporation fees, which were considerable. He is sure this was done because this was the first organization incorporated in Canada which was to be completely funded by voluntary contributions from outside the country.

A unique opportunity to formally introduce the new organization to western sportsmen then presented itself. The Manitoba Game and Fish Association was about to have their annual meeting and dinner, so it was decided to tie in the announcement of the Ducks Unlimited program with this event. A special printed program dedicated to Ducks Unlimited (Canada) was prepared for the banquet, and the speeches given by John C. Huntington, W. G. Ross, and E. B. Pitblado were published in the 1937 Spring Issue of the Manitoba Game and Fish Association Bulletin. (See Appendix I)

SPRING ISSUE
1937

MANITOBA GAME & FISH ASSOCIATION

"Ducks Unlimited (Canada)" Number

The Story —

Speeches by:
    John C. Huntington, New York, Originator.
    W. G. Ross, K.C., M.L.A., Moose Jaw, Canadian Director.
    E. B. Pitblado, Winnipeg, Manitoba Game and Fish Assn.

Approval —

Getting Underway

In order to expedite the functioning of Ducks Unlimited (Canada), eight members of the firm of Pitblado, Hoskin, & Co. had been installed as provisional members and directors of the corporation. This was done so they could quickly run off the general by-laws, or whatever borrowing by-laws might be required. Throughout 1937, these eight temporary directors met merely for the purpose of establishing the Chairman of the meeting, the Secretary, and Treasurer.

At a meeting on March 22, 1938, the provisional representatives transferred their responsibilities to the new members and directors. The formal transfer, in which each individual temporary representative resigned in favour of a specific new member and director, was the first item of business at the first meeting of Ducks Unlimited (Canada) held in Winnipeg at the Fort Garry Hotel on April 1 and 2, 1938. The following directorate was installed to take effect the 1st day of April, 1938:

Arthur M. Bartley of New York
Louis M. Barkhausen of Chicago
Butler F. Greer of San Francisco
Harold W. Story of Milwaukee
S. S. Holden of Ottawa
James A. Richardson of Winnipeg
W. G. Ross, K.C., of Moose Jaw
O. Leigh Spencer of Calgary

Front, left to right: Judge William G. Ross, Louis H. Barkhausen, James A. Richardson. Rear, left to right: Arthur M. Bartley, Edward B. Pitblado, and Harold W. Story.

Greer, Holden, and Spencer were absent but sent their proxies. E. B. Pitblado, while not a Director, was asked to continue as Secretary, a position he held until 1973.

The Chairman, Harold W. Story, addressed the group on the origin of the Ducks Unlimited idea, and then advised that Ducks Unlimited, Inc., at their meeting in Chicago, March 11 and 12, 1938, had passed a resolution making $100,000 available to Ducks Unlimited (Canada) for the period April 1 to December 31, 1938.

He pointed out "that not all people contacted had a real conception of the breeding picture and, accordingly, an educational program would have to be conducted before it would be possible to develop the full purpose and objectives of the corporation. It was, therefore, necessary to make an immediate start on the work in Canada and develop advertising material for making further progress in raising money in the United States . . ."

This statement, extracted from the minutes, is of interest not only from the historical point of view, since it records the first transfer of money from Ducks Unlimited, Inc. to Ducks Unlimited (Canada), but it explains why, in the early days of the corporation, the senior officers — T. C. Main and E. S. Russenholt — spent such a high proportion of their time on speaking engagements in the United States.

Bartley advised that the money would be available as follows:

$50,000 in cash
$30,000 on July 1, 1938
$20,000 on October 1, 1938

The first cheque for $50,000 was actually deposited to the credit of Ducks Unlimited (Canada) in the Bank of Commerce in Winnipeg on April 7, 1938.

A tentative budget was prepared and discussed. In speaking to the budget, Mr. Bartley suggested that two objectives should be aimed at:
(1) To allot the largest possible amount toward field work for increasing the duck crop.
(2) To allot a sufficient amount for:—
   (a) Publicity in Canada and for preparatory work for activities in 1939, and
   (b) Gathering and preparing material for publicity needs in the United States.

The following budget was then approved:

MANAGEMENT
(Overhead)

General Manager @ $6,000 per year	$4,500	
All other head office expense	8,500	$13,000
FIELD WORK		
Restoration of former breeding grounds		40,875
Special controls		8,500
Technical surveys		6,000
Field Force	$10,725	
Equipment and travelling expense	11,350	22,075
SELLING EXPENSE:		
Photographic records, moving pictures, slides, etc.		8,000
RESERVE — Contingencies		1,550
		$100,000

The detailed minutes of the meeting reveal the concern of the American directors with the difficulty of obtaining support for the Canadian program, due to a lack of understanding by American duck hunters of both the importance of the Canadian breeding grounds to the waterfowl resource, and the current water situation in Canada. This concern explains the relatively substantial item in the budget for photographic records, moving pictures, slides, etc.

It is interesting to read of the opposition, although based on false premises, which had already developed against Ducks Unlimited (Canada).

James Richardson described these prejudices and suggested there was missionary work to be done in Canada, too. Many Canadians, he said, believed that ducks were shot on the Illinois River all through the spring, and in Louisiana all year round. They therefore saw no reason why they should curtail their own kill. Some also believed that Ducks Unlimited was a scheme to reserve all the best shooting grounds for Americans who would come to Canada in droves. Ross said these fears had been somewhat allayed and provincial game and fish associations were now anxious for the corporation to begin work.

In discussing the 1938 program, it was decided that one large project should be built in each of the Prairie Provinces that year. The crow and magpie control program by sportsmen's groups and school children would also be promoted.

Officers for Ducks Unlimited (Canada) elected at this first meeting were:

President	W. G. Ross, K.C.
First Vice-President	L. H. Barkhausen
Second Vice-President	O. Leigh Spencer
* Secretary	Edward B. Pitblado
Treasurer	Harold W. Story
* Assistant Treasurer	J. Gray Mundie
Executive Committee	Arthur M. Bartley
	W. G. Ross
	L. H. Barkhausen
	Harold W. Story
	James A. Richardson

* Not directors

After the election of officers, the first item of business for the meeting was the selection of a General Manager. While the way had been cleared by James Richardson with the Canadian National Railways for T. C. Main to be considered, applications from several other suitable candidates had been received.

Discussion resolved that T. C. Main was the preferred candidate and when the meeting reconvened on April 2nd, Richardson, Ross, and Pitblado were appointed a committee "with full authority to make whatever appointment in their opinion was in the best interests of the Corporation, Mr. Main having indicated it would take two or three days to ascertain the pleasure of the Canadian National Railways by whom he was employed". The Committee selected Main. This action was approved at the Directors' Meeting of April 14, 1939, (a full year after his official appointment as General Manager), but apparently the appointment was for one year only since at that meeting, he was re-engaged as General Manager for the coming year.

From the standpoint of both personality and professional background, the corporation could not have chosen a better man for General Manager at that time. Colourful, enthusiastic, and knowledgeable of water problems of the Prairie Provinces, Tom Main was clearly the man to sell the concept of Ducks Unlimited (Canada) to American duck hunters, which he did — with huge success. With his great shock of snow-white hair, his injured eye, rumoured to be the result of being hit by a falling mallard, (something that he never really affirmed, but was too good a showman to deny!) and his great enthusiasm for the job he was trying to do, Tom Main made a tremendous impression on duck hunters who attended the meetings arranged in the larger cities in the United States. His personality and talents, combined with the equal enthusiasm and public relations skills of E. S. Russenholt, who became his Assistant General Manager, must be credited with establishing the fledgling company securely with American duck hunters.

At 52, when he became General Manager, Tom Main had had a long association with western water problems. As Prairie Surface Water Engineer for the Canadian National Railway, his was the responsibility, in the mid-1920's, of locating and developing new sources of good water across the prairies for the new and larger locomotives which were then coming into use. To augment his income, he was also in the habit of taking his holidays in the spring, when he gave technical advice to three municipalities in south-central Saskatchewan, mostly on road building, but also on water supply and dugout locations.

After five months in Bermuda in late 1930 and early 1931, where he was on loan from the C.N.R. to assist with engineering and water problems on the island, Main returned to Winnipeg to the drought and depression which gripped Western Canada. He was almost immediately loaned to the Province of Saskatchewan to assist in any way he could with their drought problems.

Main was also a prime mover in establishing the "Canadian Conservation Institute". This organization apparently began in 1928 with informal meetings in Winnipeg of civil engineers and other individuals concerned with problems of Western Canada, particularly those of water and land use. The organization appears to have been a loose informal one without fees or structure, much like some of our modern environmental groups. It assumed much greater importance as the drought deepened and it began to attract more influential people, in particular Premier John Bracken of Manitoba, and James Richardson.

Through W. L. MacTavish, who was an enthusiastic member of the Institute, and editor of the Winnipeg Tribune newspaper, wide distribution of the releases of the Institute were obtained through the Southam newspaper chain. Air time was provided by James Richardson's chain of radio stations across the west.

While T. C. Main was undoubtedly the best man to get Ducks Unlimited (Canada) underway, the path was made easier by the pioneer work of the Institute, and the powerful support of influential people. Also of great importance was the co-operation of the fish and game associations in the three Prairie Provinces.

Tom Main viewed the waterfowl problem in Western Canada as primarily one of water, though as we shall see, he realized that other factors — predation, agricultural encroachment, etc. — had a depressing effect on waterfowl populations.

Consequently his first action was to find a suitable engineer. He had one in mind, D. M. Stephens, who was at that time employed by the Manitoba Provincial Government in the Department of Public Works. Main arranged to have Stephens loaned to Ducks Unlimited and he joined the company in early May, 1938. It was a short loan however, for Stephens was recalled on August 23rd by the Provincial Government to become Deputy Minister of Mines and Resources, and later Chairman of Manitoba Hydro. He was replaced as Manitoba Supervisor by George R. Fanset, who had worked for Main for three summers as an under-graduate while he was with the C.N.R. Fanset later became Manager of Ducks Unlimited (Canada) when Main left in October, 1946.

For an Assistant Manager, and particularly one to assume the public relations responsibility for the organization, Tom Main could have done no better than turn to his old friend, E. S. (Ed) Russenholt, whose imagination, enthusiasm, and skill with words and sketch pen, were just what was needed to dramatize the emergence of a new concept.

Conservation, which he defined as "The use of all resources of land and water for the greatest good of the greatest number of people over the longest time", had been part of Russenholt's credo for many years — the result of study, experience on the Saskatchewan prairies, and association with the Canadian Conservation Institute.

At the time he was contacted by Tom Main, Russenholt was in Toronto (which, he hated) working as Director of Public Relations for the Wawanesa Insurance Company. Main's message to him was also characteristic, "Come on home, we've

Edward S. Russenholt.

Bertram W. Cartwright.

got the chance to do the job we've always wanted to". Russenholt joined Ducks Unlimited in the first week of May, 1938.

T. C. Main knew something about waterfowl but, by his own admission, not enough to carry out the work he had undertaken. Fortunately, B. W. (Bert) Cartwright, a prominent Winnipeg naturalist, was interested in working for Ducks Unlimited (Canada) and had indeed been one of the applicants for the position of General Manager. Within a few days of T. C. Main's appointment, Bert agreed to join the new organization as Chief Naturalist effective May 1, 1938.

Bert brought impressive credentials with him. Born in England, he had emigrated to Canada as a young man and settled in Winnipeg where he was one of the founding members of the then Manitoba Natural History Society (now the Manitoba Naturalists' Society) and the Manitoba Museum. He was a well known authority on birds, and in particular their calls, an enviable skill. For many years he had written a column, "Wild Wings", for the Winnipeg Tribune, and had been keenly interested and involved in all areas of conservation. His experience with the waterfowl and upland game bird censuses of the Manitoba Game and Fish Association was of great benefit to him in organizing the waterfowl surveys he would carry out for Ducks Unlimited.

One of the things his younger co-workers remember most vividly about Bert Cartwright, was his ability to fly on aerial surveys through the roughest air, without apparent discomfort. While men much younger than he were going through the agonies of air sickness in the back of the aircraft, Bert bounced happily up and down on the front seat, recording ducks, geese, pelicans, and anything else that interested him.

It was exceptionally fortunate for the new company that these particularly gifted men were available and that drought and depression had conditioned the people of Western Canada to

George R. Fanset.

welcome such an organization. Without these favorable circumstances, it is quite possible that the fledgling company would not have survived. Truly, they were the right people in the right place at the right time.

In his memoirs, T. C. Main records that his first visitors as General Manager were E. B. Pitblado and his father, Isaac Pitblado, a well known sportsman. They said they would have office space for him by afternoon, and they did. It was only one room in the Bank of Hamilton Building at the corner of McDermot and Main Streets in Winnipeg, but it sufficed for the short time until adequate office space was found in the Commercial Building (now demolished) on Notre Dame East. Early in 1941, the Commercial Building was taken over by the Royal Canadian Air Force and the company moved to the mezzanine floor of the Bank of Commerce Building near the corner of Main and Lombard Streets. As the staff grew, more space was required and the office was moved in 1960 to the 6th floor. The next move was to 1495 Pembina Highway on June 28, 1968, and then in July of 1977, the company purchased its own building in Buffalo Place on Waverley Street and McGillivray Boulevard, and moved in May of 1978.

At the first Directors' Meetings, there was considerable pressure from W. G. Ross, the President, to locate the Head Office in Regina because of its central location. The decision was finally left to the General Manager and the office remained in Winnipeg.

Main began to gather the support staff he needed immediately. His first acquisition was Dorothy Cartwright, who began work as a secretary even before her father joined the organization. A retired Bank of Commerce Manager, E. B. Walker, was hired as an accountant. In an organization like Ducks Unlimited, what other name could he be given than "Hiram"! And, as "Hiram" he was known, until he left the company early in 1947.

An early D. U. Party. Angus H. Shortt, Betsy Shortt, Irma Main, Dorothy Cartwright, Renee Deschamps, Zoe Parsons, Irene Knocke.

Very soon Irma Main was also hired as a stenographer. As she recalls, it was on a rather uncertain basis. Because he was afraid of being accused of nepotism, and because she had not yet completed business college, her father fired her as soon as he returned from the field. For some time the game went on. Dorothy Cartwright hired her when T.C. left town, and he fired her on his return. Irma spent eight happy years with Ducks Unlimited, although she says she was never formally hired — T.C. finally just forgot to fire her! In June, 1938, Renee Deschamps became secretary to Ed Russenholt.

Ducks Unlimited, Inc. loaned Alex Camerle to assist in getting the new organization underway. He was paid by the American corporation but his expenses were picked up by Ducks Unlimited (Canada). He was also provided with a secretary, Violet Jackson, who was always known as "Jackie". H. C. (Cam) Cormode was Office Manager during the summer, then permanently in 1939. He left in 1950.

With this Head Office staff, Ducks Unlimited (Canada) began. Many sources remark on the great camaraderie that existed at that time. Starting this new organization was tremendously exhilarating — and particularly exciting with personalities like Main, Russenholt, and Cartwright generating an idea a minute. Renee Benningen (Deschamps) says it was a joy to go to work, because something new and stimulating was always happening, and because there was a great and sincere feeling of mutual commitment to make a really worthwhile project succeed.

George Fanset reaffirms this mood, and recalls when he went to the office on a Sunday to get in a couple of hours of quiet work, it was quite customary to find nearly all the office staff there. As Irma Main says, "Stories have been told that we all worked ungodly hours, with an almost religious fervor for the work — those stories are true! Probably Dorothy and I were caught up in the excitement of our elders — certainly we spent

DUCKS *Unlimited* (CANADA)

A Permanent Work in Sport and Conservation

505 Commercial Bldg.,
Winnipeg, Man.,
August 23, 1938.

Mr. E. B. Pitblado,
395 Main St.,
Winnipeg, Man.

Dear Mr. Pitblado:

      I have your letter of the 12th inst. in
which you intimate that the Searle Grain Company would be
willing to carry our publicity to their many correspondents,
along with the market quotations and reports. This is a
very happy suggestion indeed, and I am quite sure we will
avail ourselves of it. Please be good enough to arrange a
meeting for Russenholt and myself with Messrs. Gilchrist and
Strange and yourself at a convenient time for all concerned.
Thank you very much for this contact. It is very pleasing,
also, to note that such men as Mr. Leslie Moffat and Mr. G.
Montegu Black are pulling for our Company.

      Yours very truly,

      T. C. Main,
      General Manager.

TCM/J.

To Increase and Perpetuate the Supply of Ducks

35

William G. Campbell.

countless evenings at our desks, and I recall being there at least part of every weekend as well, that first year. It was years after I left DU before it occurred to me that some people got paid if they worked overtime."

In order to carry out the objective of building one large project in each prairie province, as decided by the directors, Main developed his provincial staff while personnel for the Head Office were still being assembled.

W. G. (Bill) Campbell was hired at the beginning of May to undertake the survey and construction of Big Grass Marsh in Manitoba. Bill was a hardened fieldman with many years of winter surveys behind him, living in tents in wilderness situations. He took the job on what he then thought was a temporary basis, and as a welcome respite from rough bush living. For a temporary job, it lasted a long time! For Bill retired from the company with honour in October, 1972, after a dedicated and productive career, principally in the Eastern Irrigation District at Brooks, Alberta.

In Saskatchewan, Main found a Provincial Supervisor, (the term "Manager" was not used at this time) F. T. (Frank) Clarke, a Past-President of the Saskatchewan Fish and Game League, who had assisted in the 1935 waterfowl census by The More Game Birds in America Foundation. An engineer, Hugh C. Ritchie, was hired as a temporary field assistant. Their chief assignment for the year was to survey and build the dam on Waterhen Marsh near Kinistino. "Jackie" Jackson, who had begun work with Ducks Unlimited in Winnipeg, was the first Saskatchewan stenographer. But by early fall of 1939 she had left, to be replaced first temporarily by Irma Main and then by Alma Clarke, the wife of the Provincial Supervisor, who continued as secretary through several succeeding Provincial Managers until late 1950. Pearl Irvine then assumed the position and continues in that capacity today.

The first Alberta Supervisor was Col. T. Newcomen. The date he was hired is not recorded, although reference is made to him in October, 1938. The first stenographic help in Alberta was Mary O'Brien. Irma Main also spent some time in Edmonton in 1939 and 1941. Betty Harley, wife of Rennie Harley who became Provincial Manager in February, 1941, provided stenographic services for the next four years on an almost gratuitous basis ($25.00 per month.) She was succeeded by Renee Benningen, originally of the Winnipeg staff, for two years, then a series of girls, and finally by Helen Pollock on July 1, 1956, who remained until 1975.

The co-operation of the three provincial governments was readily achieved. The Saskatchewan Government provided free space for the Ducks Unlimited office for many years, and thereafter an annual grant in lieu of rent until 1975. A similar arrangement for free office space in Edmonton was also made by Tom Main with Premier Aberhart of Alberta, which continued until 1976.

His first meeting with Aberhart had another significant result. Main suggested that a company such as Ducks Unlimited shouldn't have to pay for the use of crown lands. Aberhart agreed, and gave him such an undertaking in writing. Main immediately advised the Premiers of Manitoba and Saskatchewan of this arrangement, and had a similar agreement from them in a very few days.

A most useful concept also evolved from these agreements. Main determined from authorities in the United States that they were paying an average of $16.00 per acre for land to be reserved for wildlife. He used this figure in his speaking engagements in the United States for computing the value of the Canadian contribution to the objectives of the company.

Main also realized that the company would be unable to make any significant progress if they were forced to buy land from private owners. Consequently, the policy evolved of obtaining free easements from private landowners to develop waterfowl habitat on their land. In the first years, verbal consent was sufficient, but as the company grew, a more formal type of agreement was considered necessary.

With his Head Office staff selected and his provincial organizations established, Main was now ready to move into his first year of operation.

The First Year

4

At the first Directors' Meeting on April 1st, Arthur Bartley, representing Ducks Unlimited, Incorporated, set forth the objectives for 1938. First, to allot the largest possible portion of expenditures for field work to increase the duck crop at minimum cost and maximum result per dollar expended. He noted, "A big sales argument will be how many ducks are produced with this money". Second, to allot a sufficient amount for (a) publicity in Canada and preparation for expansion in 1939, and for (b) gathering and preparing public relations material needed to build up the organization in the United States.

The field work was to consist of restoring and managing former breeding areas. It was also to include such other activities to increase waterfowl production as control of predators, fires, botulism, and the salvage of ducklings, etc.

To publicize and gain support for Ducks Unlimited, he said it was absolutely necessary to operate in the three Prairie Provinces, building a major project in each. If approximately 100,000 acres could be restored, with pictures taken before and after, it would be a very tangible achievement to show subscribers in the United States.

Bartley stated that because an annual report of the status of the duck population was also considered to be extremely important, a suitable amount was provided in the budget for survey and census, and that there was no better way to acquire these data than by the staff of Ducks Unlimited right in the breeding area. He further stated that publicity should be a part of the responsibility of the operation.

There is no written account of these general guidelines being transmitted to Main. Presumably it was done orally, or by reference to the minutes of the meeting. Probably some guidance came from Camerle. Things must have been somewhat difficult,

Big Grass Marsh, April, 1938.

however, since Main's memoirs do not suggest a very high regard for Camerle's understanding of the situation on the prairies. Camerle spent much of the year taking movies of projects and other activities, which were shown with great success in the United States the following winter.

The first staff meeting to organize the 1938 program took place in Winnipeg on Wednesday, April 20th. Present were:—

T. C. Main	General Manager
Don Stephens	Manitoba Supervisor
Ed Russenholt	Assistant General Manager
Bert Cartwright	Chief Naturalist
Dorothy Cartwright	Stenographer

Although Bert Cartwright did not officially join Ducks Unlimited until May 1, he apparently attended the meeting.

This meeting and subsequent discussion revealed that there would be a large project available in each province for construction in 1938: Big Grass Marsh near Langruth, Manitoba; Waterhen Marsh near Kinistino in Saskatchewan; and Many Island Lake, north and east of Medicine Hat, Alberta. These areas were well known to provincial fish and game groups and, after years of drought, local residents were psychologically prepared to co-operate in re-establishing them as waterfowl marshes. This made the task a good deal easier. In any case, available projects did not seem to be a problem. T. C. Main, in a letter to A. M. Bartley of April 26th, reports 52 additional potential projects written up for consideration but worries about time and personnel to inspect them.

Big Grass Marsh, west of Langruth and Lake Manitoba, became Ducks Unlimited (Canada)'s first project, but a long history predated the involvement of the organization.

The marsh, some 40,000 acres in extent, was drained between 1909 and 1916 as part of a proposed 100,000 acre reclamation project. It was found unsuitable for agriculture and in the drought of the '30's was ravaged by dust storms and peat

Building the dam on Jackfish Lake, Big Grass Marsh. Ducks Unlimited's first structure.

Dam was completed December 5, 1938; project reached full supply level 1942.

fires. The two municipalities involved were in serious financial difficulties because the drainage levies still had to be paid.

As early as 1935, E. B. Pitblado, on behalf of the Manitoba Game & Fish Association, was already vigorously advocating the restoration of Big Grass Marsh. His main supporters were the solicitor for the Municipality of Westbourne, Stan H. Fahrni, and the Member of the Legislative Assembly for the area, W. Morton. Ducks Unlimited, in their search for a large Manitoba project in their initial year, were thus able to take advantage of a situation where much of the groundwork had already been done.

It was first inspected by Ducks Unlimited (Canada) personnel — Don Stephens, Bert Cartwright, and T. C. Main — on April 21st, 1938, the day after the corporation's first management meeting. These investigations confirmed the potential of the Big Grass Marsh Project.

Bill Campbell was hired May 2nd and immediately sent to the marsh to make the required surveys. As no transportation was available for him, he boarded with a farmer on the west side of the marsh and walked to work. Later moving to the east side of the marsh, he did the same thing.

His first job was to construct a temporary wood and rock dam on the outlet from Chandler Lake to the drainage ditch at the south end of the marsh. This was begun May 4th and completed on the 10th. A farmer had already built a pole and earth dam on the drainage channel from Jackfish Lake at the north end of the marsh, and although it leaked, it held about one foot of water. In the late fall, Ducks Unlimited replaced it with a stop log rock and timber dam. A similar dam replacing the temporary structure was also built on the drainage channel to hold water in Chandler Lake. Both were completed on December 5, 1938. Combined costs were $4,919.30 plus $400.00 for the Consulting Engineer, who supervised the construction by Macaw & Macdonald of Winnipeg. The designed elevations had the potential

Big Grass Marsh before . . .

. . . after.

of restoring approximately 10,000 acres of the former marsh. In 1939, a 37-foot steel observation tower was built, as well as a Ranger's cabin and tool shed, and over the next two years both standard and electric fences were installed.

To permit development of the project, the Municipality of Westbourne leased 49 quarters of land to Ducks Unlimited for 21 years at an annual rental of $5.00. After an extension of 10 years, a new agreement was drawn on November 1, 1968 for another 21 years with no rental fee. The Lakeview Municipality entered into a similar agreement on January 14, 1939 for 77 quarters of Municipal lands at a rental of $200 per year. This was also extended for 10 years and then a new agreement drawn for a further 21 years on June 21, 1971. No fee was charged, but the corporation agreed to deepen the drainage ditch to speed the passage of flood waters. The number of quarters presently under lease in the new agreement is somewhat less than the original, but those withdrawn are part of the uplands, and total acreage under lease from the two municipalities is almost 99 quarter sections, or, 15,840 acres. Separate agreements with the few private landowners in the marsh were obtained. Crown lands affected were reserved from sale or lease by the provincial government. The whole area had been made a bird sanctuary in 1926. In all agreements, Ducks Unlimited has been held free of all taxes and assessments.

The original rock and timber dams were replaced by concrete structures in 1953 and an 8,500 foot dyke constructed on the southwest side of Jackfish Lake to protect against flooding. Two smaller projects were built to flood attractive areas on the east side of the drainage ditch in 1954.

Big Grass Marsh brought great satisfaction, despite some disappointments. The marsh was under relatively intensive management by Ducks Unlimited on a year-round basis beginning in 1939, first for a short period by Ralph Fryer, and then by R. D.

Bert Cartwright at Big Grass Marsh Headquarters. Ranger's cabin and tower.

Harris. In 1942, Harris enlisted in the Royal Canadian Air Force and was reported missing after air operations on March 11, 1945. Under his supervision the fencing was completed, fireguards kept black, and haying, unauthorized grazing, and muskrat poaching controlled. Subsequent managers were employed by the Big Grass Muskrat Management Ranch to handle the muskrat aspects of the operation.

In 1941, preliminary planning for a P.F.R.A. (Prairie Farm Rehabilitation Act) community pasture in the Municipality of Westbourne began. At first this was welcomed by Ducks Unlimited as a relief from the continual problems with hay permittees and illegal grazing. It proved, however, to be a two-edged sword. The P.F.R.A. were sufficiently influential with the Municipality to insist that, in order to facilitate the pasture operation, water levels had to be kept so low that the Chandler Lake section of the project has always operated below its potential.

The first four years were disappointing in that run-off was deficient. It was not until the fall of 1942 that the marsh reached full supply level and water first flowed over the dams. From this time on, the marsh flourished. The muskrat population boomed and B. W. Cartwright effectively organized a muskrat management committee composed of representatives from the two municipalities with Ducks Unlimited as consultants. Called the "Big Grass Muskrat Management Ranch", it was a highly successful operation and contributed substantially to the municipal coffers, as long as the price of muskrat remained high and the catch good. The adjacent table summarizes the history of muskrat trapping on the project to 1958.

In 1943, after it had been demonstrated to the municipalities that intensive management of the marsh was a money-making proposition, it was turned over to them for operation as a self-supporting profitable enterprise.

Year	House Count	Population Estimate	Maximum Quota	Authorized Quota	Actual Catch	Average Price	Total Gross Revenue
1938	—	50	—	—	—	—	—
1939	—	—	—	—	—	—	—
1940	—	—	—	—	—	—	—
1941	37	180	—	—	—	—	—
1942	549	2745	700	700	700	2.05	1442.00
1943	1649	9894	5000	5000	3340	3.01	10071.00
1944	4064	24384	12000	10000	9309	2.16	20149.26
**1945			1500	1500	1384	1.41	1953.22
1945	4497	26894	15000	10000	10052	2.61	26300.64
1946	5402	30,000	20000	15000	16003	3.23	51750.68
1947		Marsh flooded			10880	2.12	23063.13
1948	2304	11520?		8000	4773	2.10	10123.88
x1949	2312	11000		5000	4368		
x1950	2515	12000	6000	4200-6000	2315		
x1951	2263				3020		
x1952	3636	(Everett Schneider)			1271	1.00?	1271.00?
*1953	1716	(Gordon Arksey)			2559	.95	2431.25
*1954		(Gordon Arksey)			2244	.92	2064.48
*1955		No Quota			2344	.88	2062.72
1956		(Indian Affairs)			13029	.71	9331.30
1957				23000	13020	.53	6949.96
1958				5000?	3128	.64	2016.45
							170980.97

x Owing to breakdown of management by the B.G.M.M.R. figures for these years are not available.

* The B.G.M.M.R. made deals with individuals from 1953-55 until arrangements were made with the Indian Affairs Dept. of the federal Government to manage the muskrat resource.

**Probably a fall trapping season.

This was a mistake. For when a series of flood years came, the muskrat crop deteriorated and small deficits were incurred. The area was neglected by the municipalities, and with fireguards unmaintained and poaching uncontrolled, fire swept the marsh from end to end, even damaging the timber control structures.

Ducks Unlimited then resumed control and in 1953 replaced the wooden structures with concrete. In 1956, the municipalities turned trapping operations over to the Indian Affairs Department for a percentage of the catch.

The wet years brought other problems for Ducks Unlimited. Heavy rains from June 21 - 27 in 1947 caused floods on the upper drainage of Jackfish Lake and the Grassy River. Alleging that flooding of agriculture land had resulted from the Ducks Unlimited dam on the drainage ditch below Jackfish Lake, the local farmers supported a lawsuit for damages against the corporation by Chris Brickman. The corporation retained M. A. Lyons as a Consulting Engineer. He established beyond a doubt that the dam was in no way responsible for the flooding, since the inflow into the marsh from the excessive rains, augmented by numerous drainage ditches, far exceeded the capacity of the drainage ditch below Jackfish Lake. The case was argued in September of 1951 and judgement given in favor of the corporation with costs assigned against the plaintiff.

Throughout the years, Big Grass Marsh has continued to produce substantial numbers of waterfowl, and to provide a valuable moulting area for ducks and an important staging area for ducks, geese, and cranes. However because of landowner complications, it has never been possible to develop the full potential of the Chandler Lake part of the project. At the present time, there are proposals to use the area as a retention basin to assist in alleviating floods in the Whitemud River Watershed. Ducks Unlimited disagrees with this intent and has suggested alternative proposals.

In 1961, the project was dedicated to Isaac Pitblado, a life-long sportsman and conservationist, and father of Edward B. Pitblado, long-time Secretary of Ducks Unlimited (Canada). A suitable cairn with a plaque was built.

The major project selected in Saskatchewan for 1938 construction was Waterhen Marsh, near the town of Kinistino, about 65 miles southeast of Prince Albert. The situation was remarkably similar to that at Big Grass Marsh. Both Waterhen Lake and Waterhen Marsh at the headwaters of the Carrot River (which empties into the Saskatchewan River just west of The Pas in Manitoba), were drained independently in 1920 for development into farmland. The lake, really a shallow marsh, was finally brought under cultivation although there were initial difficulties to the point where the Saskatchewan Government even attempted to restore it in 1933 by means of a small dam in the drainage channel.

The marsh was very different. Peat accumulations were much greater and attempts to cultivate it failed. The peat dried out, caught fire, and the smoke became both a nuisance and hazard to local farmers, who were sometimes unable to return to their homes from town due to the dense smoke.

The Waterhen Lake and Marsh were thus well known in Saskatchewan. It was a dramatic place for Ducks Unlimited to begin work in the province. It was also a place where they would find a welcome!

W. G. Ross, first Ducks Unlimited (Canada) President, suggested the area as a possible project at the inaugural meeting of the corporation. His suggestion was quickly acted upon. Frank Clarke, the Saskatchewan Supervisor and his Field Engineer, Hugh C. Ritchie, met with the Kinistino Board of Trade on May 11, 1938. The Board passed a resolution that its officials "interview the permit holders on Waterhen Marsh with a view to having them give their consent and to petition the government to have the marsh raised to, or near, the old level before it was drained".

By May 13th, all affected parties had signed. Consent to proceed was given by the government by phone on the same day. Construction began on an earth plug in the drainage canal on the 14th and was completed on the 17th.

Construction was by team and scraper, and by hand. Total cost $50.00 — team and teamster 40 cents per hour, labor 30 cents.

Relinquish Hay Permits to Re-Flood Marsh

Twenty-two members and twelve farmers were present at a special meeting of Kinistino and District Board of Trade, held Wednesday evening, for the purpose of discussing the Waterhen Lake project with Messrs Ritchie and Clark, representing Ducks Unlimited.

The aims of the organization were outlined by these gentlemen and it was pointed out they were at present interested in flooding the marsh portion of the Lake for a game sanctuary. To do this it would be necessary for the Department of Natural Resources to obtain the consent of present holders of grazing leases before flooding could be attempted. Af-

After considerable discussion the following resolution was passed on motion of Mr. W. Iredale: "That the Board of Trade interview permit holders on Waterhen Lake marsh with a view to having them give their consent, and to petition the Government to have the marsh raised to or near the old level before it was drained."

Consent was readily given by the grazing lease holders to this project and a coffer dam has been put in so that drainage might occur to allow the work of building a dam to be proceeded with.

Kinistino Times, May 18, 1938.

The permanent dyke, 4,400 feet long and containing 11,920 cubic yards, was completed on October 31st for 15 cents per yard. Repairs to the wooden bridge over the drainage canal, which had been designed as a control structure, brought the total cost of the project to $5,610.00 and would hold water on 3,760 acres of former marsh. In 1947, the original dam was replaced by a concrete stop log structure.

For those who might believe that the concept of nesting islands for waterfowl is new, it is interesting to relate that twelve 200' x 100' islands were built in the marsh, and 20 parallel to the dyke, using the stripping from the borrow pits, at a cost of $2,500.

The lake and marsh, and considerable upland acreage, was made a game preserve by Order-in-Council on June 15, 1939. Because some landowners farming the uplands objected to having their land included in the preserve without their consent, which they refused largely because of crop damage, the preserve was reduced in early 1940 to include the lake and marsh and a strip 600 feet wide around it. Since then the strip has been narrowed, eliminated, and re-established, but the marsh and lake have always remained preserves.

In compliance with an agreement made with the Saskatchewan Department of Natural Resources that Ducks Unlimited would appoint a marsh manager for the Waterhen Marsh, W. G. Leitch was hired May 19, 1939, in Winnipeg and arrived at the marsh with B. W. Cartwright on the 21st. Leitch remained with Ducks Unlimited until February, 1941, when he took leave of absence to join the R.C.A.F. Returning in 1946, he supervised the biological program in Saskatchewan and Alberta, becoming Chief Biologist in 1951, a position he held until 1976. He retired December 31, 1977.

During the summer, a biological survey of the project was made, waterfowl censused, nest searches and brood counts con-

44

ducted. In addition, bulrush and sago pondweed were planted and the islands sown to brome grass and sweet clover.

Since October 1939, while there has been no resident manager, the project has not been neglected. Management of water levels has been carried out for a very nominal fee by the Porter brothers, first Fred and then Morris, adjacent farmers who have supported the project since the beginning. In addition, there was also intense interest in the resident goose breeding flock, and a goose banding program began after the war and con-

tinued for several years. This resulted in frequent visits by Ducks Unlimited fieldmen. As well, biologists from several different organizations engaged in other specific studies and spent the entire breeding season at the marsh.

In 1939, Leitch recorded two pair of breeding geese. In 1971, Kent Brace, a student studying the Canada geese on the project, found 145 nests. Of these, 28 were on "Goose Island", 5.9 acres in extent. The attractiveness of this natural island for nesting waterfowl is demonstrated by the 170 gadwall nests

Real horsepower built the dyke on Waterhen Marsh.

The original wooden structure was rebuilt as a control . . .

. . . and the marsh restored.

found on it at one time by Jim Hinz, another student, who was studying this species. The nests were actually confined to 2.2 acres of snowberry. Nesting success was 82%. If all waterfowl could achieve this success, there would be no need for Ducks Unlimited!

Canada geese have reached a maximum of 70 nests on this island, but at this density, territorial conflict at the nest site significantly reduced nesting success. Such conflict is not a factor with gadwall. Gadwall eggs collected here have been transported to the Coniagas Ranch in British Columbia to establish a breeding population of this species in the lower Fraser Valley.

In 1969, Edward G. Hennan, a student who became a permanent Ducks Unlimited employee in May, 1970, carried out an evaluation of level ditching in an overgrown section of the marsh. This necessitated the construction of a series of ditches and three observational towers which were reconstructed from old windmill towers.

In 1947, Waterhen Marsh became an Iowa donor project. Through the years, it has been an extremely successful and productive project. Water levels have varied but only minimally and waterfowl production has remained uniformly high.

T. C. Main always had a particularly soft spot in his heart for Alberta, no doubt because, although he was born in England, he was brought up at Pincher Creek. At any rate, when Many Island Lake in southern Alberta, about 40 miles east of Medicine Hat, was chosen as the first project for that province, T.C. took particular interest in it. In a memorandum he states that Head Office will be quite busy enough in administering the construction of Big Grass Marsh and Waterhen, and that he would take responsibility for Many Island Lake himself. Col. Newcomen, an engineer, was already established as the Alberta Supervisor, so T.C. had the engineering assistance that he needed.

The concrete dam was built in 1947 and the marsh became an Iowa donor project.

Canada Geese now use the old drainage ditch spoil banks for nest sites.

Ducklings concentrated on the fast disappearing water of Many Island Lake were rounded up, transported, and released on permanent water.

Main first saw Many Island Lake in 1910 and described it as magnificent. A. C. Bent, the celebrated ornithologist, in *The Auk* of October, 1907, describes it in similar glowing terms. In wet years it no doubt was, for it covered over 8,000 fertile acres with shallow water and had a long, flat, sinuous shoreline. Unfortunately, it also typified the characteristic hydrology of southern Alberta shallow grassland lakes — fluctuating between flood and drought, depending on the unpredictable whims of winter snowfall and spring run-off.

Seen at its best, then, it was magnificent, and such must have been the case when the greater part of the area was made a Dominion Bird Sanctuary in 1920. By 1935, the situation was quite different. The lake was dry, and in 1936, J. Dewey Soper, then Chief Federal Migratory Bird Officer for the Prairie Provinces, recommended cancellation of the sanctuary, and substitution of another area which would be more productive.

Main, though he saw the area in 1910, may have been redirected toward it by C. H. Miles, a Bank Manager in Saskatoon, who had been stationed at Medicine Hat and had shot on the lake. Correspondence seems to confirm this. This contact led to one with the Medicine Hat Fish and Game Association, and ultimately to the owners of a shooting lodge on the lake, in a critical area which was not in the sanctuary. The members strongly encouraged Ducks Unlimited to restore the water in Many Island Lake. As an inducement, they offered to give up their shooting privileges within the sanctuary. The fulfillment of this obligation was to cause them great agony (and Ducks Unlimited much anxiety), when waterfowl responded to the return of water in the lake!

Main and Sam White from Maple Creek, who worked for Ducks Unlimited during the next two summers, inspected Many Island Lake on July 25, 1938. The only water they found was in hoofprints, and covered about thirty acres. Main reported

Under the lone tree at Many Island Lake, Tom Hargraves rancher, centre, gives Tom Main left and Sam White, permission to proceed with the project.

thousands of ducklings and 50 goslings stranded, dependent on the little water that remained. He arranged for Sam White to have local school children assist in driving the birds into a pen, loading them on a truck, and transporting them to permanent water some distance away. Alex Camerle came from Winnipeg to record the salvage operation with still and movie cameras. Shown with great success the following winter, these pictures helped fulfill T.C.'s obligation under the 1938 budget to provide educational material for use in the United States.

From an engineering standpoint, Many Island Lake presented a problem quite different from the simple dams and dykes on the drainage ditches of Big Grass and Waterhen Marshes.

Here, except for occasional years of heavy run-off, the lake was too large for the watershed of McKay Creek which supplied it. Water spreading out shallowly over such a large area soon disappeared in this region of high evaporation. T.C.'s plan of development, which has since been used many times by Ducks Unlimited, consisted of reducing the flooded area by a restriction dam at a narrow point of the lake so that the impounded area more closely matched the average run-off from the watershed. A greater depth of water would thus be stored to offset evaporation and provide some carryover for years of low run-off. At the same time, in years of abundant water, the entire former lake would be filled — but only after the primary restricted area was full.

Diversion of additional water from Ross Creek into McKay, and thence to Many Island Lake was considered but was judged too expensive, although it might not be so considered now. Had this been done, the subsequent history of the lake might have been quite different. In retrospect, it seems an exceptional opportunity was missed. Although considering the financial constraints at the time, and the necessity to distribute construction across the three Prairie Provinces, it is difficult to see how any other decision could have been reached.

Surveys were completed on August 25, 1938 by Col. Newcomen and work started September 29th by Gibbs Bros. of Lumsden, Saskatchewan, under sub-contract from Poole Construction of Edmonton. The work was completed on November 3rd.

As well as an earth dam, a ditch 2½ miles long was built to convey the water from McKay Creek to the reservoir. This was to prevent it from spreading out from the ill-defined channel of the creek through a low area enroute and thus being lost to evaporation. Over the years this ditch led to problems for the local rancher, who had depended on this natural irrigation from the creek for his hay crop. Although Ducks Unlimited provided a structure in the ditch for him to carry out the same irrigation procedure on a controlled basis, it never seems to have worked to his satisfaction.

The project which, when developed, established 700 acres of the 8,360 acre lake as a reservoir between 4 and 5 feet deep, was named Lone Tree Lake for the single tree which grew on its shore in the wide open prairie. The 2½-mile ditch contained 11,-700 cubic yards of earth; and the 977 foot dam, 14,678 cubic yards. Total cost was $4,609.06.

The project presented a host of problems right from the start; problems which Ducks Unlimited would experience on many other projects in future years and from which basic operating principles would evolve.

Overgrazing was a serious concern and in order to improve cover, Ducks Unlimited purchased a fraction of a section which they owned until 1975. They also became involved in a fencing program to control grazing pressure on the sanctuary uplands. Here they learned, (even though a local rancher, a conscientious and co-operative man, was paid a retainer fee to manage the area) that fences in grazing lands, unless they are maintained and enforced at an almost unacceptable level, are ineffective in preserving grass for nesting cover. The better grass inside the fence, particularly in dry years, is almost irresistible to a rancher with hungry cattle and a pair of wire cutters in his pocket. In some instances, fences meant to exclude cattle or horses were used to hold them on what were meant to be cover areas. This experience no doubt had much to do with the Ducks Unlimited policy on fencing, which is one of extreme caution, unless adequate supervision is guaranteed.

On this project, too, the corporation became involved in establishing the new boundaries of the sanctuary. This exasperating experience, combined with a similar occurrence at the Mormon Church Ranch Project, also in Alberta, no doubt motivated Main to outline Ducks Unlimited's policy on the establishment of sanctuaries in a letter dated May 27, 1942, to D. W. Hays, one of the members of the shooting lodge at Many Island Lake. This policy which evolved early from harsh experience is still followed today, and is basically one of non-involvement.

As might be anticipated in an area where precipitation is highly variable and unpredictable, Many Island Lake had good years and bad. Sometimes the whole complex was flooded and highly productive, and sometimes, even with the ditch from McKay Creek, the reservoir was almost dry. To be fully effective, the project needed the diversion from Ross or Battle Creek, but, after the original investigation, this seems to have been forgotten.

In 1946 and 1947, plans were made to improve the existing works and develop two other basins. In 1948, a very heavy run-off prevented further work and since that time, nothing more has been done. Recent investigations show that the original dam requires repairs, and that during the dry years, several gas wells were drilled in the dry bed of the reservoir. While these were not insurmountable obstacles to the rehabilitation of the project, the unreliability of the water supply remains, for which there may now be no solution. The water from Ross Creek is fully allotted for the Ross Creek Irrigation Scheme, and to obtain water from Battle Creek is a complex problem, since it is both interprovincial and international.

Main had better luck with a fourth major project he was able to build with the 1938 budget. Stalwart Marsh, about 50 miles north of Regina, was a real bargain. For $209, using horses and scrapers, field engineer Hugh Ritchie was able to build an earth dam and spillway on the outlet and improve water levels on 767 acres of excellent cattail-bulrush marsh. This simple earth dam has since been replaced by a concrete structure and additional water has been diverted into the area. Islands have been constructed and the marsh still operates today as a most productive project.

Neither the Ducks Unlimited Charter nor the terms of reference for the 1938 budget, as laid down by the Directors, restricted Main to the exclusive use of water storage as a means of increasing the duck population.

Although undertaking one project in each province was the primary 1938 objective, Bartley specifically stated that "Consideration should be given to allotments for preventing marsh fires, cattle trespass, in crow, magpie, and other predator control, in curbing grazing losses, in cleaning up disease areas and for such matters as drought losses, duck census, photographic work, etc."

Main began the management phase of his program in Alberta, selecting the Mormon Church Ranch in the southwestern part of the province as one area, and the Ministik Lake Bird Sanctuary, thirty miles due east of Edmonton, as the other.

He was directed to the Mormon Church Ranch in mid-July, 1938, by a chance meeting in Cardston with Seymour Smith, a local rancher. Such meetings were a common thing with T.C., who was a friendly gregarious person. Smith showed Main over his ranch but suggested that the Mormon Church Ranch, near Caldwell, had greater possibilities for waterfowl. He then arranged for the Mormon Church Ranch manager, J. R. Frodsham, to show Main the ranch.

It comprised 30,000 acres and contained, according to Main's report of August 6, 1938, between 60 and 100 attractive small lakes or sloughs. He was impressed with the wetlands, but the area was heavily overgrazed, and predators, specifically skunks, crows, and magpies, were said to be particularly numerous.

Apparently Frodsham indicated to Main that the Church might look favorably on his suggestion that Ducks Unlimited manage the ranch for waterfowl production. On his return to Winnipeg, T.C. wrote to E. J. Wood, President of the High Council of the Alberta Stake of Zion, making that suggestion. En route to Winnipeg, he met Dr. C. W. Watson in Regina who was Assistant Director of Waterfowl Activities for More Game Birds in America, and in Canada inspecting bird refuges and sanctuaries. Main asked him to proceed to Cardston and see if he could come to an agreement with the Mormon Church Ranch on behalf of Ducks Unlimited.

On September 18th, Watson was able to report a tentative agreement with Frodsham on behalf of the ranch for a 20-year period. The official agreement with the President and the High Council was signed on November 29th, but only for 10 years. Seymour Smith had intended to have his ranch included but apparently never got around to making the necessary application to the Alberta Government to have his land made into a game preserve.

Frodsham was employed October 1, 1938, to carry out Ducks Unlimited's plans for the ranch in addition to his duties as ranch manager — salary $125 per year plus $25 for ammunition for predator control. The major effort was to be directed toward predator control and patrol of the area to prevent hunting. At this time, Main had not yet learned his lesson on setting up game preserves, and had persuaded the Church to have the ranch made into a preserve. In fact, he was particularly determined that this be done. He was to regret it.

On January 28, 1939, Assistant General Manager Ed Russenholt, at the Annual Meeting of the Alberta Fish and Game League in Edmonton, found strong opposition to the Church Ranch game preserve from local hunters. And on April 18th, Col. Newcomen, the Alberta Manager, ran into a veritable meat grinder when he attended a Lethbridge dinner inaugurating a new fish and game club to be known as the "Southwestern Alberta Fish & Game Club". (Strangely enough, in view of what followed, Main was made one of the Honorary Vice-Presidents!)

The members were violently opposed to the Mormon Church Ranch being made a game preserve because it was, they said, the only place in the area where they could hunt ducks. Ducks Unlimited was accused of establishing sanctuaries along the southern border of the province so ducks could mass undisturbed by Canadians, and then cross the border to waiting American hunters. One speaker claimed he had made investigations in the United States, and from these, was convinced that Ducks Unlimited was not "sincere".

That Newcomen had a bad night is confirmed by the concluding sentence in his report, which states, "May I suggest, that in order to offset any such arguments as the above, we confine our activities further north, so that Canadians will have a chance at migrating birds before they cross the border."

The project turned out to be a disappointment. Through the ten-year agreement with the ranch, water conditions were highly variable. In some years nearly all of the ponds and sloughs were dry and in others quite productive. In 1939, one slough, about 10 acres in size, was fenced to provide better nesting cover. The remainder of the ranch was heavily grazed.

In the same year, W. Ray Salt, a well known Alberta ornithologist who worked for Ducks Unlimited that summer at this project, and at Many Island Lake, transplanted bulrush into some of the open water areas. He also banded half a dozen ducks which he was able to catch by hand.

But the predator campaign never did really get underway, in spite of urging from Bert Cartwright at the Winnipeg office. Frodsham, who was supposed to report monthly, turned out to be a poor reporter and this further aggravated the situation. Finally, payments to him were stopped at the end of November, 1943. Fanset (then Chief Engineer) in a letter to Frodsham, pointed out that due to gasoline shortages, the company had to localize their activities in each province, and were thus unable to give the ranch the attention it deserved, and that the agreement would be carried on in name only until the situation changed. He made the suggestion however, that it might be possible at some time to divert irrigation water into the ponds and sloughs on the ranch.

This possibility was explored in 1946. Leitch, on October 23rd, after an inspection of the area, was impressed with its potential and particularly with the excellent cover (grazing practices had obviously changed). He recommended that the company proceed with plans to divert Crooked Creek through the ranch. However, investigation revealed that the water was already all allotted for irrigation. When the lease came up for renewal in 1948, Ducks Unlimited advised the Church Ranch that they would not request an extension, and in 1949, it was written off the official company project list.

Much greater success attended the management by Ducks Unlimited of the Ministik Bird Sanctuary about 30 miles east of Edmonton. The Sanctuary, as established by Order-in-Council by the Canadian Government in 1920, totalled about 15,680 acres with approximately 4,000 acres in Ministik Lake proper. To the east of the lake, the Sanctuary included a large number of attractive small wooded ponds, which contributed significantly to production from the area. H. E. Williams, a local farmer, whose sons, Francis, and then Keith, were to have long association with Ducks Unlimited, was employed by the Canadian Government as Warden, at a salary of $125 per year, plus a boat.

The Sanctuary was turned over to the Province of Alberta by the Federal Government when the natural resources were transferred in 1930. Williams was discharged by the Federal Government and not replaced by the Province. At first, the Sanctuary was retained inviolate, but gradually, under local pressure, haying and grazing leases — some long term — were granted. Poaching became common, fires swept the area and over-grazing was rife. It was apparently under these conditions that Dr. C. W. Watson on his 1938 survey of sanctuaries for More Game Birds in America first saw the project.

Tom Main appeared to have great confidence in Watson. After a two month period in Canada, in 1938, Watson returned to the United States, whereupon T.C. wrote him a highly complimentary letter offering him employment with Ducks Unlimited should he ever so desire. Watson returned to Canada in 1939 and took a very active part in establishing the Ministik project. Although he never assumed the title, he acted as Alberta Provincial Manager (Newcomen having departed) from January, 1940, until early 1941, at which time he returned to the United States and disappeared from the Ducks Unlimited story. During his time with Ducks Unlimited, he exerted considerable influence

Ministik Lake and adjacent potholes.

on the policies and attitudes of the organization, and particularly on T. C. Main.

The first reference to the Ministik project is by Main in a memorandum to file under date of June 15, 1938. This refers to an attached report on Ministik, likely by Watson, which apparently described deplorable conditions on the Sanctuary, but which unfortunately has not come to light. On the basis of this report, T.C. recommended that the appropriate officials of the Provincial Government be approached to eliminate grazing leases, to have the area fenced, and to appoint a game guardian. (The Alberta sportsmen had recommended this course of action to the Government on several occasions without success.) It was suggested that an approach by Col. Newcomen and Main might be effective, and the Fish and Game League officials believed there would be more chance of success if Newcomen and Main went alone, without a delegation of sportsmen.

There are no details, but apparently the approach was made either by Newcomen or Main, or either one with Dr. Watson. In a report to Main on Ministik, dated August 26, 1938, Watson refers to his investigations of bird sanctuaries in Alberta for Ducks Unlimited from August 1-14, and the fact that local sportsmen, particularly in the Edmonton area, and the Provincial Government, were anxious to have something concrete done in Alberta that year.

The Alberta Game Commissioner suggested that Ducks Unlimited funds might be most effectively and economically spent by instituting proper management on provincial game sanctuaries, since government funds were unavailable for this purpose. Ministik was mentioned by the Game Commissioner as one that would be most productive under management. Thus the door was opened for Ducks Unlimited to make a proposal to the Alberta Government to take over management of the Ministik Sanctuary.

This is illustrative of the welcome given by the prairie governments to Ducks Unlimited at this time. One of the reasons was, of course, that the prairies were just beginning to recover from drought and depression, and anyone who would spend new money in the province was very welcome. But the game commissioners were also pleased to have someone do what they knew should be done but for which they had had no resources themselves. A third reason, and probably as important, was that there were no professionals in the provincial wildlife organizations at that time, and Main, Watson, and Cartwright represented a new approach to wildlife management based on the principles contained in the newly published bible for wildlife managers by Aldo Leopold, *Wildlife Management*. So, when approached by an organization both eager and financially able to implement new concepts, the prairie governments, having no money themselves, were willing to give it a chance.

During a three-way conversation between Main, Bartley and Watson at Prince Albert, Saskatchewan, on August 16th, (probably during the aerial survey of northern waterfowl populations) the idea developed that Ducks Unlimited might well take over the Ministik Sanctuary and create a model project there. It could serve as a pattern for management of other sanctuaries, and, being close to Edmonton, its publicity value was obvious. As far as possible, and this was considered to be of primary importance, the project should be made self-supporting through the utilization of its own resources — not only to relieve Ducks Unlimited expenditures, but to demonstrate that such a thing was possible for all sanctuaries.

Muskrats were considered to have the greatest potential for that purpose. No water control structures were contemplated, for, although the lake had fallen 5 feet below its normal level of 1923 and this shrinkage had established the shoreline as much as one-quarter of a mile from the high point, there were no well-

defined inlets or outlets. The lake appeared to be an exposed water table augmented by local run-off.

In a letter to the Alberta Game Commissioner dated August 30, 1938, Watson made a formal proposal that Ducks Unlimited take over the management of the Ministik Bird Sanctuary. Although a 20-year lease was discussed, it was considered that a statutory commission would be the best vehicle by which revenues from the Sanctuary could be ploughed back into its management and development. Watson was dreaming beyond the Ministik Sanctuary, for the idea of managing sanctuaries by commissions seemed to open the door to opportunity all across the west. "Imagine", he says, "such a commission in each province with the General Manager of Ducks Unlimited sitting on all of them . . . Ducks Unlimited would become an integrating force between the provincial commissions." Unfortunately, it was not to be.

In summary, the proposal by Ducks Unlimited to the Alberta Game Commissioner contained the following:

1. That Ducks Unlimited (Canada) take over the complete management of the Ministik Lake Sanctuary for a period of twenty years for the purpose of developing an ideal waterfowl sanctuary there. During this period Ducks Unlimited will finance all operations. It is proposed that the sanctuary be made as self-supporting as possible through utilization of natural resources and that the revenues be expended to maintain the sanctuary. In other words, Ducks Unlimited funds will be used to "prime the pump".

2. That a statutory commission be set up by an Order-in-Council under the Companies Act. That this commission take a direct lease on the Ministik Sanctuary lands. That the commission make a contract with Ducks Unlimited for the latter to manage the area.

3. That the commission will act in an advisory capacity on matters of management of the sanctuary but in a control capacity

in the matter of revenues from the sanctuary and their reinvestment therein.

4. That revenues be paid directly to the commission but that disbursements be made through Ducks Unlimited as managing agent.

5. That the contract between the Sanctuary commission and Ducks Unlimited give the latter a degree of freedom of action which will encourage quick and efficient management of the project.

As might be expected, once the subject of land lease to Ducks Unlimited, or the formation of a commission to operate the Sanctuary, reached the inner legal sanctum of the government, it ran into difficulties. In spite of repeated attempts by Ducks Unlimited to clarify and confirm their legal position at Ministik, they were forced to operate only by the authority of a letter from the Minister of Lands and Mines, dated November 25, 1938, which agreed only to recommend the appointment of a commission. It was found that to create such a commission would require the introduction of a private bill into the legislature, and, in this arena, the concensus was that it would be highly contentious. Thus, the first of T.C.'s hopes for the project — that it could demonstrate self-sufficiency — was shattered.

Nevertheless, due, it seems, to confusion within the Lands and Mines Branch, Ducks Unlimited continued to assign grazing and haying leases, to collect the fees for them, and to sell the predator pelts trapped by the Warden, Francis Williams. There was some doubt about what to do with the money since, without a commission, Ducks Unlimited did not feel they could spend it to offset their costs in operating the Sanctuary. As a result, it was sent to Winnipeg and put in a trust fund.

In December of 1942, B. W. Cartwright wrote to the Alberta Game Commissioner, drawing to his attention that Ducks Unlimited was operating only under the authority of the November 25, 1938 letter, and asked how tenure could be placed on a more satisfactory basis. He advised that Ducks Unlimited had continued to put all revenues into the trust fund but without a commission they felt that no disbursements could be made.

The Game Commissioner's reply pointed out that under the Transfer of Natural Resources Agreement of 1930, it was impossible to give Ducks Unlimited a lease on what had been a Dominion Bird Sanctuary. In view of Ducks Unlimited's work and expenditure, however, the government was sympathetic to the organization having some sort of recognized presence in the area. But the trust fund would have to be turned over to the province for inclusion in general revenue.

At a meeting with the government on March 12, 1943, it was suggested that Ducks Unlimited act as an agent of the government, but there is no record of this being formalized. However, Francis Williams, the resident Ducks Unlimited Manager, was to make recommendations on all hay and grazing permit applications and send them to the Ducks Unlimited office in Edmonton for approval. They would then be forwarded with the fees to the provincial government. In lieu of the government's matching the revenue from Ministik, which had been one of Main's objectives, and in recognition of the work done for the government by the Ministik Manager, the government agreed to pay $20.00 per month toward his salary.

This financial arrangement continued well into the 1950's. Keith Williams, the present Ducks Unlimited Northern Area Supervisor, whose responsibilities include management of the Ministik Sanctuary, still controls the issue of haying permits on the Sanctuary. Grazing has now been practically eliminated.

On March 13, 1943, the money in the Ministik Trust Account, a total of $1,544.35, was turned over to the government.

Shallow bay, Ministik Lake.

Management of the area by Ducks Unlimited was not really formalized until August 7, 1959, when a "Licence of Occupation" for Ducks Unlimited to manage the Sanctuary was issued under date of May 14, 1958 — "for as long as required". This recognition resulted from long negotiations by Bob MacEwing, the Ducks Unlimited landman, beginning in 1955. Another problem was to secure tax exemption for the half section of land Ducks Unlimited had been forced to buy in order to establish a viable management unit. This exemption was not obtained. In 1963, the company sold the land privately.

But the story of the Ministik project is really that of the Williams family, without whose dedicated interest, which went far beyond the employment the sanctuary provided, the project would never have succeeded.

The father, H. E. Williams, had been the Warden in charge of the original Ministik Federal Bird Sanctuary from the time it was established in 1920 until it was turned over to the Provincial Government by the Federal Government in 1930. During the period 1930-38, the Sanctuary was without official supervision although Col. Newcomen, the Ducks Unlimited Alberta Manager, stated that Francis Williams, son of the former Warden, "does what he can in the time he can spare from his farm work". Presumably, Francis had some sort of authority at this time — probably that of a Voluntary Game Warden — for which of course he was unpaid.

On November 5, 1938, Francis was hired by Ducks Unlimited to manage the Sanctuary. Salary was $70 per month plus $20 for upkeep of saddle horses — since this was the only way that the Sanctuary could be patrolled — and ammunition for predator control, etc. The $20 was paid by separate cheque, which led to much humourous comment that Ducks Unlimited was the only organization with a horse legitimately on the payroll! Even more humourous was that the horse also had an

expense account! On Francis' weekly report, the item often appeared — meal for man — oats for horse —.

Francis tackled a formidable job. Virtually unsupervised for nearly a decade, the Sanctuary, through neglect, had become almost common property. Long-term haying and grazing leases had been issued, shooting and trapping were carried on almost openly, and uncontrolled fires swept the area.

The cancellation of long-term leases and removal of the Sanctuary as an area of common use, aroused great resentment in the community. Francis had to demonstrate the authority of Ducks Unlimited in the area. And this he did with above average tenacity and courage.

Twenty-five miles of fence were built by the end of 1938, delineating the boundaries of the Sanctuary. Francis laid out his trap lines for skunks and coyotes and began his lifelong battle with magpies all year and with crows in the summer.

He also began his patrols of the area to control muskrat and deer poaching. Many of these were made at night, in the winter, on horseback. In his weekly reports, Francis often mentioned being up all night waiting for a trapper to return to his traps.

His report of the week ending November 3, 1949, dramatically describes the hardships and risks he endured in carrying out his duties.

Colonel T. Newcomen
Dear Sir:

I would like to submit my weekly report ending November 3, 1939.

Date	Left H.Q.	Returned H.Q.	Miles	EXPENSES		
				Gas	Horse	Man
October 28	9.00 a.m.	6.00 p.m.	9	none	none	none
October 29	8.30 a.m.	5.00 p.m.	21	none	none	none
October 30	7.00 a.m.	5.15 a.m.	42	none	none	none
October 31	8.00 a.m.	8.00 a.m.	16	none	none	none
November 1	9.45 a.m.	1.00 a.m.	22	none	none	none
November 2	8.45 a.m.	11.00 p.m.	28	none	none	none
November 3	9.15 a.m.	7.00 p.m.	19	none	none	none

REMARKS

Monday, October 30 discovered traces of night trapping of muskrats. Watched till 5 in the morning but trappers didn't appear. No trappers Tuesday or Tuesday night. Wednesday discovered the trappers trapping around a small lake. Waited till dark and hid beside rat run. At 10:00 p.m. caught . . . and . . . with 10 rats and eight traps. These fellows had horses and kept them within ten feet of themselves all the time for a quick get away. I laid the information with Magistrate Chapman of Tofield and Constable Austin of the R.C.M.P. has agreed to prosecute the case for me. Mr. Bacheldor assisted in the capture. When I shone my flashlight on the trappers, . . . rushed at me with fists flying and Mr. . . . ran for the horses but Mr. Bacheldor had already caught the horses so their little scheme to slug the guardian and beat it failed. When they found that there was two of us they submitted quietly to arrest.

Yours sincerely,
(signed) Francis Williams

If Francis had been of overpowering physical presence, adventures such as this would not have been so remarkable. But he was relatively slight and often in poor health — yet of courage, dedication, and honesty, he had more than his share.

His winter program for 1939, as submitted to Col. Newcomen, forecasts a busy season:

Colonel T. Newcomen
Dear Sir:

I would like to submit a program of winter and fall work for your approval:

Finishing construction of log cabin at observation tower.
Finishing construction of log barn at observation tower.
Finishing trail to observation tower and on to lake where it crosses line near centre line of section 22, Twp. 50, Rg. 21.
Widening and improving all trails which could be used in emergency in the fenced area of the sanctuary.
Establishing a long trap and snare line for coyotes and skunks before October 15.

Trap all muskrats which have located in unsuitable locations right after freeze-up.
Establish a trap line for weasels as soon as weasel skins are prime.
Moving boat house out to deeper water when ice is thick enough to support horses.
Construction of pier to boat house.
Cutting 300 fence posts to be stored for use in general repair work on Ducks Unlimited fence.
Brace each poplar telephone pole with willow fence posts.
Measure all hay permitted in the sanctuary.
Keep poachers out by systematic patrols around area.
Improve one rat run in each slough and small lake in area so water could be available for putting out fires.
Removal of some fire traps within a few feet of fence which if allowed to remain would seriously damage fence in case of fire.

Yours sincerely,
(Signed) Francis Williams

But in spite of lease problems, muskrat and deer poachers, fires set to divert Francis to other parts of the Sanctuary so that these illegal activities could be carried on, and fires set maliciously as a protest against the Sanctuary, B. W. Cartwright was able to report to the Alberta Game Commissioner, under date of December 30, 1942, as follows:

We fenced the Sanctuary, at a cost of approximately $6,000; appointed a resident wildlife manager, who patrolled the area and put an end to illegal shooting, trapping, grazing, wood-cutting and haying. With the cooperation of the Government, long-term hay and grazing leases were cancelled — and new permits were arranged on a yearly basis. A 40-foot, steel lookout tower was erected, cabins built, and telephone line installed. The settlers were organized into an efficient fire-fighting force; and fires have been attacked and brought under control with promptness and despatch. Strict attention has been paid to the proper administration of the revenues derived there from fur and from grazing and haying permits.

As regards waterfowl management, we have controlled their predators effectively. These include crows, magpies, skunks, coyotes, and mink. The fur-bearers have been taken off when their pelts were prime, and delivered to the Department for sale by auction. Proceeds, of course, go into the Trust Account. We have banded approximately 3,000 waterfowl on this Sanctuary; and the returns have been mapped, showing the distribution over the continent.

To sum up — Ministik is now functioning as a first-class Bird Sanctuary, as it was intended to do under the Migratory Birds Convention Act.

In June, 1945, the project, but not the Sanctuary, was expanded to include Joseph, Oliver, and Larry Lakes and sold as a donor project to the McIntyre brothers, who owned the Munroe Auto Equipment Company at Munroe, Michigan. The project became the Maeco-Ministik donor project, referring to the first letters of the company name, and with the additional area now comprised 41,000 acres. However, effective control was never extended to include the three lakes.

Francis reported faithfully every week and his reports give a continuous picture of events on the Sanctuary. In his annual report dated January 8, 1946, is an excellent description of the devastating effect of a hailstorm on waterfowl. Since Francis was not given to exaggeration, this can be considered an accurate account of what occurred.

Unfortunately a very bad hailstorm swept along the south side of the main lake July 28, 1945, and as a large percentage of the newly hatched lesser scaup and canvas-back were concentrated in this area, the damage was heavy. At least 2000 young scaup died and many other birds such as full grown crows, hawks, robins noted killed or crippled . . . several trees had pieces of bark knocked out by large hailstones.

In 1949, eight small areas were developed in the pot-hole complex in the eastern part of the Sanctuary to distribute perma-

Sago pondweed was harvested, stored, and then dried on wire frames by Francis Williams.

nent water through the complex. These totalled 294 acres. A further extension was added in 1961 which increased the acreage under water control by an additional 40 acres.

Beaver, which were once numerous but had been trapped out, were re-introduced into the pot-hole complex in 1953. By 1976 they were abundant and had created more permanent water in the area. On the other hand, muskrats, which Main had hoped would be the financial mainstay of the project, increased very little over the years in spite of protection. Limited good habitat, and the fact that the water levels of Ministik Lake could not be manipulated to provide it, were no doubt the reason.

By 1950, most of the problems of the project were under control and the local people had begun to accept the fact of the Sanctuary. Francis was able to extend his activities to include other projects which had been developed in the general area. Beginning in 1952, sago pondweed was harvested at Ministik Lake and shipped to other Ducks Unlimited projects for planting. This process required the plants to be harvested, using a garden rake, then dried and the seed separated from the dried plant. To simulate the normal process, the seed was stored in wire containers under the ice of the lake through the winter. It was then exposed to bright sunshine to break the dormancy, dried, and shipped principally to Saskatchewan.

In 1951, Canadian Well Services was given permission to drill for oil in the Sanctuary under stiff regulations evolved by consultation between the Game Commissioner and Ducks Unlimited. No producing wells were found.

Francis Williams died in March, 1954, and his position was taken over by his brother, Keith, who had been doing the work for his brother some months prior to his death.

Since that time, the Ministik Sanctuary gradually became only another project among many supervised by Keith Williams,

Keith Williams.

and his work expanded into all the aspects of an area manager's responsibility.

The Sanctuary needed much less attention once its existence became accepted by the local people. The Ducks Unlimited fence is still functional but the upkeep is done by the landowners to keep their cattle *out* of the Sanctuary. Haying permits must still be approved by Keith Williams. At one time, no haying was permitted until August 1st, but now it can begin July 15th. Experience demonstrated that haying was not detrimental to waterfowl production if controlled, and gradually eliminated the Canada thistle problem which resulted from over-grazing.

Deer have increased greatly, to the point where a two week season is permitted in order to avoid over-populations. At the time the Sanctuary first came under Ducks Unlimited management, Francis estimated there were two resident moose. In 1976, they were plentiful. So much so that the Alberta Wildlife Branch were using the area to study this animal.

Ministik Lake has always been a very productive area for diving ducks, particularly lesser scaup, and to a lesser extent, white-winged scoters and canvasback. The surface species were more confined to the potholes in the eastern part of the Sanctuary. On July 26, 1940, Francis Williams reported 1,600 young scaup on the lake and 56 going nests of which he knew. On September 19, 1940, he estimated 159,000 ducks of all species in the Sanctuary. Canada goose populations have increased steadily over the years both as breeding birds and as migrants. The Sanctuary has become an important fall staging area for these birds.

Thus, for the most part, the Ministik project has fulfilled Main's ambitions for it, and though government restrictions prevented it from becoming self-supporting, this was perhaps an unrealistic expectation.

Including Ministik with Big Grass Marsh, Waterhen Marsh, Stalwart Marsh, Many Island Lake and the Mormon Church Ranch — Main, by his calculation, reached the 100,000-acre target suggested for 1938 by Arthur Bartley at the Directors' Meeting April 1st and 2nd. In fact, he exceeded it by 55,000 acres.

In later years the method by which these acreages had been computed was considered overly generous. It was assumed that the area for a mile around each project had been improved for waterfowl by creation of the project, and what was quoted was the "improved acreage". A more realistic method of calculating acreages was adopted soon after the war and the acreage originally assigned to these projects reduced to conform.

For a first year and $100,000, this was a creditable enough showing. But T.C. had other programs underway, in addition to planning for work in the north in 1939.

Local Restaurant Habitues Eat Crow—and They Like It

It's Dished Up as Pie and Tastes Almost Like Pigeon

CHICAGO restaurant proprietors are offering ten cents each for crows to serve to customers in crow pies, but in Winnipeg they are still cheap and appear on the 25-cent lunch.

On recommendation of a local sportsman, who also supplied the birds, a Main st. lunch put "Individual Crow Pie" on the menu Monday. The novel dish, vieing with c h i c k e n croquettes, steak and onions, and other favorites, was a sell-out.

Popular Dish

"It was just an experiment," said Paul Bachek, chef and co-owner of the business with John Cleland. "We had ten birds. I made nine pies, baking the birds with onions and peas. The dish was quite popular, and one or two of those who tried it took home extra orders to their wives."

Winnipeg Tribune, June 23, 1936.

A breakfast customer, who had tied into the crow pie Monday, told The Tribune that the birds tasted more like pigeon than anything else. They were very fine and not nearly as wild in taste as prairie chicken. The meat, however, was a bit darker.

Aversion Disappears

"One has a bit of natural aversion to crow meat," he said, "just as many people turn up their noses at rabbit or duck. But after the first two or three bites, the aversion begins to disappear, and the crow tastes all right."

Mr. Bachek states crow pie will be again available to customers as soon as he can get more birds.

Crows are scarce in the south, but are quite plentiful in Canada. The sportsman who promoted the local use of the bird remembers eating many a crow pie in his younger days in Eastern Canada.

The crow control program was a big item from a publicity standpoint and initiated co-operation with the prairie game and fish associations. These campaigns had been carried on each summer by the governments of the three prairie provinces and the provincial sportsmen's organizations. Ducks Unlimited hoped, by the infusion of additional money, to increase the scope and effectiveness of the campaigns. By late May, arrangements had already been made to assist sportsmen's groups in each of the provinces in their crow "control" activities.

The government program in Alberta consisted of four competitions: for adult organizations, (game associations, gun clubs, municipal districts, etc.), individual adults, schools and individual students. Competition was by points on the following scale: gopher tail — one point; crow or magpie foot — two points; crow or magpie egg — four points. Numerous prizes were offered in each competition. Total prize money paid by the Alberta government in 1937 was $4,195.

The results given for the 1937 Alberta campaign show that a lot of crows and magpies were eliminated by this program.

	Crows & Magpies	Gophers	Crow & Magpie Eggs
School Children	51,477	492,663	126,596
Adults	17,950	203,708	17,670
Totals	69,427	696,371	144,266

We know today that such control programs have little effect on either the population of predators or the nesting success of waterfowl, but the activity did keep wildlife groups interested and actively involved at what they considered a conservation project, and identified their obligation to the resource.

In addition to the government campaign, the Alberta Fish and Game League sponsored a crow and magpie control campaign of their own. The Calgary branch paid 2 cents per foot before May 15th, and 1½ cents thereafter; for young magpie feet ½ cent and eggs ½ cent. First prize was $15; second $10; and

PROVINCE OF SASKATCHEWAN

DEPARTMENT OF NATURAL RESOURCES, GAME BRANCH, REGINA,

ANNOUNCES

PROVINCE - WIDE CAMPAIGN

FOR THE CONTROL OF

CROWS AND MAGPIES

which cause havoc to game and other useful birds by destroying their eggs and young.

Contest Opens **MAY 1,** and Closes **DEC. 1, 1938**

388 crows and magpies will be banded with numbered bands and released in all parts of the Province.

$4500 - CASH PRIZES - $4500

The prize money will be divided as follows:

1 PRIZE	of $500.00	- - - -	$500.00
2 PRIZES	of $250.00	- - - -	$500.00
5 PRIZES	of $100.00	- - - -	$500.00
10 PRIZES	of $ 50.00	- - - -	$500.00
20 PRIZES	of $ 25.00	- - - -	$500.00
50 PRIZES	of $ 10.00	- - - -	$500.00
300 PRIZES	of $ 5.00	- - -	$1500.00
			$4500.00

In addition to the prizes listed above, $2.00 will be paid for the return of any band used by this Department in 1936 or 1937.

This contest is open to all residents of the Province of Saskatchewan with the exception of employees of the Department of Natural Resources and their immediate families.

Anyone securing a band from a crow or magpie should communicate at once with E. S. Forsyth, Game Commissioner, Department of Natural Resources, Regina, Saskatchewan.

IN ADDITION TO THE ABOVE PRIZES, Mr. T. C. Main, General Manager, Ducks Unlimited (Canada), announces that the Corporation will assist the Campaign for control of crows and magpies carried on by the Department of Natural Resources and the Saskatchewan Fish and Game League by awarding the following prizes for crows' and magpies' feet delivered to the Office of the Corporation at Regina.

1 PRIZE	of $200.00	- - - -	$200.00
1 PRIZE	of $100.00	- - - -	$100.00
20 PRIZES	of $ 25.00	- - - -	$500.00
25 PRIZES	of $ 10.00	- - - -	$250.00
50 PRIZES	of $ 5.00	- - - -	$250.00
			$1,300.00

Prizes will be awarded on the basis of highest number of feet of either crows or magpies delivered by competitors. Each shipment should consist of at least forty feet, and should be forwarded by parcel post to Ducks Unlimited (Canada), 30 Canada Life Building, Regina, at any time between May 1st and November 1st, 1938. Costs of shipment will be remitted to the sender by Ducks Unlimited (Canada), together with receipt for feet received. This contest is open to any resident of the Province of Saskatchewan. Pooling of feet will be permitted, but no transfers of credits can be made after receipts have been issued. No credit will be allowed for feet received by the Corporation after November 1st, 1938.

J. R. HILL, Deputy Minister   **W. F. KERR, Minister**

5M - 4-38-965.

Nest destroyed by crows.

third $5. In addition, a cup was offered for the largest number of crows and magpies shot by a seven-man team. The Edmonton branch had a different program in which a box of shotgun shells was awarded for every 15 crow or magpie feet turned in to the Secretary of the league.

Total league expenditures in 1937 had been about $300 and approximately 10,000 crows and magpies had been killed. In 1938, Ducks Unlimited made $1,300 available to the Alberta Fish and Game League to be distributed to the two campaigns by a committee of three members, one of whom, Wm. C. Fisher, was to become the third President of Ducks Unlimited (Canada).

In Saskatchewan, the government also carried on an annual campaign "for the control of crows and magpies which cause havoc to game and other useful birds by destroying their eggs and young". This program featured a different approach and while it promised much, the actual payout wasn't that great.

Banded crows were released throughout the province and prizes offered to hunters who were lucky enough to shoot one of them. Total prize money was $4,500: a first prize of $500; 2 of $250; 5 of $100; and, in descending order, 380 other prizes. Considering the liabilities assumed, this turned out to be a cheap campaign. Only $600 was paid in prize money in 1936 and $380 in 1937. Obviously the chances of shooting a banded crow weren't very great. The results of the Saskatchewan program were, of course, hard to assess. Estimates ran as high as 250,000 crows killed but this is difficult to believe.

In 1938, Ducks Unlimited undertook to supplement the Saskatchewan campaign by offering prizes for the largest number of crow and magpie feet delivered to the Regina office. A total of $1,300 was made available with a top prize of $200.

The Manitoba government also had a campaign "for the protection of the nests, eggs, and young of migratory and upland game birds". It is interesting to note that the 1937 campaign had

followed the same pattern as that of the Saskatchewan government — the release of banded prize crows. One hundred and thirty-seven crows were banded and released. Only four were shot and returned for a total outlay in prizes of $28. If the sportsmen put much effort into trying to shoot a prize crow, it was certainly a disappointing return and they were quickly disillusioned by the odds. The 1938 program was to take a different turn. Certificates for a box of 12-gauge shells were to be given for each 25 crows' feet. This program was estimated to cost the government between $500 and $1,000. Cash prizes were donated by Ducks Unlimited for a draw using duplicates of the certificates issued by the government.

The Manitoba Game and Fish Association had sponsored a vigorous crow campaign for many years. A crow egg contest was established through the schools (one can imagine the clamor this would cause today!). Thirty-five schools in the vicinity of important marshes were organized for the campaign. Restricting the program to areas where crows might be causing damage to waterfowl showed more than usual insight into the problem. Two cents per egg was to be paid, one cent by Ducks Unlimited and the other by the Game and Fish Association. Ducks Unlimited also agreed to provide prizes for the most crows' feet submitted under the government plan. Total amount made available for the crow campaign in Manitoba was $500. In addition, the Manitoba Game and Fish Association offered 5 cents per pair for the first 24,000 feet turned into the Ducks Unlimited Winnipeg office — dubbed the "Crow Control Office" — and for each 50 feet a certificate would be issued for a prize draw, with awards totalling $400.

This part of the program turned out to be a nightmare for the Winnipeg office staff. Renee Benningen (then Deschamps); one of the first Ducks Unlimited secretaries, still recalls with horror the ordeal of counting mounds of crows legs in various stages of decay, and Irma (Main) Young echoes her revulsion.

In all, Ducks Unlimited spent $3,204 on crow-magpie campaigns in 1938 with the following results:

	Crows & Magpies Destroyed	Crows Eggs Destroyed
Manitoba	6,658	8,220
Saskatchewan	12,201	—
Alberta	27,301	—
	46,160	8,220

A balance of about $500 left in the Alberta account was used for a winter magpie control program. At the end of March, 1939, 7,992 additional magpies had been collected.

These annual cooperative crow and magpie campaigns of various types continued at about the same level until the mid-1960's. A record was established in 1945 when 469,031 units were collected. Long before 1960, it was realized that they were ineffective in controlling the numbers of these birds. But they were continued as a public relation activity to keep the provincial game and fish associations viable as a potential force of possible assistance to Ducks Unlimited.

School children were paid for crows' eggs.

Kee-Men come from many backgrounds — but are united in their love of waterfowl.

In 1938, the organization also carried out a waterfowl census similar in scope to that of The More Game Birds in America Foundation in 1935, comprising both ground and aerial surveys. For the ground surveys, Ed Russenholt had organized a volunteer force of fieldmen and named them Kee-Men. Their administration became the responsibility of B. W. Cartwright. In June, 1938, an initial broadside (including an introductory letter, copies of two radio broadcasts, a report form and return addressed envelope) went out to 5,528 individuals, most of whom were likely selected from those who took part in the 1935 census. On July 5th, a follow-up mailing (consisting of a 2-way postcard) went to a list of 5,882. These mailings brought some 1,200 reports on water and nesting conditions, and provided the basic list of Kee-Men for the 1938 census. Census forms were distributed to them and reports received from 1,089. By November, the Kee-Men corps had increased to 3,200, about 50% of whom made a fall report on migration, water, and freeze-up.

The census, as conducted at this time, required a Kee-Man force of this size, since an actual count was attempted. In 1947, the attempt to census waterfowl and arrive at total duck populations was abandoned as impractical. It was decided that population trends would be sufficient for the purposes of the organization.

To establish a trend required only an opinion type of questionnaire which was sent to the Kee-Men in the spring, summer, and fall. After 1952, the major source of data on water conditions and waterfowl populations were the surveys carried out by Ducks Unlimited staff. The Kee-Men reports were invaluable as back-up data for these surveys. Up to 1960 however, the Kee-Men were encouraged to continue making actual counts for the summer report, which could be compared with those of previous years.

"Keeman's" Ground Census Report Sheet . . .

DUCKS *Unlimited* (CANADA)
A Permanent Work in Sport and Conservation

1938 WILD DUCK CENSUS - SUMMARY REPORT

This form is for your Summary of all the information gathered by yourself and the co-operators you enlist to help you.

A separate Tally Sheet and Plat should be used by each field investigator. Each Tally Sheet and Plat should refer to only one township. When an investigator covers areas in two, or more, townships he should use one Tally Sheet and Plat for each township covered.

Number each Tally Sheet and Plat, so you may tabulate the results in the columns below. Insert on each Tally Sheet number of sections, township

and range; name of the field investigator; and your own name and address—before you distribute these sheets to the co-operators you enlist.

The census begins July 16. The last day set for field work is July 24. You can help greatly by completing investigations and making returns before the last day.

Tabulate below the results from all Tally Sheets. Attach Tally Sheets and Plats to this Summary. Sign your name and address below; and mail your complete report as soon as possible, but not later than Monday, July 25, in the stamped envelope addressed to Ducks Unlimited (Canada).

TALLY SHEET NUMBER	AREAS INVESTIGATED			NAME OF FIELD INVESTIGATOR	Total number of ducks seen with broods	Total number young ducks	Total number old ducks without broods	Total number of ducks—young and old
	Sections	Township	Range					
1		6	16	Gordon Hanna	255	1189	225	1669
2		6	15	H Box	197	796	49	992
3		5	16	H Box	168	997	136	1281
4		5	15	Gordon Embury	350	1529	154	2033
5		4	15	Harold S Box	65	393	36	494
6		4	16	H Box	0	0	0	0
7		3	15	Gordon Hanna	132	578	401	1111
8								
								7580

Name of Kee-man *H Box* P.O. Address *Belmont, Manitoba*

Ducks Unlimited (Canada) "Keemen" consolidated reports of their co-operators on this sheet and mailed it to provincial headquarters.

PRAIRIE DUCKS AND GEESE

DUCKS UNLIMITED (CANADA)

DUCKS UNLIMITED
Census 1938 & 1939

and

KEE-MAN
RECORD BOOK

Waterfowl in Canada

Ducks Unlimited (Canada)

Cooperation Unlimited –

A Conservation Manual
for Ducks Unlimited
Kee-men

Aerial survey and crash at Cumberland House.

Since fewer Kee-Men were needed, their numbers were permitted to decline; and for the past several years, they have been maintained at about the 350 level, evenly distributed across the three Prairie Provinces. (See Appendix VII)

The aerial part of the 1938 census was organized by A. C. Camerle. In general, it followed the 1935 census route of More Game Birds in America. Ducks were counted or estimated on a ducks per acre basis, and on larger areas or streams, as ducks per running mile of shoreline. Bert Cartwright flew the "Blue Route" from Winnipeg to Great Slave Lake, which took 49:45 hours. He was accompanied by J. C. Huntington and R. E. Benson of More Game Birds in America as far as Prince Albert, and by A. M. Bartley from Prince Albert, Saskatchewan to Great Slave Lake in the Northwest Territories. The much shorter "Green Route" (12:40 hrs.) from Prince Albert to Lac La Biche, Alberta, was flown by Camerle, E. S. Russenholt and F. T. Clarke, the Saskatchewan Manager.

The aircraft used were cabin, single-engine, high wing monoplanes on pontoons, flown by experienced bush pilots. Unfortunately, the only logs available do not record the make of aircraft.

It was an adventuresome flight for the Blue Route crew — Cartwright, Huntington, and Benson. In taking off at Cumberland House in northern Saskatchewan, with the famous bush pilot, Tom Lamb, at the controls, the aircraft failed to retain flying speed when airborne, and crashed into the bush. Bert Cartwright's log under date of August 13, 1938, gives a dramatic account of this experience.

10:00
Takeoff from Cumberland House.
10:13
Crashed in bush half mile from Hudson's Bay Post of Cumberland House. The takeoff was sluggish and the plane was barely over the trees when she lost flying speed and started to wobble. Tom Lamb behaved very cool and when he could not do anything else, he set the ship down among the willows. The right float was folded under plane and I was the first to fall out among the willows. I scrambled to my feet and ran blindly through the bush away from the plane, being fearful of fire. When a little distance away, I looked back and saw Ray Benson staggering away from the wreck with blood streaming down his face. The other two were still in the plane and I heard Tom Lamb call, "Anybody hurt?" I called back that I was alright and then returned to the wreck. Tom Lamb was okay and John Huntington climbed out and I saw he was alright also. Huntington went to the assistance of Ray Benson, down whose face blood was streaming from cuts on the head. His head had gone through the side window on my side. Indians now began to arrive from the

post and assisted us to retrieve our equipment. I recovered my camera and proceeded to take pictures of the wreck and salvage operations. Anthony La Rocque took Benson away to the nurse at the post for treatment. He insisted that he was alright and, as he was not the least dizzy, Huntington bound his head in a clean handkerchief and Benson started in to take photographs also. That is all. I am now going at 11:15 a.m. to study birds on the beach at Cumberland Lake.

It took more than an air crash to divert Bert Cartwright from his passion for bird watching!

Ray Benson was able to get a flight to Prince Albert with another party the next day so he could receive proper medical attention (the gash below his eye required three stitches). Later the same day, Cartwright and Huntington continued the survey to Prince Albert with an aircraft chartered from Mason & Cross, a pioneer bush flying company from Prince Albert.

But their problems were far from over. The weather turned foul, with high winds, turbulence and blinding rain. They were forced to land on the Saskatchewan River before they reached Nipawin. Cartwright records it as a "bumpy downwind landing. Raining in sheets and lightning and thunder awe inspiring."

The long night was spent on the riverbank with the aircraft tied to the willows along shore. Each man stood a three-hour watch to make sure the aircraft did not break away in the strong wind. After a breakfast of hardtack and honey, and warmed by a fire on the riverbank, Bert Cartwright was his old self and proceeded to make a list of the birds in the area. By now they were able to take off once more and, ironically, as so often happens in these situations, found they had spent a miserable night less than a mile from a Forestry cabin and a farmhouse! At 1:50 p.m. they landed safely at Prince Albert.

But sometimes hard luck never seems to end. On August 17th, a plane arrived from Lac du Bonnet, Manitoba to continue the survey. Airborne in good time on the next day the aircraft was almost immediately forced to return to Prince Albert with a faulty generator, and that day was lost. The 19th was also lost due to bad weather, but the 20th was clear and cool and they were finally away. Except for a day lost in Fort Chipewyan due to the weather, the rest of the flight as far as Fort Resolution on Great Slave Lake was completed without further incident. The party arrived back in Winnipeg on August 24th.

The conclusion drawn from the ground and aerial surveys was that there were 49,044,000 ducks in the area covered, an increase of about 20% over the 1935 census.

Substantially the same procedure was followed in 1939 except that the aerial portion only went as far north as the Peace-Athabasca Delta. The total population for that year was computed to be 59,682,164 ducks, an increase of 21.7% over 1938 and 47.4% over 1935.

The 1940 census was another exciting one for Bert Cartwright, Vic Solman (a summer student) and Ormal Sprungman (a free lance photographer). The first pilot was a stranger to the north, and with the added difficulty of reduced visibility due to smoke from forest fires was lost most of the time, much to Cartwright's annoyance, since flying time was limited by wartime gasoline restrictions.

The pilot was replaced by Cec McNeal, in whom Cartwright had great confidence and who remained his hero for the rest of his flying years. Departure was from Prince Albert on August 25th in a Bellanca. Trouble started before the survey reached Ft. McMurray, when an oil leak began to throw oil over the windscreen. By the time the flight reached Fort Chipewyan two days later, it was necessary to reach out and wipe the oil off the window every ten minutes.

Then, at Fort Chipewyan smoke closed in and grounded the flight for ten days. Sometimes visibility was less than 100 yards,

Angus Gavin, General Manager, Ducks Unlimited (Canada), wishes Bert Cartwright left, Gordie Hoffus pilot and Tom Sterling, good luck on departure of aerial waterfowl survey.

In addition, the plane was declared unserviceable and a replacement, a Norseman, had to be flown in from Edmonton. On September 6th, the crew were off once more, and after two long hard days flying lakeshores and marshes, reached Prince Albert.

The duck population was estimated to be 71 million, an increase of 18.7% over 1939.

The 1941 aerial census was apparently so curtailed by the wartime gasoline shortage that it extended only as far north as Lac la Biche. The estimated duck population on the prairies and in the north was 75 million.

Aerial surveys continued to be restricted until after the war. Annual populations were computed using Kee-Man reports from the prairies and other sources of information from the northern areas. From these reports, total waterfowl populations were estimated as follows:

1942	97 million
1943	125 million
1944	140 million
1945	140 million
1946	106 million
1947	110 million

In 1946, the full aerial routes were flown once more and total waterfowl populations estimated. After 1947, because of the controversy generated by the discrepancy between population figures published by Ducks Unlimited and those of the U.S. Fish and Wildlife Service, the two organizations decided with the Canadian Wildlife Service that, instead of publishing annual population figures, the changes in populations from year to year would be expressed as trends or indices.

Many observers participated in the aerial surveys but the main responsibility was borne by Cartwright and Leitch through the early 1950's, and Leitch and various observers through the

late 1950's to 1961. Other Ducks Unlimited personnel then took over. R. T. Sterling covered northern Saskatchewan and eastern Alberta from 1962 to 1966, and Fred Sharp the Edmonton area and western Alberta north to the Hay Lakes. The final survey was flown in 1967 by Allen Spelay and Dennis Hooey in Saskatchewan, and Sharp in Alberta.

For several years after the war, the entire survey was flown from Winnipeg. In later years, it was divided into provincial segments. Manitoba was flown by a number of individuals after 1954, including Angus Gavin, Cartwright, and Ted Dillon. The Saskatchewan and eastern Alberta segment was flown out of Prince Albert and after 1958, the Edmonton area and western Alberta was flown out of Edmonton.

Before the surveys were divided provincially, Lamb Airways, then based at The Pas, usually provided the aircraft for the entire survey. These included progressively, a Fairchild 24, Cessna 170, and finally for most surveys, a Cessna 180, with one of the Lamb boys (usually Greg) as pilot.

After the surveys were divided, Athabasca Airways of Prince Albert supplied the Saskatchewan aircraft, a Cessna 180, piloted by Floyd Glass; and in Alberta, the aircraft was usually furnished and flown by Walter Staheli, a director of Ducks Unlimited (Canada). Lamb Airways continued to do the Manitoba section.

Using the same pilots year after year made the job much easier, for they knew how the observers wanted to fly. The aircraft was flown at an altitude of about 100 feet and had to be throttled back as far as safety would permit to reduce the ground speed for good observation. Often in the turbulence along lakeshores on windy days, the stall horn seemed to be making more noise than the engine! It was rough, hard flying for the whole crew.

There were some close calls. Sterling remembers repeated forced landings with the Fairchild 24 due to carburetor heat

Bert Cartwright makes his counts.

A low flying plane met a low flying mallard.

coming on unexpectedly. Leitch and Moulding will never forget a take-off from The Syne at Fort McMurray, when a heavily loaded aircraft plus a sudden change of wind put them into a very tight spot.

But ignoring turbulence and air sickness, flying the aerial survey was a tremendous experience, and in those years Ducks Unlimited observers were extremely knowledgeable of the important waterfowl lakes between the northern fringe of agriculture and the Pre-Cambrian Shield. Beside the thrill of seeing great masses of waterfowl, there were many moose, usually up to their withers in a lake, an occasional elk (in Manitoba), woodland caribou, bear, wolves, colonies of cormorants and pelicans, and the great herds of buffalo around Lake Clair in the Wood Buffalo National Park in the Peace-Athabasca Delta of Alberta.

A memory that will always remain with anyone who made the trip is of nights spent over the Chinese restaurant at Fort Chipewyan! And the restaurant itself, where everyone insisted on eating eggs, even though they might be weeks old and had been exposed to the sun all the long trip by barge down the Athabasca River from Fort McMurray.

The aerial surveys were continued through 1967, at which time it was decided that, since use of the data had declined to the point where it provided only a line or two in the September *Duckological*, it was no longer worth the cost nor the considerable risk to the personnel involved.

In the first year, Ed Russenholt undertook his responsibility for public relations and education with his characteristic energy, enthusiasm, and imagination. By May 24, 1938, he had the first Ducks Unlimited broadcast to Western Canada on the air from Winnipeg, Regina, Yorkton, Edmonton, Lethbridge, and Calgary on free time mostly supplied by the James Richardson network. Forty-six 15 minute weekly broadcasts were given on a wide variety of conservation topics by different staff members to the end of the fiscal year March 31, 1939. (See Appendix II)

These broadcasts continued until November 1, 1940, when they were terminated due to lack of staff time to prepare them. In all, 131 consecutive talks were given.

In 1947, weekly radio broadcasts, now limited to five minutes, were again initiated on free time over 9 western radio stations by H. C. Cormode, who took over responsibility for Education and Records when Russenholt resigned on April 15th of that year. In 1950, Cormode left Ducks Unlimited and the responsibility for the broadcasts was taken over by the new Public Relations Officer, Alton Cleland, a former newspaperman. In the 1950-1951 series, 33 programs, for the most part dramatized sketches, were written and broadcast on free time over a network of 12 western stations. (Appendix III) Twenty-five were prepared for the 1951-1952 series. They were terminated at the end of 1952 due to production difficulties and the problems of obtaining good free time.

Material written for most broadcasts during the Russenholt period was reprinted as *News Flight*, a slick paper release sent to Ducks Unlimited Kee-Men, dailies, weeklies, radio stations and outdoor magazines. Copies in bulk were sent to New York, Chicago, and San Francisco to help fund raising in the United States. Selected *News Flights* were sent to western Members of Parliament and members of the prairie governments. From 1,500 to 2,000 copies of each issue were distributed, and of some particular issues, considerably more. During 1938, total distribution exceeded 125,000 in Canada and 35,000 in the United States.

Senior staff also addressed 43 meetings in 1938, varying from game and fish groups to the Credit Granters Association. Five reels of film were also produced for use in the United States and in Western Canada.

At the first Annual Meeting in 1939, Russenholt also presented the format for a slick-cover monthly magazine for western distribution to be called "The Mallard". It was intended to inform the public about Ducks Unlimited and, in general, teach conservation. Russenholt expected the game and fish leagues to support it at 10 cents per member, for it would carry their news. Other costs would be covered by the sale of advertising. The proposal was rejected by the directors ". . . in view of the generally unsettled world condition and for numerous other reasons . . ." No explanation of the "other reasons" is given.

An interoffice publication did appear, called first, *Ducks and Drakes (at Home and Abroad)*, and then, *Duck Doings*. It persisted on a sporadic monthly basis, depending upon who was around to write it, until after the war.

Bert Cartwright as head of the Ecological Department also had a busy year as the summary of his Annual Report for 1938 shows:

> The Ecological Department has conducted 22 ecological surveys during the period under review and published reports on same. Formulated two Questionnaires to more than 3,000 Kee-Men. Conducted Ground and Aerial Censuses and prepared report of same. Has been responsible for securing movie and still photographic record of all work. Conducted salvage operation at Buffalo Lake, Alberta. Banded 496 ducks. Investigated losses through disease, drought, fires, floods, illegal shooting and farm operations. Investigated waterfowl food plants, and prepared mounted collections of aquatic flora and fauna. Conducted analysis of 70 duck stomachs. Prepared Wildlife Management Plan for projects. Conducted predator control campaign. Prepared and gave addresses, broadcasts and other publicity material. Attended meetings and conferences and assisted in developing general policy.

On October 24, 1938, Dr. A. J. Bajkov joined the company as Aquatic Biologist. Though a competent biologist, Bajkov was an eccentric and his eccentricities were to provide the Ducks Unlimited staff with anecdotes far beyond his relatively short time with the company. A White Russian, he had escaped from Russia and skied his way into Western Europe by travelling at night. How he got to Canada is unknown, but he had been employed as a biologist by the Canadian government until his unpredictable behavior severed that relationship. His experience with the north must have appealed to Main who was planning an extensive northern program for 1939. Bajkov did carry out several northern winter biological investigations for Ducks Unlimited before he left the company, in late 1939, and became Arctic Advisor to the U.S. Army.

The high morale and camaraderie in the organization at this time is illustrated in Main's memoirs where he records that on his departure on January 5, 1939, for an extended speaking trip in the United States, the entire senior staff, and their wives, were at the station to wish him "God speed".

Into the North

5

The year 1939 marked Ducks Unlimited's major movement into the North. T. C. Main called it "No Man's Land". That strip of waterfowl habitat lying between the northern fringe of agriculture and the Pre-Cambrian Shield, and stretching from The Pas in Manitoba to the Peace-Athabasca Delta in northern Alberta.

His proposed program of work for 1939 outlines his evaluation of the potential for waterfowl production of this area and his plans for it:

> The area lying south and west of the Precambrian Shield; north of the agricultural belt and east of the Rocky Mountains, we call No Man's Land. It is of paramount interest to Ducks Unlimited. Our duck factory must be located in this territory. . . .

> This Corporation, and its affiliates south of the international boundary, has been organized to increase the continental waterfowl population. After carefully studying the situation for a year, I am certain that this objective can be attained to the satisfaction of our contributors in the United States. Further, I believe that a substantial population increase can be made each year; and that the total cost will be well within bounds.

> The question now is, 'Where will our duck factories be located? Where can we get best results, most efficiently and economically?'

> The original proposal anticipated that our work would be chiefly in the Farmland belt. Let us examine this idea. Approximately 15% of the continental ducks nest in this agricultural area. (Main is referring here to what was, unknown to him, an abnormal short term situation due to drought.—W.G.L.) Undoubtedly, a much larger percentage nested here a few decades ago. Their vast nesting areas have been plowed down, overgrazed and over-cropped; marshes and lakes have been drained; cover and food have been destroyed; and, the productiveness of the duck nesting area in the agricultural country has been greatly reduced.

Col. Terry Newcomen on northern survey.

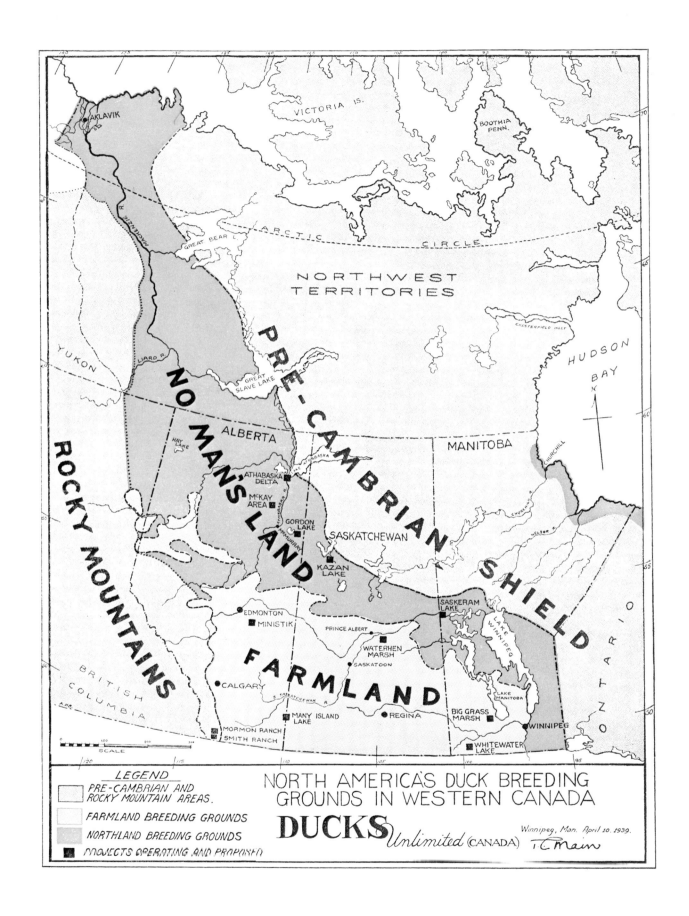

NORTH AMERICA'S DUCK BREEDING
GROUNDS IN WESTERN CANADA

DUCKS *Unlimited* (CANADA)

Winnipeg, Man. April 10. 1939.

LEGEND

PRE-CAMBRIAN AND
ROCKY MOUNTAIN AREAS.

FARMLAND BREEDING GROUNDS

NORTHLAND BREEDING GROUNDS

PROJECTS OPERATING AND PROPOSED

The projects that we have completed in 1938 were all in the Farmland belt. They have already increased — and will continue to increase — the duck population. The scope for further efficient development in this area is decidedly limited. Due to land ownership and other problems connected with the advance of civilization, projects here will be costly. Even if we develop the agricultural belt to the full extent practicable, we can only hope to about double its present duck production. This might mean an increase of 7,500,000 in the waterfowl population of the continent. If this is to be the full extent of the increase that we are hoping for, we might as well roll our tents and gracefully fade away. Another drawback to development in the south is the probable antagonizing of sportsmen due to turning some of their hunting grounds into sanctuaries.

Further, we are working in close co-operation with the P.F.R.A. in the Farmland belt. They have thousands of water projects and over forty community pastures, totalling more than 1,000,000 acres. Many thousands more water projects will be built. The pastures will be increased to 3,000,000 acres. These pastures are all game preserves. Cooperation in these projects offers Ducks Unlimited the best opportunity for increasing duck production in the Farmland belt.

I am now convinced that our major activities should be in No Man's Land. Here, with competent wildlife management, it is possible to at least treble the duck production of that area. This would mean an increase to at least 100,000,000 ducks. Incidentally, if something isn't done in the North the duck population will be reduced much more quickly than we can hope to bring it back in the south. . . .

At the same time, to my mind, it is more important to save a good duck breeding area that is in process of destruction than it is to secure control of a duck breeding area that is to all appearance close to optimum production now and is in no immediate danger.

Summing up then, the policy now recommended is as follows:

Concentrate on —

(1) Major projects in No Man's Land.

(2) Encourage Governments and private corporations to improve the situation in the north.

(3) In the Farm belt:—
   (a) Manage the projects we now have.
   (b) Assist the Provincial Governments to make existing sanctuaries more effective.
   (c) Cooperate with the P.F.R.A. in wildlife management on their projects and Community Pastures.
   (d) Develop high class projects upon the recommendations and with the cooperation of sportsmen's organizations and other interested citizens.

(4) Carry on educational work amongst the people of Western Canada to make them conservation-minded — for their own good; for the good of the country; and at the same time to help in the production of more waterfowl.

Preparation for the northern work began in 1938. D. M. Stephens, Manitoba Supervisor, made a reconnaissance of The Pas area in mid-August and from his notes, George Fanset prepared a report and with Angus H. Shortt (who joined the company January 1, 1939, as an Artist-Technician and Naturalist) made a further survey at the end of that month. Controls were recommended for the Saskeram, Pasquai and Reader Lake areas.

Head office staff were deployed through the prairies wherever there was a void. Thus between June 30 and July 4, 1938, Stephens had also made a reconnaissance of the remote Leaf Lake area at the headwaters of the Overflowing River near Hudson Bay Junction in east central Saskatchewan. This project was finally built in 1977. Then in late February, 1939, travelling by team and cutter and on snowshoes, Fanset and Shortt carried out a reconnaissance of the Meadow Lake country in north central Saskatchewan but decided that conflict with haying precluded any development by Ducks Unlimited. It was not until 1965 that the area was again investigated by Ducks Unlimited. Flood

Men and supplies had to be flown into these remote areas.

Travel was difficult.

control was then sold to the farmers and ranchers as a means of increasing both hay and waterfowl production. Many excellent projects were developed under this concept.

Col. Terry Newcomen and Dr. Bajkov made the original investigations of the areas proposed for development in the "No Man's Land" section of Alberta. These included MacKay Lakes, Gordon Lake, and the Athabasca Delta. Again these were winter surveys beginning on February 9, 1939, and extending over 34 days.

It was a rugged trip. The MacKay area, actually about 40 miles due west of Fort MacKay on the Athabasca River, which included Namur and Gardener Lakes, locally called Moose and Buffalo Lakes, comprised 21 townships. Eleven townships of the Athabasca Delta were explored and 12 townships of the Gordon Lake area. The weather was clear and cold, and snowfall had been well above normal. Travel, especially with dogs whose condition was so poor they were unable to pull any reasonable kind of a load, was very difficult. It was slow going on snowshoes, all 232 miles of it. Old unused cabins were utilized for overnight camps and, at Gordon Lake, they camped out in the bush.

The situation was just as difficult in the Manitoba section of "No Man's Land" where W. L. Bunting, following the earlier investigations by Fanset and Shortt, made the detailed surveys in The Pas area for the coming construction season.

Bunting, who joined the organization on February 1, 1939, as a field engineer with the expectation that the job would be short-lived, was to go on to a long and productive career with the company, becoming successively Saskatchewan Engineer, Saskatchewan Manager, and Chief Engineer before leaving in the spring of 1951.

Bunting surveyed the original cross sections for the Bracken Dam at The Pas which controls the Saskeram Project. He states that his greatest recollection of that survey was that he wouldn't

Bracken Dam.

do it again for anybody. It was —40° (F.) and after the first hour, the Zeiss level became so cold and the bubble so elongated that it was useless. So it was back to The Pas for another instrument and then back to work, rather than quitting for the day.

Further surveys in the Root and Rocky Lakes area just north of The Pas followed. Life in a tent at extreme temperatures was not easy. Bedrolls froze to the ground when willows had to be used as a bed in place of spruce boughs. Dinner was pre-cooked bacon and beans which had to be broken up with an axe before they could be heated.

Such adventures can be fun if winter camping is the objective. But at the end of a hard day's work, it is an entirely different matter.

Four projects finally resulted from these winter surveys at The Pas. The Saskeram was built in 1940, and the Pasquai and Watchi Bay developments in 1941 under the supervision of Frank Dagg, an engineer hired for that purpose. The Reader Lake Project was not built until 1954.

The Bracken Dam, named for the incumbent premier of Manitoba, was built on the Saskeram River to act in the dual role of controlling flooding from the Carrot River on the 14,000 acres of Saskeram Lake and to hold water in the lake in dry years. This continues to be a highly successful project, and in 1962 the dam was rebuilt.

The Knapp Dam, named for Joseph Knapp, who had been the prime driving force behind the inauguration of both More Game Birds in America and Ducks Unlimited, was built on The Pas River to hold water on the 35,000 acres of Pasquai Lake. This project operated successfully until 1952 when it was made inoperative by the P.F.R.A. reclamation scheme for the Carrot River Valley. Attempts to reactivate the project are still underway.

Saskeram Lake.

BRACKEN DAM

DUCKS UNLIMITED
RESTORATION PROJECT

BUILT 1940 WITH FUNDS
CONTRIBUTED BY 20,000
UNITED STATES SPORTSMEN.

OPERATED BY THE
MANITOBA GOVERNMENT
TO DEVELOP WILDLIFE
IN SASKERAM LAKE.

Departure from The Pas for opening ceremonies of Bracken Dam.

The Honorable John Bracken, Premier of Manitoba, opens the gate. On the left George R. Fanset, Chief Engineer, Ducks Unlimited (Canada).

The Knapp Dam.

Pasquai Lake — before.

Pasquai Lake — after.

Victor E. F. Solman at Gordon Lake.

A Saskatchewan project was also included in the thrust into the north. Kazan Lake, north of Ile a la Crosse, had been seen on the aerial surveys to support a very heavy duck population. It was speculated that raising and stabilizing the water level would make the area even more productive.

In retrospect, one wonders why time and energy would be expended on an area that was already so productive. Ironically, subsequent aerial surveys demonstrated that Kazan Lake was more attractive to waterfowl at lower levels rather than high.

Nevertheless, just before spring break-up, Lloyd Bunting, Bill Campbell, and Fred Bard surveyed the lake. Fred Bard was an assistant at the Saskatchewan Museum of Natural History and his responsibility was to carry out a biological assessment of the area. Under several feet of snow and ice, this was rather a difficult assignment. Bard subsequently became Curator of the Museum, and established an international reputation for his work with whooping cranes.

Although the winter work was followed up by a summer program in 1942 when Tom Randall, a competent naturalist, spent four months at the lake and confirmed the high productivity and waterfowl use, it was never developed as a Ducks Unlimited project. However, the Saskatchewan Department of Natural Resources did build a rock and timber dam on the outlet to raise the water level for increased fish and muskrat production. By 1976, this dam was no longer effective and the project again became an active one for Ducks Unlimited but this time with the objective of lowering — not raising the water level!

But T. C. Main's greatest thrust into "No Man's Land" was scheduled for the 276,000-acre Gordon Lake area in Alberta, and for this project he had great expectations. He hoped to demonstrate that by proper management, control of predators, trapping and fires, and the reintroduction of beaver, the area could produce sufficient revenue from fur to pay for such management, and also support a local population of natives.

The great experiment began on May 18, 1939, when Bunting, Victor E. F. Solman, and Sigfus Arnfinson were flown into Gordon Lake to establish a headquarters and begin management of the area. A cook, Les Rutherford, was included.

Vic Solman, a biologist from eastern Canada, had just completed his Master's degree. During the following three summers he spent with Ducks Unlimited, he made many biological investigations for the company. One of which, the impact of northern pike as predators on ducklings, was carried out east of The Pas in northern Manitoba and became the dissertation for his Ph.D. His skill and interest in photography added both movie footage and stills to the company's library.

Arnfinson was an able bushman, and his expertise with axe and saw was needed to build the headquarters' log cabin. A magnificently built man, just over 6 feet tall, blonde, Icelandic, he needed only the horned helmet and sword to be accepted as a present day Viking. "Fusi", as he was known, spent his career with Ducks Unlimited at Gordon Lake, many lonely weeks completely by himself, and for a month without flour or gas for the lamp. The lake was sixty miles east of Fort McMurray with access only by air during the summer, and by dog team in the winter, which he didn't have. During fall freeze-up and spring break-up, there was absolutely no access. Leitch, who joined Ducks Unlimited as a field biologist in May, 1939, spent the winter of 1939-1940 with him. Fusi left Ducks Unlimited to join the R.C.A.F. in the summer of 1940. He was replaced by Gaylord Ransom and his wife, who, with various assistants, chiefly a man by the name of Wallace, managed the area until the company withdrew in February of 1942.

In spite of the best efforts of the fieldmen involved, the project was doomed from the start, due primarily to a lack of un-

Gordon Lake from Cabin.

derstanding by senior management of the practical difficulties and requirements of managing 276,000 odd acres of wilderness, but also due to the shortage of funds at that particular time to provide the equipment and people necessary to do the job. Main had dreamed a great dream but never seemed to appreciate the practicalities essential to its realization.

In this instance, the Alberta government could hardly have been more co-operative. The 12 townships which comprised the Gordon Lake project were made a game preserve on October 24, 1939, at the request of Ducks Unlimited, and the corporation was given a 20-year lease on the area dated from January 1, 1940 for $1.00 per annum.

Establishing the game preserve meant evicting some trappers from their traditional trap lines. Main intended that there would be sufficient work in connection with the project to compensate them. They would be paid in kind from the store to be established at the project.

Stocking the store led to these amusing comments by T. C. Main on Col. Newcomen's original list of required merchandise:

Leitch, left, and Arnfinson at Gordon Lake Cabin, 1940.

Arnfinson tries to contact Fort McMurray.

November 2, 1939

T. Newcomen
Supplies for Gordon Lake

Dear Terry:

I note with considerable concern that you have ordered several pairs of ladies' bloomers for the trade at Gordon Lake; and with even greater apprehension that they must be red in color..... If you have first hand knowledge of these matters, will you be good enough to submit a report on our standard form describing your investigations and supporting your claim by photographs, etc. in the regular way? If you do not have sufficient first hand knowledge, kindly obtain advice from others who are well-known authorities on this important matter. I refer, of course, to Bill Wallace and George Spargo. You might also discuss this problem with Dewey Soper, Charlie Gould and Doc Watson who recently carried out an exhaustive study of this in Alberta. I am waiting your report with keen interest.

Yours very truly,
T. C. Main
General Manager

But food and other merchandise had to be flown into Gordon Lake from Fort McMurray. This made prices higher than in Fort McMurray and quickly disillusioned the few natives who did seek employment. After the first months, only occasional sales were made to passing natives.

Controlling fires over such a large area was impossible with so few men and no equipment. Bunting, Solman, and Arnfinson did their best. But until late summer, when back packs and hand pumps were sent in, they had no fire-fighting equipment. Worse still, they had no transportation other than a canoe and paddles — no outboard motor. In addition, the poor distribution of waterways made it a very difficult area in which to travel and much of it could be reached only on foot through rugged terrain.

Winter Camp, Gordon Lake.

Arnfinson and Leitch were without transportation of any kind during the winter of 1939-1940, but after Ransom took over in late 1940, a dog team was supplied and an outboard motor — which seldom worked but generated voluminous correspondence!

Although a radio was provided to communicate with Fort McMurray, it was very unsatisfactory, in spite of repeated adjustment and repairs. For weeks, particularly at break-up and freeze-up, no one really knew whether the people at Gordon Lake were alive or dead.

The senior staff were not all in agreement with the concept of this project. Witness extracts from a letter to T. C. Main by Bert Cartwright under date of February 27, 1940:

> . . . No expenditure of funds by DU in this area is likely to make any substantial difference in the duck population . . . Only effective thing we can do is fireguard and that would be better exercised on more important duck breeding areas . . . Considered solely from its duck producing potentialities, this great area is in no immediate need of attention, nor can anything we do make any great difference in the duck crop.
>
> As a demonstration area designed to convince the Alberta Government that by wildlife management practices fur and big game can be restored in highly profitable measure, probably the project has merit . . . I regret I cannot support the Gordon Lake project. I consider it a mistake and if we go ahead with it we lay ourselves wide open to the accusation of the misuse of funds.

Cartwright added that funds would be required for fire patrols and if this was the function of Ducks Unlimited, fine, but if the purpose was to raise ducks — no.

Trappers petitioned to re-open the area for trapping. At the same time, the Alberta government began to promote registered trap lines in the northern part of the province. By assuming that occupants of registered trap lines would carry out the same

On patrol, Gordon Lake: Rennie Harley and Gaylord Ransom.

85

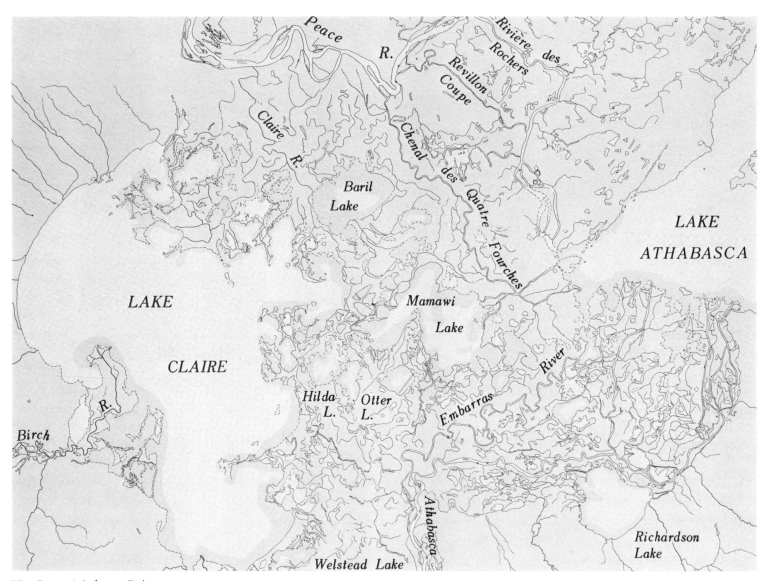

The Peace-Athabasca Delta.

management practices with the same objectives as those of the company, Ducks Unlimited was able to withdraw gracefully from the lease — probably with a sigh of relief. Ransom and his wife left the project in March, 1942 and the employment of Ducks Unlimited at the end of April. The lease was formally cancelled December 23, 1943.

The MacKay Lake adventure was even shorter lived than that at Gordon Lake. A five-man crew was flown into the area on May 25, 1939, to establish a headquarters and to lay the groundwork for a management program. The crew consisted of T. II. Nicholson, the engineer in charge; D. A. Ross, a biologist; and two helpers, Polson and Wylie, as well as a cook.

A cabin and storehouse were built, but Main, after visiting the area July 13-18, decided that the original evaluation made during the winter by Bajkov and Newcomen was wrong, and that the area had little waterfowl potential as most of the shoreline was rock. He terminated the project, disbanded the party, and discharged Nicholson and the crew except for Ross, who was sent to the Peace-Athabasca Delta to continue biological investigations there.

The possibility that Ducks Unlimited might work effectively in the Peace-Athabasca Delta was apparently suggested by the Alberta Government to T. C. Main at the same time as the MacKay Lakes and Gordon Lake. Thus began an involvement in the area which was to continue at varying levels of intensity until the present time.

The winter surveys in the Peace-Athabasca Delta had been restricted to the area southeast of the Embarras River and estimated by Newcomen to comprise about 11 townships (253,440 acres). The entire Delta is over a million and a half acres but most is in the Wood Buffalo National Park and controlled by the National Parks Branch of the Federal Government. At this time, Ducks Unlimited did not attempt to carry out any ground surveys in the Park, though it was regularly covered in the annual fall aerial survey of waterfowl populations.

In the spring of 1939, Bajkov again visited the area, this time in company with Ray Salt. While Newcomen had recommended the construction of five dams in the Delta to stabilize water levels, Ray Salt did not agree that they would be worthwhile. Salt was more concerned with the spring and summer kill of waterfowl and the collection of eggs by natives. Ross's reports indicate that Salt may have received exaggerated reports on the number of eggs collected, and that most of the eggs picked up were those easiest obtained — those of coots and Franklin gulls.

Salt did pinpoint the role of jackfish as predators on ducklings, based on information obtained from native trappers, and seems to have been the first in the Ducks Unlimited organization to do so. No doubt this stimulated the further investigations by Ross in the Delta in 1940 and 1941 on pike-waterfowl relationships, and those of Bajkov and Shortt in the Saskatchewan River Delta near The Pas in the same year. These studies culminated in the intensive work by Solman in The Pas area in 1940 and 1941, and publication of his results in Ecology, Vol. 26, No. 2, April, 1945.

Ross was headquartered at Webel's trading post on Big Point Channel in the Athabasca Delta after leaving MacKay Lakes in 1939. When he returned for the 1940 field season, he built a headquarters near the trading post to live in and to store equipment during the winter. He banded in 1939 and 1940, which was probably the furthest north in Canada this had been done up to that time. He also made biological investigations and waterfowl censuses preparatory to a possible development program by Ducks Unlimited. The company was unable to employ him in 1941 due to budgetary restrictions, and he turned to a career in entomology.

Ducks Unlimited headquarters in Fort Chipewyan. Angus and Phyllis Gavin, left, with friend.

After Ross left the organization, interest in the Delta appeared to wane. Or perhaps nothing more could really be done because, due to the war, it was impossible to obtain suitable personnel. However, a local trapper, Steve Brace, continued with the banding program from 1944 through 1949, with the exception of 1945.

At the end of the war, there was another great surge of interest in the area, both in Canada and the United States, stimulated by the suggestion that it be developed as a "Living Memorial" for both Americans and Canadians who had lost their lives in the war. This proposal was abandoned in 1947 for no apparent reason, but keen interest in the Delta continued.

The area fascinated Main and he made several trips to it. He was preoccupied by plans to control the flooding, which occurred first from the spring melt in the local tributaries, and later from the melt in the mountains. Planning included such grand schemes as a direct diversion of the Athabasca River into the Peace. It is ironic that when controls were finally built, they were designed to prevent the Delta drying up!

It was in connection with the Athabasca Delta that Angus Gavin, who was subsequently to serve as the General Manager of Ducks Unlimited (Canada) from 1951 to 1968, first appeared. He was hired by Ducks Unlimited on November 1, 1945, to spearhead the biological and engineering investigations on the Delta.

Angus had almost as much color as Main. Born in Scotland, he had spent 16 years in the Arctic as a Hudson's Bay Company Factor. A keen hunter and naturalist, he came to the attention of Ducks Unlimited when he discovered the breeding grounds of the Ross goose in 1938. Before joining the company he served as a Kee-Man, reporting from his Arctic posts.

With the glamour of his adventure-filled Arctic background and his thick Scottish brogue (which took some association to un-

derstand!), Angus had great appeal for American audiences and, during his years with Ducks Unlimited, particularly while he was Saskatchewan Manager, he was a very successful spokesman for the company in the United States.

Gavin went to the Delta in February of 1946 to establish a headquarters at Fort Chipewyan, and to begin preliminary engineering and biological investigations. He was joined by an engineer, George Charles, from January to August, 1947, at which time the company interest in the Athabasca Delta cooled for a number of reasons.

In the first instance, Main left the organization in the fall of 1946 and took much of the enthusiasm for the project with him. Also, reports by Rennie Harley, the Alberta Manager, that the plan to control flooding was, if not impractical, then just too big for Ducks Unlimited to undertake alone, were convincing. In addition, the company had made itself unpopular in the area by the unfortunate release to a Winnipeg newspaper of parts of an internal company report by Angus Gavin. Just how the report got to the newspaper is unclear, but it dealt with spring and summer shooting of waterfowl in the Delta by native people and caused such an uproar in Fort Chipewyan that it was thought best to remove Gavin from the scene. This was done in late summer of 1947. He then spent two years as an area manager in southwestern Saskatchewan on his way to becoming Saskatchewan Provincial Manager and then General Manager in 1951.

Except for the banding program under Steve Brace, which continued until 1949, and the annual aerial fall surveys of the waterfowl population, there was no further activity in the Delta until 1964. In that year, Tom Sterling, as a result of flying the fall aerial survey, was stimulated by the obvious potential of the Delta to again initiate studies for controlling the disastrous spring and early summer floods.

High water in the Peace-Athabasca Delta.

This new activity began with flights over the area June 1st and 2nd, 1965, by Sterling with another staff member, and a member of the Canadian Wildlife Service. In September of the same year, Sterling and Gunner Campbell, a senior Ducks Unlimited engineer, spent considerable time on ground surveys. These resulted in a preliminary development plan to control the Delta floods over some 510,000 acres in the Wood Buffalo Park on the west side of the Delta. Basically, this called for a 75 mile main dyke, and secondary and tertiary dykes on individual impoundments. The cost estimate for the major dyke alone was in the $7.5 million range and the total development from $8-10 million.

At this point (July, 1966), Gavin, then General Manager, realizing that the concept was beyond the resources of the company, wrote to the Canadian Wildlife Service suggesting that it become a co-operative project with the federal and provincial governments. To acquaint the Canadian Wildlife Service and the Alberta Wildlife Branch with the area and proposed development plan for it, Ducks Unlimited, in September, 1966, sponsored an aerial reconnaissance which included personnel from both government agencies. Considerable enthusiasm for the project resulted. Much effort was then expended in preparing a combined Canadian Wildlife Service and Ducks Unlimited brochure to promote development of the Delta, but this was never produced.

It appeared for a while that the main dyke might be built as an access road from the south to Fort Chipewyan and Fort Smith. The road did not materialize. Then in 1968, a dramatic reversal of the fundamental and long term water problem in the Delta began when lack of water, rather than flooding, invalidated all previous plans for development. This change was caused by the British Columbia Hydro when they began to fill the Williston

Low water drained the shallow lakes.

Great mud flats appeared.

Lake Reservoir, impounded by the Bennett dam on the Peace River.

The Bennett dam effectively controls some 50% of the flow in the Peace River at the point where it affects Lake Athabasca. And since high flows in the Peace River not only flooded the Peace-Athabasca Delta, but also acted as an hydraulic dam to impound outflow from the Athabasca River floods to the south, reduction of the flood flow in the Peace River had a drastic effect on the Delta water levels.

In 1969, Herman Dirschl of the Canadian Wildlife Service, began intensive biological studies of the effects of lower water levels on the ecology of the Delta. These continued through 1970, Ducks Unlimited contributing financially to the study. In the period 1968 to 1971, the Alberta Water Resources Branch also gathered considerable engineering data.

On June 29th, 1970, *Time Magazine*, in an article titled "Death of a Delta", gave concern for the Delta dramatic and international scope. A public symposium in Edmonton on January 14 and 15, 1971, heard papers on the situation in the Delta and discussed solutions.

In response to this public concern and demands for action to save the Delta, an intergovernmental interdisciplinary study group was formed to investigate the effects of low water levels on the resources of the Delta and upon the local people. Intensive ecological, hydrological, and sociological studies were undertaken. Leitch represented Ducks Unlimited on the Technical Advisory Committee and E. G. Hennan, a company biologist made the breeding pair, brood, and fall staging surveys during the two summers of the study, and for two subsequent years. Waterfowl

The Caron Potholes.

populations continued to be monitored by government agencies through 1976.

The cost of the investigation was about $1.5 million and extended over 20 months. Since so many departments of both federal and provincial governments were involved, it is a tribute to the leadership of D. M. Hornby, the Project Director (since deceased), that so many divergent viewpoints and interests were finally resolved into the concrete recommendations put forth in the voluminous report of 1972.

One of the major problems was the requirement to maintain the water levels in the Wood Buffalo National Park as close to the natural regime as possible in order to satisfy National Park Policy. A fixed control on the Riviere des Rochers was finally recommended. The structure simply compensates for the loss of natural control by the Peace River and restores the ecological conditions on the Delta to approximately what would occur naturally, though floods from the Peace itself will still be reduced. The dam on Riviere des Rochers and a smaller structure on the Revillon Coupe were built in 1975 and 1976 for $2 million, cost-shared 50% by Canada, 45% by Alberta, and 5% by Saskatchewan. A federal-provincial committee is monitoring the effects of the dam on fish, muskrats, waterfowl and ungulates.

A combination of unusual events can still cause floods in the Delta, and did in 1973 and 1974. However, these will be infrequent due to the effect of the Bennett Dam. The drier years of 1976 and 1977 saw the dam function as planned in retaining water in the shallow lakes and ponds of the Delta.

So ends the long involvement, up to the present, of Ducks Unlimited in the Peace-Athabasca Delta. Although the organization had no part in construction of the dams on Riviere des Rochers and Revillon Coupe, it played a significant catalytic role through the years in focussing attention on the great potential of this famous Delta.

Although the thrust into the north was the major interest of 1939, a vigorous and successful program was also carried out on the prairies where projects were developed using standard engineering methods, e.g. dams on outlets of shallow marshes, stream diversions and area reduction by restriction dams.

Several new techniques to increase waterfowl production from the prairies also appeared that year. One of these was the establishment of small salvage ponds through pothole areas using a variety of techniques. A great deal had been written about the loss of ducklings to summer drought when their home ponds went dry and they were forced to wander in search of water. Much of the finest waterfowl production habitat is subject to such periodic drought, and some of the best of it lies in the knob and kettle terrain of the Missouri Coteau. This stretch of low hills arches through Saskatchewan in a great, interrupted crescent, from the international border in the southeast, to the vicinity of North Battleford in the northwest.

Potholes in this area can reach as high as 100 per square mile and in wet years produce large numbers of ducks. In dry years they attract no ducks, but when they contain a small amount of water, they still entice nesting birds. A dangerous situation then develops if they are dry before nesting season is over. A significant part of the year's production is then lost.

Simple earth dam stores permanent water.

August brood count.

It was to alleviate this loss that the concept evolved of constructing deeper salvage areas, distributed through the pothole region, which would last through a dry year. These were known as Keewaters. The first were built in the fall of 1939 in the Missouri Coteau southwest of Moose Jaw. This development became known as the Caron Potholes project.

Several construction techniques were used. The best was to divert additional drainage into a pothole increasing the average annual depth so that it would outlast adjacent temporary potholes. In some instances, several ponds were partially drained into one to be sure that at least one water area would survive in a dry year. One such development has never been dry since it was built almost 40 years ago, and annually carries a large number of broods in August. In other cases, a dam was constructed across a small flowage. As a last resort, a dugout was built in the middle of a dry marsh.

It was planned that the projects would be located so that ducklings would have to travel no more than a mile to permanent water. This ideal spacing was not always possible due to lack of construction opportunities in the required locations.

It was not until after the war that there was sufficient manpower to evaluate this program, and it was found that ducklings did indeed move to the larger, more permanent areas. The Caron Pothole Study Area, as it became known, has a continuous record of breeding pair and brood counts from 1947 to 1976, as well as more intensive data for the 1947 through 1950 period.

Counting broods in the heavy cover and the muddy uneven bottoms of the potholes was hard work in hot weather and many young field assistants found out whether they really wanted to be waterfowl biologists!

With the soundness of the pothole program established by the Caron investigations, similar programs were later developed in other pothole areas in both Saskatchewan and Alberta.

Ducklings were also known to be lost on large shallow prairie lakes in late summer when they dried up during dry years. Frequently these lakes had no possibilities for the usual engineering developments by dams or stream diversions, etc. There was no way by which additional water could be impounded. To salvage these ducklings, dugouts were blasted in the deepest parts of the basin where the last of the water would be. Lakes that have never been dry since were so treated, including Whitewater Lake in southern Manitoba, and Tatagwa Lake in Saskatchewan. These lakes were at the bottom of the dry cycle when the work was done. They are no longer considered active Ducks Unlimited projects.

The year 1939 was then one of new ideas and experiments, as one would expect when a new problem is first attacked. No other period would be so innovative.

Public Relations

6

While T. C. Main spearheaded construction on the prairies and penetration into the North, Ed Russenholt, following the original plan for the Ducks Unlimited (Canada) operation, which included an allocation for publicity in Canada and for gathering and preparing material for publicity needs in the United States, was laying the foundations of public relations programs that would persist for many years.

On January 1, 1939, Angus Shortt, who was to play a major role in this function for over 34 years as a writer and artist-technician, joined the organization. His skills combined with the talents and fertile imaginations of Main, Russenholt, and Cartwright resulted in an aggressive and innovative public relations program, which has never been matched.

Of Irish descent, Angus never neglected to wear his green tie on St. Patrick's Day. His dry wit, good humour, and co-operativeness made him a joy to work with. An excellent naturalist, he was able to combine his field experience with his artistic and writing skills for the immense benefit of Ducks Unlimited.

New ideas proliferated at a prodigious rate during these early years. Many appeared in the weekly broadcasts: for example, "The Loop of Death", Russenholt's descriptive term for the drought area of southern Alberta and southwestern Saskatchewan.

Monthly reports on current waterfowl conditions distributed to Ducks Unlimited supporters and news outlets in the United States and Canada officially began on June 10, 1939. In July, 1940, this report was named "The Duckological". It is still a valuable public relations tool in both the United States and Canada. While no one is entirely sure where the name came from, the general consensus is that it was from Russenholt, after a brainstorming session in which many suggestions were bounced around.

Angus H. Shortt.

Ducks as Angus Shortt sees them.

The *Duckological*, issued monthly while the ducks were on the prairies, combined and digested information on waterfowl and habitat conditions from every available source: reports from Kee-Men and Ducks Unlimited fieldmen; weather reports; data from aerial surveys; incidental and sporadic reports from interested individuals; and, since 1950, from transect ground surveys — all went into the melange. (Appendicies V & VI)

In the early years, the *Duckologicals* sparkled with the clever caricatures of Ed Russenholt. The "Ducko", as it became known, was signed by whoever happened to be in the office to compile it; frequently Ed Russenholt or Bert Cartwright, but often T. C. Main himself.

The day the *Duckological* went out — "Ducko Day" — was always exciting for one reason or another. Angus Shortt recalls running it off on an old hand-operated duplicating machine when each copy had to be interleafed with another sheet of paper to control the static electricity so the other side could be printed. In the midst of all the paper, ink, and confusion, Main would sometimes arrive from a trip across the west with "hot off the griddle news" — and it was stop the press and back to square one.

Everyone in the office, great and small, participated in stuffing the Ducko envelopes which at this time numbered 1,500. As time went on, a more modern, powered duplicator was purchased which, as it aged, became so attached to Doris Kuntz that only she could operate it. Rumour had it that knowing where to apply a good kick was the secret! With an increasing volume, a crew of women was then employed to stuff the envelopes. In due course, the Ducko was printed commercially. By 1977, circulation had reached 80,000. It continued to be written in Canada, but was printed in the United States for reasons of economy and, except those for Canadian addresses, mailed from Chicago.

Even before Main and Russenholt left the organization in late 1946 and early 1947, respectively, the Ducko became the responsibility of Bert Cartwright, and remained so until his retirement in 1960. Leitch then wrote the Ducko for Angus Gavin's signature until Gavin's retirement in 1968. It then began to appear under Leitch's own name and did so until the end of 1976, when it became the responsibility of the new Chief Biologist, Dr. A. J. (Sandy) Macaulay.

Another public relations tool combined the clever verse of Bert Cartwright and the cartoons of Ed Russenholt to produce the promotional posters "Jake the Drake", and then "Jake the Drake and Mary the Mallard". These became well-known characters throughout the United States. Christmas cards designed by Ed Russenholt were a delight to send and receive.

The *News Flight*, a series of informational pieces on waterfowl and general conservation topics, were continued. These were distributed to 200 writers and publications in the United States in order to achieve widespread publicity. In the 1941-42 year, 77 of these *News Flights* were published.

In the minutes of the annual meetings of 1941, 1942, and 1943, general reference is made to the proposed production of a book by Ducks Unlimited, tentatively titled *Ducks and Men*, which was to be paid for by a sponsor and sold. The idea disappears after 1943 but was probably fulfilled by *"The Ducks Came Back"*, written in 1945 by Kip Farrington, a professional American writer.

Other ideas came thick and fast but not all survived. Special shirts were designed and worn in the United States by Ducks Unlimited members. But Ed Russenholt went too far when he suggested that Alberta fieldmen should also wear the traditional 10-gallon hats. Opposition from the field was strong and the idea was abandoned.

96

Jake, the Drake — and Mary the Mallard

The curly-tailed, green-headed Jake
Led the way over prairie and lake.
  With a quack that was harsh,
  He espied Big Grass Marsh —
And immediately put on the brake.

With Mary, his sweet bride-elect,
He landed, the dam to inspect.
  She said: "Jake, forsooth,
  You told me the truth.
We'll stay here — a home to select.

So Mary got down to her duties;
And waddled around on her tooties.
  With down from her breast
  She lined her grass nest;
And laid fifteen eggs. They were beauties.

For nearly a month she sat dumb—
While Jake, her mate (the big bum)
  Played ducks and drakes
  For very high stakes;
And lost all his feathers, by gum!

One sunny day the proud mother
Felt eggs pop — one after another.
  Great was her pride
  When she saw by her side
The reward of her patience and bother.

When she led her flock to the lake,
The first drake they met was her Jake.
  He did look a mess
  In his nondescript dress;
The ducklings (in chorus) yelled "Fake!"

Said Mary "Tut, tut! That is bad!"
(They looked again — and felt sad)
  "When his new feathers grow
  He'll be handsome I know;
And then you'll be proud of your Dad!"

The young Jake-a-loos grew apace;
The credit and pride of their race.
  They fed — and grew fat on —
  The potamogeton
And other pondweeds on the place.

Says Jake — to his friends in D.U. —
"We're seventeen ducks, just from two;
  And there's millions of drakes
  (If you restore lakes)
Who will multiply ducks — all for you!"

Yours for Ducks Unlimited,
Bert W. Cartwright   (his words)
Ed Russenholt   (his drawing)

Good Hunting, Brother!

Remember- they told you, when you were a lad,
You'd get nothing from Santa Claus if you were bad;
But- tho' you might be the bad boy of the block,
On Christmas, there always were gifts in your sock!

By-an'-by, you discovered that all you were given
Was from generous hearts (where Santa was livin').
Then- when you put childhood away on the shelf,
You found YOU must be Santa Claus to yourself!

So- streamline old Santa the duck hunter's way-
Pack Ducks Unlimited into his sleigh!
Trade his mythical team of reindeer de luxe
For unlimited flights of actual ducks!

Be happy and smile- like the chaps in the bed
Get into D.U. for five years ahead!
Then- every duck shooter can have his sock filled-
And sleep with clear conscience for those he has killed.

Then will Christmas be merry- and all the New Year
The ducks will be working for you, that is clear;
You'll have "Good Hunting, Brother"- and be able to brag
You put two ducks on the wing for each one in your "bag."

During these early years, the idea of donor projects evolved (Angus Shortt believes it was 1941; he knows it was going strong in 1942). These were to be projects which would be privately paid for and dedicated to individuals, or sponsored by organizations, states or cities. In 1943, one was proposed in memory of Carole Lombard, the movie actress wife of Clark Gable, who was killed in a plane crash. It was believed $100,-000 could be raised by movie stars donating their time for a radio broadcast. Although the movie colony was said to support the idea, nothing came of it.

The donor concept resulted from Tom Main's speaking trips to the United States. Russenholt and he believed it had a great fund-raising potential. It would provide money apart from the annual budget for projects which became unexpectedly available,

and upon which quick action was essential. Russenholt soon came up with appropriate words to give the program appeal — "The Lake that Waits" — implying that the potential lay there, ready to be developed and all that was needed was the money.

Folders were prepared with the words "The Lake that Waits" printed in gold across the dark green binding. In each folder was a packet which contained a standard set of photographs of ducks, duck nests and broods, and other illustrations prepared by Angus Shortt — about 8 to 10 pages in all. For each specific presentation, the details of "the lake that waited" were added to the folder, including photographs, plans, and written material. By 1943, the program was putting great pressure on the engineering department, and particularly George Fanset, the Chief Engineer, to produce enough projects and prospectuses to satisfy the demand.

The donor program was so successful that it soon became part of the regular fund-raising activity in the United States, rather than the special program with segregated funds, visualized by Russenholt and Main. "The Lake that Waits" was replaced by the "Your Project" appeal. Later, the approach was changed and the brochure became more a recognition piece for donors than a sales vehicle. In 1949, a "Donor Management Fund" was established with monies which had been subscribed in excess of the cost of individual donor projects. This caused administrative problems and the excess funds were finally taken into general revenue.

Some of the brochures were truly works of art, with ducks carefully chosen for the donor's preference or flyway, painted on the covers by Angus Shortt. In some instances, for state brochures, the state flower was featured. In his career, Angus

prepared some 270 of these brochures. At the end of 1977, there were 348 donor projects.

The first project named to honor an individual was built in 1939 on Bullpound Creek in central Alberta, south of the town of Hanna, and was dedicated in 1940 to John Coleman, then President of Ducks Unlimited, Inc. This was not quite the same thing as a donor project since it was built under the annual budget and then named to honor Coleman. The first donor project in the usual sense was Lake San Francisco — Cassils Lake near Brooks, Alberta, which was built in 1942 from funds donated specifically for that purpose by the Pacific Rod and Gun Club in San Francisco. The money had been raised from trap and skeet shooting competitions.

The first project named for a state was the Louisiana Lakes, just east of Brooks, Alberta, built in 1943. A. G. (Pops) Glassell

Later cairns were not as elaborate as this — the first one.

of Shreveport, Louisiana, energetically promoted this project and collected some $20,000. It was to be the stimulus for the many other state projects which followed.

Fund raisers in the United States, and Tom Main himself, believed a movie illustrating the work of Ducks Unlimited in Canada to be absolutely essential. Production of an annual movie for this purpose was the responsibility of Ducks Unlimited (Canada), and specifically that of Angus Shortt, from 1939 through 1954.

The first scripts were products of the fertile minds of Main, Russenholt, Cartwright, and Shortt; but after the departure of Main and Russenholt, movies became more and more the responsibility of Angus alone, following general guidelines with casual input from other staff members both in Canada and the United States.

A general theme was suggested by Ducks Unlimited, Inc. and the movie was then produced by Ducks Unlimited (Canada). Although they were made for fund raising in the United States, the movies were very popular in Canada and widely shown to sportsmen's groups, service clubs, and schools. Such showings were part of the winter program for Ducks Unlimited staff for many years.

The story of how the early movies were made is best told in Angus Shortt's own words:

During the year 1939 I worked closely with our movie man, Percy Brown, who had been a newsreel photographer with Pathe News and had done some movie work as well. Tom Main and Ed Russenholt decided that a movie film was a 'must' to generate interest in the U.S. and in fund raising campaigns.

Our first film was a black and white effort, showing construction of three of D.U.'s first projects; it was appropriately titled "A Dam Site More Ducks".

Plans were underway for a color film in 1940 but the outbreak of World War II cancelled this, although a lot of footage had been taken and a preliminary assembly made. It was to be called "Bringing Back The Ducks".

With the U.S. not yet at war, our $100,000 budget was approved by the American directors and it was decided to proceed with a full-length movie for 1941. For this, we were fortunate in obtaining a top free-lance photographer and writer in Ormal Sprungman of Minneapolis.

Title of this production was "Seven Out of Ten", the story line stressing the losses in eggs and ducklings that occurred on the Canadian waterfowl breeding grounds before young ducks reached flight stage. The completed film ran 1200 feet and was replete with explanatory, hand-lettered titles, colored, animated cardboard cut-outs and graphics depicting loss factors such as fire, drought, predators (crow, magpies and jackfish). It was quite a film, packing a real punch.

Prints were distributed through the D.U. headquarters in New York and were widely and successfully used at fund-raising dinners, etc., in many States.

In December, 1941, following the Japanese attack on Pearl Harbor and the U.S. entry into the war, there was a natural reaction among some D.U. directors that operations should be suspended. Tom Main strongly opposed this view and forthwith launched himself on an intensive lecture tour in the U.S. during the three months, January, February, and March of 1942. In the meantime, strict spending curbs were imposed for D.U. (Canada) which meant shelving the D.U. movie.

In order to carry on until a decision had been reached, all senior staff agreed to serve without remuneration pending the final outcome.

There is little doubt that, but for Tom Main's initiative and drive at this critical time, D.U. would have ceased to exist, at least for the duration of the war.

As it was, operations in Canada got the green light when fund raising activities were continued and accelerated in the U.S. Assured of our $100,000 budget again, film making was given a high priority. Ormal Sprungman, although now in the U.S.

Naval Reserve, returned on movie making assignments in 1942, 1943, and 1944, when we produced "On The Trail of Ducks Unlimited", which starred Tom Main as he traversed the prairies on an inspection tour of D.U. projects, both completed and under construction.

In 1943 came "In Defence of Ducks" — this had a wartime theme, the battle by ducks against drought, fires, etc. Interspersed throughout the film were clips of actual battle scenes from the war raging in Europe.

In 1944 what was to prove one of our outstanding films was made, titled "The Big Marsh Lives Again". This was the story of Big Grass Marsh, near Langruth, Manitoba (D.U.'s first project). The history of the area lent itself admirably for our purpose and the script written by Ed Russenholt, unfolded the picture of land speculation on the Canadian prairies as it was following World War I, when two dollars per bushel of wheat was the lure that precipitated the land rush. Drainage of land totally unsuited to agriculture such as Big Grass Marsh, became widespread.

Live actors took part in this movie. George Waight, well-known Winnipeg actor, played the part of the smooth-talking land salesman and head of the firm called "Skinner and Crooks". We had several posters printed with this name prominently displayed in a Main Street store window, and filmed, representing a real estate office. The part of an old-timer who was totally against its drainage, knowing the land to be worthless, was taken by George Secord. A young couple played the roles of a newly married couple with visions of quick wealth on a wheat farm. Sequences were filmed showing the young couple attracted by the real estate window sign, hesitating, and then entering and quickly falling for the 'sales talk' and putting down their entire savings on a tract of Big Grass Marsh land. Flashes visualized their early hopes, then successive failures, until finally they were destitute and abandoned the farmstead, now nothing but a few dilapidated and run-down buildings.

Called to active service, Ormal Sprungman was lost to us for three years, returning in 1947 to make five more excellent films, including our first sound production "Water Is Life" in 1951.

In 1941 we moved to the mezzanine floor of the Canadian Bank of Commerce head office building, which was only a block from that famous "corner of Portage and Main", renowned for the icy blasts which in winter make it as difficult to navigate on foot as the North Pole! Our new working area consisted of what had been one of the Bank Manager's private offices — a large, high-ceilinged room complete with a big fireplace.

It was in this room that all our film work was carried out. Here scripts were written, revised (we used the word 'rehashed') and finalized, film editing took place, all main introductory and explanatory titles were produced and filmed, as well as colorful graphs and animated sequences.

In most instances, Ormal and I worked at night when the office was clear and we could position our material and photoflood lamps as required. We often worked past midnight, for once we were set up, it was essential that the sequences be completed.

A great deal of planning and many "dry runs" were necessary before we achieved the results we wanted. With our limited resources, invention and ingenuity were called upon to produce special effects which were part of each film presentation. For example, in one sequence portraying the closing down of the Western Canada Duck Factory by winter, we prepared a color map of North America on a half sheet of Beaverboard. This was placed on the floor, the camera and tripod straddling it, all secured against the least movement (sometimes by driving nails into the floor!). A flour sifter filled with powdered borax (flour was found to be too fine) was then held over the northern areas of the map and the powder gently sifted down until Western Canada was "buried beneath a mantle of snow!" The effect was excellent — and dramatic.

On another occasion we were depicting waterfowl migration routes from the Western Canada breeding grounds, based on D.U. band recovery data. Using the same map as a base, we purchased a sheet of glass for use as an overlay. On it I painted in opaque red poster color a series of arrows indicating flyways and tributary routes to the U.S. Under photoflood lamps and with Ormal exposing film 2 frames each time, I carefully scraped off with a razor blade ⅛" of each arrow, a painstaking, slow job. This was filmed in reverse so that when spliced into the finished

Ormal Sprungman "shoots" Gunner Campbell, D.U. Engineer.

production, the red arrows were shown advancing southward through the various States to their destinations.

One effort which created a great deal of interest was one on waterfowl migration — again using the North America base map but with tiny cardboard ducks! For this epic we had a steel-cutting die made to the outline of a flying duck as viewed from above. With this we had one hundred ducks stamped out of black cardboard; each one had a wingspan of ¾ of an inch!

The sequence opened with groups of these ducks concentrated on main migration staging areas on the prairies. Then migration got underway with my moving each duck "southward" ⅛ of an inch at a time as Ormal filmed at 2 frames speed!

During the three years that Ormal was in the services, we completed our annual film, relying largely on our stock of film taken by him on his field excursions plus some obtained from other wildlife photographers. We were fortunate too, in obtaining another Minneapolis movie man — Dan Billman — for the indoor shooting for our 1945 production, "Good Hunting Brother".

Due to space problems and a growing staff, it was decided in 1946 to move our film operations elsewhere. We obtained space on the second floor of the Wilson Furniture building on the opposite side of Main Street, about two blocks away. Here our cameraman was a Winnipeger — Paul Chipman — who made an excellent job of the filming required to complete "The Big Duck Factory" in which was told the story of duck production on D.U. projects. Our new quarters proved inconvenient and considerable time was lost commuting with our main office; in the end we moved back into the bank.

In 1947 we put together two 400-foot films utilizing stock plus new footage taken by Paul. It was found that the longer films were unsuited to many of the D.U. and Service Club meetings when a speaker was featured; films of 800 feet being more acceptable. With this in mind, we produced "Bred On The Waters" and "For Good Hunting".

These could be shown together or individually and ample

time could be permitted for a speaker; this was particularly adaptable to the popular luncheon meetings lasting one hour.

In 1948 with the return of Ormal Sprungman, we launched production of a totally new 800-foot movie, this length of film being expressly requested by our U.S. directors. With the catchy title "Lucky Ducks" the value and necessity of marsh restoration on the prairie breeding grounds was the theme.

In our 1949 film "Meet The Ducks", correct field identification was stressed with some of my waterfowl paintings filmed and used along with live footage of various species to accentuate the distinguishing features of each.

1951 marked our entry into sound films with "Water Is Life". Eight hundred feet in length, this film was an instant success and remained in constant demand into the 1960's. Work on it was extremely interesting as we taped the commentary while playing recorded music in the background, while screening the film to get the overall effect. One session continued until 2 a.m.

1952 saw the completion of "Wings Across The Border" dealing with the arrival in spring of waterfowl from the U.S., their nesting in Canada, and subsequent departure to the U.S. in fall. This was the last film Ormal made for us.

In 1953 our New York office commissioned M.P.O. Studios in that city to make a film called "Canada Goose". This was the first film on which I did not work, the entire job being completed in the U.S.

In 1954, however, movie making returned to Winnipeg when another local cameraman, Frank Holmes, was contracted to produce a feature film for us. This 1200-foot effort was called "Each Year They Come" and was made from entirely new footage taken from spring through fall. I worked closely with Frank throughout. A radical departure planned for the presentation was the use of wooden duck models (these models I carved from balsa wood) which waddled about on stiff plastic legs and weighted feet! The legs were suspended inside the balsa wood body as a unit, secured to a metal collar. Much work was required before a satisfactory "walking duck" was achieved.

In this we had the professional assistance and advice of a local metal working firm, where suspension and correct angle for the legs and feet were solved. A number of "movie sets" were constructed from the dried stalks of flagreed, bulrush and three-square bulrush. These gave an authentic "marshy background" for the models. In addition, I made full size, hollow duck heads. Constructed in two halves, the lower mandible was hinged and rotating eyes were inserted. These latter were made from brown and yellow marbles (from a Chinese checkers game) on which I painted black pupils!

To synchronize the movements of the duck's bill with the film sound track, an attachment to a telegrapher's key was rigged up to a vertical metal rod inside the head to the lower mandible. Similarly a rod fastened to a pressure plate rotated the eyes as required. Although this grandiose scheme was successfully completed and the sequences filmed, it was found that they added too much footage — over 200 feet — and the film itself was 1200 feet. In the end only a couple of short sequences of the "talking" heads were used. This was my last involvement in film making.

From 1955 onward, a number of outstanding films were donated to D.U., particularly those produced by the late Edgar M. Queeny of St. Louis, Missouri, for many years a director of D.U., Inc. and a wildlife photographer of the first order. Among his most celebrated films for D.U. were "North To The Wavies", "Mike", "Prairie Wings", and "The Great Country".

During his career with Ducks Unlimited, Angus Shortt's reputation as a wildlife artist, particularly of waterfowl, became increasingly well established. In 1948, he collaborated with Bert Cartwright on a waterfowl identification booklet for "Sports Afield". He later produced an intriguing series of caricatures for Ducks Unlimited exaggerating the characteristics of each species.

Each year he produced a waterfowl painting for auction at the annual dinner of the New York Chapter of Ducks Unlimited, Inc. where it was the pièce de résistance. No doubt this was the origin of the outstanding successful auctions which are now part of all Ducks Unlimited dinners.

Angus Shortt became particularly well known for his canvasback paintings.

His last year with the company was devoted exclusively to painting for Ducks Unlimited, Inc.; forty canvases were stockpiled for future auctions. Still being produced for the print media are the Marsh World panels, illustrating the ecology and wildlife of marshes, which Angus began in 1970.

In 1950, the first full-time Public Relations Officer (Russenholt had many other duties), Alton Cleland, was hired. He remained with the company until 1967.

The War Years

7

The war brought problems in money, manpower, materials and transportation. That the program was able to continue at the pace it did was due, not only to the strong management group in the head office, but also to the strength in the provinces — W. L. Bunting in Saskatchewan, whose career with the company has already been related, and R. M. (Rennie) Harley in Alberta. The Manitoba program was the responsibility of the head office at this time.

Harley came to Ducks Unlimited as Provincial Engineer in May, 1940, with an excellent background for the job. He had been working as an engineer with the Province of Alberta developing irrigation and domestic water supplies. The contacts he had established in this position were to prove immensely valuable to Ducks Unlimited not only in their coming work in the irrigation districts, but in developing co-operative water management programs with the Alberta Government, particularly in the North. T. C. Main once said that hiring Rennie had resulted in half of Alberta working for Ducks Unlimited! He became Provincial Manager in February, 1941, and Western Manager in 1951. In 1958 he became Director of Public Relations in Winnipeg, and left the organization in 1960.

The most critical period for Ducks Unlimited came in 1940, even before the entry of the United States into the war. A ban was placed on the transfer of money out of the country and, for a while, it appeared that Ducks Unlimited, Inc. would not be able to send money to Canada. In the end, the transfers were considered to be in somewhat the same category as those of the Red Cross, and were permitted. Nevertheless, Ducks Unlimited (Canada) did experience a serious financial crisis in 1940 — the only one in its 40-year history.

Instructed to plan on a budget of $130,000 in American funds for the 1940-41 fiscal year, which at the prevailing rate of exchange was $150,000 Canadian, the corporation budgeted for

Staff meeting March, 1942. Left to right: Tom Main, Bert Cartwright, Rennie Harley, Lloyd Bunting, Ed Russenholt, George Fanset.

Milwaukee Sentinel, fall, 1944.

a $125,000 program. Unfortunately, probably due to the anxieties caused by the intensifying war in Europe, collections were less than anticipated, and only $95,000 was actually sent to Canada.

In spite of drastic cuts in staff, re-organization, and economies of all kinds, the company was almost out of money as the calendar year-end approached.

There are two versions of what then occurred. The official minutes of the directors' meeting held in Winnipeg, May 2, 1941, record as follows:

> Mr. Bartley inquired as to contributions made by the staff when funds were not coming in at regular intervals. He understood that some of the staff had contributed part of their salaries and suggested that the General Manager return the gift from funds appropriated for 1941. Mr. Main advised that he had asked the staff for funds and in addition had contributed $1,000.00 of his own money but all contributions had been repaid and it was moved by Mr. Bartley and seconded by Mr. Barkhausen and carried that the Directors express to the staff the thanks of the Board.

Main gave a somewhat different account in his interview with Leitch in June of 1974. According to his version, he personally borrowed $25,000 from the bank and used it to help the company over this difficult time. Irma (Main) Young confirms that her father did borrow the money.

Another crisis came when the United States entered the war. According to Angus Shortt, there was serious soul-searching in the U.S. as to whether Ducks Unlimited could, or even should, continue. But continue it did, with slowly increasing budgets through the war years.

Reports of these years are replete with references to the difficulties of operating with a shortage of trained staff. This problem extended to senior management. A. M. Bartley, the General Manager of Ducks Unlimited, Inc., and the focal point of the fund raising program, was recalled to the Navy in July of 1943. This increased the demand for Tom Main's services as a speaker and fund raiser in the United States (he had attended 70 meetings even in the 1941-1942 fiscal year) to the point where he was spending as much as four months a year away from Winnipeg. Ed Russenholt was similarly involved, though to a lesser degree.

The absence of Main threw an additional burden on the head office staff. Much of the administration, budgeting, annual reports, etc., was handled by George Fanset, the Chief Engineer, since the major expenditures were in the engineering field.

Manpower problems in the field were even more acute, and intensified as the war progressed. Engineers, other than summer students, were simply not available. Skilled tradesmen, such as carpenters and machine operators, were just as scarce.

Construction materials were also difficult to obtain. In fact, permission to construct anything had to be granted from the Federal Controller of Construction. Use of reinforcing steel had to be authorized by the Steel Controller of the Department of Munitions and Supply. War seems to have lent wings to the postal service, undreamed of in this day, and spurred bureaucracy to unbelievable efficiency, for when George Fanset applied for reinforcing steel for Lake Barkhausen in Alberta on September 8, 1942, he had his reply, though negative, on the 11th!

Obtaining cement was particularly difficult. The situation was better in Alberta than elsewhere because most of the work was being done in the irrigation districts where it was considered to be of direct agricultural benefit, particularly for stock watering. For this reason, Harley was able to bring in cement and other materials for the projects he was building.

Transportation was a real problem. Gasoline was strictly rationed, and the shortage of tires in particular presented great

"The Major". Left, Bob Gibb, Kane-Gibb Equipment; George Fanset, Chief Engineer, Ducks Unlimited (Canada); Walter Kane; Joe Kokinsky and Marcel Caron.

Oregon — Plover Lake, Alberta, 1940. The last Ducks Unlimited dam built with horses.

Major — Dirty Lake, Alberta. In 1941, "The Major" was hard at work; a new era had begun.

Mrs. T C Main "launches" The Major's Lake with Irma Main and Betty and Rennie Harley.

difficulties. Herb Moulding (a long-time employee of Ducks Unlimited) recalls that everyone carried a hand pump and a patching kit. On a trip from Brooks to Hanna, Alberta, about 100 miles, he had to fix 6 flats using tire irons and a hand pump. To save travelling by car, operations were localized, and provincial managers travelled between their offices and the work area by train or bus.

The Keewater program of blasting survival dugouts in dried lake bottoms was discontinued, due not only to a scarcity of dynamite, but also to the responsibility of making certain it didn't fall into the hands of saboteurs! Toward the end of the war, movie film also became very difficult to obtain. In spite of many shortages, the feeling expressed in the annual reports was that the organization was being dealt with very fairly by the government regulatory bodies.

The scarcity of materials brought out everyone's ingenuity. Lloyd Bunting recalls authorizing an expense account from one of his field parties for a considerable amount of lime, which he wondered about at the time, but dismissed from his mind. When a subsequent expense account contained an item for more lime, he decided to investigate on his next trip into the field. The explanation was simple. The fieldmen had discovered by experiment that adding lime to the unrationed purple gasoline reserved for agriculture would remove its colour in a few days. They could then use the gasoline without detection and avoid the penalties for misuse. Rightly or wrongly, Lloyd didn't challenge any further charges for lime.

As the war progressed, there was plenty of work for contractors building everything from airfields to latrines, and they were more and more reluctant to bid on the relatively small jobs offered by Ducks Unlimited.

Tom Main discussed this problem while on a speaking trip in California in 1941, and received the offer of dirt-moving equipment from Major Max Fleischmann: a crawler tractor, bucket and dozer, a truck to transport it and a trailer for the crew. The "caravan" was christened "The Major" in honour of the donor. To further honour him, the first large project built in Alberta with "The Major" was called Major's Lake. This was followed by Lake Traung, named for Louis Traung, a close friend of Major Fleischmann, and finally in 1943 by the Lake Fleischmann-Crab Lake project.

Acquisition of this equipment enabled Ducks Unlimited to operate more independently of contractors, and as the war continued, additional equipment was purchased, until at the end of the war, three dirt moving outfits were in operation. A dragline was obtained in 1946. By this time, contractors were again becoming available, and the directors instructed that they be used as much as possible and company equipment kept to a minimum. The large equipment was gradually disposed of but smaller items have always been essential for repairs and small projects. But "The Major", since it was the company's first large piece of equipment and obtained in such a unique way, had a special spot in everyone's heart. This was enhanced by the personality of the operator, Joe Kokinsky, who worked with "The Major" through its career with Ducks Unlimited and for many years afterward. Joe could neither read nor write but he was the best "cat skinner" in the business and could fix anything.

Stories about Joe are legion and are sure to be told and retold whenever Ducks Unlimited oldtimers get together. One of the best has several versions and locales, but nevertheless a solid basis in fact. Joe was frugal and rarely cashed his pay cheques while in the field, living almost entirely off his expense account. Sitting in his lonely trailer one night out on the prairie, he began to worry about the number of cheques he had accumulated. Finally, he got up, put the cheques in a can, went outside and hid them in a gopher hole. In the morning, he couldn't find the right gopher hole! By mid-morning, when George Freeman (the Strathmore Area Manager) came by to see how the job was going, he found Joe and his assistant had plowed up a great area around the trailer looking for the cheques. Joe finally found them, but the area in the Strathmore district is still known to Ducks Unlimited people as "Joe's Garden".

The war years saw the beginning of Ducks Unlimited's work in the irrigation districts of southern Alberta; the Eastern Irrigation District centered on the town of Brooks, and the Western Irrigation District at Strathmore. At this time, work in these districts was not only attractive because of assured water, but because it offered the opportunity to work intensively in a small area and reduce the travel problems resulting from the war.

It was a profitable partnership for both Ducks Unlimited and the irrigation districts. Ducks Unlimited had the free use of land on which to develop waterfowl habitat using the return or "waste" water from the irrigation operation; the irrigation districts benefited from permanent water established on grazing land where use had been restricted due to lack of stock water. This partnership exists to this day as Ducks Unlimited continues to expand its activities in these regions, particularly the Eastern Irrigation District.

Rennie Harley's earlier association with L. C. Charlesworth, who had been Director of Water Resources for Alberta prior to retiring and becoming Manager of the Eastern Irrigation District, and with P. M. Sauder, who followed the same route to become Manager of the Western Irrigation District, provided a quick entry into the co-operative programs with the districts.

The first project in the Eastern Irrigation District designed to use irrigation water was the Edgewood Project, southwest of Brooks, built in 1941. However, the irrigation features of this project were not developed until much later, so the first functional irrigation projects were the Lake San Francisco Project at Cassils Lake, just west of Brooks, and the Lake Barkhausen Project, north of Bassano on Crawling Valley, both of which were under construction in September of 1942.

Operations really got underway in the Eastern Irrigation District when W. G. Campbell became Ducks Unlimited's resident manager at Brooks on April 1, 1944, the first Area Manager appointed by the company. About half the development work had been done on the Louisiana Lakes during Bill's absence in the Army in 1943. From this point on, with a resident manager on the job, construction moved ahead swiftly. Bill formed a close friendship with Wes Crook, the engineer for the Eastern Irrigation District, which has lasted to the present when both are retired. He has often expressed his gratitude for the help Wes gave him in those early years. The fine relationship between the Eastern Irrigation District and Ducks Unlimited has continued under the present Manager, R. T. (Bob) White.

Accommodation was difficult to get in Brooks both for the resident manager and for Ducks Unlimited personnel on inspection trips, so a log siding cottage was built with a large garage and "bunkhouse" for transients. Brooks became the showplace for the organization in the later years of the war and for some years thereafter, and the "bunkhouse" was the social centre for Ducks Unlimited in the area. The guest log lists many of the prominent personalities in Ducks Unlimited through the years. Its cozy warmth and the friendliness of Ellen and Bill Campbell made it an oasis to many a weary Ducks Unlimited fieldman.

Campbell was succeeded as Area Manager in 1972 by Lloyd Dimond, and he in turn by Craig Gordon in May, 1975.

Development still continues, and to date, 36 projects (many containing several water bodies) totalling 20,236 acres and 361 miles of shoreline have been completed in co-operation with the Eastern Irrigation District. Of particular note is the substantial donation given to Ducks Unlimited by the Richard King Mellon

Gilbert Patrick.

George Freeman, left, Southern Alberta Supervisor, and Jimmy Robinson of Sports Afield, long time supporter of Ducks Unlimited, at the Fresno-Honens donor project in the Western Irrigation District.

Foundation in 1971 to underwrite construction of two large reservoirs that greatly increased the number of areas which can now be supplied with water for waterfowl production.

Progress was somewhat slower in the Western Irrigation District due to the lack of a resident manager. But at the end of 1944, the company hired Gilbert Patrick. He had been the engineer for the Western Irrigation District until he retired from the Canadian Pacific Railways, which originally developed both the Eastern and Western Irrigation Districts beginning in 1903.

Things then began to move swiftly. George Freeman, who worked with Patrick after the war and succeeded him as District Manager, says that Patrick behaved as though the C.P.R. still owned the system, and the local residents weren't entirely sure from his behaviour whether they did or not! Consequently, he did things that he never would have been able to otherwise.

Patrick was one of the real Ducks Unlimited characters. Claiming to have driven a Stanley Steamer, he considered himself (perhaps for that reason though the relationship is obscure) a particularly good driver. Those who worked with him didn't share that assessment!! It was customary, when several Ducks Unlimited fieldmen were working together in an area, to use every subterfuge possible to trick someone else into using their car. Driving was no treat for Ducks Unlimited fieldmen. With Patrick, it was different. Everyone volunteered to take their car — so that Patrick wouldn't take *his*!

Both Pat and his wife were kindly people and when a few garter snakes decided to overwinter in the stone basement of their home, they didn't molest them. Word quickly got around in the world of the garter snakes and soon they owned most of the house. This still didn't bother Pat all that much, though his visitors found them somewhat nerve-wracking. One winter when he rented the house, the renters left in horror almost immediately. Stern measures were required to restore the home to its right-

ful owners. It was amazing how quickly the surviving snakes learned they were no longer welcome.

Patrick retired from Ducks Unlimited in 1950 and was replaced by George Freeman. George had returned from five years' service overseas and had worked part time for Patrick before becoming Area Manager. Born in Strathmore, George was an excellent replacement for Patrick because he knew the irrigation district equally well and everyone in it. An excellent naturalist, his contribution to the company in this field rivals his work in project development.

George's quick wit has made association with him, both personal and by correspondence, a continuous battle of one-upmanship. His ingenuity saved senior management from embarrassment when, on a field trip with the directors at the Mellon Tilley project near Brooks, the lunch failed to arrive in the field on time. George promptly demonstrated how to snare gophers, to the delight and distraction of the directors who didn't realize that lunch was late. Freeman was promoted to Southern Alberta Supervisor in April, 1975, and now has responsibility for the entire southern part of the province, including both the Eastern and Western Irrigation Districts.

To date, 26 projects comprising 6,203 acres and 166.5 miles of shoreline have been built in the Western Irrigation District, utilizing irrigation water. In addition, many other projects using irrigation water have been built in co-operation with other irrigation companies in southern Alberta.

Repairing main canals.

Cleaning lateral ditches.

Building drop structures.

Constructing controls.

Building dams on individual lakes.

Broods seemed to appear from nowhere as soon as water was turned into a new area.

Louisiana Lakes, Alberta — main canal, lakes, and dams.

Louisiana Lakes Dedication. Left, A. C. (Pops) Glassell of Shreveport, La. and Wes Crook, Chief Engineer, Eastern Irrigation District.

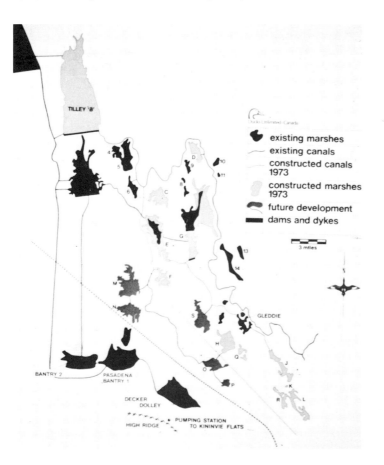

existing marshes
existing canals
constructed canals 1973
constructed marshes 1973
future development
dams and dykes

Through a generous gift from the Richard King Mellon Foundation in 1973, Ducks Unlimited was able to build two large reservoirs, Tilley A and B, and greatly expand the program with the Eastern Irrigation District.

Fred Sharp.

R. C. Cardy.

Irrigation projects require considerable management. Experience in running water is essential so that the maximum amount is taken from the system while it is available, without overtaxing the ditches and structures. Fred Sharp was sent to manage the Eastern Irrigation District projects in May, 1946. He was located at the town of Tilley, 12 miles east of Brooks, to be near the Louisiana Lakes. A naturalist, he had joined Ducks Unlimited in Winnipeg in March, 1945, banded in Manitoba that year and winter banded in 1946 near Calgary. Until 1960, Fred remained in southern Alberta, running water, battling muskrats that tunnelled into dams and ditch banks, and struggling with crop damage. Well known through the southern part of the province, he later became involved out of his own district as far north as the Hay Lakes project in the extreme northwestern corner of the province.

Big old Fred, as he was affectionately known (though he wasn't old), was a great raconteur, and not deterred by hyperbole if it improved a story. As Freeman has often said, at a gathering of Ducks Unlimited employees everyone spoke for the first 15 minutes and then just Fred. A keen hunter, he was an excellent shot with both rifle and shotgun.

Fred became Alberta Provincial Manager in 1966 and retired from the Company at the end of 1975. As Fred Sharp's activities expanded, the responsibility of running water was taken over by Martin Jolitz, who had originally joined the company as a summer construction worker in 1946, and finally retired in December, 1975. Big, slow-talking Martin was a joy, and his dry humour delightful.

During the war years, contact was made with another agency and a long co-operative association established. The Special Areas Board of the Alberta Department of Agriculture had been established at Hanna in 1939 to manage and rehabilitate land in east central Alberta abandoned by farmers during the dry years

114

After.

of the 1930's. These normally arid plains had been brought under cultivation in a land rush, prior to and during the First World War, which happened to coincide with an abnormally wet period for the area. When normal conditions returned, farms were abandoned wholesale, and to try to restore grass cover, plantings were made and rigid grazing restrictions imposed on natural grasslands by the Special Areas Board. Much of the area is drained by well-defined tributaries to the Red Deer and the Battle Rivers. These offered numerous opportunities for Ducks Unlimited to build impoundments to store spring melt water on these temporary flowages. Land problems were easily solved in an area starved for water. The Special Areas Board offered every encouragement on lands they controlled, and the private landowners all wanted as much water as they could get.

The first project in the area was built on Bullpound Creek in 1939 and created a new shallow 2600 acre lake. All the land was made available by the Special Areas Board, except for one privately-owned quarter section. In June, 1940, it was named Lake Coleman.

Bruce McGlone discusses a project with machine operator.

As the number of projects in Special Areas grew and opportunities continued to appear, a full-time Area Manager was required. R. C. Cardy held the position from 1954 to 1965, and then Bruce McGlone until 1976 when he moved to a new posting north of Edmonton and was replaced by Gordon Edwards. Office space has always been supplied rent free by the Special Areas Board.

Up to the present, 187 projects have been built in the Hanna area, totalling 36,959 acres and 861 miles of shoreline.

Muskrat trappers watch fire in Libau marshes.

Although emphasis during the war years was on engineering, Bert Cartwright, in addition to managing Big Grass Marsh and developing the muskrat co-operative there, made a short-lived attempt at a similar organization for the marshes south of Yorkton, Saskatchewan. He also launched a program to improve waterfowl production from the great Netley and Libau marshes, some 50,000 acres in extent, in the delta of the Red River about 30 miles north of Winnipeg.

As early as June 25, 1938, a Mr. C. Harvey brought to the attention of Ducks Unlimited the losses to waterfowl from fire and floods which were taking place in the Netley and Libau marshes. Bert probably was already aware of this, for even in the writer's experience, the red glow in the night sky north of Winnipeg from the burning marshes was almost an annual spring event.

Fires were usually started for one of three reasons: by permittees on crown hay leases to get rid of old grass in preparation for harvesting the current hay crop; by muskrat trappers to make easier walking through the marsh and to expose rat houses; or by irresponsible people who just wanted to see a fire.

The effect on nesting ducks was devastating. Direct losses occurred when burning was delayed until after the ducks had started to nest, as it often was. Indirect losses occurred when the cover was burned on the high ground, forcing the ducks to nest at lower elevations where they were flooded out by the tides generated by strong north winds on Lake Winnipeg. Later nesters, using new cover, were destroyed by haying operations which were begun before the nests had hatched, although the law said otherwise.

It was not until February, 1940, that Bert Cartwright was able to begin a program. At that time he met with Arthur F. Anderson, a lifetime resident of the marsh edge, to discuss what could be done to control fires and flooding in the Libau marsh.

He could not have made a better contact. While Art Anderson was paid for the work he did for Ducks Unlimited, his interest went much further than that, for he truly loved the marsh. And from him, during his association with Ducks Unlimited, came a steady stream of suggestions to improve the management of the area. As the program grew, he gradually assumed administration of the entire field organization.

By personal contact and then by letter, Cartwright advised the Manitoba Lands, and Game and Fisheries Branches that Ducks Unlimited was prepared to spend $2,000 to organize the burning in the Libau marshes on the east side of the Red River. Permission was granted. The Municipality of St. Clements also promised co-operation "as long as it didn't cost them any money". Bert shrewdly had the marsh designated as a "wooded area", which brought it under jurisdiction of the Forestry Branch, and under much stricter burning regulations. For example, no fire could be started unless a minimum of six men were present to keep it under control.

The Lands Branch co-operated by stressing to hay permittees that no hay could be cut prior to July 10th (it had begun as early as the fourth week of June in some years), and no mowing was to be done closer than 100 feet from the water. The Director of the Branch reserved the right to limit cutting on any part of a permit which might adversely affect waterfowl nesting, and to withdraw from haying any claims where the value to waterfowl outweighed that of the hay. If the permittee burned the area and the fire got out of control, he would be subject to prosecution and would lose his hay permit. One could hardly ask for more co-operation than that!

Anderson and another fire guardian were employed through the spring, and for 2 days a week during the summer. There were no uncontrolled fires and the rules under which hay could be cut were enforced for the Lands Branch.

Ducks Unlimited fire tower, Libau marshes.

Art Anderson starts backfire with Hauck flame gun.

Redhead hen escapes rising water on Libau marsh by building up nest.

Eggs from flooded nests.

By the end of October, when the program was shut down for the year, 8½ miles of fire guards had been plowed, and the marshes cut into blocks by mowing or scything 20 foot swathes through the emergent vegetation to the water's edge so that accidental fires could be isolated. A total of $1,845 had been spent. Cartwright estimated that, at the end of 1940, Ducks Unlimited had 25,000 acres under management on the east side of the river.

During the summer, Cartwright also made arrangements with the Lands Branch and the Municipality of St. Andrews to have the program extended to the Netley Marshes on the west side of the Red River in 1941. He also asked the Delta Waterfowl Research Station to make a survey of the effects upon waterfowl nesting success of mowing as early as July 10th. Peter Ward, now Director of the Station, and Lyle Sowles, a student, made the survey. It revealed a loss of 25% of the nests in hay meadows due to haying operations. Cartwright then successfully convinced the Lands Branch to set back the date when haying could begin to July 20th.

The year was marred, however, by a severe outbreak of botulism in the marsh due to the low water levels. An estimated 35,000-50,000 ducks died. These very high losses reflect the large number of ducks which must have been using the marsh at that time — far in excess of anything seen today. The duck carcasses were gathered up and burned or buried by the Game and Fish Branch and Ducks Unlimited.

Early in 1941, the Lands Branch approved the extension of Ducks Unlimited's activities to the Netley Marshes, as Cartwright had already made preparations to do. The Branch cooperated by making it compulsory for hay permittees to arrange for burning their claims under supervision of Ducks Unlimited fire guardians. All burning had to be completed by April 20th. Ducks Unlimited employed 2 guardians on each side of the river at $3.00 a day under the general field supervision of Art Anderson. The wage for men employed to blacken fire guards and scythe was 21 cents an hour since they were classified as agricultural workers.

Cartwright took a keen interest in the program and made many trips to the field to see how the work was progressing. He estimated that there was now 48,000 acres under management. Three fire towers were built in the Libau marshes for $18.00 each. The marsh, since the water level had increased, was said to be in the best condition since 1920, and there was estimated to be three times as many ducks as in 1940.

Through the 1940's, the Libau marsh was particularly outstanding for the large number of redheads it produced. Botulism again broke out and the Game and Fisheries Branch gathered and buried the dead ducks, while Ducks Unlimited collected and hospitalized those that were sick.

The program was expanded in 1942 to include the Beaconia marshes on Lake Winnipeg, east of the Libau Marshes, and was put under the supervision of the Game and Fisheries Branch. Ducks Unlimited hired and paid the fire guardians but the general field direction was given by the local game warden. In addition the company staked the hay claims 100 feet from the water so that the regulation would be obeyed. Upon their recommendation, several claims were withdrawn from haying which "had more value as waterfowl nesting cover than hay".

High water in 1943 reduced the burning problem but substituted the old one of flooding, which could not be as easily solved. Surveys in the Libau Marsh from 1941 through 1943, resulted in a plan for water control on 6,000 acres of water and 16,000 acres of cover. The original estimate was $60,000 but this was soon increased to $100,000. This was considered too big a project for Ducks Unlimited alone, and it was hoped that assistance would be forthcoming from the provincial government.

It wasn't. And not until well after the war was the corporation able to build dykes to try, unsuccessfully, to control flooding.

The burning control continued, though a series of high water years, beginning in 1945, reduced the area to be burned. The Grand Marais marshes were included in 1944 and the program expanded to the Riverton and Hecla Island marshes in 1948. Cartwright estimated 60,000 acres were under control in 1948 for a cost of $1,300 annually.

Art Anderson now completely organized and supervised the field work, working smoothly with Game and Fisheries Branch personnel, and doing an outstanding job of obtaining the cooperation of landowners as well as permit holders. In 1950, he estimated 100,000 acres were under spring fire control.

In 1957, the burning control program was extended to the Big Grass Marsh area on the west side of Lake Manitoba. These burning programs were all terminated in 1963 when investigations showed that high water had so reduced waterfowl nesting populations in the Netley-Libau marshes that the program was no longer justified, and that the situation had now been brought under control by the municipalities at Big Grass Marsh.

Since that time there have been low water years, but fire has not been the problem it was before initiation of the program. The attitude of local landowners has changed, and a greater responsibility in the use of fire assumed. For this, Ducks Unlimited can take credit.

Beginning in 1948, a series of high water years, and subsequent flooding from Lake Winnipeg wind tides, stimulated the farmers adjacent to the marsh to undertake a dyking program. Ducks Unlimited was approached to assist and agreed to do so on the basis that they would pay 1/4 to 1/3 of the cost of a dyke, depending on the value to waterfowl.

H. C. Moulding.

Ten and a half miles of dyke were built in 1948 and 1949, designed to withstand flood levels similar to those of 1948, the highest in recent history.

Unfortunately, in 1950, water levels were well above even those of 1948. This, combined with the resulting extreme high wind tides from Lake Winnipeg, almost completely destroyed the dykes which had not had time to consolidate. In 1951, it was decided that they could not be economically repaired. The culverts were removed and the project abandoned. Since Ducks Unlimited had agreed with the farmers to maintain the dykes, the corporation, in order to fulfill their obligation, refunded the money of those who had contributed.

Dykes built between 1957 and 1959 to control flooding on the west side of the Red River were less extensive, but more successful. The 3½ mile Goldeye dyke just south of the Netley Marshes protected some 7,500 acres from flooding, and a control structure on the outlet of the adjacent Goldeye Lake stabilizes water levels on the lake, except for extreme floods.

During the war years, several young engineers who were first employed as summer students became permanent employees, two of whom have had long productive careers with Ducks Unlimited.

H. C. (Herb) Moulding joined the company as a rodman at Brooks in 1943, and became an instrument man in 1944. In 1945 and 1946, he worked in the Western Irrigation District in Strathmore under Gilbert Patrick. Moulding graduated in 1947 and worked out of the Edmonton office, chiefly in the Hanna and Peace River districts. In the latter area, he carried out the

Hart River Diversion Survey for the Kimawin and Winagami projects under extremely difficult conditions. The story is that he was once lost for 16 hours. Herb denies this, claiming that you can't get lost if you use aerial photos — though it may sometimes be difficult to get from point 'A' to point 'B'. Herb moved to Regina as a field engineer in 1950, and became Provincial Manager in 1951. He moved to Winnipeg in 1973 to become Manager of the Special Projects Team, a position for which he was well suited.

G. A. E. (Gunner) Campbell was another engineer who began a long career with the company as a summer student. Employed during the summer of 1944 and 1945, he joined the permanent staff in the spring of 1946 and became Saskatchewan Provincial Manager later in the year when Lloyd Bunting moved to Winnipeg as Chief Engineer. He left the company briefly in 1949, returned as Manitoba Provincial Manager in 1951, was transferred to British Columbia as the first Provincial Manager when Ducks Unlimited expanded to that province in 1969, and left the company in February, 1973. Gunner was a reconnaissance engineer of above average talent. Many of the projects based on streams flowing into the Quill Lakes in east central Saskatchewan were conceived by him, an excellent example of which is the J. "Ding" Darling — Campbell Project near Wynyard. The great expansion in The Pas area of Manitoba during the 1960's was under his direction, including the development of the Cumberland Marshes and Helldiver Complex in northeastern Saskatchewan, and the great Del-Mar project in the Saskatchewan River Delta east of The Pas.

Other summer students who became permanent employees but stayed for a shorter time included Hayden Wilks and Frank Farrish.

Hayden Wilks was a contemporary of Gunner Campbell. He joined Ducks Unlimited in Saskatchewan in 1946. In January,

Frank Ward.

1949, Wilks replaced Frank Farrish as Manitoba Provincial Manager, a position which he held until he left in 1951.

Frank Farrish began as a rodman in Saskatchewan in 1940 and after graduation divided his time between Ducks Unlimited and the University of Manitoba. He became Manitoba Provincial Manager in 1946 and left the company in 1948.

With Frank Ward, he built many of the smaller projects in the Baldur-Mariapolis district of southwestern Manitoba, as well as the Otter Lake and Proven Lake projects near Erickson. These were subsequently named for the well known wartime aircraft manufacturer — Glenn Martin. Frank recalls when building the Rice Lake project just west of Saskatoon, Saskatchewan in 1942, that he had the Bently brothers of hockey fame — Max, Doug, and Jack — working on construction for him. Though Max and Doug were big stars in the National Hockey League at that time, you would never have known it from the way they conducted themselves on the job.

Farrish also recalls a period when Ducks Unlimited must have been very short of money. He was given a car and a tent and sent to Saskatchewan to survey. He pitched the tent close to any job where he happened to be working. Fortunately, he had a meal allowance of $1.20/day which permitted him to eat in restaurants most of the time.

Frank Ward was another interesting character who came to Ducks Unlimited during the war. He had already had a career as a rancher and farmer on the edge of the Shoal Lakes northwest of Winnipeg, when he joined the company on April 1, 1944. Frank was a good practical naturalist, had been a market hunter, and had guided such famous ornithologists as T. A. Taverner, and numerous others from the United States. He was an uncle of Peter Ward, now Director of the Delta Waterfowl Research Station.

Tall, straight, and proud, with tanned lined face, he was everyone's old outdoorsman. He was hired primarily to help with land negotiations, and with his farming and ranching background, he was good at it. Furthermore, he had a good stage presence, and made a great impression when he showed Ducks Unlimited movies to school children or game and fish groups. With the latter, he was a favourite.

His tales of the early days of plentiful game at "the turn of the century" established his authority as a wildlife expert. Ward had little time for biologists or modern game management. He once complained that the company was being 'biologized' to death. His battle (although he finally lost) against a doe hunting season in Manitoba was an epic. He left Ducks Unlimited in 1956 and died shortly thereafter.

At the end of the 1945 fiscal year (March 1, 1946), the last of the war years, Ducks Unlimited had under control or management "165 projects that improve 1,263,200 acres". This very large total was arrived at by including such management projects as Gordon Lake (322,000 acres) and by assuming that a project improved waterfowl habitat for a mile back from the full supply level. In some cases this was true when the project supplied reliable brood water for temporary potholes in the surrounding area. But it was hardly a measure that could be applied arbitrarily since projects differed so radically. In the years following the war, some management acreages were written off, projects reevaluated, and acreage reduced to that of the water area alone.

In 1945, *"The Ducks Came Back"*, the story of Ducks Unlimited, was written by Kip Farrington, an independent

American writer. The account greatly exaggerated Ducks Unlimited's role in increasing the waterfowl population to what was then an acceptable level. The book proved to be a source of great embarrassment to the company, and temporarily estranged many other organizations with whom they had worked on behalf of waterfowl.

Russenholt's annual report for 1945, as Director of Operations, expressed the concern of management with this problem. "A vital part of our work must be to do everything possible to ensure the accuracy of material circulated about DU — by our own DU people and by independent writers. This requires endless tact and watchfulness. It is not possible to positively check material produced independently. Nevertheless, we must invest time and effort to do so. In presentation, one mistaken effort can do more damage than many good efforts can heal."

At the annual meeting at Ottawa in 1946, Arthur Bartley expressed the attitude of the Canadian directors when he said, "Our job, as I see it, is important. Do the job, tell the truth, and we will not need to worry about public relations."

One of the major causes of friction with other organizations was the conflicting reports on waterfowl numbers, particularly between the United States Fish and Wildlife Service and Ducks Unlimited. In 1945, the Trustees of Ducks Unlimited, Inc., in order to remove this irritation, agreed with the Service not to give publicity to census figures. Changes would be expressed as trends.

A conference in Washington, February 9 and 10, 1948, was attended by Bartley, Cartwright, and Leitch on behalf of Ducks Unlimited. Here they met with representatives of the Fish and Wildlife Service, the Canadian Wildlife Service, and the Wildlife Management Institute, to discuss census techniques and population data.

At this conference it was decided that there would be an exchange of information between the organizations on June 15th each year, and again in September, with the object of releasing information on which all could agree. The integration and analysis of all available data was expected to greatly improve relations among the organizations, and with the public generally.

Fieldmen did meet in June and at the end of the field season for two or three years, but due to the difficulties of coming together during the field season, the meetings were discontinued.

A free exchange of data, however, continues to this day, with a strong bond of mutual co-operation toward a common objective.

At an Executive Committee Meeting in Winnipeg on May 11, 1945, and again at the annual meeting in Saskatoon on September 28th, Tom Main summed up the accomplishments of the organization to date and the outlook for the future. By the end of 1944, the year on which he was reporting, the company had spent a total of $850,000 and he believed that the objectives of the company could be achieved for the $3 million originally planned. He estimated that, for every dollar spent by Ducks Unlimited, governments had spent ten. If land and services had been paid for, it would have cost the company about $9 million. (In 1975, a similar calculation was made of the value of land leased free to Ducks Unlimited. This was estimated at $130 million current value.) Main estimated that a continental duck population of 250 million could be maintained in balance with industry and other interests.

Postwar

8

The immediate postwar years are closely identified with the tenure of George R. Fanset as Manager of Ducks Unlimited (Canada). Main retired in October, 1946, and was officially replaced by Fanset at the Regina Directors' Meeting of May 30, 1947.

Main felt he wasn't meant for a chair and needed to get out and do things. He wrote to the President in this vein and added that since Ducks Unlimited had grown, they now needed a good executive, which he did not feel he was.

He was retained on a consulting basis from the end of October to February 28th, the end of the fiscal year. The Executive Committee then recommended that he be further retained as consulting engineer to April 13, 1947. During this period he assisted in a special fund raising campaign in the United States.

When Main resigned, Arthur Bartley became Manager of both Ducks Unlimited (Canada) and Ducks Unlimited, Inc. George Fanset was made Executive Officer until he was appointed Resident Manager at the meeting in Regina.

A basic administrative change was made at this meeting when Bartley's title became that of Executive Director, with overall responsibility for both companies. This was a relationship which might have existed before in principle, but had never been formalized during Main's tenure. Until his retirement from the position of Executive Director in 1962, part of Bartley's costs were budgeted by Ducks Unlimited (Canada). In addition to numerous short trips, he annually spent at least two weeks on field inspections in Western Canada.

For Ducks Unlimited (Canada), the title of General Manager was replaced with Resident Manager. It never came into common usage and Fanset simply signed himself as "Manager". Russenholt resigned in April, 1947, and his title, "Chief of Operations", which had been devised in 1945 to give him added prestige for his speaking trips into the United States,

was eliminated. His department, Education and Records, was taken over by H. C. Cormode. The position of Chief Engineer became Engineering Assistant, but the original title was recreated when Bunting was transferred to Winnipeg in 1947. The positions of Chief Naturalist and Chief Biologist were unchanged.

Fortunately, George Fanset was the capable administrator that Main believed the organization now required. During Main's absences in the United States, Fanset had done much of the administration so the staff changes were made with surprisingly little disruption to the Canadian operation.

The first Annual Meeting held after the war was in Saskatoon on September 28, 1945. With the cessation of hostilities, the mood was one of optimism and plans for the future, when men and materials were expected to again become easily available.

Improvement took much longer than anticipated. It wasn't until 1949 that the supply situation was said to have eased somewhat. Even then, materials, particularly cement, had to be procured when available and stockpiled. It is apparent, too, that management, almost nostalgically, anticipated a return to prewar costs for labour and material, and deferred some construction in this expectation, which of course never materialized.

At the Saskatoon meeting in 1945, the Ducks Unlimited (Canada) staff were closely questioned on their present program and their plans for the future. Most questions came from American directors who demonstrated a determination to ensure that the money entrusted to them was being spent to the best advantage.

A similar critical and constructive attitude characterized the Annual Meeting of April 9, 1946, in Ottawa. The directors refused to accept the budget as presented, and were critical of the lack of detail. It was referred to the Executive Committee for

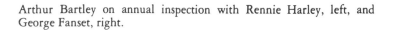

study and amendment. The policy was established that in future the budget was to be broken down, and passed by the Executive Committee prior to presentation to the directors.

The return of Arthur Bartley from the Navy to his former position of Manager of Ducks Unlimited, Inc. no doubt stimulated the new aggressive attitude of the American directors. Though aggressive, it was constructive, and demonstrated that the keen interest and drive to accomplish something worthwhile for waterfowl had not been lost to the exigencies of war — or to the apathy of time.

Throughout Fanset's career as Manager, this keen interest by the American directors continued, and resulted in many interesting and spirited discussions at annual meetings. It led to new administrative alignments and policies; and new programs and activities evolved as the money sent from the United States increased from $247,556 in 1946 to a peak of $325,000 in 1948 and 1949, and declined again to $250,000 at the end of the period.

At the annual meetings in 1946 and 1947, great concern was expressed by the American directors, particularly A. C. (Pops) Glassell, an energetic and colourful director from Louisiana, for the security of tenure of the projects in which they had invested. Glassell wanted leases or easements on all projects. He considered

the system then in use valueless for raising money. He also felt he was deceiving his contributors who believed that land for the projects had been granted permanently by the Canadian government.

He was right. Many projects had been built on a simple verbal agreement from the landowner, and as the company grew, some better form of security was required. Leitch recalls, when on a reconnaissance with Bunting prior to the war, a project was inspected, the dam site surveyed, the landowner interviewed (he happened to be passing by on a load of hay), and the contract let (to the farmer), all in one afternoon! The whole operation was carried out to everyone's satisfaction. The verbal land agreement was never challenged, and the project is still in operation. That was the way to get things done with little money and staff, but it would no longer do.

After a long discussion at the 1946 meeting, the directors decided that definite action must be taken to have appropriate agreements signed for leases, flood easements, etc., which would be registered against the land by caveat. The staff pointed out the difficulties and the time required to carry out this directive but the directors remained firm, and further suggested that a legal person be appointed in each province to approve the agreements before the project was built. Management was instructed to prepare a report on the land status for every project which had cost in excess of $2,000.

In response to the directive which was again emphasized at the annual meeting in Regina in 1947 by Glassell, George Du Pre was transferred from Education and Records to the engineering branch to carry out formal land negotiations. He had been hired as Chief Kee-Man in February, 1946, to rebuild the Kee-Man organization by eliminating those who were inactive and appointing replacements. During this period, he helped Russenholt produce the Kee-Man booklet, "Co-operation

Ed Russenholt addresses one of his many meetings in the United States. The live ducks on stage were a unique and imaginative feature of this meeting.

Unlimited''. Du Pre had little aptitude for land work and left the organization at the end of April, 1947.

He was replaced by Robert MacEwing who joined in July, 1947. A dour Scot, and a former landman with the Canadian Pacific Railway, MacEwing was an excellent choice for the position of Landman, which he filled admirably during his time with the company. He and Ed Pitblado, the company solicitor, designed legal forms which didn't terrify the farmer with their complexity and yet gave the company the protection it needed. ''Mac'', as he of course became known, had an honest and forthright approach to landowners which inspired confidence and made him a very successful negotiator. When he died in July,

1958, he left a well-organized operation to his successor, W. T. Watt, who continued successfully until he, too, died in December of 1968. John Paxton carried on for the following year, but he was no longer required when, in 1969, with decentralization of the company, the provincial organizations became responsible for their own land negotiations.

The determination of the directors to mount an effective program which would produce ducks also led to a significant increase in the biological activities of the company. Following the analogy of the ''Duck Factory'', a Production Department was formed, and Leitch, who had returned to the company from the R.C.A.F. in 1946, became Head of the Department and in

125

charge of biological programs in Saskatchewan and Alberta. B. W. Cartwright retained this responsibility for Manitoba.

Glassell reinforced the move to increased project management at the Annual Meeting in Winnipeg on April 7, 1948, when, based on his inspection of 50 to 60 projects the previous fall, he proposed that no project should be proceeded with unless fencing rights had been obtained. Both staff and the Canadian directors pointed out the many difficulties of obtaining fencing rights on all projects, and that they were not always necessary. It was finally decided and officially adopted that, "The policy for 1949 is that no projects in excess of $3,000 where rights to fence have not been obtained shall be gone on with without the specific authorization of the Executive Committee or the Board."

At the 1949 Annual Meeting held in Reno, Nevada, subsequent to that of Ducks Unlimited, Inc., management reported that fencing rights were more difficult to obtain than flooding rights. Attempts to secure them had seriously hindered land negotiations. They suggested to the directors that serious consideration should be given to revising the policy of requiring fencing rights on all projects. The directors then decided that if sufficient data on each project were presented to them, they would then determine if fencing was required.

Fifteen miles of fence had been constructed on 8 projects during 1948. Barbed wire was still in short supply but a carload had been sent from the United States by a now unknown donor. Unfortunately, it was very poor quality, stretchy and difficult to tighten and keep tight. Most of it was used in the Eastern Irrigation District in southern Alberta, where Campbell was the Resident Manager. Ten years later mention of the Will J. Reid Project fences still made Bill's face red and increased the pitch of his voice!

The impossibility of carrying out the fencing policy, and still maintaining a construction program, led to it being generally ig-

Robert MacEwing.

nored by management, though attempts were made to obtain fencing rights whenever possible, whether there were plans to exercise the right in the immediate future or not. In the Special Areas of central Alberta however, permission to flood also carried permission to fence a hundred feet back from the water's edge. This was seldom exercised because fences are only of value if they are maintained and supervised, and at this stage in its career, Ducks Unlimited did not have the field staff to do this effectively.

In the same meeting, Glassell also suggested that, effective in 1949, no project should be built within five miles of a town or city "unless every means had been taken to have the appropriate authorities declare the area about the project as a sanctuary". This was far from an unreasonable suggestion, except, as he himself pointed out, where the proposed project already had an established hunting tradition. But it should apply, he believed, where an area was restored to usefulness after a period of no water or no ducks. For some reason, this proposal was not carried to a vote, though through the years it did have an influence on staff decisions.

At Reno, the directors again expressed a desire for more details on proposed projects, so they could determine if the money was being well spent; specifically, whether a proposed project, in their estimation, was worthwhile.

Ducks Unlimited (Canada), Directors meeting, Winnipeg, April 7, 1948. Front, left to right, Dr. Walter F. Tisdale, Chief Justice W. M. Martin, Gordon E. Konantz, L. M. Barkhausen, M. W. Smith. Back row, left to right, E. B. Pitblado, Harold W. Story, A. C. Glassell, Arthur M. Bartley, Judge L. T. McKim, Col. W. F. W. Hancock, O.B.E.

It was decided that in the future each proposed project would require a "work order". Directors were to receive copies of work orders 30 days prior to the annual meeting at which the decisions would be made. Bartley pointed out that in the beginning the major consideration had been the restoration of water, while now the emphasis was becoming more and more biological — hence the need for work orders. It is ironic, that for years thereafter, although work orders were prepared (with great input of staff time and considerable expense), in the writer's memory, none of them were seriously challenged.

Through the Fanset years, a shortage of contractors who would bid on the small jobs that Ducks Unlimited had to offer still continued and led to a build up in company-owned dirt moving equipment and construction personnel. This reached its peak in 1948 when the company was operating five tractor and scraper outfits, a dragline, and five construction crews. Key foremen were kept on staff during the winter to overhaul equipment. Trailers were built and repaired at Brooks for summer housing of crews on the job.

With so many construction units in the field, it was inevitable that accidents would occur. In the late fall of 1946, Allen Simpson from Brock, Saskatchewan, who had worked with

E. W. Burkell, Alberta Manager, and secretary Shirley Kormondy, 1952.

fieldmen were probably the best cadre of mud road drivers in the country.

Bill Campbell injected a new term into the Ducks Unlimited lexicon at this time. Asked how he had got through a particularly bad mud hole, he replied, "Well I just backed up and put her in leaping gear." From this time on, every Ducks Unlimited vehicle had a "leaping gear"!

During this period, many young engineers spent their undergraduate summers with Ducks Unlimited, first as rodmen, then instrument men, and then either continued with the company after graduation or pursued careers elsewhere. One of these, E. W. (Ted) Burkell, has had a long career with the company, beginning as summer rodman for Rennie Harley in Alberta in 1939-1940 before joining the Army. Because he was born and brought up in Hanna in the centre of the Special Areas, his personal contacts and intimate knowledge of the district were a tremendous asset in locating and building the many projects the company now has in that area.

Burkell returned to Ducks Unlimited as a summer employee in 1948 and 1949, and became a permanent staff member in April, 1950, in charge of the Strathmore and Hanna districts. He moved to Edmonton as Southern Alberta Supervisor and became Provincial Manager in 1951. In 1965, he was transferred to Winnipeg as Chief Engineer and left in July, 1973, to become British Columbia Provincial Manager. At the beginning of 1976, he became Pacific Regional Manager in charge of both British Columbia and Alberta.

Burkell has always had great success in what were often difficult negotiations for the company, not only because of his skill and personality, but because it has seemed that every engineer or individual in an important position has been either an army buddy or a classmate!

Ducks Unlimited as a cat operator for several seasons, was killed while repairing a small Ducks Unlimited tractor at Baldur, Manitoba. Another fatal accident occurred in September, 1969, when R. J. (Rod) Galbraith, the Area Manager for southeastern Saskatchewan, and an employee since 1956, was killed on the Baldwin Project of the Saskatoon Southeast Complex, while supervising excavation for a culvert.

With the millions of miles which Ducks Unlimited employees have driven, it is amazing that there have been no fatal accidents, though S. T. (Ted) Dillon, a Manitoba Provincial Biologist, suffered permanent injury from a car accident in 1960. During the period after the war and through the 1950's, a series of wet years coincided with major highway development and relocation all across the prairies. At this time, Ducks Unlimited

R. T. Sterling and Rowdy on waterfowl survey.

A contemporary of Burkell, Max Wopnford, worked as a summer student in Alberta in 1947 and 1948. He became a permanent employee in April of 1949, and subsequently Northern Alberta Supervisor. Wopnford left in September, 1951, for a successful career with Shell Oil.

The biological or production aspects of the program expanded as well during the postwar years. In his annual report for 1948, Leitch stated that for the first time the Production Department had begun to assume leadership in reconnaissance and in the selection of projects for future construction. This statement was somewhat optimistic as it turned out. He continued, "This expansion is a planned growth from a two-year period of inspection and evaluation of existing projects. It is a natural step from this phase to one of active leadership in the selection and development of future projects."

In his proposed program of work for 1949, Fanset planned for seven project managers to be appointed to handle "contacts with Kee-Men, local land negotiations, duck damage and related problems, detailed management of projects and fence maintenance." Six of these project managers were active by the end of 1949.

In presenting his proposed program for 1950, Fanset again emphasized the need for better project management. In reply to Arthur Bartley's query as to whether the company was not getting too far away from their original objective of impounding water, he said,

> We find that we are to a large extent an engineering organization. Our projects when completed were not getting sufficient management. We were building them and almost forgetting about them. During the war years, we wanted to do something about it but were unable to. Getting around to see these projects takes a lot of gasoline. As soon as gas and cars became available we developed the idea of project managers . . .

Their duties are to take a group of 20 or 25 projects, inspect them periodically, look after the fences, report on the number of ducks . . .

On this basis, the Production Department staff expanded between 1949 and 1951. Summer students carried out small-scale research programs on the waterfowl use of typical prairie and parkland marshes, and on areas planned for fencing prior to construction. Bulrush roots were planted on projects deficient in emergent cover, and sago pondweed harvested and planted.

Several individuals, who would have long and productive careers, joined the organization at this time. On May 1, 1951, R. T. (Tom) Sterling, a biologist, after two years as a summer student in the Brooks district with Fred Sharp, was stationed at Wynyard to manage the group of projects based on the Quill and Kutawagan Lakes areas. Tom Sterling is still with the organization. He became Saskatchewan Provincial Biologist when the biological activities in the province were consolidated at Saskatoon in 1957. He pioneered the expansion of Ducks Unlimited into British Columbia in 1967 and 1968, and became the Provincial Biologist for that province in 1969. From 1975 to 1977, he provided biological assistance for the first project built in Mexico by Ducks Unlimited de Mexico.

R. J. (Bob) Caldwell, also a biologist, was hired at the beginning of May, 1951, to manage the projects in the Swift Current area, replacing Bob Turner who had occupied the position as a

Pintail nest.

Canvasback on nest.

Mallard nest.

Sometimes ducks nest in queer places. This mallard chose an old crow's nest.

Predators destroy many nests . . .

. . . and so does fire.

summer employee. Bob Caldwell remained with Ducks Unlimited until 1963 when he joined the Saskatchewan Wildlife Branch.

Gordon Staines was hired as additional biological support staff in Saskatchewan in 1956, and left to join the Saskatchewan Wildlife Branch in 1964.

With this expansion of the biological staff, the Production Department was able to partially carry out the responsibilities outlined by Fanset, and to increase waterfowl breeding population and production surveys by establishing a permanent transect system of sampling in the agricultural area of the three prairie provinces. Transects provide a sample of a square mile of waterfowl habitat by counting the waterbodies and waterfowl for a distance of ⅛ of a mile on both sides of the road along a four-mile stretch. Beginning experimentally in 1949, the transects were expanded and became part of the annual program in 1950. They were, and are, run in mid-May to assess habitat conditions and to determine the return of waterfowl to the prairies to breed, and again in mid-July to ascertain how the water is lasting and to obtain a subjective evaluation of the success of the breeding season to that date.

A long term series of annual brood counts on representative projects was also begun at this time and continues to the present. These data have been used through the years as background for the *Duckological* and other reports on habitat conditions and waterfowl populations by Ducks Unlimited (Canada). They have also been made available to the United States Fish and Wildlife Service and the Canadian Wildlife Service.

The postwar years also saw the beginning of the co-operative cost-sharing programs between Ducks Unlimited and the prairie governments. Prior to the war, the governments were helpful but poor; now they had money to spend.

There was great concern at this time that the return of veterans would result in the same land rush, with the same attendant poor land-use decisions that characterized the period immediately after the First World War. The prairie governments seemed to be aware of this possibility, and both Saskatchewan and Alberta entered into co-operative programs with Ducks Unlimited to protect the marshes on the northern fringe of agriculture. But in Manitoba, although Premier John Bracken was a good friend of Ducks Unlimited, friction had developed between T. C. Main and the Minister of Mines and Natural Resources, and things moved more slowly in that province long after Main had departed.

At the Annual Meeting in Saskatoon in September, 1945, Main told the directors that the company had entered into an agreement with the Saskatchewan government whereby 1¼ million acres in the Saskatchewan River Delta would be investigated for its wildlife potential. Ducks Unlimited would assist in the surveys to the extent of $10,000 and would spend another $90,000 on engineering improvements. The intrusion of settlers into the area would be curtailed until the evaluation was complete. T.C. was afraid that once the settlers became established they would immediately promote drainage. Later experience in the Carrot River Valley at The Pas confirmed his apprehension.

W. M. (Bill) Morrison was hired in May of 1946 as Area Manager for The Pas, Manitoba, to survey, and to look after the interests of waterfowl and Ducks Unlimited in the Saskatchewan River Delta in both Manitoba and Saskatchewan. Although he only remained with the company until September, 1948, his many reconnaissances laid the groundwork for subsequent work by the company in the area.

Under this co-operative program with Saskatchewan, surveys were made in the winter of 1946 on the opposite side of the river, to the north and west of the Cumberland Marshes which

Alberta Water Stabilization Board, 1946. Left to right: Frank L. Grindley, Ben Russell, Eric Heustis, Rennie Harley. Standing: Boney Watkins.

Ducks Unlimited is presently developing. Main was able to report at the 1946 annual meeting that the Saskatchewan government had voted $75,000 to develop the area. In 1947, the government had completed one dam. Two more were to be built, and two crawler tractors and a dragline were in the area. A tremendous flood in 1948 severely eroded the dams, and the project was not finally completed until 1951. In 1952, another huge flood washed away large sections of the dams and the Saskatchewan government abandoned the project.

A further agreement had been reached with the Saskatchewan government in 1947 whereby they would charge an additional royalty on all wild fur to accumulate a fund for habitat development. The government was to carry out land

negotiations (this would be particularly helpful to Ducks Unlimited) and pay 60% of construction costs. Ducks Unlimited would do reconnaissance, surveys and design, and pay 40% of construction costs. Several projects were built under this program.

In Alberta, Rennie Harley, working with Frank Grindley, the Chief Engineer of Water Resources for the Alberta government, conceived the idea of a co-operative program which would benefit both Ducks Unlimited and the Alberta government. As a result, the Water Stabilization Board was formed in 1946, and operated successfully for many years thereafter. The original members were Frank Grindley; Ben Russell, Director of Water Resources; Eric Huestis, Game Commissioner; Boney Watkins, Director of Fisheries; and, Rennie Harley of Ducks Unlimited.

Basically, the Board co-ordinated the efforts of the government and Ducks Unlimited in areas of mutual interest. If the proposed project benefited the government most in terms of fisheries or other wildlife, they paid 2/3 of the cost. If the project benefited waterfowl most, Ducks Unlimited paid 2/3. The program was successful in preserving many excellent marshes from drainage. The active support of the provincial government made many projects possible which would have been very difficult to develop otherwise. Twenty-four projects totalling 212,-404 acres of water with 623 miles of shoreline were built under this program.

Although it must have been discussed informally many times previously, the need to expand into eastern Canada to help the black duck is first mentioned formally in the minutes of the 1945 Executive Committee Meeting in Winnipeg. L. M. Barkhausen, director from Chicago, queried the sum of $9,480 set up in the budget for Eastern Canada Construction and Surveys. Main replied that a Mr. Peters, Flyway Biologist for the U.S. Fish and Wildlife Service, had been making extensive studies of black duck breeding habitat in Eastern Canada, and had offered the information to Ducks Unlimited. He had in mind several areas that might be managed for this species. Main was to meet with Peters and the governments of New Brunswick and Nova Scotia during May and June. Bartley supported this move, with the comment that anything that could be done to improve shooting along the eastern seaboard of the United States would have a very beneficial effect on donations from that area.

At the Annual Directors' Meeting in Saskatoon on September 28, 1945, Main was able to report that the trip east had been very successful. He was received in New Brunswick by several cabinet members and the Game Commissioner. (Main also added that approaches had also been made to the company to expand into British Columbia and Quebec.) At this meeting, Bert

Cartwright advised that Bruce Wright, recently discharged from the Navy, had been employed to make a major study of the black duck. The University of New Brunswick had provided office space, and Wright had begun his investigations in the lower estuary of the St. John River. He had made the first waterfowl survey of the study area, some 36,000 acres, on July 16, 1945, by canoe and outboard, and on foot. During the fall and winter of 1945-46, Wright remained on the Ducks Unlimited payroll and carried on his research at the University of Wisconsin under Dr. Aldo Leopold.

Brian Carter, who was to subsequently become Director of the Wildlife Branch of New Brunswick, joined the staff in the spring of 1946 as a biologist. A technician, Andrew W. Skeed, also joined at that time. So, at the beginning of May, 1946, the Eastern office of Ducks Unlimited consisted of Bruce Wright, Brian Carter, and Andrew Skeed.

During the 1946 season, the primary work consisted of standardizing breeding pair counts in the lower St. John River Valley. The pattern established was used for many years. Other important breeding areas, many coastal, were also investigated, as was the role of beaver ponds in black duck production.

During the winter of 1946-47, Ducks Unlimited and the Wildlife Management Institute met and decided to establish the Northeastern Wildlife Station at the University of New Brunswick, which again agreed to supply office space and stenographic help. This station was to be the eastern counterpart of the Delta Waterfowl Research Station in Manitoba. Bruce Wright was named Director.

After that, Ducks Unlimited took little active part and left administration of the Station to the Wildlife Management Institute who continued financial support until 1963. The station was finally taken over completely by the University of New

Black duck habitat, St. John River Valley, New Brunswick.

Beaver ponds are important black duck breeding habitat.

Black ducks — the gold standard of the Atlantic Flyway.

Black duck nest on tree base above flood water.

Bruce Wright.

Brunswick, and with Bruce Wright's death in 1975 ceased to exist.

In 1950, Wright recommended the construction of the Fullerton Marsh Project on Prince Edward Island. This, the first Ducks Unlimited project in the Maritimes, was built in 1951.

Evidence of a continuing desire to undertake some operation which would increase waterfowl populations on the east coast of the United States is found in the minutes of the June 3rd Annual Meeting of 1950, where the Executive Committee and management were authorized, in reply to a request from E. Herrick Low, Chairman of the New York State Ducks Unlimited Committee, to ship mallards or mallard eggs to the east coast.

Strangely enough, this proposal had the support of such eminent biologists as Dr. Clarence Cottam and Dr. Fredrick Lincoln of the United States Fish and Wildlife Service. Today it would be greeted with horror by those intent on preventing further pollution of the black duck gene pool by mallards. There is no record that the transplants were ever made.

One of the problems throughout the war had been the lack of men trained in wildlife management. With the war over, the company, at the suggestion of the Executive Committee, prepared a comprehensive training scheme for returning veterans, but it was not implemented by the government officials to whom it was submitted.

Also at this time (1945), the question of soliciting donations in Canada was first officially broached, and the Executive Committee instructed to give the matter consideration. There were arguments pro and con. Since that time, it has been discussed at innumerable Executive and Annual Meetings, but whether the company should embark on a Canadian solicitation program is still not completely resolved.

Attempts began in 1947 to have unsolicited donations to Ducks Unlimited (Canada) considered charitable for income tax purposes. President Judge Ross, just before his death in December of that year, was given a negative decision by Ottawa. Fanset then began working with Director Senator Paterson and other western Senators to develop an approach which might be successful. New representation was made in 1949, but there was no progress until 1954, when Rennie Harley, then Western Manager, went to Ottawa. With the help of contacts there, he was able to have the company recognized as a charitable organization, and to obtain income tax exemption for donations.

At the September 1945 Annual Meeting, Bert Cartwright reported that the company had banded 42,016 ducks up to that point. A rather remarkable achievement in view of the transportation difficulties of the war years and Main's confession as late as 1946, that "cars and trucks were purposely made available for the Engineering Department, sometimes at the expense of the Ecological Department . . ." Cartwright also reported that an official request had been received from the U.S. Fish and Wildlife Service for Ducks Unlimited to participate in attempts to save the Whooping Crane from extinction.

It was agreed that the company should help. Kee-Men were asked to report Whooping Crane sightings on their reports, and for years these were assembled and forwarded to Fred Bard, who co-ordinated the work from the Saskatchewan Museum of Natural History in Regina. These reports, which were numerous, were not only of great value in establishing migration dates and routes for Whooping Cranes through Western Canada, but also provided a check on their numbers.

An intriguing mystery surrounds the disappearance of the idea promoted at this time by Harvey Sorenson of California for a project to commemorate the men killed in the war. The concept was enthusiastically accepted by the Trustees' Meeting in Milwaukee in 1946, and an emotional letter from Sorenson read to the Canadian directors at their Annual Meeting in Ottawa on

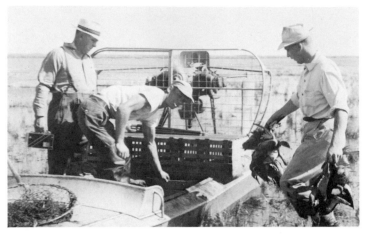

Using the airboat to collect ducks sick with botulism on Whitewater Lake, Manitoba, 1950.

Ducks in recovery pen at Whitewater Lake.

Irrigation water added to Stobart Lake, Alberta, brought botulism there under control.

April 9, 1946, led to complete endorsement. S. S. Holden in putting the question to the meeting said, "I do not think it necessary to put the question. Anyone in my opinion who would fail to vote for such a proposition . . . should be laid on an icicle bed in a churchyard where the asparagus does not grow." It was carried unanimously.

Sorenson had suggested the project be financed by "a million dollar club" consisting of 1,000 members who would contribute $1,000 each. The Canadian directors believed that both the federal and provincial governments would want to contribute. The projects suggested as possibilities were the Athabasca Delta (a strong favourite), the Saskatchewan River Delta, and the Netley-Libau Marshes. This apparently excellent idea which was so enthusiastically received and had such potential public appeal disappears completely from the official record after this meeting.

During a series of low water years after the war, botulism was a serious problem on many shallow lakes in Western Canada. Ducks Unlimited operated a hospital at Whitewater Lake in southern Manitoba in 1949 and 1950, under the supervision of Frank Ward, for ducks sick with the disease. Botulism patrols on Old Wives Lake, south of Moose Jaw, Saskatchewan, and at Stobart Lake, near Strathmore, Alberta, were also carried on for several years. A supply of anti-toxin was assured in case of an outbreak. The Stobart Lake problem was solved by the diversion of irrigation water to the lake and construction of a dam on the outlet. There are no engineering solutions to the situations at Old Wives Lake and Whitewater, and the danger of a major outbreak is always present in low water years.

The need for efficient transportation over shallow water and wet mud for botulism work led to the purchase of Ducks Unlimited's first air-thrust boat. Sharp and Leitch went to the Bear River Marshes in Utah in September of 1949 to observe the methods used there in coping with botulism outbreaks. While

Isabel Curwain.

there, they ordered an air-thrust boat (at that time they were handmade from aluminum), which was delivered in June of the next year. The airboat proved to be such an efficient vehicle for marsh transportation that additional boats were added in subsequent years. In 1977, the company had a fleet of eight of these boats (now fibreglass) distributed across Western Canada.

Although the directors kept a much tighter rein on the program after Bartley returned from active service, they were quick to respond to the problems of the staff. It was customary for T. C. Main to be voted a bonus at each annual meeting (this was not continued with the following General Managers) in recognition of a successful year. In 1944, he was given an extra bonus of $500 to help defray the very heavy expenses he had accrued as the result of the prolonged illness of his wife. At the 1950 annual meeting in Calgary, it was decided that $5,000, the carry-over from the previous year's budget, be used "for the purpose of providing for flood losses of members of the staff in Winnipeg, to the extent of the difference between the total loss sustained and the money received from other sources, and that distribution of the fund be left to the Executive Committee".

Staff pensions first received attention during the immediate postwar period and were the source of much debate. First official mention was at the 1947 Annual Meeting in Regina, when the Executive Director, Arthur Bartley, in consultation with the Executive Committee, was instructed to consider the matter further and, if they could agree on a proposal, to set up a pension scheme. In 1948, at Winnipeg, Bartley reported that he could not recommend a pension plan because his smaller contributors were opposed to having their money used in that way. He believed a higher salary scale would be received more favorably. This solution was adopted by the meeting.

In 1951, the pension question was again raised at the Annual Meeting in Des Moines by Harold Basford, an American director. He stated that his view had changed over the years, and he was now of the opinion that the corporation should reconsider a pension plan. On his motion, seconded by Will J. Reid, another American director, the Executive Committee was instructed to consider the matter again and to set up a plan. At the Annual Meeting in 1952, the directors ordered that the pension plan be implemented that year, and made the necessary financial arrangements for it.

Reflecting the belief still prevalent as late as 1947, that wages and prices would finally return to prewar levels, a new salary scale became effective on January 1, 1948, which included a bonus on the first $200 monthly salary of ½% for each point the cost of living index rose over 130. The bonus was paid by separate cheque. By 1956, it was apparent there would be no return to prewar conditions. The bonus was eliminated and salaries increased to compensate.

The last of the Fanset years saw further changes in the original staff and the introduction of a new member who was to give long, efficient, and faithful service to the company.

E. B. "Hiram" Walker, the original highly respected and beloved bookkeeper had died in 1950, after retiring in 1947 due to ill health. A. W. Meadows, his replacement, died that same summer and was replaced by C. W. Duncan.

Isabel Curwain came to Ducks Unlimited on April 1, 1950 (a date which still amuses her) as secretary to George Fanset. She soon became involved in the accounting and, when Duncan retired in 1962, took over his responsibilities and also became Office Manager.

Isabel is still with the company — a continual source of cheerfully given information, both current and historical.

In wet years, innumerable wetlands dot the fields.

The Wet Fifties

9

When Angus Gavin became General Manager in 1951, Ducks Unlimited was almost immediately faced with entirely different problems, quite at odds with the original concept. Suddenly there was too much water, bringing with it drainage and crop depredation. Waterfowl biologists working at that time, still look back on the period from 1951-1957 as the golden age of waterfowl in the modern sense. Bag limits in Saskatchewan in 1955 through 1957 were 15 ducks a day with 45 in possession, and could be achieved. These generous bag limits were as much in response to farmers' complaints about duck damage to crops as they were to the abundance of birds.

While there had been high water years in the 1940's, drainage programs were not initiated due to the priorities of war. In the 1950's, it was different. Flooding was severe and prolonged, the country prosperous, and money available for drainage programs. The actual and potential loss of valuable waterfowl habitat became an immediate concern for Ducks Unlimited, although construction carried on as usual and expanded with increasing budgets.

The drainage problem was most severe in Saskatchewan and largely resulted, paradoxical though it may seem, from government policies during the drought years of the 1930's. At that time, the government encouraged the sale of marsh lands, which were then dry or greatly reduced in size, to adjacent farmers. In other instances farmers just illegally encroached on exposed Crown land. These accrued lands were mostly used for pasture but a considerable amount was brought under cultivation. When these former marshes refilled in the early 1950's, the accrued lands were flooded and the immediate cry was for drainage. Many farmers believed that since the government had sold them the land, it had a moral obligation to provide drainage.

Ironically, prompted by the dry years of the late 1940's, the Saskatchewan government in 1949 established a Conservation

Angus Gavin.

```
3-55    copy              REPORT      FORM
4-56
1-57              SASKATCHEWAN  MARSH  RECONNAISSANCE
11-57

Name    Coyocari Slough       File #        72 H-31  Classification        D-2

Sec   30    Twp  9      Rge  23    W   2   Engineering File #

Direction & distance from nearest town

Observer   Tom Sterling                    Date          June 9/56

Contact    Mr. Syhlouyk, Kayville

Physical
                                                          average    1.5'
         Number of acres   650        Miles of shoreline  6.5
                                                          Maximum    2.5'

         Present level in relation to F.S.L. at F.S.L. old shoreline

         Area at F.S.L.    605          Shoreline at F.S.L.  6.5

         Source of water    local runoff

         Profile medium shore flat bottom   Contour      somewhat irregular

         Turbidity    clear to bottom 2.5'        Salinity    fresh

         Analysis      T.D.S.       pH          Alkalinity-phth

                                                         mo

         Bottom   firm sandy clay

         Adjacent water areas   other large D areas, some with dugouts

         Local topography    rolling

Biological

         Submergents   some sago, both star and lesser duckweeds abundant



         Emergents    70% whitetop grass, 5% slough grass and smartweed, trace of

         cattail and spikerush.



         Shoreline and upland vegetation   less than 5% grass remainder cultivation.
```

First page of Saskatchewan Wetland Inventory Program report form.

Drained marsh.

and Development Branch, whose responsibility was the conservation and development of provincial water resources. But when the wet years began, it soon became an efficient drainage organization.

It is difficult to argue effectively against the drainage of patented cultivated lands. But the drainage obsession once underway tends to snowball, and land under any waterbody, private or Crown, becomes a potential bonanza in the minds of drainage advocates.

Ducks Unlimited's role in the drainage program became one of pointing out to the government the wildlife values of Crown wetlands, particularly for waterfowl, and providing biological and historical background data on individual wetlands for the Saskatchewan Wildlife Branch.

The establishment of the Saskatchewan Water Stabilization Committee in the early 1950's through the efforts of Rennie Harley, then Western Manager, provided a vehicle for this material to reach the government. The Board was composed of representatives from the Conservation and Development Branch, the Water Rights Branch of the Department of Agriculture, the Wildlife Branch of the Department of Natural Resources, and Ducks Unlimited.

One of the major programs of the Production Department in Saskatchewan (Ducks Unlimited's biological arm at that time) thus became that of assessing the wildlife values of areas proposed for drainage. Close association with the Conservation and Development Branch, through the Water Stabilization Committee, made plans for drainage schemes available to Ducks Unlimited. In the 1954 field season, 22 such schemes were evaluated and reported upon. Most were lands long under cultivation, whose drainage would have little effect on waterfowl. In cases where waterfowl habitat was involved, a sympathetic hearing was accorded.

It became apparent, however, that when plans for drainage had been finalized, contracts let and the draglines standing by, not to mention the political commitments made, only a miracle could prevent a scheme from proceeding. So instead of chasing draglines and hurriedly grabbing what data (always inadequate) could be obtained on short notice, the Production Department decided to get ahead of the game and begin a Wetland Inventory Program so that the basic wildlife data for an area would be on file when drainage proposals were first made.

This program, which began in 1955, to catalogue the biological and historical aspects of every water area in the southern part of the province over 640 acres in size, was planned, directed, and vigorously promoted by Sterling, Moulding, and Leitch.

During the program, which extended into the early 1960's when a return to drier prairie conditions diverted drainage programs northward, surveys were made and reports prepared on over 1,200 areas. These were summarized by topographic map sheet in the southern portion of the province, and on a watershed basis in the more northerly and eastern parts. Fifteen topographical map sheets and 6 watersheds were completed, a total of 102,199 square miles. The data were made available to the Saskachewan Wildlife Branch to use in their efforts to preserve waterfowl habitat. They were also made available to the Canadian Wildlife Service for the Land Capability Classification for Canada program under ARDA (Agricultural Rehabilitation and Development Act).

The Saskatchewan Wildlife Branch once stated that in many instances during this period when they attended meetings dealing with the disposition of a specific wetland, the only information they had on the area, and the only data with which to argue for the preservation of it for wildlife, were contained in the Ducks Unlimited reports.

Needless to say, these arguments were not always successful. But they did demonstrate to advocates of wholesale drainage, that there were values in wetlands which had to be considered and measured against the sometimes marginal agricultural benefits of indiscriminate drainage. During this period, wildlife gradually became accepted as a public good and, in 1961, "use for wildlife" was recognized under the Saskatchewan Water Rights Act.

The Wetland Inventory in Saskatchewan also served as reconnaissance for the Ducks Unlimited construction program, and where no water control was possible, recommendations were made for marsh management works, such as level ditching, island building, vegetation control, etc., in order to increase production and to identify the area for waterfowl, and thus forestall alienation for other purposes. These recommendations are now the basis for the marsh management program presently underway in Saskatchewan, and provide a valuable historical perspective to planning.

To quote Rennie Harley's 1957 Annual Report to Ducks Unlimited (Canada), "in Alberta a saner view was taken". This perhaps was to be expected. Due to higher rainfall, a much greater percentage of Saskatchewan is cultivated, and the province presents the ultimate in the conflict between waterfowl and agriculture in both drainage and crop depredation. With more arid land, and a greater dependence on stored water for irrigation and stock-watering, Alberta has traditionally been more aware of the need for water conservation.

This was reflected in the attitude taken in regard to accrued lands and drainage in Alberta. In 1957, a government Conservation Board was established which included the departments of Agriculture, Lands and Forests, Fish and Game Branch, and Power Commission, and other agencies that influenced or were affected by water control. It took the view that drainage of lakes for agricultural purposes provided only sub-marginal land, that there had never been a lake reclamation scheme that had been entirely successful, and that it was much better to have too much water in a natural basin than not enough. They adopted a no-drainage policy except when approved by the Board.

It was suggested that privately-owned lands accrued on lakes due to low water levels should be purchased by the Crown, and the entire lake then reserved for all time for the benefit of wildlife and recreation.

Through membership on the Alberta Water Stabilization Board, Ducks Unlimited participated in this program. Up until the late 1960's, a significant part of the biological program in Alberta consisted of inspecting and evaluating the waterfowl potential of areas suggested for drainage or other disposition. Most of these inspections were at government request and Crown reservations were placed on many valuable wetlands as a result.

Except for the northern Interlake, and the Carrot River Project at The Pas, most of the drainage in agricultural Manitoba took place prior to the establishment of Ducks Unlimited, so the wet 1950's did not see such an upsurge of drainage as it did in Saskatchewan. A wetland survey in the Interlake of areas in excess of 200 acres was made by air and checked for ground truth. A total of 241 areas were so inspected by Charles Lacy, Ducks Unlimited's Manitoba Provincial Biologist at that time. The Manitoba Wildlife Branch was able to put reservations on 61 of the better areas for a total of 128,405 acres. A similar aerial coverage was made of the Westlake area (along the west side of Lake Manitoba) where 64 wetlands were inventoried. The Manitoba program was reactivated in 1965 when an additional 54 wetlands were covered.

Illustrating the seriousness with which management and directors regarded the drainage threat, Rennie Harley was transferred to Winnipeg in 1958 as Director of Public Relations, to deal with the problem, with the expectation he would be able to use his considerable skills in public relations and negotiation more effectively from that position.

As mentioned earlier in this chapter, the wet years of the early 1950's resulted in greatly increased waterfowl populations. This coincided with a wholesale change in harvesting techniques which saw stooking and threshing replaced by swathing and combining. Crops lying in swath were much more vulnerable to waterfowl damage than when stooked.

Although the spectre of crop damage had been with Ducks Unlimited from the beginning (it was the reason for the determined community resistance to the proposed sanctuary surrounding the Waterhen Marsh project in 1938), and although it was mentioned at the 1943 directors' meeting and discussed again in Saskatoon in 1945, probably as a result of the high waterfowl populations of that time, it was not until the Annual Meeting in October of 1953 that it suddenly became a major concern of the directors. After this time, at almost every annual meeting for the next few years, someone enquired about the duck damage situation.

What had focussed attention on the problem was described by the American directors at the October meeting. They reported that exaggerated accounts of duck damage had circulated in the United States in 1952, along with newspaper stories that Canadians were poisoning ducks to get rid of them. These stories had had an adverse effect on contributions in some areas. Cartwright was able to report that "exhaustive enquiries" had failed to reveal any poisoning or attempts to poison.

Although as previously mentioned, nothing had appeared in the official minutes of directors' meetings about crop damage prior to 1943, and no serious recognition was given until 1953, management had long been aware that it could become a major problem and the company was already involved in programs to find a solution.

At the 1953 Annual Meeting, Bert Cartwright reported on the results of a questionnaire sent to farmers in 1952 by the Alberta Fish and Game Association and distributed through the Alberta Hail Insurance. Ducks Unlimited had analyzed the returns as their share of the program. The questionnaire was designed to determine what percentage of farmers suffered from duck damage, and whether they were interested in a crop insurance program. Of the 9,086 replies, 1,305 had had damage and 81% were interested in an insurance program.

A similar investigation was carried out in Saskatchewan in the spring of 1953 by the Provincial Wildlife Branch. This was a personal contact survey in the heavy crop damage areas of the province. Tom Sterling, then stationed at Wynyard, made the survey on the western side of Last Mountain Lake. The Saskatchewan Crop Insurance Program was inaugurated that fall as a result of these surveys.

In 1954, Leitch was a member of a committee established by the Technical Section of the Mississippi Flyway Council, "to suggest how the technical section could assist in evaluating the problem of crop damage in Western Canada". The committee recommended a U.S./Canada joint undertaking and outlined a program, but no action was taken.

In the meantime, Ducks Unlimited followed the policy of giving farmers as much help as they could to protect their crops. This included arranging for parties of hunters and demonstrating scare techniques such as scarecrows, flashers, etc., but the corporation would make no cash payments for duck damage. This was a management policy as there is no record of it being formally proposed or adopted by the directors. Fieldmen attended farmers' meetings on crop depredation which were, to say the least, very unpleasant. Freeman recalls one meeting which he attended at Blackie, in southern Alberta, where, as the atmosphere heated up, he began to wonder if the rafters really would support a body!

At the August 6th meeting of the Waterfowl Advisory Committee in Washington in 1958, a program for the inspection and assessment of duck damage was proposed. Such action, at this level, indicates the importance with which the problem had come to be viewed. Personnel were volunteered from the United States Bureau of Sports Fisheries and Wildlife, the Mississippi Flyway Council, the provincial game branches, Ducks Unlimited, and the Canadian Wildlife Service.

Sometimes things do move swiftly! Two weeks later (August 25th) an organizational meeting was held in Regina and field work was begun on the 27th in Saskatchewan and Manitoba. Alberta decided not to participate. One wonders if such speed would be possible today.

The first year's program was, of necessity, exploratory, and designed to determine how extensive crop damage really was, how effective control methods then utilized (feeding stations, pre-season shooting permits and other scaring techniques) really were, and also how satisfactory the Saskatchewan Crop Damage Insurance Program was from the farmers' point of view. Preliminary findings in these areas would provide direction for the 1959 program. Ducks Unlimited supplied a man to help evaluate the feeding program in Manitoba and one for the work at Nokomis, Saskatchewan. At Nokomis, the Canadian Wildlife Service tested the effectiveness of a noise-generating machine in keeping the ducks out of farmers' fields. It wasn't successful, but did demonstrate the ingenuity of the local youths. They were able to start it up one night and, had they discovered how to switch to full volume, would probably have broken all the windows in town!

Ducks Unlimited personnel attended meetings on February 1, 1959, in Minneapolis, and in Regina on the 19th to design the program that year. The objectives were to test known and new devices for preventing duck damage, and to evaluate the losses in terms of dollars or bushels, The latter part of the program was expanded to include Alberta. Ducks Unlimited supplied a man and vehicle to help with the evaluation of scaring techniques at Meadow Lake, Saskatchewan, particularly that of Zon exploders, six of which the company supplied for the experiments.

The 1959 program showed that exploders were effective within a quarter mile radius and would protect small fields. The 1960 program in the Meadow Lake area was then designed to determine if the technique merely moved ducks around or would keep them from field feeding entirely throughout a large area if sufficient exploders were employed. Ninety-eight exploders were used in a 220 square mile block and fifteen fieldmen, drawn from the U.S. Bureau of Sports Fisheries and Wildlife, Canadian Wildlife Service, six states in the Mississippi Flyway and one state from the Atlantic, and a Ducks Unlimited representative, placed and serviced the exploders and evaluated their effect. Ducks Unlimited also provided 14 of the exploders. A man and vehicle were supplied in Manitoba to continue evaluation of the feeding stations maintained at the southern end of the Delta Marsh as a deterrent to field feeding.

Crop damage control in Canada once again created a serious problem for Ducks Unlimited, Inc., in the United States when one of the American members of the task force at Meadow Lake returned home with the story that over a million ducks were killed annually in Alberta in pre-season crop protection shooting. This figure was shown to be inflated beyond belief. The number was more like 50,000 (based on comparative Saskatchewan data). But waves from such dramatic stories take a long time to subside in spite of well-documented repudiation.

Canada goose goslings — free of the egg at last — now it's on to other adventures.

W. J. D. Stephen, of the Canadian Wildlife Service, who headed the investigations in the Meadow Lake area in 1959, and again in 1960, concluded after the last year:

> that if a satisfactory model of automatic acetylene exploder is developed, systematic and prolonged harassment can reduce duck damage in areas where depredation is a serious problem without deleterious effect on ducks. It is also concluded that the effectiveness of harassment can be increased if alternate field feeding areas (i.e. harvested fields), are available.

He added that ducks forced by harrassment to feed on harvested fields should be protected from disturbance by hunters until the danger of crop damage in the area is past.

The techniques learned at Meadow Lake never came into general use, mostly because of the very high manpower requirements. The Ducks Unlimited exploders were used in late summer for several years to frighten ducks away from botulism areas in both Saskatchewan and Alberta, and were loaned to farmers suffering crop damage adjacent to projects.

Crop damage control has since centered on lure crops and feeding stations in susceptible areas, financed by the federal and provincial governments. Provincial governments have concentrated on developing and evaluating these techniques. In 1970, the Alberta Wildlife Branch began a three-year study in the Peace River area to determine the relative effectiveness of lure crops and feeding stations. Ducks Unlimited participated by supplying the required aircraft coverage. Feeding stations were found to be the most effective and economical.

George Freeman checks bulrush planting on a project in the Western Irrigation District.

While Ducks Unlimited has assisted in defining the scope of the crop damage problem and possible solutions, the organization has steadfastly refused to become involved in overall preventative and compensation programs. As a private organization, the company has no specific responsibility for the waterfowl resource. This is a federal obligation under the Migratory Bird Act. Ducks Unlimited has chosen to assist governments to discharge their responsibility to the resource by preserving and developing habitat. In turn, it expects the federal and provincial governments to fulfill their commitments by providing the administrative and other costs of management, including hunting season regulations and enforcement, research, and crop depredation.

The 1950's, with project managers now in Saskatchewan and Alberta, saw the beginning of more intensive management of Ducks Unlimited projects, as forecast by Fanset early in the decade.

Under the Production Department, projects were inspected almost annually, and biological improvements undertaken on many. By 1960, a total of 138 projects in the three prairie provinces had been worked on, including planting programs involving bulrush and sago pondweed, island construction, goose nesting sites, level ditching, and shoreline improvement.

For several years, beginning in 1953, sago pondweed seed was harvested at the Maeco-Ministik project, east of Edmonton, and shipped to other areas, principally Saskatchewan, where stands of this valuable food plant were successfully established.

When his expanding responsibilities made it no longer feasible for the Maeco-Ministik Manager to harvest the seed, sago pondweed tubers were purchased from aquatic nurseries in the United States. In 1959, 14,000 sago pondweed tubers were planted on Saskatchewan projects.

Fencing was done on fourteen projects which could be visited frequently and the fences thus maintained. A total of 69¼ miles had been built by 1960. Little has been added since that time, probably because of a report on the problems of fencing prepared by Leitch for the directors at the 1960 annual meeting.

Through the 1950's, the company not only undertook investigations of its own, but also assisted other organizations with research applicable to the Ducks Unlimited program, without itself becoming involved in long term studies.

Habitat assessment, along with breeding pair and brood counts in the Caron Potholes Study Area southwest of Moose Jaw, Saskatchewan, were begun in 1947, and are still a yearly activity, valuable for the insight they provide into annual waterfowl nesting success. On the basis of the Caron Pothole data, the pothole development program was reactivated in the mid-1950's. A similar study, north of Southey, Saskatchewan, in cultivated parkland (to monitor parkland waterfowl production and compare it with grassland habitat typified by the Caron Potholes) was begun in 1952 and continued through 1957.

In co-operation with the U.S. Fish & Wildlife Service, who required the data for air/ground comparison of waterfowl surveys, two intensive study areas were established in southern Alberta in 1953. One was of short duration; but the other, between Strathmore and Calgary, was run by George Freeman through 1973 and supplied the same data for that area as the Caron Potholes did for Saskatchewan. In June, 1955, Leitch accompanied the U.S. Fish & Wildlife crew on their annual survey of waterfowl populations in the western Arctic.

Ducks Unlimited (Canada) has been fortunate that its headquarters are located within sixty miles of the Delta Waterfowl Research Station which also began operations in 1938 at the edge of the Delta Marsh. A close mutually stimulating association of research and management has extended over the entire forty years.

In 1953, Ducks Unlimited commenced a co-operative program with the Delta Waterfowl Research Station in marsh management studies with funds provided by the R. Howard Webster Foundation of Montreal. The research program was to be directed by representatives from the United States Fish and Wildlife Service, the Wildlife Management Institute, two American and two Canadian universities, and Ducks Unlimited. The corporation was to provide management areas for study, field quarters, field assistants, and travel facilities on their areas, as well as heavy earth-moving equipment for special studies.

Under this program, Lloyd Keith carried out a 5 year (1953-1957) Ph.D. study of waterfowl ecology and populations on the Will J. Reid Project, northwest of Brooks, Alberta, where an artificial pothole complex had been created using irrigation water. This included an evaluation of fencing in increasing waterfowl production. Also, at the Louisiana Lakes, north and east of Brooks, Bob Webb, and then in 1954, Robert I. Smith, studied the breeding ecology of pintails. Ducks Unlimited's dragline was used to construct special study plots at Delta the same year. Through to 1960, the company supplied assistants or facilities in most years for the Webster students.

From 1954 through 1956, P. G. Hanson studied the effects of fluctuating water levels on production of sago pondweed at Long Island Bay in Lake Winnipegosis, a major staging area for canvasbacks, redheads, and lesser scaups. A banding station was also operated. This study was supported by Ducks Unlimited, but accommodation, transportation, and guide service were supplied by R. M. Gaylord, a Trustee and past president of Ducks Unlimited, Inc., who owned a shooting lodge on the Bay.

Further study into the life history of sago pondweed was stimulated by a donation for this purpose by Guido Rahr, a member of Ducks Unlimited from Milwaukee who had a shooting lodge in Saskatchewan, first on Buffalo Pound Lake, and then on the Big Arm of Last Mountain Lake. Research began on these areas in general in 1955, but became a study of the life history of sago pondweed through 1956 to 1958 when it terminated. The research was done by graduate students under the direction of Dr. R. T. Coupland of the Department of Plant Ecology, University of Saskatchewan. Travel and other incidental expenses were paid by Ducks Unlimited.

From 1967 through 1971, the Delta Waterfowl Research Station and Ducks Unlimited co-operated in investigations to determine if breeding populations of mallards could be re-established in under-utilized habitat using hand-reared wild strain birds raised at the Delta hatchery. Much of the hatchery expense was supported by grants from the Ducks Unlimited Foundation. While it was shown that this could be done, it was also found that nesting success of both released and wild birds was extremely low, because of heavy predation in the limited nesting cover. This naturally led to an investigation of the possibilities of increasing nesting success by providing cover sown for that purpose. This was carried out on a co-operative basis from 1972 through 1975.

One of the interesting sidelights to the mallard introduction program was the use of the excess drakes for northern banding experiments, since only the hens were used in the introduction program. In 1971 and 1972, with the co-operation of the United States Fish and Wildlife Service, these birds were banded and then flown to remote release areas north and east of Lake Winnipeg where a large natural population of mallards was known to nest. It was impractical to band in this area and it was assumed that the banded birds introduced into the population would migrate normally with it. This they apparently did and yielded new information on the migrational behaviour of this mallard population.

From 1969 through 1972, Ducks Unlimited provided field support and an assistant for A. J. Macaulay during his study of the taxonomy and ecology of roundstem bulrush in Manitoba. As previously mentioned, Dr. Macaulay became Chief Biologist of Ducks Unlimited (Canada) in August, 1976.

In 1972 and 1973, the company supported research by R. M. Donaghey into waterfowl productivity at the southern edge of the boreal forest in Alberta. Productivity studies were also carried out in that province by Peter Davidson on the Ribstone Creek Flood Irrigation Project and the water management techniques required to maximize production were determined.

June 18, 1975. General Manager D. S. Morrison, left, and directors Lorne M. Cameron, Douglas C. Groff and John D. McDiarmid, inspect cover crop.

The 1950's also saw a great change in banding techniques. It was found that ducks and Canada geese could be caught in large numbers by driving them into wire pen traps during the flightless period. Very few geese had been banded in Western Canada prior to this time and the acquisition of airboats made this a highly efficient and cheap way of banding waterfowl. The initial drives were made on the Louisiana Lakes and one year were photographed from the air and on the ground by *Life* magazine for a feature article. The record catch of 5,475 ducks in one drive was made in 1957 at the Pel Lake Ducks Unlimited project, west of Wynyard, Saskatchewan, by a crew under the direction of Tom Sterling. The returns from these bandings were analyzed by Sterling in 1966 for his M.A. thesis.

R. M. Gaylord also established a fund for canvasback banding, and attempts were made to band flightless moulting canvasbacks by driving at Lamb Lake in 1951, and by nightlighting at Driftwood Lake in 1956. Both lakes are in the Saskatchewan River Delta, east of The Pas. Further attempts were made at Wynyard, Saskatchewan in 1957, at MacCallum Lake in northern Saskatchewan in 1958, and at Big Stick Lake in the southwest in 1959. Only at Big Stick Lake was there any success, for even though canvasback could be driven, the formidable armada of men, boats, and aircraft required to conduct the activity on a significant scale was more than Ducks Unlimited could muster at that time.

In response to continuing pressure from Ducks Unlimited members on the eastern coast of the United States to do something about the black duck in the Atlantic Flyway, a banding station was established at Nain in Labrador in 1954 and 1955, and at False River near Fort Chimo, Quebec in 1956. The State of Virginia provided a biologist for the project and Ducks Unlimited supplied equipment (including a small seaworthy boat), an assistant, transportation, and supplies. Terrain,

Drive banding — a record catch.

Flightless moulting pintail.

Leitch bands blue winged teal caught by night lighting. (Photo by R. Dodds)

logistics, and lack of large enough concentrations of black ducks with which to work made the operation expensive and impractical, and only a few were banded. In 1957, Ducks Unlimited contributed toward a black duck banding station at Lake Manuan in Quebec.

Bert Cartwright analyzed all the duck banding records, and, in 1952, they were published in booklet form titled, *Waterfowl Banding 1939-1950*. The publication was updated in a second edition of December, 1956, which included all bandings through 1954 and all recoveries to March 31, 1955. At the end of the decade, 122,954 ducks and 1,647 geese had been banded.

Although the program base broadened greatly during the 1950's, the main thrust was still in project construction, as the annual income from Ducks Unlimited, Inc. increased from $300,000 in 1950, to the milestone of half a million in 1956, and $550,000 in 1960. By the end of that year, a total of 568

projects had been built, mostly on the prairies, comprising 975,-500 acres with 4,600 miles of shoreline.

Several projects were built under the co-operative program with the Water Stabilization Committee in Alberta in the early years of the decade, but after that point, this program had pretty much run its course except for joint maintenance of the projects. With the establishment of an office in Hanna in 1957, a major program began in the area to develop the many water storage opportunities of the watercourses flowing into the Red Deer and Battle Rivers, utilizing the co-operative attitudes of the Special Areas Board and the local farmers. Numerous small projects were developed in the Strathmore area using irrigation water, and construction also continued in the Brooks irrigation district.

In Saskatchewan, construction was concentrated around the Quill Lakes-Nokomis area where many smaller projects were built. In 1953, a pothole development program began again in the Missouri Coteau. This program, based on the original Caron Pothole work of 1939, sought to establish permanent brood water by partially draining adjacent potholes into one, throughout the drought-prone Coteau, where waterfowl breeding populations are high. A similar program was initiated in the Big Valley Potholes west of Hanna, Alberta.

Manitoba continued to develop small projects, particularly in the area surrounding Brandon in the southwestern corner of the province. A major structure sponsored by Kansas City was built on the outlet of the Oak and Plum Lakes in 1958, which has preserved this outstanding 18,000 acre lake and marsh against repeated attempts at drainage. Another large project, Reader and Root Lakes, totalling 27,000 acres, was built at The Pas.

But the project which really gripped everyone's imagination was Hay Lakes, in the extreme northwestern corner of Alberta. Comprising 70,000 acres of shallow marshes, this area, located in the flood plain of the Hay River, was a major staging area for ducks and geese en route to and from the Arctic. It also supported a significant breeding population, including a surprising number of canvasback in some years, and was used for moulting habitat as well.

Acting on rumours that this great area was now dry, Rennie Harley, Ted Burkell, and H. B. Watkins of the Alberta Game and Fish Department, made an aerial inspection in September of 1953. The rumours were found to be true. Burkell returned in late fall and made the engineering investigation necessary for construction of a dam on the Amber River which drains the Hay Lakes into the Hay River. The treated timber for the dam was shipped into the site during the winter, and the structure built in September, 1954.

The contractor was Martin Overguard from Sundre, Alberta, a tough individual of the old school, able to put up with any hardship the bush might put in his way. Standing over six feet tall and weighing in excess of 200 lbs., he commanded respect from the Indians whom he frequently employed in remote areas. His glass eye fascinated the natives, who had never seen one before. Martin was aware of this, and the story is told that while building the Hay Lakes dam, when he had to leave the site for a while, he would remove the glass eye, and setting it on a convenient stump, jokingly tell the Indians to keep working because he was watching them!

The dam was built as a co-operative project with the Alberta government under the Water Stabilization Board, whereby they paid 1/3 of the cost. Martin had built many projects for the Board and was adept at using local material for his dams, which were usually timber rock crib overflow structures. He built many such structures for Ducks Unlimited in Alberta and Saskatchewan, and "Overguard Structure" became a common term in the Ducks Unlimited vocabulary.

Martin Overguard centre, Arthur Bartley left, right unknown.

Overguard structure on Ducks Unlimited's Lac St. Anne project.

Original Hay Lakes dam.

New dam under construction, 1969.

152

The road to Hay Lakes, 1957. Ted Burkell ponders a problem.

Martin backed away from very little. Once during a trip into the Hay Lakes with Burkell, after leaving the highway for the 60-mile trip on undeveloped trails into the project, they were immediately confronted by deep water-filled ruts, and streams in flood. For a while they pondered the wisdom of attempting the trip; then characteristically Martin said, "Well . . . we signed on as tough S.O.B.'s . . . let's go!" And they did.

Sharp, Burkell, Leitch, and Dr. Robert McCabe, Professor of Wildlife Management at the University of Wisconsin, had much the same experience in July of 1957, when, with a four-wheel drive winch-equipped truck and pulling an airboat, they set out from the highway at Upper Hay to drive band ducks on the Hay Lakes.

There had been heavy rains for the past week and it took 5 days to cover the 60 miles. One day they made only 10 miles and winched out six times, mostly after digging in "deadmen", for frequently there were no trees close enough to be reached by the winch cable — they had been torn out by previous expeditions. An Indian, "Joe Bulldog", and his team had been hired, and his

skill with an axe was needed to bridge a stream where the crossing had been washed out. Frequently, the airboat had to be dragged through the mud by the horses. The truck finally was abandoned and the party proceeded on foot, walking most of the way through water fighting hordes of mosquitoes. Because the horses were in such poor condition, it was all they could do to pull the wagon and the airboat.

Upon finally arriving at Hay Lakes, it was disappointing to find that the large concentration of moulting ducks which had been reported was not there. So, after inspecting the dam and carrying out some further reconnaissance, the return trip began.

Very heavy rain had continued all the while the party was at Hay Lakes; unofficially, 10 inches was said to have fallen. It was decided to leave the airboat there to be brought out after freeze-up. On the return trip, the whole countryside was flooded and most of the distance was covered on foot, walking through water, fighting mosquitoes, and trying to find a spot dry enough to camp at night. The streams were all in flood (Angus Gavin would have said "in spate"), and, with the bridges gone, had to

be forded. The truck was left behind to be brought out after freeze-up, and the Ducks Unlimited group joined forces with a train of seven Indian wagons going to the Upper Hay Post to haul merchandise for the Hay Lakes Hudson's Bay store.

When the MacKenzie Highway was finally reached, the problems were not over. The Ducks Unlimited car, which had been left at Upper Hay Post, had to be towed by a semi-trailer fish truck through a quarter mile of water three feet deep on the highway, which flooded the floor of the car to a depth of six inches. Once the town of High Level was reached, conditions continued to improve southward.

Some directors also have pleasant memories of Hay Lakes. In September of 1955, R. M. Gaylord, Robert Winthrop, Lloyd Stevens, and Colonel Hancock spent a few days in the area under canvas at a camp set up by Martin Overguard. The goose flights were spectacular but it is said that Mrs. Wigham's hot cinnamon rolls made as great an impression. Mrs. Wigham, on many occasions, had cooked for Overguard's crews. Her skill, often under the most primitive of conditions, was legendary.

In 1960, a second structure was built on the Habay section of the southwest Hay Lakes complex to flood an additional 17,000 acres. Burkell's technique in surveying this project was adapted to the situation. The pilot was used as a rodman, and on the open marshes where long shots could be made, he used the aircraft to taxi on skis from one shot to the next. As Ted puts it, that was the most expensive rodman Ducks Unlimited ever employed!

In 1958, all lands affected by the dams, and a large surrounding area, totalling about 520,000 acres, (water area 70,-

Directors of Ducks Unlimited (Canada) and senior staff at Zama Lake Headquarters of Hudson's Bay Oil and Gas Company, Hay Lakes, September 13, 1975.

000 acres), were set aside for waterfowl and other wildlife by an Alberta Order-in-Council. This action subsequently preserved the area from drainage and uncontrolled oil development. In 1965, when a major oil field was discovered around the lakes and drainage was suggested as a means of developing it, the Ducks Unlimited dam and the established full supply level forced the oil company to use other than conventional drilling techniques. Rigid requirements for drilling in the lakes, with considerable input from Ducks Unlimited, were established by the Alberta Oil & Gas Conservation Board. The oil companies co-operated willingly and completely with these restrictions. When the new dam was being built on the Amber River in 1969, Gulf Oil, who had by then built a road into the area, permitted Ducks Unlimited to use it free of charge, while other companies were charged $2.50 per ton.

High water continued for many years on the Hay Lakes. It became apparent that the drought conditions which had first brought Ducks Unlimited to the area were very infrequent and of short duration. The real problem was high water caused by flooding from the Hay River. An accumulation of waterfowl records, not available when the dam was first built, showed that when the area was flooded, waterfowl use was much reduced. So an investigation was begun to see how water levels could be controlled for maximum waterfowl production.

In 1969, the original dam was replaced by a new structure about 3½ miles downstream. This stop-logged structure gave better water control, permitting utilization of the entire channel to get rid of floodwaters. However, Ducks Unlimited was aware that this was only a partial solution to the flooding problem, so from 1973 to 1976 inclusive, intensive engineering and biological investigations were carried out. The Hudson's Bay Oil and Gas Company, which has an operational oil field in the area contributed a total of $39,800 toward the costs of the investigation over a four year period.

In September, 1975, in conjunction with an Executive Committee Meeting in Edmonton, the directors were flown over the Hay Lakes on a glorious autumn day and were guests for lunch at the Zama Lake headquarters of the Hudson's Bay Oil & Gas Company.

It is regrettable that no economically feasible method was found to control the wholesale flooding on the Hay Lakes, though several smaller projects are possible.

One of Fred Sharp's best stories originated from the early trips into Hay Lakes. According to Fred, they were down to their last can of beans. Someone put the can on the fire without punching a hole in it. In due course, it blew up. Fred says, "The only bean I got was one that stuck behind my ear!"

The closing years of the 1950's brought increasing activity and supervision by the directors in the affairs of the company. Through the early years of the decade, the Executive Committee seldom met. Arthur Bartley, in his capacity of Executive Director, carried out the supervisory function on a personal basis.

In 1955, when R. H. G. Bonnycastle became a Director, the situation began to change. Dick Bonnycastle was to play a very influential role in the affairs of the organization through four years as President, 1957 to 1960, and his term as Chairman of the Executive Committee, 1960-1967. He was also Chairman of the Management Sub-Committee from 1962 until 1966, when its functions were absorbed by regular meetings of the Winnipeg-based members of the Executive Committee. His death from heart failure in October, 1968, while landing his aircraft at Long Island Bay on Lake Winnipegosis, was a great loss to Ducks Unlimited.

At the Annual Meeting of Ducks Unlimited (Canada) at Kansas City in 1956, Bonnycastle advised that the Canadian

R. H. G. Bonnycastle.

directors had already met in Canada to go over the management's report and discuss plans for the coming year. At the preliminary meeting, the view had been expressed, he said, that the annual statement and balance sheet should be expanded so the directors would be better informed when they attended the annual meetings, which were then being held in the United States in conjunction with those of Ducks Unlimited, Inc. These meetings of Canadian directors prior to the formal annual meetings became routine thereafter, even though since 1969 the official Canadian annual meetings have been held in Canada.

At the Annual Meeting in 1958, the second year of his Presidency, Bonnycastle suggested that an independent agency should be engaged to examine and evaluate each active project so that the company would have an impartial appraisal of the effectiveness of their work. This would be helpful to management, and would aid the Board in determining the extent to which expenditures were being wisely made and the overall objectives achieved. The President was made a committee of one to determine the ways and means of having the appraisal done.

In reporting on this subject at the 1959 Annual Meeting, Bonnycastle advised that he had been in communication with the Canadian Wildlife Service regarding the appraisal, and they had agreed to carry it out beginning that year. Nothing was actually done in 1959 due to shortage of Canadian Wildlife Service personnel, but at the 1960 Annual Meeting, further progress in planning was reported. The program was to extend over two years and the Canadian Wildlife Service had assigned a biologist to the project. Twenty-four areas, some Ducks Unlimited projects and some natural wetlands, were reported as inspected by the biologist in 1961. But, much to the disappointment of the directors, the program never really did get underway, as Angus Gavin reported to the Annual Meeting in 1963. At the 1964 meeting, it was noted that the Canadian Wildlife Service was unable to

Staff meeting Regina, December 17, 1957. Seated left, Rennie Harley, Col. Fitzgerald (Assistant to Arthur Bartley), Bert Cartwright, Angus Gavin. Standing, left, George Freeman, Ted Burkell, Al Burns, Dick Cardy, Bill Leitch, Bill Campbell, Gunner Campbell, Keith Williams, Bob Caldwell, Herb Moulding, Bill Hooey, Rod Galbraith, Gordon Staines, Tom Sterling, Don Kimberly.

proceed with the appraisal. It had degenerated into an evaluation of artificial loafing sites on two Ducks Unlimited projects near Edmonton.

Bonnycastle made personal contacts with the provincial governments and the Canadian Wildlife Service in an attempt to increase their co-operation. One interesting result of his efforts, and those of Rennie Harley, was the visit of Premier Manning of Alberta to California in 1960 to address two Ducks Unlimited fund-raising meetings. A rather exceptional achievement.

It was also reported at the 1959 Annual Meeting that because of excellent work by the landman, only 64 land agreements on the projects built to that time remained to be formalized. Although two additional lawsuits had been filed against the company, neither was as serious as that originating at Big Grass Marsh some years before, which had been decided in favour of the company. The Van Wezel action pertaining to the Craigantler project near Strathmore, Alberta, was concluded when the company closed the inlet and abandoned the project. The Pressman suit at Grant's Lake, 30 miles west of Winnipeg, was settled out of court for a small sum.

An era ended at the Annual Meeting in 1960, when Arthur Bartley requested that his title of Executive Director of Ducks Unlimited (Canada) be dropped. He felt that he was only acting in the role of advisor, and that the responsibility of carrying out the wishes of the Board and the Executive Committee was that of management. The Executive Committee was increased in size and a Management Sub-Committee formed in 1962 to work more closely with management. The sub-committee met each month.

September, 1960, also saw the retirement of B. W. Cartwright, the last of the original senior management of the company. His responsibilities were assumed by Leitch.

In 1957, the Saskatchewan biologists were moved to Saskatoon, under Tom Sterling as Provincial Biologist, to better integrate their activities, particularly pertaining to the Wetland Inventory.

S. Tennison (Ted) Dillon became the first Manitoba Provincial Biologist in 1958. C. H. Lacy took his place in 1961 when Dillon was injured in a car accident. Lacy remained in Manitoba until 1966, when he was transferred to Edmonton as Provincial

Biologist, leaving in 1971 to pursue a career as a wildlife artist. He was replaced the same year by E. W. (Ernie) Ewaschuk, who spent six productive years with the company.

In 1955, W. E. (Bill) Hooey began his long and successful career with Ducks Unlimited as Swift Current Area Manager. He was transferred to North Battleford, Saskatchewan, in 1964, where his gregarious and outgoing personality, and ability to work under difficult conditions were largely responsible for the early success of the company's program in the Meadow Lake district. In May, 1969, he was moved to Creston, British Columbia, to begin an equally difficult job in that area. His position at North Battleford was filled by Dale Brydges, who had begun his career in Manitoba as a bio-technician in 1965. D. P. (Don) Mitchell, who joined Ducks Unlimited in 1963, continued with the program at Meadow Lake.

The year 1956 is also important in the history of the biological program of Ducks Unlimited (Canada), for in that year, Doris M. Kuntz became Secretary to the Chief Biologist. For 17½ years, with helpful suggestions and quick and ready wit, she retained order on the edge of chaos, even through July deadlines, *Duckologicals*, and banding records. She retired in 1973.

Doris M. Kuntz.

Pearl Irvine — backbone of the Saskatchewan office since October 25th, 1950.

Reorganization and Expansion 10

The first half of the 1960's saw the Ducks Unlimited (Canada) budget stabilized around the $600,000 mark. Then in 1965, with the appointment of Dale Whitesell as Executive Director of Ducks Unlimited, Inc. (later Executive Vice-President), income rapidly increased, reaching a million dollars in 1968, and more than doubling the 1965 figure by 1969. The increase continued at better than 20% compounded annually to 1977, when $9.6 million was sent to Canada.

This great increase required reorganization at the Head Office and expansion in the field, so that the money could be spent wisely for the greatest benefit to waterfowl.

The increasing interest and closer involvement of the directors was further illustrated when the Chairman, Dick Bonnycastle reported that in 1961, seven meetings of the Executive Committee were held.

At the Annual Meeting in 1964, Bonnycastle stated, ". . . the Canadian directors felt that in view of increased monies becoming available, and increasing demands on management, it was desirable to strengthen the Canadian organization and recommended engaging Riddell, Stead & Co., who had performed the audit of the Corporation from its inception, to make a thorough study of the administrative organization, and recommend improvements they found advisable." The proposed review was no doubt stimulated by the fact that the corporation was under-expended by $125,000 on the 1963 budget of $671,000. This occasioned much critical comment of management at the directors' meeting of March 20, 1964. A quotation of $7,500 for the study, plus travelling expenses, had been received. The Management Sub-Committee was instructed by the directors to proceed with the study.

The study was carried out in 1964 and produced the usual trauma throughout the organization, particularly since those assigned to it came from Toronto, had little understanding of what Ducks Unlimited was attempting to achieve, or the field problems it faced. However, the investigation did result in a new bookkeeping system where, by a coding technique, a much finer breakdown of expenditure could be made for the directors' scrutiny. The same basic system, with minor modifications, is still in use today.

In addition, E. W. Burkell was moved in the fall of 1964 from his position of Alberta Manager to that of Chief Engineer in Winnipeg, in order to supervise engineering programs and exercise budgetary control. This position had been vacant since Lloyd Bunting left in 1951. Gunner Campbell had prepared the year-end engineering reports, in addition to carrying out the responsibilities of his official position as Manitoba Manager.

At the 1964 Annual Meeting, the Management Sub-Committee also emphasized the need to establish a backlog of alternate projects so that the debacle of 1963 would not be repeated. Emphasis was also placed on the need to revamp and increase the Kee-Man organization to provide more data for Ducks Unlimited, Inc. to use in discussions on United States hunting regulations. All Kee-Men were interviewed and evaluated during the following year.

Changes in construction policy also took place in the early 1960's. By 1965, the company had disposed of all its heavy equipment and, except for repairs and small projects, for which smaller units were retained, particularly in the irrigation districts and The Pas, all work was done by contract. A further milestone was reached in May of 1969, when Ducks Unlimited bought their first aircraft, a Piper Supercub, for ease of access to remote areas in The Pas area. Gerry Townsend, The Pas Area Biologist, was the first pilot; when he left in 1970, Ron Schiedel was hired as Bio-technician and pilot.

With increased budgets, and assurance they would be met, the long range planning essential for good management was now possible.

Although the way sometimes had been lost, long range planning was not new to the organization; in fact, the original 1937 concept was for a five-year program which would spend $600,-000 each year. Three million, it was believed, would restore the Canadian breeding grounds to their previous productivity. The war interfered and the $600,000 annual level was not reached until 1962. However, even by 1952, when $3 million had been sent to Canada, it was obvious that the job to be done was much greater than originally anticipated.

In 1951, at Des Moines, Leitch suggested in general terms, what course the company should take in the next ten years, and, although the report was never accepted as a 10-year program, it may have had some influence on policy during the following years. The need for a definitive, long range plan, was again stressed by Directors Bawden and Auger at Pasadena in 1963. In 1965, primarily as a result of the report by Riddell Stead, Leitch prepared a long range program in co-operation with Gavin and Burkell (the three were designated The Technical Committee), again in general terms and based on the submissions of senior personnel. Titled *Waterfowl Problems and Ducks Unlimited Programs,* the report was thoroughly discussed at the Annual Meeting in New Orleans in 1965, but no official action was taken on it.

At a meeting of December 1, 1966, the Management Sub-Committee once again emphasized its desire to advance reconnaissance and surveys to the point where a five-year program could be plotted. Gavin pointed out that the provincial staffs at their present levels could do no more than keep pace with annual programs. He was instructed to report to the Committee how reconnaissance and surveys could be expedited, either by

reorganization, or by hiring additional personnel, in order to formulate a five-year plan, since it was essential to plan further ahead.

Gavin reported to the Annual Meeting in 1967, that a five-year program was gradually becoming a reality. Experienced personnel were being freed from other duties so they could concentrate on acquiring a good backlog of projects.

When Gavin became Senior Vice-President as the Annual Meeting in Milwaukee in April, 1968, (he left the company in December, 1968), he was succeeded as chief executive officer by Elswood Bole.

Bole, who had been a director of Ducks Unlimited (Canada) since 1966, was asked to head the organization as Managing Director. The appointment was temporary and on a part-time basis. His major assignments were to find a new General Manager and to recommend, and when approved, implement, a plan for expanding the organization in line with the increasing availability of funds, as well as to develop long-range planning, including projects in British Columbia and Eastern Canada.

Bole's first action was a rapid decentralization of the company, giving much greater authority to the provincial management. The biological and engineering head office line function was eliminated, and a staff group formed in its place. All provincial personnel reported directly to the Provincial Managers, who in turn reported to the Managing Director. A public relations specialist and an assistant to the Managing Director were added. The head office was moved from its long-term location in the Canadian Bank of Commerce building on Main Street near Lombard to larger and better quarters at 1495 Pembina Highway.

In December, 1968, Bole became full-time Managing Director of the Corporation, no suitable candidate for General Manager having been found.

At a Directors' Meeting in Winnipeg on December 16, 1968, Bole reviewed his long range proposals. He pointed out that if adopted, these proposals would call for an excess of expenditure over revenue in 1969 of $250,000 and in 1970 of $150,-000, a considerable amount of which would be incurred in developing projects for the future. The plan was discussed at some length, but there is no record of its being adopted.

At the Annual Meeting in Victoria in 1969, Bole suggested that the long range objective of the organization should be to assure that six to six and a half million acres of prime habitat was preserved and managed for waterfowl. This figure was based on a Canadian Wildlife Service unofficial estimate that this much habitat would be required to maintain the waterfowl population at the average level of the period 1956 to 1962. This level was considered satisfactory, and included both good and poor production years. Ducks Unlimited had approximately 1½ million acres under control at the end of 1965. Four and a half million additional acres were required to meet the objective.

The plan was not that Ducks Unlimited alone would acquire or develop that amount of acreage, but that, acting as a catalyst, they would stimulate both provincial and federal governments to achieve the objective with them. Bole believed that this objective could be reached in the next ten years with the active cooperation of governments. The cost was estimated at $65 million.

Unfortunately, the 4½ million acre figure was taken out of context in subsequent publicity releases, and became erroneously identified as the company's own construction and reservation objective, against which the annual performance of the company was embarrassingly measured by some contributors. The minutes of the annual meeting do not record that the 10 year objective as outlined by Bole was formally adopted.

At the Executive Meeting in Regina on May 24, 1970, a Long Range Planning Committee was finally formally established. By this time, Elswood Bole was no longer with the company, having resigned in December of 1969. D. Stewart Morrison, his Administrative Assistant, had been appointed Co-ordinator with the authority of General Manager. He was confirmed as General Manager June 1, 1970, and Executive Vice-President at the Annual Directors' Meeting in Regina in 1977. A graduate in commerce, with experience in the arms and ammunition industry and a sincere interest in hunting and the waterfowl resource, Morrison was an excellent choice to lead the organization through the difficult days of rapid expansion which lay ahead. His organizational training, combined with the experience of senior professionals on staff and excellent new staff aditions, brough the organization safely through this critical period.

The Long Range Planning Committee established in 1970 had as its Chairman, Mr. R. O. A. Hunter, and as members: L. M. Cameron, S. R. Lyon, G. W. Malaher, S. P. Rattray, R. A. White, and D. S. Morrison. Inputs from staff were solicited and enthusiastically contributed.

D. Stewart Morrison.

The plan was for the period 1973 to 1977, and was by far, the most comprehensive and explicit ever produced for the organization. It made the following recommendations:

1. *Gain Control of Large Wetlands*

We should try as quickly as is feasible to gain control of the large key prairie and parkland wetlands which still remain, including reservoir sites for future downstream development on a watershed basis. This means establishing the water base first, and then building management capability into the basic design of these projects. We need new tools to accomplish this in order to obtain control of these *key areas* and to provide land for waterfowl habitat development.

If it is deemed unwise for Ducks Unlimited to be involved financially in land acquisition, the Canadian Wildlife Service and provincial governments will continue to be encouraged to acquire land which Ducks Unlimited may then develop.

2. *Improve Production by Better Nesting Facilities*

We should begin to deal with all factors in western Canada which have a depressing effect on waterfowl production, rather than just water, though it is readily admitted that this is the basis of any waterfowl activity. We should, therefore, experiment with, evaluate and develop intensive marsh management practices in all regions with a view to increasing waterfowl production from all types of projects and natural areas. *In essence, make more efficient use of the water we have by exploiting the high reproductive potential of waterfowl.*

Depending upon the intensity of management, it is possible to double the nesting success on most marshes. The additional pairs which can be attracted are an extra bonus.

3. *Investigations*

Investigations into waterfowl productivity and the management of potential areas, where such knowledge is presently lacking, should be undertaken by Ducks Unlimited or through other agencies better suited for the task. For example:

(1) Northern edge of parklands

(2) Boreal Forest

(3) River deltas and flood plains

(4) Coastal marshes — including the estuarine marshes in British Columbia and the Maritimes

(5) Other areas of Canada; example Ontario, Quebec, etc.

4. *Gain Agriculture Co-operation*

Integrate as fully as possible with the agricultural sector in multi-use projects where waterfowl habitat is endangered. Every reasonable effort should be made to influence agricultural activity to the benefit of waterfowl.

5. *Experimental Use of Equipment*

Continue with the experimental use and development of special equipment to open up marshes dominated by cattail and bulrush.

6. *Promote Canada Goose Program*

Begin to actively manage our projects for Canada geese as well as ducks in order to broaden our appeal to the general public and as a public relations tool to help preserve natural wetlands. A production flock will be required to provide goslings for transplant to our projects and to natural areas.

7. *Duck Cost Criteria*

Determine if some practical duck cost criteria can be established so that the project construction and management activities can be more definitively evaluated.

In addition to the above specific recommendations, a Special Projects Team to undertake large investigations was also proposed.

Funding for the 5 year period was estimated at $20.5 million. The plan was officially adopted by the directors at the March, 1972 Annual Meeting in Regina. By 1977 approximately $27,450,000 had been spent on an expanded program.

At the Executive Meeting in June, 1975, a new Long Range Planning Committee was established to update the old plan. Sterling Lyon agreed to act as Chairman, but pressure of other commitments forced him to resign in favor of D. C. Groff. The Committee was composed of 16 directors, including for the first time six Americans. Again staff input was encouraged and freely given. The plan, as prepared for the period 1977 to 1981 was approved at a special meeting of the Board of Directors held in Yorkton, Saskatchewan, in September, 1976. Since the plan was to be subject to annual revision, the Long Range Planning Committee remained constituted to deal with any proposed changes.

The plan reaffirms the basic objectives of the company, but places more emphasis on new philosophies and techniques which, although contained in the Charter, had not been significantly employed. These include habitat manipulations on natural areas where Ducks Unlimited has no water control, programs with agriculture where waterfowl may be benefited, marsh improvement on existing projects, and research and evaluation.

It was estimated that the program costs for the period 1977 to 1981 could be $68,550,000.

The increasing interest of the directors in the operation of the company was further demonstrated when the first Executive Committee Meeting in the field was held at The Pas on August 19, 1966, under the chairmanship of Dick Bonnycastle. Since then the practice has been to hold some executive meetings in the field each year, at which all directors are welcome. These are held at locations in the vicinity of major activities of the corporation and have included Brooks, Alberta, adjacent to the Tilley developments; Fairmont, British Columbia, near the Columbia River development; Edmonton, which included a day-long air trip to the Hay Lakes; and, Prince Edward Island to see the Maritimes operation. These field trips have been popular and well attended.

From an operations standpoint, rapidly increasing budgets after 1965 required an increased field staff to efficiently carry out the expanded program. This was done by establishing additional area offices, strengthening existing offices, and increasing the professional staff at the provincial level.

There had been area offices at Brooks and Strathmore ever since 1944, when the company first began to work intensively in these irrigation districts. In 1954, an office had been established at Hanna to work with the Special Areas Board. Now Ministik Project Manager Keith Williams' activities were expanded to include area manager responsibility for the northeastern part of the province. In 1972, another area was established, based at St. Paul de Metis, which came under Williams' supervision as Northern Alberta Supervisor in 1977. A Peace River Area was also established in 1977. A. S. (Al) Glover had been appointed Provincial Engineer in 1973.

In Saskatchewan, there had long been a project manager at Swift Current, first on a seasonal basis, and then permanently, with the assignment of a biologist to the area in 1951. An engineering technician was added in 1955. In the Wynyard area, a temporary manager was replaced by Tom Sterling from 1951 until 1957, when he was transferred to Saskatoon.

Increasing emphasis on parkland fringe projects resulted in an area office being opened in North Battleford in 1964. An office was opened in Wadena in 1970 but later closed, and one established at Yorkton in 1971 with Allen Spelay, a biologist-engineer who joined Ducks Unlimited in 1964, in charge. The southern part of the province, including the Swift Current area, was by this time managed by an area manager working out of Regina. R. M. (Bob) Wallace was added to the Regina staff as the Administrative Assistant in 1969 and A. R. (Dick) Iverson became Provincial Engineer in 1975.

The Engineering Year — reconnaissance, survey, construction and operation.

Mel Pavlick.

Lawrence Kelly.

Manitoba established area offices at Brandon in southwestern Manitoba in 1969, and The Pas in 1964. Lawrence Kelly, who joined Ducks Unlimited in 1952 as a construction worker, was made Area Manager of the Brandon district, a job which requires all his charm, wit, and skill in public relations to keep a good program going. The position at The Pas was filled by Mel Pavlick who joined Ducks Unlimited in 1954 as a machine operator. His willingness and ability to work in the north under harsh winter conditions, and that of Tom Heape who joined the organization in 1957, were largely responsible for the success of the company program in the Saskatchewan River Delta surrounding The Pas. An office was opened at Ashern in the Interlake in 1972, and in 1975 was relocated at Dauphin. J. L. (Jim) Woolison, who joined Ducks Unlimited in September, 1968, had carried out the Area Manager's responsibilities for the Interlake before the office was opened in Ashern. He became Administrative Assistant to the Manitoba Manager in 1974.

At the outset, the area manager's job was a one-man operation which included all company functions — reconnaissances, land negotiations, construction, project inspection and repairs, and public relations. With increasing budgets, area staffs were expanded to include bio- and engineering technicians, surveyors, and construction specialists.

In 1969, the organization passed an engineering milestone, when well over a million cubic yards of earth were moved that year. Over three million cubic yards of earth and rock riprap were moved in 1976.

In 1973, a Special Projects Team was established at Head Office to undertake investigations, surveys, and conceptualization of large projects beyond the capabilities of the provincial staff. Construction and development of these projects would then become a provincial responsibility. Examples of some of the major projects are the Cumberland Marshes in Saskatchewan, now under development, the marshes associated with the Columbia River in British Columbia, and the Hay Lakes in Alberta.

To head the team H. C. Moulding, long time Saskatchewan Provincial Manager, was transferred to Winnipeg, and two biologists, E. G. Hennan and A. J. Macaulay, along with an engineer, Marc Pelletier, were assigned as the original support staff. Macaulay subsequently replaced Millard Wright as Saskatchewan Provincial Biologist in 1974, and became Chief Biologist at Winnipeg in August, 1976.

With the continuing increases in annual budgets, manual bookkeeping methods were now found to be inadequate, so the company adopted computerized accounting in February of 1970. Some bugs, of course, had to be ironed out of the system, particularly when the first printout showed $6,000,000 had been spent in one month on temporary employees' benefits — in the middle of the winter when there were no temporary employees on staff!

A Controller, Gunnar Helgason, was also hired in March of 1972. He resigned in 1973 and was replaced by R. B. Fowler, who became Manitoba Manager in 1976, and was replaced by Hellar Nakonechny, and then by L. W. Warren in 1977. The accounting staff was further increased when a senior accountant, K. A. (Ken) Swanson, was added in 1977.

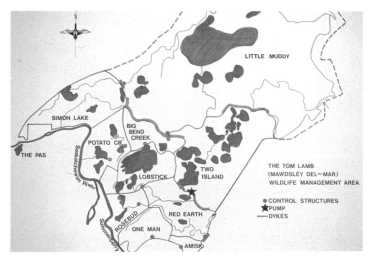

Ducks Unlimited developments in the Tom Lamb (Mawdesley Del-Mar) Wildlife Management area.

Tom Heape and corduroy road built over muskeg for access prior to construction.

Constructing the perimeter dyke.

Typical marshes in the Two Island Area.

Pumping to lower water levels in the Two Island Area.

Paul Winslow and Tom Heape check out pump installation.

Dr. A. J. Macaulay.

These increased budgets gave Ducks Unlimited the opportunity to become involved in much larger projects than ever before, and demonstrated the corporation's professional capability to carry them through to completion.

For instance, when the Grand Rapids Hydro-Electric Dam was built in Manitoba in the early 1960's, it flooded out almost a million acres of the highly fertile marshes of the Lower Saskatchewan River Delta east of The Pas. To limit the destruction of waterfowl, muskrat, and moose habitat, the northern part of the Delta, some 510,000 acres, was to be protected by a dam at the Moose Lake Narrows. This protected area was first referred to as the Mawdesley Wildlife Area but was later renamed the Tom Lamb Wildlife Management Area to honor an outstanding pioneer of The Pas. Ducks Unlimited, under the authority of a 21 year letter of agreement with the Manitoba government, was asked to develop the waterfowl potential of this huge area.

During the period from 1968 to 1974, twenty-seven miles of external dyke was built in the Tom Lamb Area, as well as internal impoundment dykes and ditches. When the dam at the Moose Lake Narrows failed to prevent flooding of the general area, a pumping station had to be constructed to reduce water levels in the internal impoundments. The name of Paul Winslow is closely associated with the development of this area and the projects in the Delta west of The Pas. Coming to the company as a summer employee in 1957, he joined the permanent staff in 1960, carrying out the surveys in The Pas area often under difficult and hazardous conditions. He is still with the company serving as a Civil Technologist.

Over a million dollars has been spent on the project so far. Since much of the basic cost was underwritten by contributors from the States of Delaware and Maryland, the general area was called the Del-Mar project. Discrete units within the area have been sponsored by eight additional groups or individuals, with the costs of the pumping station underwritten by Illinois.

Great potential exists for further development of the area if water levels can be reduced on North Moose Lake. The company continues to press the Manitoba government to carry out their obligation in this regard.

While most projects result from extensive and often frustrating reconnaissance and investigation, by contrast, Cumberland, the largest project both in size and financial commitment, that Ducks Unlimited has undertaken so far, was volunteered.

One day in 1960, G. W. Malaher, then Director of the Manitoba Wildlife Branch (now retired, and a director of Ducks Unlimited), came with Don Denmark, Supervisor of Fur Production for the Hudson's Bay Company, to see Angus Gavin, then General Manager of Ducks Unlimited. They advised him that the timber dam built by the Hudson's Bay Company on the Birch River to hold water on the eastern section of the Cumberland Marshes, south of Cumberland House in northeastern Saskatchewan, was no longer operative, and had to be replaced. The Hudson's Bay Company was abandoning the project, due to low fur prices, and would not replace the dam. If it was permitted to disappear, the marshes would soon be dry and the whole area vulnerable to agricultural encroachment. Neither Malaher nor Denmark wanted to see that happen, but neither had authority or the means to prevent it.

The Cumberland Marshes were well known to Ducks Unlimited for their waterfowl production. The first investigation of the area, before the Hudson Bay dam was built, had been made by Angus H. Shortt and Dr. Alex Bajkov in 1939. These marshes were also sometimes covered on the annual fall aerial survey of northern waterfowl concentrations.

A. C. Burns.

In 1961, Ducks Unlimited rebuilt the dam, but located it farther downstream to develop additional water area. The company was given a 15-year lease by the Saskatchewan government on the area, which totalled 320,000 acres, with 19 larger named lakes comprising 73,400 acres and innumerable small ponds and meandering creeks. Ducks Unlimited's reliable wilderness contractor, Martin Overguard, built the structure. The curved concrete dam, the largest and most expensive structure built by Ducks Unlimited to that date, is a monument to the tenacity and ingenuity of Overguard and Burns. A. C. (Al) Burns joined Ducks Unlimited in 1957 as Provincial Engineer, becoming Manitoba Provincial Manager in 1968, and Alberta Manager in 1975.

In 1963, an inlet control structure was built on the "Dragline Ditch", which had been dug many years before by the Hudson's Bay Company to bring water into the Cumberland Marshes from the old channel of the Saskatchewan River.

Coincident with the construction of the dam in the summer of 1961, biological investigations were begun by G. H. Townsend, then a Ph.D. candidate from the University of Wisconsin. These studies extended over a four-year period, and gave Ducks Unlimited the most comprehensive ecological and waterfowl data they have ever had on such an area. This not only provided a basis for management of the area, but also for the intensive internal development program which began in August of 1975.

Townsend joined Ducks Unlimited on a permanent basis in May of 1966, becoming successively, biologist in charge of all projects in the Saskatchewan River Delta as well as the Cumberland Marshes, and then Manitoba Provincial Biologist. He left the company in November, 1970. Before doing so, he had demonstrated the value of drawdowns in improving these marshes for waterfowl and muskrat production, and had begun a large scale drawdown program in the Cumberland Marshes.

From May of 1964 to September, 1966, co-operative biological investigations were carried out in the Cumberland area by the Canadian Wildlife Service and the Wildlife Branch of the Saskatchewan Department of Natural Resources. These studies were designed, to quote from the report *Wildlife in the Saskatchewan River Delta*, "(1) to determine the potential of the area for the production and utilization of big game, furbearers, and waterfowl; and, (2) to propose a form of land use development for the Delta through which the wildlife and aesthetic resources of the Delta could be conserved and fully utilized in harmony with other desirable forms of land-use development."

The studies confirmed, "that the marshes and lakes of the area are capable of producing large numbers of waterfowl and muskrats on a sustained basis, if the habitat is maintained through sound management . . ." The report also stated that the technical knowledge to develop this type of habitat for agricultural production and to maintain that production indefinitely was lacking and suggested that the area was unsuited for immediate large scale agricultural use.

It specifically recommended that ". . . about 400,000 acres consisting of the Cumberland Marshes, and the stagnant bog area south of the Birch River be developed as a wildlife management scheme. Implementation would include the following:

> The wetlands would be divided into a series of interconnected compartments by a system of dykes, canals, and control structures, permitting manipulations of water levels to create optimum conditions for production of waterfowl and muskrat."

Gunner Campbell and H. C. Moulding of Ducks Unlimited provided the engineering input for this part of the report and produced a plan for development, estimating the cost at $2.3 million.

With their lease from the Saskatchewan government on the Cumberland Marshes due to expire in October of 1975, Ducks

Original Hudson's Bay Company dam on the Cumberland marshes.

The new Ducks Unlimited dam, built 1961.

Muskeg Lake, typical habitat, Cumberland marshes.

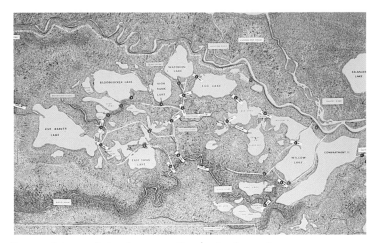

Proposed internal development, Cumberland marshes.

Draglines at work on canal.

A major canal and dykes near completion.

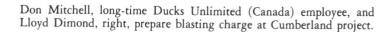
Don Mitchell, long-time Ducks Unlimited (Canada) employee, and Lloyd Dimond, right, prepare blasting charge at Cumberland project.

Unlimited management presented a proposal for development of the area to an Executive Meeting held at The Pas on June 22, 1974. The proposal was based on the original compartmentation concept of Campbell and Moulding, and the cost to develop the area estimated at $3.3 million (including contingencies) in 1973 dollars. This was later revised to $3.7 million following further engineering investigations and refinements.

The new agreement, signed on January 1, 1976 with the Saskatchewan government, granted Ducks Unlimited a five-year construction period followed by a 33-year lease — a total of 38 years on the 332,000 acres now included in the Cumberland Marshes. Negotations were long and difficult. They involved Al Burns and Bernie Forbes working with the natives at Cumberland House, and Stew Morrison and Forbes working with the Saskatchewan Government. Five years were given to develop a plan of management for an adjacent 180,000 acres to the south prior to further lease negotiation.

Work began in August of 1975 under the on-site supervision of Lloyd Dimond, who was transferred from the position of Brooks Area Manager. Dimond had joined Ducks Unlimited in May, 1969. At the end of 1977, the project was ahead of schedule and 70% complete, and three million dollars had been spent. Due to inflation, total costs to completion in 1980 are estimated to be $5 million.

While development and preservation of waterfowl habitat are the acknowledged objectives of Ducks Unlimited, the company has always considered an essential part of its role to be catalytic — to make things happen which will benefit waterfowl. Though not always reflected in the acres and miles of shoreline statistics at each year end, it may well be their most important function. Provincial governments control the use of land and water, and it is only by working in close co-operation with them that this catalytic function can be realized.

Such co-operation, on a grand scale, was demonstrated in the development of the Hay Lakes project in Alberta, the Cumberland Marshes in Saskatchewan, and the Tom Lamb Wildlife Management Area in Manitoba. Less spectacular but equally important have been the integration of annual programs of water conservation and waterfowl habitat development with all three provinces.

In Alberta, beginning with the era of Rennie Harley and the Water Stabilization Board formed just after the war, and continuing to the present, through many committees with many names, there has been close co-operation between the Provincial government and Ducks Unlimited.

In 1960, the Alberta government, recognizing the value of water in the southern part of the province, agreed to pay for half of all projects built, up to $25,000 per year, in the area south of Hanna. This co-operative program lasted for many years. In 1970, approximately $320,000 out of a total provincial budget of $400,000, was spent on cost-shared projects with the Alberta government. Sixteen such projects were built in 1971, and 30 out of a total of 47 in 1972. These projects were, and are, built on a "value to waterfowl" basis. The Ducks Unlimited contribution is based on the value to waterfowl; the remainder of the cost is

Dennis Hooey.

picked up by the Alberta government for the value to other resources, or for flood control. Because the Alberta government could solve the land problems, many excellent projects have been constructed which would have otherwise been unobtainable for Ducks Unlimited.

The co-operative program today is at the municipal level with the local branches of the Department of Environment. The initiative to manage a specific area for flood control frequently comes from the Municipality. However, their share of the costs may be greater than they can afford. If it is in the best interests of waterfowl, Ducks Unlimited may then step in and provide the additional money for the project, with concessions for waterfowl an integral part of such participation.

Saskatchewan is a more difficult province in which to work, for here, land-use conflicts between waterfowl and agriculture reach their greatest intensity. In view of the agricultural pressure, it is surprising that waterfowl have received the consideration they have.

During the 1960's, Ducks Unlimited co-operated with the Saskatchewan Wildlife Branch to preserve waterfowl habitat from further agricultural encroachment by means of the Wetland Inventory, which has already been described. In addition, in 1968, key easements were bought by the Saskatchewan Water Supply Board (a Crown corporation established to allocate South Saskatchewan River water from the irrigation system) so that work could proceed on Ducks Unlimited's development of the Saskatoon Southeast Project. The Canadian Wildlife Service also purchased some essential acreage. The Little Nut Lake project was also developed co-operatively by Ducks Unlimited with the Saskatchewan Department of Conservation and Development, along with the Local Area Authority, as were Mudie Lake, Carmen, and Pelican Lake.

In 1972, to resolve the conflict of interest in Saskatchewan between water conservation agencies, wildlife agencies, and agriculture, a Wetlands Committee was formed consisting of the Deputy Ministers of the Departments of Agriculture, Natural Resources, and the Water Resources Commission. An Advisory Committee was established from Agriculture and Wildlife, of which Ducks Unlimited was a member and for which it supplied much of the waterfowl input from 1972 through 1974. Ducks Unlimited also assisted in the study of the Qu'Appelle River system which has great waterfowl potential. The late T. H. McLeod — a long time Ducks Unlimited director from Regina, Saskatchewan — was a member of the Public Advisory Group to the Qu'Appelle Basin Study Board.

In 1970, the company tried a new approach in their efforts to have Saskatchewan wetlands set aside permanently for waterfowl. This pilot program sought to have landowners sign easements, reserving their wetlands in their natural state in perpetuity. When complete marshes were signed up, the government would then be requested to set them aside permanently by Order-in-Council. Dennis Hooey, a Ducks Unlimited Bio-technician since 1963, and who had demonstrated considerable skill in public relations work, undertook this program. Interviewing farmers with leases on wetland acreage, he was able to obtain easements on four complete marshes, which, including the areas that were partially signed up, totalled 2,517 acres. In 1971, a similar program was undertaken to see if easements could be obtained on patented land. Six marshes were completely signed up which, again including those partially obtained, amounted to 1,635 acres. The program concentrated in the western part of the province during 1972, where cereal crops rather than mixed farming was the major agricultural activity. Here, water areas were shallower, more temporary, and landowners more reluctant to give easements. All agreements were obtained on two wetlands and the total acreage brought under easement was 585 acres.

The program demonstrated that in the mixed farming areas of Saskatchewan, a significant number of farmers were willing to sign easements to preserve their wetlands whether leased or patented. The agreements completed, however, were not considered to have sufficient legal status to support order-in-council action, so this part of the pilot project was eliminated.

At this point, the program was turned over to the Saskatchewan Wildlife Federation as a proven method for preserving natural wetlands. It helped form the basis of their "Acres For Wildlife" program in which farmers were asked to sign agreements preserving wildlife habitat, both upland as well as wetland, in perpetuity. This program is still actively promoted by the local branches of the Federation. Co-operating farmers are identified by a sign placed in their yards. A total of 19,000 acres has been pledged to wildlife thus far.

In Manitoba, in a co-operative program with the Manitoba Wildlife Branch, Ducks Unlimited carried out an inventory of larger wetlands in the Interlake and Westlake area. Based on this inventory, many areas on Crown lands were then reserved for waterfowl habitat by the Branch.

In January of 1964, the Manitoba Department of Natural Resources called a meeting of agencies interested in the future of the Delta Marsh at the southern end of Lake Manitoba. A committee was formed to study the situation in these marshes and to make recommendations for their preservation and management, particularly in view of the Assiniboine River Diversion, which was being constructed to divert the flood flows from the river to the lake.

Ever since its inception, Ducks Unlimited had been involved sporadically in the Delta Marsh. In 1939, dams had been built on two small creeks flowing out of the marsh; then in 1947, a series of ditches, dams, and structures were built at the northern end of the area in conjunction with the Manitoba government program to improve water supply and distribution in that part of the marsh. In 1964, in co-operation with the Manitoba Wildlife Branch, carp screens which are still operative were installed on the main inlets to the marsh.

Ducks Unlimited was represented on both the Delta administrative and technical committees established by the January meeting. These included: members from the branches of Wildlife, Fisheries, and Water Control and Conservation, of the Department of Mines and Natural Resources; the Canadian Wildlife Service; the University of Manitoba; and the Delta Waterfowl Research Station.

The biological field work was done primarily by the Canadian Wildlife Service, with W. R. Miller of that organization as project leader. Members of the Botany Department of the University of Manitoba made the required plant surveys under the direction of Dr. Jennifer (Walker) Shay. Field work began in July of 1964, and continued through 1966. Ducks Unlimited engineering crews mapped the underwater contours of the marsh; and an engineering feasibility study and cost estimate was done by the consulting engineering firm of M. M. Dillon and Company. A comprehensive report was compiled by the committee and a summary report prepared for public distribution by E. F. Bossenmaier, titled "The Delta Marsh, Its Values, Problems, and Potentialities".

Land assembly and further biological investigations are presently underway in the marshes. An agreement has been signed by the federal and provincial governments for implementation of the plan or some version of it. Ducks Unlimited will likely again be involved, when a clear program of action is finalized.

In addition to the foregoing study, Ducks Unlimited provided data for the many and continuing altercations between wildlife and agriculture interests over the elevation at which Lake Manitoba should be maintained. Briefs have been prepared for the many government committees which have studied the problem and similar reports have been prepared for the Lake Winnipeg marshes. Biologists from the Special Projects Team are presently completing an extensive study of the effect of various water level regimes on all the marshes of the Lake Manitoba Basin.

Ducks Unlimited has also participated in a number of projects where the Manitoba government acquired the land and the company helped develop the waterfowl potential. The Oak Hammock Marsh, some 20 miles north of Winnipeg, is a prime example. This area was known to Ducks Unlimited in the middle 1940's as St. Andrew's Bog, and, except for the truculence of one of the two local municipalities involved, the company would have developed it then, though on a somewhat more modest scale than it was finally built.

In 1973, the provincial government completed the land assembly of 8,000 acres and built the main dyke. Ducks Unlimited constructed the east-west dykes and the controls, and built sixty nesting islands in the three impoundments which hold 3,800 acres of water.

Co-operative and catalytic action also saved the waterfowl potential of the Dog Lake Marshes. Flooding was a serious problem and the simplest solution was to drain the lake into Lake Manitoba. Ducks Unlimited participated in the planning and design for flood control, and by providing additional funds assured that Dog Lake would be retained at the best level for waterfowl in relation to the other objectives of the development.

The company is also participating in the development of the flood control program for the Whitemud Watershed, which dis-

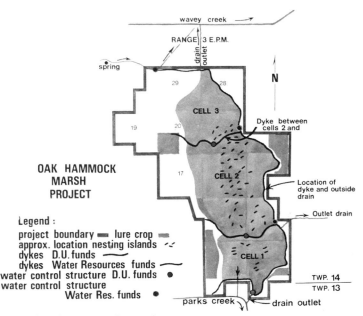

Plan of Oak Hammock marsh.

Marsh partially filled, east-west dyke and constructed islands.

Islands constructed to increase waterfowl nesting success.

Level ditches open up overgrown marshes.

charges into the southern end of Lake Manitoba by the Whitemud River. Intensive engineering and biological surveys are being made in order to take advantage of all opportunities to develop or preserve waterfowl habitat.

Although there has been much co-operation between prairie governments and Ducks Unlimited, the legal complexity of carrying out the company's program increased greatly during the 1960's, and this trend is continuing. Where once easements from landowners affected by a project sufficed for permission from the respective provincial water resources branches to proceed with construction, an increasing list of requirements now encumber and inhibit the company's efficient operation.

The lead time from project initiation to construction has been greatly increased by the number of government steps through which a proposal must pass before it can be implemented. Procedures differ between provinces and on whether the proposed project is on private or Crown land, but such requirements as municipal resolutions, approval from government departments other than water resource branches, advertising and posting of an intent to construct, delay progress and cost money.

Comment must also be made on co-operation with the Canadian Wildlife Service during recent years. In addition to the key land purchases made by the Service so that Ducks Unlimited could build projects in the Saskatoon Southeast development, land was also purchased so the Stalwart Marsh Flats, Last Mountain Lake and Tway Lakes projects could be built in Saskatchewan. Their experimental small pond paid easement program also made it possible for Ducks Unlimited to construct some smaller projects which would not have been otherwise possible. In eastern Canada, their purchase of the Tantramar National Wildlife Area gave the company the opportunity to develop excellent waterfowl habitat there.

A co-operative attitude has always existed between the United States Fish & Wildlife Service and Ducks Unlimited fieldmen. Free exchange of information and assistance has been characteristic. John J. Lynch, Allen Smith, Arthur S. Hawkins, Ross Hanson, Jerry Stoudt, Duane Norman, Hortin Jensen, Arthur Brazda, and Mort Smith have always worked closely with their Ducks Unlimited counterparts on the prairies.

Beginning in the late 1960's, an increasing biological emphasis characterized the Ducks Unlimited programs. The objectives of the company came to be recognized as biological, and development of waterfowl habitat much more complex than simple storage of water. Acknowledgement of this fact has resulted in greatly increased biological input at the senior administrative and planning levels, and has been reflected in the field by programs which demonstrate an ecological understanding of waterfowl and their total environmental requirements.

Level ditching programs, island construction, control of emergents, and nesting cover plots all reflect an understanding of this relationship. These refinements are now included in all basic project planning. And such internal developments now constitute a major program where the company may have no water control, but where it can be seen that their use will enhance waterfowl production.

This type of development required new equipment. The "Cookie Cutter," a machine designed to open up overgrown marshes, purchased in 1975 for use in the Maritimes, was so successful that a second machine was given to Ducks Unlimited in 1976 by the Wisconsin State Ducks Unlimited Committee and stationed in Manitoba.

The company philosophy now seems to have come full circle. In the earliest years, under the influence of B. W. Cartwright as Chief Naturalist and T. C. Main as General Manager, there was a much wider appreciation of the biological complexities of the

"Cookie Cutter" breaks up solid stands of cattail or bulrush.

waterfowl problem than in the intervening years, when water acres and shoreline miles tended to be the sole criterion of progress.

Part of the philosophy of the Ducks Unlimited program — and a valid part — was to establish a waterfowl priority for as much wetland habitat as possible, by whatever techniques would accomplish it — realizing that the time when this could be done was short. Water control was the method most frequently used, and many examples can be cited where this technique has successfully preserved waterfowl habitat from other exploitation. The plan was always to return to these areas at some later time and add the other management refinements which would ensure maximum waterfowl productions.

With increased budgets and biological staff, these refinements are now being implemented. The addition of habitat development biologists to the prairie provincial biological staffs in 1976 now permits a review of the older projects with the intent of upgrading their waterfowl production. The concern of the directors, that management of our projects was inadequate, was reflected in 1977, when critical triennial evaluations of all projects became part of annual provincial biological programs.

Until the 1960's, biological staffing had been based on a provincial biologist in each province. Additional biological staff were then hired either as junior biologists or at the bio-technician level, Dennis Hooey was the first of these. With the establishment of the Kelsey Institute of Applied Arts and Sciences in Saskatoon, well-trained bio-technicians became available. The company was able to recruit many excellent people from this source and has profited from their competent and dedicated service. The first of these was Dale Brydges, who became a permanent staff member in 1965, followed by Keith Pugh, Rollie Wilkins and Ed Harris.

Another characteristic of the 1960's was an increased involvement with Canada geese, which the drought of the 1930's had almost extirpated from the prairies. With the return of breeding geese to the prairies, beginning in the 1950's, interest was aroused in how these birds could be increased both in numbers and distribution, and how the known public affection for them could be used to stimulate public co-operation in preserving marshes.

The first Canada geese were banded by Ducks Unlimited in 1949, a semi-captive flock at the Alf Hole Sanctuary at Rennie in southeastern Manitoba. In 1951, a co-operative banding effort with U.S. Fish & Wildlife Service personnel on the Bow River, west of Brooks, Alberta, demonstrated the technique and potential for drive banding Canada geese during the July flightless period of the annual adult moult, and before the young of the year could fly. The next year, Ducks Unlimited purchased their own equipment, and July banding of Canada geese in Alberta

and Saskatchewan, and transplants of young birds to vacant habitat, has been part of annual provincial biological programs ever since.

The focus of the Alberta banding has been in the Brooks area on the irrigation projects, where the co-ordinator for many years was Fred Sharp. The program has long been a co-operative one with the Alberta Wildlife Branch. Using the Brooks area as a source, new breeding flocks have been established on many Ducks Unlimited projects in the Hanna area, and on projects and natural areas east of Edmonton.

The leader in the Canada goose work in Saskatchewan was Tom Sterling. Drive banding began in the western part of the province, primarily in the southwestern corner, in 1958, and expanded to include Ducks Unlimited's Waterhen Marsh in northeastern Saskatchewan the following year. In 1961, 29 geese were banded along Red Deer River in Alberta and Saskatchewan.

The Canada goose transplant program in Saskatchewan was based on the free-flying flock established in 1953 at Wascana Park in Regina by Fred G. Bard, the curator of the Saskatchewan Museum of Natural History. In 1959, Bard wrote to Ducks Unlimited asking for help in locating areas into which the excess geese from Wascana might be released. He saw the flock as a production centre from which geese could be reintroduced into many new areas in the province.

From 1960 until 1969, when Tom Sterling was transferred to British Columbia, and when the Saskatchewan Wildlife Branch established a Canada goose production unit at Eyebrow Lake, Ducks Unlimited worked closely with Fred Bard and the Saskatchewan Wildlife Branch on a Canada goose release program. These releases resulted in the establishment of new goose breeding flocks in several areas of the province, the most successful of which were in the southeastern region where, centered on the Ducks Unlimited Montmartre project, 472 birds were released between 1963 and 1968. On the project, and the surrounding area, a breeding flock of approximately 125 pairs has been established. In a unique program, pairs of Canada geese were given to selected farmers along Moose Mountain Creek in the same area of the province. These birds, which were wing clipped, successfully raised broods and stimulated interest in Canada goose programs.

Prior to the releases from Wascana, Tom Sterling and Bill Hooey, then Area Manager for southwestern Saskatchewan, had brought in Canada geese from the United States Fish & Wildlife Service Refuge at Bowdoin, Montana. These were goslings hatched in incubators and originated from nests about to be flooded by the irrigation activities adjacent to the refuge. In 1960, 86 goslings were brought in, and by 1963 a total of 259 had been released in the Kyle area, north of Swift Current. A successful breeding flock was established which spread to the adjacent South Saskatchewan River.

Introductions from the Wascana flock were also made into the Oak and Plum Lakes (a Kansas City donor project) in southwestern Manitoba. A total of 757 flightless young were released on the area between 1964 and 1968, and a further 98 in 1974. Fifty of the total release were from eggs gathered at Wascana, and incubated and reared at the Delta Waterfowl Research Station. From these transplants, the geese have spread widely over the southwestern area of the province. The Manitoba Wildlife Branch co-operated in the program by closing the area surrounding the lakes to Canada goose hunting. A spring count in 1977 found 45 pair on Oak Lake proper. Growth of this flock has been slower than anticipated due to high hunting mortality on southern migration and wintering areas. However, there is no doubt but that the presence of these geese helped preserve the lakes from drainage.

The Oak and Plum Lake releases were not the first attempt by Ducks Unlimited to establish new breeding flocks of Canada geese in Manitoba. In 1957, in response to criticism by the local municipality that Ducks Unlimited was doing nothing at the Big Grass Marsh project, the company decided to use the well known public appeal of Canada geese to stimulate local interest in the marsh. At that time, the recognized technique was to hold Canada geese at the release site until they reached the breeding age of three years. This imprinted them to the area, and protected them from the heavy mortality which occurs in the wild before maturity is reached. The project was a co-operative one with the Delta Waterfowl Research Station which provided yearling geese from their wild Station flock. The birds were confined and fed at Ducks Unlimited expense by Peter Skoropata on his farm close to the eastern side of the marsh. Releases began in 1960 when the first cohort was three years old. Annual releases were then made in subsequent years until the program was discontinued in 1962. A total of 79 geese were released but the project was not considered a success. The birds were too accustomed to human beings and attempted to nest on farm dugouts and small ponds where they were very susceptible to predation and poaching.

The most interesting goose banding was done by Tom Sterling on the barren grounds of the eastern Northwest Territories from 1963 through 1965. This was a co-operative program with the Canadian Wildlife Service, who supplied aerial transportation both for the banding and the extensive aerial surveys which were undertaken to locate other areas of importance to moulting Canada geese.

Of major and unique interest was that these were large type Canada geese, originating on the prairies, which as sub-adults, or unsuccessful nesters, had made a June "Moult Migration" to preferred locations on the barren grounds of the eastern

Driving flightless Canada geese, adults and young, into a shoreline "catch pen".

Neck banded geese ready to be transported to new areas.

A real "Giant Canada" outside Hanna, Alberta.

Favorite Canada goose nesting sites are old muskrat houses.

A raft with straw simulates the natural situation.

Round straw bales . . .

. . . set on end are particularly attractive.

Acceptance is good and success high in this type of artificial nesting structure.

Old tractor tires set on islands are attractive to Canada geese.

Northwest Territories. Here they would undergo the flightless period of the annual moult, when the large wing feathers are shed and then replaced, a period of about 25 days at this latitude. Banding sites were located in the Beverley-Aberdeen Lake section of the Thelon River. Although it had been known for a long time that large type Canada geese moulted in this area, the fact that they were present in sufficient numbers to offer a banding opportunity was first reported by the Canadian Wildlife Service during their caribou tagging operation on the Thelon River.

Local Eskimos were employed and using equipment of the caribou crews directed by Bob Ruttan of the Canadian Wildlife Service, 3,608 geese were banded over the three-year period. A partial analysis of the results of these bandings was made by Sterling and his colleague, Alex Dzubin, of the Canadian Wildlife Service, and presented at the Thirty-Second Annual North American Wildlife Conference in 1967. Additional data were given at the 1970 Midwest Wildlife Conference. A further publication is in preparation.

Sterling had some great experiences during his northern work. Some of them, like most adventures, weren't much fun when they were happening, but make great stories if one survives. In 1960, he flew exploratory flights with the Canadian Wildlife Service along the Arctic Coast, including Banks and Victoria Islands, and in 1967 and 1968, down the Thelon and middle Back River to Hudson Bay exploring and collecting for the Canadian Wildlife Service.

There were minor adventures on all these trips, but the one he remembers most vividly was the return flight of July 16, 1963 from Lookout Point on the Thelon River to Uranium City in northern Saskatchewan. They had plenty of fuel on departure, but almost immediately ran into a line squall with heavy rain and zero visibility. When they came into the clear, they were lost, and confused by inaccuracies in the map, but were able to locate themselves in about ten minutes — 40 miles off course.

Returning to track they ran into another storm, probably the same one. Tom suggested landing while they knew where they were, but the pilot disagreed. It began to get dark and the storm was as bad as the first one. There were no lights in the cockpit so Tom had to crawl to the back of the aircraft and get a flashlight from the pilot's gear. But the batteries were so weak that they could use it only for brief moments to read the artificial horizon. Breaking into the clear at dark, there was only starlight which they could see shining on bodies of water as they passed over. With only ten minutes of gas left, they decided to attempt to land. The terrain was rugged and rocky and they were out of radio contact.

Using field glasses, Tom picked up starlight on water which looked big enough for a safe landing. On their approach, when near the ground, they could no longer see the starlight and gradually landed at stalling speed, with the stall horn squalling all the time. They intended to drop the tail first and the pilot warned Tom that the aircraft might porpoise. It didn't, but stopped almost immediately, the water coming over the windshield in a great wave. They had stopped about one-quarter of a mile from a sheer rock face; a few more seconds and they would have been into it.

They waited until daylight, refilled the fuel tank with the ten gallons of emergency gas stowed in the back of the aircraft, and took off. They quickly discovered they were between Stony Rapids and the east end of Lake Athabasca, about 40 miles east of track, with enough gas to reach Uranium City safely.

Tom Sterling brought his interest in Canada geese with him when he moved from Saskatchewan in 1969 to become Provincial Biologist in British Columbia. When the Serpentine Project on the lower Mainland was built in 1973, in co-operation with

Serpentine Project.

the British Columbia Department of Recreation and Conservation, it offered an ideal location where Canada geese could be produced to re-establish a breeding population in the Fraser River Valley.

Canada geese were obtained from the Kortwright Waterfowl Park at Guelph, Ontario, through the co-operation of the Pitt Waterfowl Management Association in British Columbia, and particularly with the assistance of Richard Trethewey of the Coniagas Ranch, who is now a director of Ducks Unlimited (Canada). Eighty acres of the 101 acre project were enclosed by a predator-proof fence, and islands and channels constructed. In 1975, an additional 81.5 acres were developed.

Two hundred and six adult Canada geese were received on July 11, 1973. The females were pinioned and most of the males wing-clipped. In June, 1975, releases from the flock into the Fraser River Valley began. Production was increased by double clutching. This technique involves robbing some first nests, hatching the eggs in incubators, and thus forcing the birds to produce a second clutch. Eggs were also supplied from the Reifel Refuge and Coniagas Ranch.

The breeding flock at Serpentine was 100 pair in 1977 and will be maintained at that level for the near future. The total population in the Fraser River Valley was estimated to be 2,500 in September, 1976 and should reach near the 5,000 mark in September of 1977.

The success of this venture has resulted from the co-operation of many organizations and individuals. The British Columbia Wildlife Branch made land available for the original Serpentine project, closed the Fraser Valley to Canada goose shooting, and set aside certain islands in the Fraser Valley as nesting areas. The Pitt Waterfowl Management Association, a private group of landowners and conservationists, brought Canada geese to the lower mainland and assisted Ducks Unlimited to procure geese

The breeding flock.

"Double clutching" makes for large families!

Marsh World

DUCKS UNDER WATER — The mallard has been experimentally held alive under water as long as 16 minutes, and even 27 minutes with its trachea closed. Voluntarily, birds stay under water for much shorter times, usually less than 2 minutes. The common loon is known to stay under water for 15 minutes. To be able to dive, the bird must expel the air from his air sacs and at the same time reduce the flow of blood to the muscles. Then he can draw the oxygen stored in the muscles to permit him to dive for longer periods.

Ducks Unlimited (Canada)
1495 Pembina Hwy, Winnipeg, Man. R3T 2E2

© '77 - 219

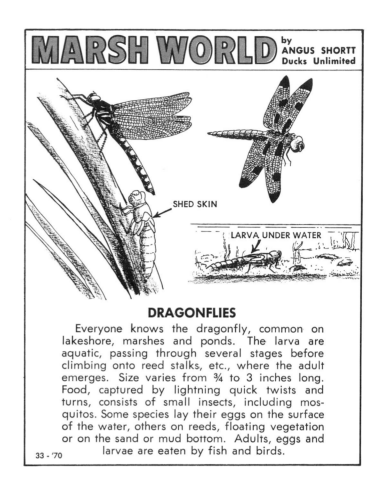

SHED SKIN

LARVA UNDER WATER

MARSH WORLD by ANGUS SHORTT Ducks Unlimited

DRAGONFLIES

Everyone knows the dragonfly, common on lakeshore, marshes and ponds. The larva are aquatic, passing through several stages before climbing onto reed stalks, etc., where the adult emerges. Size varies from ¾ to 3 inches long. Food, captured by lightning quick twists and turns, consists of small insects, including mosquitos. Some species lay their eggs on the surface of the water, others on reeds, floating vegetation or on the sand or mud bottom. Adults, eggs and larvae are eaten by fish and birds.

33 - '70

---

for their program. Douglas College, New Westminster, provided the assistance of their warden, who lives on the site. They also undertook an interpretive program at the project under the dynamic leadership of Dr. Barry Leach, who was of immeasureable assistance in establishing the Serpentine project in the first place.

The B.C. Waterfowl Society provided some geese from the Reifel Refuge, and the Canadian Wildlife Service the necessary permits, as well as barley from the Reifel Refuge for supplementary winter feeding. The B.C. Wildlife Federation and members of local naturalist clubs assisted in trapping and banding, and in releasing goslings into new habitat, as well as in censusing and recording sightings of marked birds.

In September, 1973, the foregoing organizations, along with Ducks Unlimited, formed the nucleus of the Fraser Valley Canada Goose Management Committee to co-ordinate the Canada goose propagation and release program in the Fraser Valley.

Expansion also brought rejuvenation to the public relations activities of the company. There had been no public relations officer from the time Alton Cleland left in 1967, although Angus Gavin temporarily filled the position as Senior Vice-President from April of 1968 until he left the company in December of the same year.

In the spring of 1969, Wally West injected new life into this activity which, although he left in 1971, has carried through to the present. Under his direction, the popular panel, "Marsh World", with drawings and text by Angus Shortt, was initiated. These panels now appear regularly in 950 newspapers and other publications, as well as 140 in French. The new modernized Ducks Unlimited logo also appeared at this time — the brainchild of Lorne Cameron, then President of Ducks Unlimited (Canada). Leitch, West, and Shortt collaborated to produce a pamphlet titled "Don't Burn This Spring", directed at farmers in an attempt to preserve nests and nesting cover from spring fires.

Bruce Smith replaced West and, in his short time with the company, produced with Angus Shortt, a new full-color Ducks Unlimited waterfowl identification brochure which proved to be very popular and was widely distributed across Canada. It was revised and reprinted in 1976 by Patrick Lang, the present Information Officer, and translated into French. Smith also produced the pamphlet "His Tomorrow", which is sent to potential contributors in Canada, describing how they can support the company's habitat preservation program, and "Where There's Water", which is distributed to farmers and gives general information about Ducks Unlimited and is geared to the agricultural community.

Cliff Schultz, who became Public Relations Manager in April, 1973, combined all the "Marsh World" panels into a single volume, and initiated a television film clip program which dealt with waterfowl and wetland problems. These clips were televised in all major Canadian cities. In 1977, Patrick Lang, who had replaced Schultz when he became Administrative Secretary, co-ordinated and produced a brochure titled "Working with Landowners for Better Water Management", in response to the company's concern with what appeared to be an impending drought. This illustrated the value of wetlands to landowners and suggested they write to Ducks Unlimited if they were interested in water storage projects on their lands. The brochure was inserted into the July, 1977, issue of the "Country Guide"; and the response was very gratifying.

Steadily increasing funds allowed the company not only to increase the scope of its activities on the prairies during the late 1960's and 1970's but also begin expansion all across Canada. A provincial office was established in British Columbia in 1969 and in the Maritimes during 1971. In addition, a field office was opened in London, Ontario in April, 1975, and in Quebec in January, 1976.

Ducks Unlimited had had an intermittent operation in the Maritimes from the earliest years, as has been previously described. In the beginning, it was focussed primarily on the Eastern Waterfowl Research Station. In 1951, the Fullerton Marsh was built in Prince Edward Island by the provincial government, with funds contributed by Ducks Unlimited.

Leitch visited New Brunswick in 1955, where, with Bruce Wright, the head of the Northeastern Wildlife Station, he inspected black duck habitat in the St. John River Valley and in western New Brunswick. The establishment of a black duck hatchery at the Wildlife Station, similar to that at the Delta Waterfowl Research Station in Manitoba, was considered but found impracticable.

In 1960, Ducks Unlimited paid for construction of a dam on the 1,540-acre Williamstown Lake in western New Brunswick. The company was not licensed to operate in New Brunswick at that time, so the design and construction were done by the New Brunswick government. In 1963, both Gavin and Leitch made inspections of proposed Maritime projects — Leitch with the Canadian Wildlife Service, and Gavin with the Nova Scotia Provincial Biologist. These included the Aero Lake project near Moncton, New Brunswick; Big and Front Lakes; and the Missaquash Marsh on the New Brunswick and Nova Scotia border; and also the coastal areas south and east of Amherst.

In 1969 and 1970, in order to obtain more background for their work in the Maritimes, Ducks Unlimited supported an investigation by Barry Hughson into the breeding ecology of the black duck in Nova Scotia.

But the modern era in the Maritimes really began when both Gavin and Leitch made contact in 1963 with John Waugh, then Chief Engineer for the Maritime Marshland Reclamation Administration of the Federal Government. John was to become Ducks Unlimited (Canada)'s first Maritime Manager.

From the time he met Gavin until he formally joined the organization, Waugh was a tower of strength in the Maritimes, not only suggesting projects, but on his own time, arranging for contractors and supervising construction. When he joined Ducks Unlimited on June 2, 1971, he had already built eight projects for the company. As John himself says, he had spent so much of his lifetime draining marshes (regretfully, since he was a keen duck hunter), that he certainly knew where they were, and how to reflood them! Donald J. (Doc) Black, who had been John Waugh's righthand man with Maritime Marsh Reclamation, and knew the marshes almost as well as John, joined Ducks Unlimited as Project Manager on March 1, 1971, when the Maritime office was first opened. "Doc" died suddenly on January 26, 1977. Few people have as quickly endeared themselves to an organization as he did. Not only was he respected for his competence and dedication, but his engaging personality was a delight to all who were fortunate enough to associate with him.

Keith McAloney became Maritime Biologist in April of 1972 to complete the first Maritime staff. As the work expanded, a surveyor was added in 1973 and a bio-technician in 1976. The company was registered in New Brunswick on December 12, 1967, but no registration was required in Nova Scotia or Prince Edward Island.

Much of the early work in the Maritimes was done in co-operation with the Canadian Wildlife Service. After the Service purchased the land for the Tantramar National Wildlife Area, along the border between Nova Scotia and New Brunswick, Ducks Unlimited built the structures and controls required to develop the large marsh areas it contained. The Sand Ponds project, near Yarmouth, Nova Scotia, was developed under a similar arrangement, as was the excellent 1,168-acre Germantown marsh in New Brunswick.

"Doc" Black, left, John Bain, (Director of Conservation Services for the province of Prince Edward Island) and John Waugh, inspect the control on the Forest Hills Project, P.E.I.

R. W. Coley, Chief Engineer, Ducks Unlimited (Canada) at John Waugh's prefabricated concrete spillway on the Cann's Pond Project, Prince Edward Island.

Paunchy Lake Extension — Massachusetts Project, New Brunswick.

Germantown Project, New Brunswick, partially filled — islands in foreground.

Dam and control structure on old drainage ditch, Missaquash-Delaware project, Nova Scotia.

Missaquash-Delaware, looking upstream from dam.

Corn Creek marshes, part of the Creston Valley Complex.

Close co-operation with the provincial governments of Prince Edward Island, Nova Scotia, and New Brunswick, has resulted in many other projects. To the end of 1977, a total of $1,900,000 has been spent in the Maritimes on developing waterfowl habitat and 86 projects have been built.

Ducks Unlimited also had a long "on again, off again" history in British Columbia before an office was finally opened in Victoria in 1969, and moved to Kamloops in 1973.

At the first Annual Meeting held in Winnipeg, April 14, 1939, expansion into British Columbia was discussed. It was suggested that much good might come from inclusion of that province, since a large share of the money subscribed to Ducks Unlimited had come from the western States (chiefly California) whose sportsmen were naturally interested in the western flyway.

In late winter of 1940, preliminary surveys of British Columbia were made by Main and Cartwright, and later by Russenholt. Five hundred questionnaires were specially prepared by Ducks Unlimited and distributed to game guardians and guides through the British Columbia Game Department, as well as to outdoor organizations and naturalists. These were designed to give the company a comprehensive picture of the British Columbia waterfowl situation, and to create a Ducks Unlimited Kee-Man organization in that province. In a later report, B. W. Cartwright stated that there were 126 Kee-Men in B.C., but this organization seems to have been permitted to disappear.

The proposed work program for 1940 included a preliminary survey of selected duck breeding areas in British Columbia by an engineer and ecologist. Four hundred and seventy-eight ducks were banded for Ducks Unlimited at Swan Lake, near Tupper, B.C. by T. E. Randall in 1941. The first British Columbia director, Austin C. Taylor, was elected at the 1940 Annual Meeting.

Reports on these surveys have not survived, but their essence may lie in the minutes of the 1943 Annual Meeting, when T. C.

Dyke construction on Six Mile Slough, one of the units in the complex.

Main stated that the lack of interest in British Columbia stemmed from two causes. First, they had decided it was not important as a breeding ground and that most areas were "in good shape" apart from predator control. Secondly, expansion to B.C. would add considerably to overhead.

Nevertheless, in 1953, Ducks Unlimited participated in their first British Columbia project when they assisted the Kelowna Sportsmen's Club to construct a diversion into Reisivig Slough near Kelowna. But it was not until October, 1962, when George Freeman made a reconnaissance of the Creston area and Beechers Prairie, that much further interest was shown. In July of 1963, Leitch spent a week with personnel of the Provincial Fish and Game Branch, looking at possible projects at Creston and in the Cariboo area. A year later, Gavin also made a trip to British Columbia and inspected proposed projects in the Creston area and in the Fraser River Delta. The latter was to become the site

Bill Hooey checks the Six Mile Slough dyke. Right — the dyke across Leach Lake.

Portable pumps, funded by the State of California, help manage water levels on the lakes and marshes of the Creston complex.

C. B. Forbes, then British Columbia Manager, inspects Bummers Marsh prior to construction.

of the present-day Reifel Refuge, which the British Columbia Waterfowl Society had already leased and were planning to develop along the lines of the Severn Waterfowl Trust in England.

From this point on, Ducks Unlimited's activity in the province began to grow. In 1964, considerable engineering was done for the British Columbia Waterfowl Society at the Reifel Refuge by Gunner Campbell, then the Manitoba Manager, and $10,000 was contributed toward the construction of the dykes and ponds. Engineering assistance continued through the five years of construction that followed and contributions totalled almost $39,000.

It was while Gunner Campbell was at the Reifel Refuge and through his association with Barry Leach, who was then Manager, that Ducks Unlimited became involved with the Serpentine Project where the Fraser Valley Canada goose flock was subsequently established.

But by far the most impressive area that Freeman, Leitch, or Gavin saw during their work in British Columbia were the floodplain marshes of the Kootenay River where it entered into Kootenay Lake at Creston. This was a well known staging area for migratory waterfowl and had been referred to in some popular writings as "The Valley of the Swans". Later a film by that name was produced. Waterfowl production from the area was limited by spring floods on the Kootenay River and the water level manipulation practices of the Kootenay Power and Light Company, who controlled the level of Kootenay Lake. Much of the fertile floodplain had already been reclaimed for agriculture by dyking and the remaining marshland was similarly threatened.

In 1965, 16,000 acres of land and water in the valley were established as a wildlife management area by the British Columbia Government. George Freeman returned to Creston in July of

Big Creek near Williams Lake, B.C. is diverted to supply water for the Chilco Project.

that year as part of a four-man team to carry out engineering and biological investigations. In 1968, the British Columbia government confirmed the status of the wildlife management area by Bill 65: "An Act to establish the Creston Valley Wildlife Management Area, preserving 16,000 acres of the Kootenay Valley for production, conservation and management". Management of the area became the joint responsibility of the Fish and Wildlife Branch of the British Columbia government and the Canadian Wildlife Service. A permanent manager and staff were hired in 1968.

Ducks Unlimited undertook the extensive dyke construction required to control flooding of the marshes. Gunner Campbell and Tom Sterling carried out preliminary surveys in April of 1968, and Bill Hooey was moved from North Battleford, Saskatchewan, to become Creston Area Manager in May, 1969.

Part of Chilco Project.

On December 3, 1969, Elswood Bole, then Managing Director of Ducks Unlimited, wrote to Fred Auger of Vancouver, director and former President of the corporation, who had been actively promoting the project, as follows: "I am happy to inform you that a bulldozer started work on the Creston Project yesterday morning at 9:00 . . ." A simple sentence — giving little hint of the complexities of initiating a co-operative project of this magnitude. Included were not only negotiations with two governments, but also with the Kootenay Power and Light Company, who were most co-operative once they understood what was planned, and even the International Joint Water Commission.

To date, Ducks Unlimited has spent almost a million dollars at Creston on dykes, structures, and pumps as well as internal works such as islands. The State of California has contributed $126,000 to the end of 1977 toward the cost of the company's developments in the valley. As part of management of the area,

One of the 50 wetland areas in the Chilco Project.

the Canadian Wildlife Service has built a Wildlife Interpretive Centre which provides orientation for visitors.

The British Columbia provincial office had been formally opened in Victoria in the spring of 1969, with Gunner Campbell as Provincial Manager, and Tom Sterling as Provincial Biologist. The company had been registered in the province since March 8, 1954, but was re-registered May 6, 1968.

Much reconnaissance had preceded the formal establishment of Ducks Unlimited in British Columbia. In addition to that already described, both Campbell and Sterling, mostly as a team, had carried out additional extensive reconnaissance throughout the province in the summers of 1967 and 1968, while still retaining their positions as Manitoba Manager and Saskatchewan Provincial Biologist. During these summers they identified a sufficient number of potential projects to justify a full scale provincial operation.

Gunner Campbell remained British Columbia Provincial Manager until February 1, 1971, when C. B. (Bernie) Forbes was appointed. Forbes, a farmer, had been a Kee-Man for many years before becoming Director of Wildlife for Saskatchewan prior to joining Ducks Unlimited. Campbell became Provincial Engineer and retired from the organization on February 28, 1973.

The provincial operation expanded in 1972 when an area office was opened at Williams Lake under Mike Yates, to develop the potential of the Cariboo and Chilcotin areas.

In 1973, after much debate, the provincial office was moved to Kamloops. Bernie Forbes was transferred to Saskatchewan as Provincial Manager and Ted Burkell, who had been Chief Engineer in Winnipeg for many years, became the British Columbia Manager.

To complete the shuffle, Herb Moulding, long time Saskatchewan Provincial Manager, moved to the Head Office in Winnipeg to lead the Special Projects Team, and R. W. Coley was hired as Chief Engineer in July, 1973. A provincial engineer, J. A. (Jim) Bomford, was added to the British Columbia staff in November of 1976, and became Provincial Manager a year later, succeeding Ted Burkell who has become Pacific Regional Manager responsible for co-ordinating the British Columbia and Alberta programs.

To the end of 1977, $2,400,000 had been spent in developing waterfowl habitat in British Columbia, and 82 projects have been built.

During the 1960's, pressure also increased for Ducks Unlimited to expand to Ontario, when Richard K. Moore of Toronto, who was active in the Ontario Waterfowl Research Foundation, began to campaign for a program in that province. There had been no Ontario directors appointed to the Board since the resignation of Senator N. M. Paterson in 1957. And both he and S. S. Holden of Ottawa, one of the original directors of the company who died in 1946, had been appointed for the assistance which they might be to the company in Ottawa, rather than with any idea of initiating an Ontario program.

In May of 1960, Leitch inspected part of the Lake St. Clair Marshes with Dr. C. H. D. Clarke, Director of the Ontario Wildlife Branch, but the proposed development was found to be impractical. No possibilities were found in the Ontario-St. Lawrence Park at Morrisburg near the Acadian Village, which had also been suggested.

In 1961, at the Annual Meeting in Las Vegas, Angus Gavin reported to the directors in response to their query as to whether a program should be started in Ontario, that he had had a recent meeting with a group of sportsmen and technicians in Toronto, at which he had been told there were many areas in the province where Ducks Unlimited could do worthwhile work. He suggested that money be set aside for Ontario investigations from the standpoint of goodwill and the possibility of raising funds in the east. No action was taken on his suggestion.

However, later in the same year, Gavin inspected a proposed project on the Bay of Quinte in Lake Erie near Belleville, and in 1962 Gunner Campbell was sent from Manitoba to construct it. This, the Tyendinaga Project, was Ducks Unlimited's first project in Ontario.

In 1963, Ducks Unlimited was asked by the Ontario Waterfowl Research Foundation to do some preliminary engineering and design for the waterfowl ponds at the Kortright Waterfowl Park near Guelph. The surveying was done by Angus Gavin and the structures designed by Gunner Campbell.

There was little further action until 1966 when W. C. Harris and Richard K. Moore, both of Toronto, were elected to the Board of Directors at the Annual Meeting in Winnipeg. From his new position as a director, Dick Moore vigorously continued his efforts for a full scale Ducks Unlimited program in Ontario. It was some time, however, before a program of sufficient magnitude could be identified.

In 1968, Burkell and Leitch spent three days with the Canadian Wildlife Service inspecting areas in the province which the Service was intending to buy, and where there might be an opportunity for development by Ducks Unlimited. In the same year, the company received a letter from the Honourable Rene Brunelle, Minister of Lands and Forests, encouraging them to begin operations in the province.

At the Annual Meeting of the Ontario Federation of Anglers and Hunters at Kingston in 1969, Leitch explained the Ducks Unlimited program, and discussed potential projects with the members. That September, he followed up these proposals but none proved worth developing.

Meanwhile, the Canadian Wildlife Service had been studying the productivity and development potential of the small

Richard K. Moore, left, with Bill Carrick, who produced several films for Ducks Unlimited in the 1960's.

marshes in the Aurora district, north of Toronto, and in the southwestern part of the province. In June of 1970, this program, which became known to both organizations as "The Small Marsh Program", was reviewed by Burkell and Leitch.

The Canadian Wildlife Service were able to undertake some construction under this program in 1973, but the following year their funds were frozen and they requested that Ducks Unlimited take over construction for that year. This they did, and six projects were built. In the fall of the same year, still faced with a financial problem, the Service asked Ducks Unlimited to take over the entire Small Marsh Program effective April 1, 1975, and offered to supply the necessary biological input. H. C. Moulding, the head of the Special Projects Team, made a survey that fall of the potential for an Ontario program, the results of

Typical project in the Ontario small marsh program.

which justified a continuing operation in the province. At the 1975 Annual Meeting on March 8th, the directors approved the establishment of a field office in Ontario to be located temporarily at London and to be under the supervision of the Manitoba Manager, A. C. Burns. David West was hired on April 21st as the Project Manager with office space temporarily supplied by Norval Hellofs, a Ducks Unlimited (Canada) director. This must have been a great day for Dick Moore culminating as it did over a decade of belief and persuasion.

During 1975, it became apparent that an Ontario program could not be developed by a single fieldman so far from support staff. At the Executive Committee Meeting of November 25, 1975, Morrison recommended expansion to a full time provincial office. Douglas Corbridge was hired as the Ontario Provincial Manager on March 1, 1976, and an office opened at Aurora. J. M. Collins, who, as a member of the Canadian Wildlife Service, had been deeply involved with the Small Marsh Program from the beginning, became Provincial Biologist in February,

and a Provincial Engineer was added in April, when M. S. Paradis joined the staff. Another Area Manager, Donald Borchuk, was added in September and stationed at Kingston.

Corbridge left the company in September, 1977, and was replaced by Ron Renwick, who first came to Ducks Unlimited as a field engineer in Saskatchewan in December, 1975.

But to Ontario must go the distinction of organizing and carrying out the first Ducks Unlimited fund-raising dinner in Canada. Although many sportsmen from Ontario had attended Ducks Unlimited dinners in Buffalo and Detroit, no such fund-raising dinners had ever been held in Canada, simply because Ducks Unlimited (Canada) did not have a fund-raising function, nor was it organized to promote such activities.

However, on July 25, 1974, under the leadership of Chairman Jack Rice of Aylmer, and Secretary Lloyd A. Leask of Simcoe, Ontario, a group of southern Ontario sportsmen, already contributors to Ducks Unlimited, formed the first Canadian Ducks Unlimited chapter, naming it "Ducks Unlimited Ontario

R. L. Renwick.

Marcel Laperle.

— Long Point Chapter''. To support the company's program, it was decided to have a fund-raising dinner. This was held at Tillsonburg on October 23, 1974, and was an outstanding success. Three hundred and fourteen tickets were sold and proceeds from the dinner, raffles, and auctions, generated a net total of $8,000.

Another dinner was held in 1976 by the Long Point Chapter, this time at Port Rowan. Two fund raising events took place in 1977, the Toronto Fund Raising Chapter inaugural dinner and the other again in Port Rowan. These dinners netted a total of $18,000.

Establishment of a provincial office in Quebec came about in a somewhat different manner. Although there had been occasional inquiries through the years from people in the province about the Ducks Unlimited program, no one there had been lobbying for expansion into the area in the same way that Dick Moore had in Ontario.

However, in late November, 1968, Leitch spoke to the Quebec Wildlife Federation Annual Meeting in Montreal, outlining the history and objectives of the company, with the expectation that some worthwhile projects might be volunteered. There were no direct results, though an increase in interest may have been demonstrated by the greater volume of mail from the province.

Increased activity by Ducks Unlimited in Quebec was, however, encouraged by Gaston Moisan, then Director of the Fish and Wildlife Division, and in June of 1970, Burkell and Leitch made a trip through Quebec with Canadian Wildlife Service personnel from the Eastern Region to see the areas the Service anticipated purchasing for waterfowl habitat. They were impressed by both Baie Lavalliere and Baie St. Francois in the floodplain of the St. Lawrence River near Sorel. The former is

now under development by Ducks Unlimited, though the land was finally purchased by the Province of Quebec.

In 1972, Waugh and Black, of the Maritime office, made a reconnaissance of prospective projects in Quebec. These included Baie St. Francois and Canal de Beauharnois on the St. Lawrence River, and Thurso and Baie Noire along the Ottawa. Michel Lepage, Waterfowl Biologist for the Province of Quebec, accompanied them. A year later, Waugh and Black, this time accompanied by Keith McAloney, the Maritimes Biologist, ran levels on Baie St. Francois, Thurso, and Baie Noire. McAloney also flew with a Quebec biologist to see a proposed project at the Abitibi Pulp and Power reservoir.

Thurso, the first Quebec project, was completed in December of 1973 on land transferred to the Quebec Fish and Wildlife Division by Quebec Hydro. The construction costs were underwritten by Delta Airlines and the project officially designated as the "Delta Airlines Project on Thurso Marsh". Baie Noire, downstream, was completed in 1976.

In September of 1974, McAloney made reconnaissances of several proposed areas in Quebec. In April, 1975, Moisan sent a further list of proposed Quebec projects to Ducks Unlimited and these were inspected by the Maritimes staff later in the spring.

John Waugh was impressed with these projects, and with the potential in Quebec generally for a Ducks Unlimited program. In June of 1975, he wrote to Morrison expressing this belief, and recommended a provincial organization for Quebec, "since it would be difficult and expensive to develop the areas with our Maritime staff".

Morrison recommended the establishment of a full-time provincial office in Quebec to the November 25, 1975, meeting of the Executive Committee, where it was approved. Marcel Laperle was hired as Provincial Manager in January, 1976,

Ducks Unlimited (Canada)
Canards Illimités (Canada)

SON
lendemain

DEPEND DE VOUS AUJOURD'HUI

Ducks Unlimited (Canada)

Le Monde du Marais

OIE DES NEIGES (Chen Caerulescens) — L'oie des neiges est très connue pour ses longs et spectaculaires vols de migration. De Mexico jusqu'aux lacs de la toundra et les bassins de l'Arctique, elle ne s'arrête que deux ou trois fois en cours de route. De couleur blanche, avec le bout des ailes noir, les adultes pèsent environ six livres. Le bec et les pattes sont d'un rose intense, les pattes antérieures ayant une "large tache" caractéristique. Les oies de couleur bleue, longtemps considérées comme appartenant à une espèce différente, ont un peu de bleu foncé sur la partie avant des ailes, mais sont en fait d'un gris sombre-marron, avec le bec et la tête de couleur blanche. Les deux sortes d'oies migrent et nichent ensemble.

Ducks Unlimited (Canada)   929 Boul. du Séminaire, St.-Jean, Québec
Canards Illimités (Canada)   J3A 1B6   © 234F - '78

Le Monde du Marais

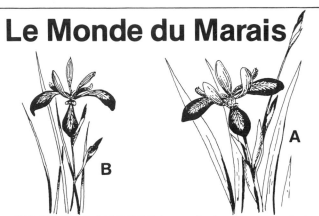

IRIS BLEU DES MARAIS (Iris versicolor et prismatica) Cette très jolie plante des marais, communément appelée "Iris sauvage" est une de nos fleurs sauvages les plus colorées. **(A)** Dans l'Ouest, ce sont de grandes fleurs avec de longues feuilles en forme d'épée. Largement répandues, elles sont d'un bleu-pourpre intense avec de fines vénules sombres, délicatement dessinées, s'évasant autour du centre jaune. **(B)** Les feuilles étroites, en forme de brin d'herbe, caractérisent la fleur des régions de l'Est. Bien que plus petite, elle est aussi très colorée. Ces deux fleurs poussent en bordure des marais ou dans les prairies humides. Elles fleurissent de mai à juin et atteignent jusqu'à trois pieds de haut.

Ducks Unlimited (Canada)   929 Boul. du Séminaire, St.-Jean, Québec
Canards Illimités (Canada)   J3A 1B6   © 235F - '78

Dedication of Delta Air Lines Project in Montreal, November 17, 1973. Left to right, Eugene DuPont III, Trustee, Ducks Unlimited Inc.; D. S. Morrison, General Manager (now Executive Vice President) Ducks Unlimited (Canada); Hugh Mackay, Director of Ducks Unlimited (Canada) from New Brunswick (now President); The Honorable Claude Simard, Minister of Fish, Wildlife, and Tourism, Province of Quebec; H. J. Canvin, Director — Canada, Delta Air Lines; and S. D. Dement, Vice-President, Marketing - Administration, Delta Air Lines.

Herman Taylor, Jr., President, Ducks Unlimited, Inc., presents 25th million dollar to R.O.A. Hunter, President, Ducks Unlimited (Canada), September 9, 1973.

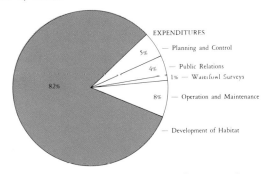

How money was used for Waterfowl.

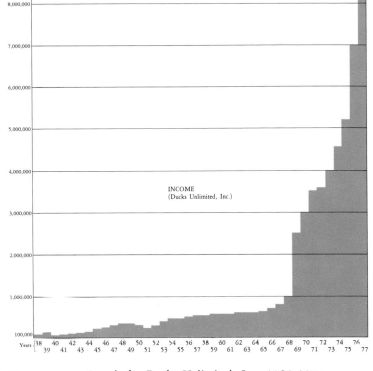

Money sent to Canada by Ducks Unlimited, Inc. 1938-1977.

Patrick Plante as Provincial Biologist in March, and a Provincial Engineer, Paul Beauchemin, in June.

With this expansion, the company became a truly coast to coast organization.

The office was in Laperle's home until June 1, 1976, when it was moved to St. Jean, just outside Montreal. The Quebec government gave financial assistance in establishing the office, and in translating and printing the Ducks Unlimited brochure into French, which was of enormous public relations benefit.

The French translation of the Ducks Unlimited name was originally to be Canard Atout, roughly "ducks are trump". However, at a Directors' Meeting in Regina on March 5, 1977, it was decided that the literal translation, "Canards Illimités", would best facilitate our operations in Quebec.

On September 9, 1973, Ducks Unlimited (Canada) reached another milestone when the 25th million dollar was sent to Canada by Ducks Unlimited, Inc.

At the end of 1977, a total of 1,462 projects had been built, of which 1,373 are still functional. Almost 2.6 million acres of land have been secured under lease or reservation to Ducks Unlimited, and of this, 1,478,614 acres of waterfowl habitat with 10,112 miles of shoreline have been developed.

The Directors

11

For the most part, this has been the story of the people who made the company go — those who initiated and carried out the programs to achieve the objectives assigned to them. But behind it all were the directors, who, though not as visible, accepted the responsibility of assuring that the money entrusted to Ducks Unlimited (Canada) was wisely spent for the purpose for which it was intended. Throughout the minutes of the corporation, the firm quiet control by the directors is obvious. And when a crisis arose, a strong figure always emerged to deal with it. The directors have kept the company on a steady path toward its goal. Seeming deviations from that path have been sharply challenged and sometimes rejected.

The relationship between directors and management was established when T. C. Main was first hired and has changed little since. The directors, and particularly the American directors, knew what they wanted done, and hired Tom Main to do it. Through the years this basic relationship between directors and staff has continued. A fine camaraderie has always existed, emanating from a mutual desire to achieve the objectives of the company.

The directors, officers, and committees throughout the history of the company are listed in Appendix IV. These people, at their own expense, gave their valuable time to guide the organization. Originally there were to be eight directors. In 1939, this was increased to 10, in 1941 to 12, in 1943 to 18, and in 1944 to 30, though for many years not all vacancies were filled on the larger board.

In July, 1972, a review of the company by-laws by directors White, Lyon, and Pitblado, not only revealed that they had been set up so soundly that they required no amendments, but also that there was no restriction on the number of directors who could be appointed. Additional directors were then added from a broad spectrum of business and professional experience to adequately reflect the geographic expansion of the company and provide a good age balance within the board. There were 50 directors in 1977. Of these, 15 were American and one Mexican.

In 1960, the position of Honorary Life Member was established for retired directors who wished to remain associated with the organization. Chief Justice Martin, President in 1955 and 1956, was the first so elected.

The members of the first board of directors were well chosen to get the new company started. L. H. Barkhausen, H. W. Story, and A. M. Bartley, the Americans who attended the first meeting in Winnipeg on April 1 and 2, 1938, brought the enthusiasm and determination of the sponsoring organization with them, which was equally matched by their Canadian counterparts, W. G. Ross and James A. Richardson. These five men translated a grand concept into action.

All presidents of Ducks Unlimited (Canada) have been Canadians and the first, W. G. (Bill) Ross, was, in Ed Pitblado's words, "a dynamo". A dedicated westerner from Moose Jaw, his fighting speech on wetlands and soil conservation while a member of the Saskatchewan Legislative Assembly, had been widely quoted in both Canada and the United States. He was also a past president of the Saskatchewan Fish and Game League.

James A. Richardson of Winnipeg had been keenly interested in conservation and waterfowl for many years. According to Tom Main's memoirs, Richardson and the Winnipeg based Canadian Conservation Institute, had been influential in inaugurating the Prairie Farm Rehabilitation Act, passed in 1935 to preserve and develop the water and land resources of Western Canada, then in the grip of drought. Through his company's chain of radio stations across the west, Richardson provided wide free publicity for the new company for two and a half years. Richardson's death in June, 1939, was a great loss to Ducks Unlimited, and to the cause of conservation generally. His com-

THE PRESIDENTS
Regretfully, picture of the late S. S. Holden, President 1945 and 1946,
is not available.

Judge William G. Ross
1938, 1939 and 1947

O. Leigh Spencer
1940, 1941, and 1942

William C. Fisher
1943 and 1944

Dr. Walter F. Tisdale
1948 and 1949

Judge Louis T. McKim
1950 and 1951

Col. William F. W. Hancock, O.B.E.
1952 and 1953

Gordon E. Konantz
1954

Chief Justice W. M. Martin
1955 and 1956

Richard H. G. Bonnycastle
1957, 1958, 1959 and 1960

Fred Auger
1961 and 1962

Dr. W. Kenneth Martin
1963, 1964, 1966 and 1968

Robert A. Kramer
1965

F. S. Sharpe
1967

Lorne M. Cameron
1969 and 1970

Robert A. White
1971 and 1972

R. O. A. Hunter
1973 and 1974

Duncan M. Jessiman
1975 and 1976

Hugh H. Mackay
1977 and 1978

Will J. Reid.

pany, however, has continued its interest in Ducks Unlimited through the years, generously contributing the boardroom for annual and executive committee meetings. Two of its top executives, L. M. Cameron and R. O. A. Hunter, have been presidents of Ducks Unlimited (Canada).

O. Leigh Spencer, although he was unable to attend the inaugural meeting, was Editor of the Calgary Herald and provided excellent exposure for the new company, particularly through his editorial pages, both before and after operations actually began. S. S. Holden of Ottawa, who was also unable to attend, was well known and influential at the federal government level and had been helpful, before he became a director, in obtaining the charter for the company.

L. H. Barkhausen of Chicago remained a central and energetic figure in both Ducks Unlimited, Inc., of which he was president in 1939, and Ducks Unlimited (Canada). He was a member of the Canadian board and a regular attendant from the original meeting until his death in 1962.

Harold W. Story had a similar long tenure as a Canadian director. B. F. Greer, the other original director, was from California and did not attend the meeting. He resigned at the end of 1942.

Arthur M. Bartley was a director of Ducks Unlimited (Canada) from 1938 until he retired in 1962. He was the senior executive officer in Ducks Unlimited throughout the same period except for two years during the war.

Through the early years and well into the mid-1950's, American directors were frequent visitors to Canada, occasionally during the hunting season. Sterling and Leitch recall many days afield with Lou Barkhausen and his long time friend, Snick Gross from Green Bay, Wisconsin, also a former president of Ducks Unlimited, Inc. The constant repartee between these two close friends was continually amusing. In one particular instance

on a long walk after sharp-tailed grouse, Snick ran out of shells. Lou refused to give him any of his, saying that any damn fool who would leave the car without enough shells shouldn't be shooting anyway!

Will J. Reid, an influential Trustee from Long Beach, California, became a director of Ducks Unlimited (Canada) in 1943, and was a regular visitor to Canada, particularly Alberta. Rennie Harley and his wife, Betty, recall these visits with much pleasure, except for an idiosyncrasy of Reid's which dictated that anything killed had to be used, preferably at once. Betty remembers, with *no* great pleasure, being huddled in the open beside a culvert, while birds were cooked over an open fire to be eaten right on location. Rennie sums it up this way, probably generously, "Sometimes it was good — sometimes it wasn't."

Another frequent visitor was A. C. Glassell from Shreveport, Louisiana. He regularly attended the meetings of Ducks Unlimited (Canada) and his emphasis on fencing programs and protection of projects adjacent to larger population centres from overshooting have already been mentioned. "Pops", as he was affectionately known, had wide experience in the petroleum exploration industry. His constant worry was that the "roughnecks", as he called them, who were coming to Canada as the western oil boom got underway, were going to shoot everything in sight. There is no evidence that they were anything else than well-behaved in this regard.

Four presidents served more than the usual two years in office. Judge W. G. Ross 1938, 1939 and 1947, O. Leigh Spencer, 1940 to 1942 inclusive, R. H. G. Bonnycastle from 1957 to 1960 inclusive, and Dr. W. K. Martin 1963, 1964, 1966 and 1968. The Martin family have had a long association with Ducks Unlimited (Canada). The father, Chief Justice W. M. Martin, was first elected to the board in 1943 and was president in 1955 and 1956. He remained an Honorary

Life Member until his death in June of 1970. Ken Martin is still an active member of the board.

Also of interest is the fact that in 1940, John Bracken, while Premier of Manitoba, was keenly interested in Ducks Unlimited and a member of the board from 1940 to 1943 inclusive. Sterling R. Lyon, a board member since 1972, became Premier of Manitoba in 1977.

Another active long term member of the board was R. M. Gaylord of Rockford, Illinois, who also served a very successful term as president of Ducks Unlimited, Inc. He was elected to the Canadian board in 1953 and served through 1973. Deeply interested in waterfowl and Ducks Unlimited, his business acumen and incisive mind greatly helped the board and management cope with the many problems of a rapidly expanding organization.

Henry G. Schmidt was also an outstanding president of Ducks Unlimited, Inc., and, as a director of Ducks Unlimited (Canada) from 1965 to 1974, he brought the same sound reasoning to decisions of the board.

The role of R. H. G. Bonnycastle in bringing the company under firmer administrative and fiscal control beginning in the late 1950's, has already been described. President Lorne Cameron was faced with similar problems at the end of the 1960's and demonstrated once more that in a time of crisis, the president and the board have always been capable of strong, positive action.

Bonnycastle began the practice of holding occasional Executive Committee Meetings in the field. Under Cameron, this became an established part of the regular board program. Meeting sites were chosen in different provinces, often near large potential projects which would require a major decision by the board.

The interaction with the field staff in these situations has been beneficial in both directions. The directors have been given a better insight into problems at the field level, while the fieldmen have come to know the directors on a personal and human basis, rather than as an impersonal list of names.

Fieldmen privileged to attend Executive Committee Meetings held in their areas have invariably been impressed by the sincerity and enthusiasm of the directors, and the efficient businesslike way in which meetings are conducted. Such experiences have strengthened trust in their leaders and pride in working for a well-run organization.

The rapid increase in income in the last decade, which is forecast to continue into the future, necessitated not only a significant increase in board members to handle the additional work load, but also an increase in the number of committees. The only regular committees struck off at the annual meetings up to 1963 were the Finance Committee and the Executive Committee. Until 1957, even these committees rarely met. Arthur Bartley, as Executive Director, fulfilled the supervisory function of the Executive Committee between annual meetings. In 1963, a Management Sub-Committee of the Executive Committee was formed, which met monthly. This continued until 1967 when regular meetings of the entire Executive Committee were substituted.

A Personnel and Staff Benefits Committee was added in 1973 and, in the following year, Pension Administration and Premises Committees. A Long Range Planning Committee was established in 1976 and produced a new five-year plan for the period 1977 to 1981.

In 1977, more new committees were added: The Biological Research and Evaluation Committee, the Head Office Capital Appeal Committee and the Head Office Building Committee. With the 1978 Ducks Unlimited, Inc. convention to be held in Winnipeg in May of 1978, a large Convention Committee, com-

Directors inspect the proposed Tilley North development, June 10, 1972.

President of Ducks Unlimited, Inc., Lee C. Howley, left, and his Canadian counterpart, Robert A. White, President of Ducks Unlimited (Canada) at gadwall nest on Tilley North Project.

R. M. Gaylord, right, and D. S. Morrison admire Angus Shortt painting given him by the Board of Ducks Unlimited (Canada) in recognition of his long and valued service. June 22, 1974, The Pas, Manitoba.

Directors at the Johnston River Project, Prince Edward Island during Executive Committee meeting September 8, 1973.

posed of directors resident in Winnipeg, was an obvious necessity.

The wide experience of the directorate in business management and finance enabled the company to pass with remarkable ease and efficiency from a relatively small to a much expanded operation. Some of the problems involved in this expansion can be appreciated when it is realized that, of the $48,246,871 sent to Ducks Unlimited (Canada) to the end of 1977, 78% has been sent in the last ten years, and 71% since 1970!

This period of rapid expansion began during the presidency of L. M. Cameron, 1969 to 1970, and accelerated through the successive tenures of R. A. White, R. O. A. Hunter, D. M. Jessiman, and continues into that of H. H. Mackay. It brought the problems of spending a rapidly increasing budget efficiently with limited experienced staff, while at the same time acquiring and training additional good people for an anticipated continuing program increase. The magnitude of the problem can be appreciated when it is realized that the permanent staff more than doubled between 1972 and 1977.

Both the directors and senior management are to be commended that the additional staff was wisely acquired and the quality of the organization undiluted.

With increased funding and thereby the capacity for undertaking larger projects, the officers and directors were then faced with major financial decisions on a scale not previously experienced. These included the Tilley A and B and Extension in southern Alberta costing $800,000; the Cumberland project totalling $3.3 million; and the $800,000 Chaplin Marsh, the latter two developments in Saskatchewan.

The reorganization and rebuilding of the board of directors by Lorne Cameron in 1969 and 1970 was an essential step toward making these major decisions. He also inaugurated the striking Ducks Unlimited (Canada) logo. Recently, he vigorously spearheaded the search for new and better quarters for the organization in Winnipeg and energetically chairs the Head Office Capital Appeal Committee to pay for the building.

Robert A. White, during his presidency of 1971-1972, found himself involved in delicate decisions relative to British Columbia staff changes, and in the controversial move of the provincial office from Victoria to Kamloops.

In addition to the problems of expansion, exemplified by the first $3 million annual budget and the 25th million dollar sent to Canada in September of 1973, R. O. A. Hunter, President 1973-1974, recalls the official establishment of the Special Projects Team as a particular highlight of his tenure. One of the major problems was the consolidation of new staff. Of particular pleasure were the opportunities to chair the dinner honoring Edward B. Pitblado and the retirement party for Angus H. Shortt.

Duncan M. Jessiman, President 1975-1976, saw the company, with expansion into Quebec, become a truly national organization. History was made in October, 1975, when ground was first broken for the Cumberland project, Ducks Unlimited's largest project to date and a critical test of professional expertise. Again increased staffing was a problem.

H. H. Mackay, elected president in 1977, became the first president from the Maritimes.

There is no doubt that Ducks Unlimited has received excellent guidance from the board of directors all through its history. Members of the Executive Committee in Winnipeg have been faithful attendants at the monthly meetings. In addition to those who have been officers, out of town members G. F. Dunn, Dr. H. Cowburn, and R. K. Moore have made a particular effort to attend the more important meetings and field trips. Rather than diminishing, enthusiasm has increased in recent years, and

Dr. Ken Martin, left, calls ducks for Charles B. Allen at dedication of Allen Project, June 10, 1970.

Mellon — Pennsylvania dedication. Left, F. R. (Rudy) Etchen, S. Prosser Mellon, Constance P. Mellon, Lt. General Richard K. Mellon, June 25, 1969.

A group of Ohionans at the Ohio Lakes dedication, including, second from left, Henry G. Schmidt, Lee C. Howley, and second from right, Dale E. Whitesell, Executive Vice-President, Ducks Unlimited Inc., July 10, 1968.

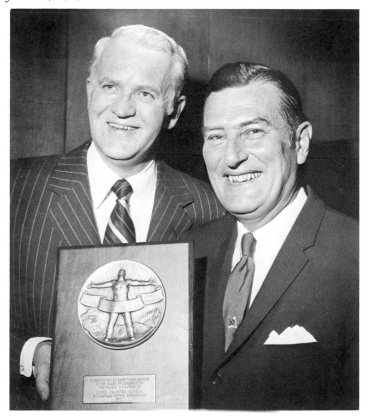

Right, Lorne M. Cameron, President, Ducks Unlimited (Canada), accepts 1970 American Motors Conservation Award from L. Rice, President. Winnipeg, December 17, 1970.

Gaylord Donnelley, President, Ducks Unlimited, Inc. and Duncan Jessiman, President, Ducks Unlimited (Canada) at field Executive Committee meeting, Yorkton, Saskatchewan, September 18, 1976.

Dale E. Whitesell, Executive Vice President, Ducks Unlimited, Inc., left, with Keith C. Russell, Regional Vice President, East Central Mississippi Flyway, and Robert D. Marcotte, Senior Vice President, Central Flyway, at Yorkton meeting.

Kahler Martinson, Chief, Management and Enforcement, U.S. Fish and Wildlife Service, Nathaniel P. Reed, Associate Secretary for Wildlife and Parks, U.S. Dept. of the Interior, Charles Carrothers, Ducks Unlimited, Inc., and William K. duPont, Senior Vice President, Policy, Programs and Liaison, Ducks Unlimited, Inc. at The Pas, Manitoba, July 12, 1971, while on inspection of Ducks Unlimited projects and habitat conditions.

St. Andrews River — Massachusetts dedication September 10, 1977. Left: Matthew B. Connolly Jr., Director, Massachusetts Division of Fisheries and Wildlife; Henry J. Nave, President, Ducks Unlimited, Inc., Vincent J. MacLean, Minister of Lands and Forests, Nova Scotia; Hugh H. Mackay, President, Ducks Unlimited (Canada).

with the excellent presidential material available on the board, augurs well for the future.

Increased interest and participation by the American Directors on the Canadian Board has also characterized the recent years. Lee C. Howley, Herman Taylor, Jr., and Gaylord Donnelley, successive presidents of Ducks Unlimited, Inc., faithfully attended the annual meetings of Ducks Unlimited

(Canada) and were frequently present at important executive meetings, as were Robert D. Marcotte and J. C. D. Bailey.

Their expression of the American viewpoint and their experience in dealing with major business problems similar to those confronting the Canadian Board were of great assistance to the Canadian directorate during the recent difficult years of expansion and reorganization.

Edward B. Pitblado, left, receives special plaque from R. O. A. Hunter, President of Ducks Unlimited (Canada) honoring his 36 years as Secretary for the corporation. Harvey K. Nelson, United States Fish and Wildlife Service, seated at right. June 16, 1973.

Ducks Unlimited (Canada) Directors meet in the James Richardson boardroom to plan the next year's operation. Counter-clockwise, beginning at left, Cameron, Whitesell, Percival, Cranstoun, Malaher, Rattray, Martin, Hellofs, Molgat, Donnelley, Bawden, Moore, McCusker, White, Schmidt, Jessiman, Purves, Groff, Pitblado, Morrison.

Canadian Co-operation

12

Ducks Unlimited could never have achieved the success that it has without the co-operation of the Canadian people and their governments.

Although its charter includes the right to own land, it must have been clear to T. C. Main at the very beginning that if the company were to make any inroads on the problems that it faced, the full co-operation of Canadians in the use of land was essential.

Consequently, his first move was to obtain the co-operation of the prairie governments. As previously described, he had little difficulty persuading them to grant the use of Crown lands, free of charge or taxes, to develop waterfowl habitat.

Without this co-operation the company would never have been able to develop the hundreds of thousands of acres of wetlands in the Saskatchewan River Delta of Manitoba, the Cumberland Marshes in Saskatchewan, or the Hay Lakes in Alberta.

Nowhere in the minutes of the corporation or in the correspondence reviewed is there evidence of a directive to Main on land policy. It emerged from a rational analysis of the situation. The policy of land tenure by free easement rather than purchase evolved as a field modus operandi, supported and enforced by the directors, but never formally initiated or adopted.

This operational policy worked because landowners, particularly in the early years with the memory of the drought still painfully clear, were eager to restore and preserve their wetlands. In many instances, land was proffered because it was in the owner's interest to have an assured water supply. However, in a surprising number of cases, they wanted water for the greenery and wildlife it would bring to the prairie landscape. Early agreements were verbal, and a handshake the bond. It was not until after the war that formal agreements were signed with landowners. Through all that time, verbal agreements had been

NINA LAKE
ERNIE SIMMONS MEMORIAL PROJECT
BUILT 1970 BY DUCKS UNLIMITED (CANADA)
NAMED IN HONOR OF
ERNEST P. SIMMONS SR.
OF OLATHE, KANSAS, U.S.A.
FUNDS PROVIDED BY HIS SPORTSMEN FRIENDS
OF THE WESTERN MISSOURI CHAPTER,
DUCKS UNLIMITED INC.

CONSTRUCTION OF THIS PROJECT
MADE POSSIBLE BY CO-OPERATION OF
THE FOLLOWING:
RURAL MUNICIPAL COUNCIL OF SIGLUNES
AND
ADOLF FREEMAN, FRANK JOHNSON,
GORDON KERNESTED, GISLI SIGFUSSON AND
JOHN SIGURDSON ALL OF OAKVIEW AND
SIMUNDUR HALLSON OF VOGAR.

Co-operation between land owners, municipality and Ducks Unlimited, controls floods on Nina Lake, Manitoba and produces both waterfowl and hay.

Water released to downstream projects from Ducks Unlimited reservoirs near Hanna, Alberta, raises both mallards and beef.

honored. Projects negotiated then and later formalized are still active today after almost four decades. (Appendix VIII)

Without this co-operation of both landowners and governments, Ducks Unlimited would never have got off the ground, for their early budgets were much too small to have any effect on waterfowl habitat if land purchase had been required.

Strong support also came in the public relations area from the Kee-Man organization, which was, and still is, invaluable to the company. In the earliest years, when waterfowl surveys were more intensive, as many as 3,000 names were on the Kee-Man roll. These men espoused the Ducks Unlimited program and did an outstanding job of publicizing and explaining the objectives of

the new company throughout the prairies. In a remarkably short time its concepts were no longer new and strange. Although the number of Kee-Men is now much reduced, they remain goodwill ambassadors for the company. Some have reported faithfully for almost forty years. (Appendix VII)

Ducks Unlimited has been, and is, people. A few professionals paid to manage and lead, and a host of people of goodwill who believe in the principles of conservation so fittingly defined by E. S. Russenholt many years ago as "the use of resources for the greatest good of the greatest number of people over the longest period of time . . . that it may be well with thee and thou mayest prolong thy days."

Ducks Unlimited Projects bring life and diversity to the landscape. In addition to waterfowl, many other wetland species thrive.

Pelicans.

The ubiquitous Coot.

American Bittern.

Marbled Godwit.

The farmers' friend, the Franklin Gull, at the nest.

First steps on a long road — Avocets.

The Red-Necked Grebe builds a soggy nest.

Long Billed Curlews, sometimes called "Flying Oilcans".

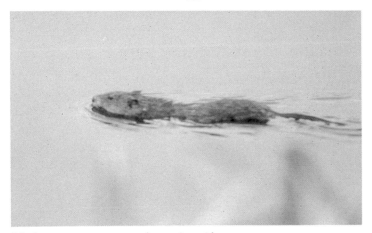

Muskrat — a year around marsh resident.

Moose thrive on northern projects.

213

Broadening Horizons

13

Ducks Unlimited, in both the United States and Canada, originally identified the decline in waterfowl populations with a lack of water on the prairies. Since both organizations began in the last years of the 1930's drought, this was obviously a valid conclusion. It led to an engineering dominated organization oriented to water storage, whose accomplishment was annually measured in terms of the number of acres of water impounded and miles of shoreline developed. This evaluation was tangible, easily measured, readily understandable, and saleable to potential American contributors.

Increasing biological input into project selection and development characterized the postwar years. But it was not until the last decade that habitat development, based on the total biological requirements of breeding waterfowl, was given equal footing with water storage and control. The Long Range Plan recognizes this increasing emphasis on management, and the 1977 budget allocated almost $350,000 to it.

The earlier years were "acquisition years" with emphasis on securing as much habitat as possible and intensive management postponed to an indefinite future. A future which, with increasing budgets, is now beginning to arrive.

Beginning in 1976, the company began a program of triennial biological project inspections. These are primarily for evaluation, but from them will emerge development programs to improve waterfowl production. Water manipulations to increase or control emergent vegetation and submerged aquatics, level ditching to open out heavy cover where no water manipulation is possible, improvement of nesting cover, and island construction are all tools for greater waterfowl production.

The horizon now broadens further toward the management of all waterfowl habitat in Canada for maximum production, whether under easement or lease to the company or not. Management programs to improve waterfowl production from Crown or private lands where Ducks Unlimited has no water control are as valid as for our own projects. Peat wetlands on the northern edge of agriculture are an excellent example. These seem secure from further agricultural encroachment. Development techniques to improve the present low production from them have significant long range potential benefits for waterfowl.

In essence, Western Canada, for example, would become one big project, managed to produce as many waterfowl as possible commensurate with other land uses.

This concept is now manifest in the appointment of an Agricultural Extension Biologist to work intensively with the agricultural community. His first priority is to evaluate the impact of agricultural activities on waterfowl production, and then to develop and promote modifications of agricultural practices which are in the farmers' economic interest but which, when adopted, will indirectly benefit waterfowl.

The urgency of such a program was emphasized by the relatively poor reproductive success of waterfowl during the good water years of 1969 to 1976. What should have been outstanding production years were, except for 1969, no better than mediocre, in terms of the high reproductive potential of waterfowl. Waterfowl appeared to be incapable of reproducing successfully in the face of intensifying agriculture.

There is a good deal of hope that changes in agricultural practice now in sight will benefit waterfowl. Such new techniques as zero tillage and increased acreage of winter wheat under zero tillage farming practices have real possibilities, not only for greater waterfowl production, but in the case of winter wheat, a decrease in crop depredation and its attendant political problems.

Basic changes in agricultural practices will not take place overnight. But a strong possibility exists that they will occur, and therein lies the great hope for the future of waterfowl.

Photo by B. N. Verbiwski.

To guide the company through the period of expanding horizons, to evolve and apply new techniques, and then evaluate them, requires a significant increase in the research activities of the organization. Much will be catalytic — stimulating other organizations to carry out research essential to Ducks Unlimited — but our own program will have to fill in where gaps occur.

In the forty years since its inception, the company has come a long way. Although the techniques have changed, the objective has not. It remains steadfastly committed, with a "Singleness of Purpose", to the preservation and increase of the waterfowl resource — through maintaining and developing habitat, and influencing for the benefit of waterfowl, all factors affecting them.

Acres of water and miles of shoreline are a poor and inadequate measure of the impact of Ducks Unlimited on the water-fowl resource, as it is hoped this history has revealed. What the company has stimulated others to do is intangible, but of much greater importance. Through their activities the value of waterfowl as a renewable resource has become recognized as it would never have been otherwise. Attitudes thus developed toward waterfowl have stimulated similar attitudes toward all wildlife species.

The author retired on December 31, 1977, after spending virtually his entire working life with the company. In retrospect, he feels privileged to have participated in a crusade begun by a small group of dedicated men, confident and determined to succeed, and carried on by following generations of similarly dedicated people in the field, the office and in the directorate.

He would have had it no other way.

Appendix I

THE CHAIRMAN: At the head table tonight we have a young man who is no stranger to Winnipeg or any part of Western Canada, even as far north as Great Slave Lake.

The son of Dwight Huntington—whose name is well known to most of you, not only as an author of books on game and game conservation but also as the father of the game breeding management movement in North America—actually at a time when such practices were illegal throughout the whole of the United States. Even as far back as 50 years ago Dwight Huntington, as the result of his part in scientific expeditions into the Northwest, foresaw the disappearance of game before the advance of civilization, not only in the Northwestern States, but even in our prairie Provinces. Consequently upon his activities game breeding laws have long since been enacted in one state after another.

Little wonder then that our guest should follow in his father's footsteps after serving overseas as Lieutenant-Commander in the Navy—where he served with the Allied fleets in European waters, participating in the occupation of Baltic Sea ports after the Armistice.

Indeed he is soon filling his father's shoes in game breeding and management work and in editing game magazines. In 1929 he founded the Game Conservation Institute in New Jersey, an experimental game farm and game management school where 250 farm youths were able to take a free two-year course in game bird restoration. The standard of this work can best be guaged when I tell you that most of these students are now in charge of Federal and State Game Farms.

In 1930 the sponsors of the More Game Birds in America Foundation induced him to accept the Vice-Presidency, and so sought after were his services that they were loaned to President Roosevelt's Committee on Wildlife Restoration—which committee, in 1934, drew up a wildlife restoration plan—providing, in part, for the present migratory waterfowl refuge system on which over $20,000,000 has already been spent.

Any wonder then that our guest should wing his way to Canada in 1935, determined to obtain accurate information on ducks—their range—breeding areas—quantities and what not. A mercy flight of some 38,000 miles.

As a result of that survey Ducks Unlimited was conceived—But he will tell you the story.

Gentlemen, I present to you John C. Huntington of New York—the Ducks' "Santa Claus."

MR. JOHN C. HUNTINGTON.

Mr. Chairman, Premier Bracken, Fellow Sportsmen:

It is a very real pleasure to me to be with you to-night and I want you to know how sincerely I appreciate the opportunity of being here.

Your Chairman has asked me to state briefly the main objectives of "Ducks Unlimited". I shall attempt to do this, in the hope that by so doing, I may contribute to that understanding of the problem involved in wild duck restoration which is so essential to success in a project of this magnitude—a project of such great economic, social and aesthetic importance to the people of Canada, the United States and Mexico.

The Wild Duck Factory

Since time immemorial the major portion of the wild duck crop of the North American continent has been produced in the vast mid-continental prairie region which extends from the sand hills of Nebraska up through the Dakotas, Minnesota and eastern Montana embracing most of the Provinces of Alberta, Saskatchewan and Manitoba and extending into the Northwest Territories to the southern shore of Great Slave Lake. This country to-day, although the southern two-thirds of it has virtually been ruined from a duck producing point of view, is still producing the bulk of the continental duck crop and always will.

Nature made this area the great wild duck factory and I doubt whether any of us will ever improve on nature when it comes to the production of wild life.

Of course there are other places on the North American continent where ducks breed but that area is the main factory, producing from 65 to 80 per cent of the ducks of the whole continent.

Depletion of Duck Crop

Starting some fifty years ago, agricultural operations in the northwestern States ruined that portion of the wild duck factory lying within our borders by draining marsh lands and drying up the small water areas which

ducks must have for breeding purposes. Thus started the downward trend in our continental duck supply which has continued uninterruptedly ever since.

Starting about twenty years ago with the development of Western Canada, and with the intensive way you went in for agriculture, what we had done to the ducks in our Northwestern States, that is, in the Southern portion of the breeding range, was repeated up here. In other words, marshes were drained, the small water areas dried up, with the result to-day, the sole remaining unspoiled breeding ground of major importance for ducks on the American continent is roughly north of your 53rd parallel and south of Great Slave Lake.

Only recently have we learned that when we destroy wild life environment in any area we soon render that area unfit for human habitation.

Conservationists Secure Action

For years, those who took the trouble to inform themselves on what was happening to the water fowl resources on the North American continent, were aware of the situation. But it was not until 1916 that official recognition was given to the subject. The signing of the Migratory Bird Convention Act for the protection of migratory birds between Canada and the United States was the first general recognition of the serious depletion of this great international resource and marked the first step in international co-operation looking toward the preservation and restoration of migratory birds.

Unfortunately, we in the United States did not take hold immediately of that programme to the extent we have in recent years. However, starting in 1918 we have progressively reduced the kill of ducks in the United States until to-day the sportsmen tell me we virtually prohibit the shooting of ducks.

Wild Life Restoration Committee

In 1934 President Roosevelt appointed a committee to study the subject of Wildlife Restoration and to make a report to him. It was my privilege and honour to work on that committee and as a result of a report filed by that committee a national programme for wildlife preservation was approved by the President. In the two following years approximately

$21,000,000 was appropriated or allocated for the work recommended by that committee. In the committee report we stressed the need for making a prompt start on the restoration of duck breeding grounds in the United States. As a result of that some $18,000,000 has already been spent and the programme will be virtually completed in about two years' time. It will require about $5,000,000 more, which the president has already promised to make available for that purpose.

When that programme is complete we will produce in the United States about 20,000,000 ducks a year, which is about four times the present production but still far short of the needs for decent shooting.

Wild Duck Census Alarming

In 1935, the More Game Birds Foundation, with which I am connected, made the first serious attempt to find out how many ducks we had on the American continent. That work, known as the International Wild Duck Census, was conducted with the co-operation of the Game Departments in the States and your Game Departments here. It was a very interesting work and it gave us a complete picture of the prairie duck situation.

When our own programme in the United States is complete, the Federal Government will own most of the worthwhile former duck producing areas in the States. I do not mean by that, that we will have restored all of the duck breeding areas we have destroyed because that is far from true, but we will have restored the best breeding grounds which are capable of restoration at the present time.

Programme of "Ducks Unlimited"

It is obvious, however, if, as I have stated, 80% roughly of the ducks on the continent are produced in Canada, that if we ever want to restore the continental duck population, we must do so up here.

The "Ducks Unlimited" programme is a five year programme which will cost $3,000,000. The sportsmen of the United States are to a large extent the beneficiaries of the wild duck crops produced in Canada and for that reason we think it is fair, in co-operation with the people up here, that we pay the cost of that programme.

"Ducks Unlimited" has been incorporated as a non-profit corporation under the laws of the Dominion of Canada and will be governed by a Board of eight directors, four from Canada and four from the United States. The directors will be outstanding business and professional men who are serving without pay, men who have a keen interest in this particular phase of wildlife restoration and who are willing to devote their business talents to this project without remuneration of any kind.

As to the programme itself, it might best briefly be described as a major restoration project. Certainly no one can improve on nature when it comes to the production of wildlife crops, particularly ducks. The programme embraces the acquisition of a certain amount of land, land unproductive and which to-day is virtually useless for any other purpose. In addition to the acquisition of worn out and comparatively useless land the programme will seek to greatly increase the annual duck crops by reducing very materially what we call the preventable losses. I do not need to tell you sportsmen there is a tremendous wastage in the production of any wildlife crop from the egg to the mature bird. Crows, disease, and many other factors

mean fewer ducks, but if these conditions are corrected the duck supply will be greatly increased.

Preservation and Restoration the Keys

This programme will seek to materially increase the duck crop in the north country, first, preserving what we have, and, secondly, building up other areas which are suitable for duck production. In the drought-stricken area the problem is almost wholly one of restoration which will be of tremendous benefit to agriculture as well as to the ducks. We in the United States feel that we have made the first step in putting our own house in order, first by materially reducing the kill which has been substantially curtailed in recent years. Our kill this year probably was not over 50% of any previous year. Having done that and having started on the restoration programme to the point where we can definitely see maximum production in the United States we are endeavouring to extend the work up here in a way that will benefit not only our own sportsmen but will materially benefit the sportsmen of the three prairie provinces. I wish to emphasize with all the power at my command that in financing the restoration of duck breeding grounds in Western Canada, sportsmen of the United States are interested in one thing and ONLY one thing—more ducks coming down in to the States each year.

And now I would be very short-sighted indeed if I failed to take this opportunity to express my appreciation of the co-operation extended by the Governments of the three provinces and to the people in all walks of life who co-operated in the 1935 International Wild Duck Census and made possible the successful outcome of that great project. Thank you.

(Applause)

THE CHAIRMAN:

Fellow Sportsmen, we also have with us to-night, an outstanding Canadian Wildlife enthusiast—a man from our sister Province of Saskatchewan—a man who, in his spare time, has been known to practice law, a King's Counsellor. At one time President of the Saskatchewan Fish and Game League, we now find him Honorary President of that organization; he is one of the Saskatchewan members of the Interprovincial Council of Western Fish & Game Associations; he is President and organizer of the Saskatchewan Field Trials; a Director of the American Wildlife Institute; one

who has largely contributed to the organization in Saskatchewan of some 20,000 children as Junior Sportsmen in Square Shooters Clubs. For seven years, he has pleaded the cause of Wildlife in the Saskatchewan legislature and, believe it or not, has converted both Government and opposition members. As an author and lecturer in the prairie areas, he has exerted and still is exerting a tremendous influence in wildlife matters.

A man who has agreed to serve without remuneration as one of the Canadian Directors of Ducks Unlimited.

I introduce to you Western Canada's No. I Wildlife Champion—Mr. W. G. (better known as "Bill") Ross, of Moose Jaw.

MR. W. G. ROSS, K.C. (Moose Jaw).

Mr. Chairman, Mr. Premier, Honourable members of the Government and gentlemen, I want to tell you that I am at a disadvantage at the present minute after listening to this recommendation or life history, whatever it was, that Ed. Pitblado gave to me. I find I am going to have quite a time living up to even a small portion of it. As a matter of fact when he was going over it I thought, perhaps, it very much resembled my friend, Ed.

Pitblado, returning from a fishing trip and describing some of the fish that he had caught, only in this case I happen to be the fish.

I want to congratulate the Manitoba Fish and Game League on the wonderful gathering you have here to-night. It is certainly encouraging to every one of us, those of us who have taken some interest in the matter of wild life conservation during the past few years, as your meeting here to-night is typical of many others I have attended the last month or so. In each case I have been able to tell those people that their meeting was the best meeting I have ever attended because each one of them was at least twice the size they used to be three or four years ago, and I think my friend, Mr. Huntington, can go back to the Atlantic Coast and to those men that are subscribing this fund of ours and he can tell them we are very deeply interested in the project he is bringing to us and in the conservation of our own natural resources.

We are very fortunate in having with us John Huntington, the acting President of "More Game Birds in America Incorporated". Mr. Huntington has come to us as that very distinguished chief of the Republic to the south of us has said, he has come to us as a good neighbour. He is in the position to offer us some help at a time when we need help very badly and I want to tell him on my own behalf and I think on your behalf as well that we appreciate very, very much indeed the action the sportsmen of the United States have taken in endeavouring to provide us with some money with which to do some work up here.

Wildlife Resources a Trust

You know when we came to the western country, whether you came as an immigrant or whether you were born in it as I was born, you and I received a very great national asset in our wildlife resources. We did not get an absolute title to those resources but we received them in trust, to administer them, not to dissipate them. We are entitled to use the increase or the interest on that capital but we must be in a position, if we are going to remain true to the trust that is imposed upon us, of being able to hand those resources over to our sons and our daughters and those who come after us intact and in a condition in which they can use them. (applause) I am not so sure that we have been fulfilling that trust. When the Great War came along there was a most intense demand for wheat. Our farmers were encouraged to grow more and more of it; the rancher was pushed off into one corner, into corners that were too small for him. Sometimes he even

turned his own plough into his pasture field and turned up acres in which a plough should never have been put at any time. There has been over-pasturage. There has been too much sheep ranching in the country I have come from—I do not think you have so much of it here—too much uncontrolled sheep ranching.

Desert Conditions Threaten West

In your country and perhaps south, the southwestern portion, there is every evidence in the world that erosion is taking place there in the same way it is taking place in the dust bowl of the United States. A lot of it has gone back to desert and where sporadic attempts at cultivation have failed mother nature is doing her best to cover her bosom with a covering of jackpine, ordinarily known as the Russian thistle.

In southwestern Manitoba, in southern Saskatchewan and Southern Alberta we have an area of 60,000,000 acres that is situated in what is potentially a drought area, the short grass country of the North American continent, the northern half of the North American basin and it is potentially a dust bowl such as we have to the south of us at the present time.

The Remedy

The whole problem so far as we are concerned as conservationists is this, whether individuals or groups of individuals that we call governments can be made to see that the proper steps are taken to stave off the day of complete destruction of that short grass prairie country. Science can clear up the causes but science cannot solve the problem. The solution depends on the application of scientific principles plus labour, and labour can only be obtained and used when it has management to guide it and capital to pay for it. It seems very certain that our Provincial Departments of Agriculture and our Dominion Department of Agriculture have a very complete knowledge of the problems and the causes and the methods of solution but it is not at all certain that even 15% of the members of our prairie legislatures and perhaps only 10% of the members of the Dominion Parliament appreciate the seriousness of the problem and the difficulty in solution. The Premier of Saskatchewan said the other day, on his return from Eastern Canada, that he was absolutely amazed at the ignorance displayed by certain members from the Eastern part of Canada in the Dominion House as to the manner in which people live west of the Great Lakes. Preventative work would have proceeded more rapidly and will proceed more rapidly if there

is a more general appreciation throughout the whole of Canada of the difficulty that we are in at the present time and the possibilities of its removal.

My friend, John Vallance, the senior Rehabilitation officer under the prairie farmers Rehabilitation Act, has one of the biggest jobs that there is on this continent to perform and if he stays on the job as long as he lives and as efficiently as he can perform the work, successors will have to be appointed for him because this fight to save the prairie areas in the west is a long and continuous one.

Droughts Will Recur

Conditions as to rainfall will no doubt improve; we expect they will improve, but just as sure as we are all in this room to-night we are going to strike another drought period inside of perhaps, two, four, five, ten years, that will be perhaps as serious as the one we have gone through. Science will demand a continuous search for the grains and grasses that will be prolific with a minimum of moisture and rainfall; it will demand the maximum of service from the short grass natural to the country and the proper allocation and the number and kind of animals that are permitted to graze on that land. Science will demand control in every possible manner of the available water supplies of this country.

Rehabilitation Act Effective

I want to say the greatest possible credit should be given to the Right Honourable R. B. Bennett for placing on the statute books the Prairie Farm Rehabilitation Act. Many of us may wish he had given it to us in 1931 instead of 1935. I may say that every credit in the world is due to the present Government of Canada for doing what governments do not very often do, namely, adopting the policy of their predecessor and carrying on the work Mr. Bennett commenced, and I may say too that a great many of us wish that the amount of money made available to those in charge of the Prairie Farm Rehabilitation ought to be just as much in 1937 as in 1936.

Coming back to the problem so far as it affects us it is only by the dissemination of a wider knowledge of this difficulty, a greater appreciation of its seriousness that we can get those people in the East who have the money to give us the assistance that is necessary in order to keep this country out here as the bread basket of the British Empire.

Individual Effort Essential

There is another point I want to deal with to-night, everything should not be left to governments to perform. As a matter of fact, I believe and I know you believe, that a great many of us lean too heavily on governments and we have got to get away from it. Private initiative has its work to perform, private initiative and capital must play its part in working out this solution, the small rancher, the land owner and the capitalist must learn to impound his own share of water on his ranch and on his farm. He must learn to plant the proper grains and grasses and he must learn to apply scientific principles of agriculture to his operations. He must see that he is not over-pasturing his land and he must do his best to plant those grasses or those trees or whatever is necessary to stop the soil that is now on the move enlarging to desert that is already on the march, and I suppose to-night among this gathering we have representatives of banks, we have representatives of mortgage companies, we have representatives here of railway companies, and I want to say to those men that they have their part to play just as well as the governments in dealing with this situation.

I want to say now that the greatest credit in the world is due to those United States sportsmen and capitalists who have formed the corporation known as "Ducks Unlimited". Perhaps it might have chosen a better name—I do not know that I like the name myself—but if by the use of that name the sponsors of this organization can go to the sportsmen of the United States and collect $3,000,000 to help us increase our surface water supplies, then we are to be mightily appreciative of the name and mightily appreciative of the efforts of its sponsors.

"Dried Out, Blown Out, Burned Out—No Ducks"

Five years ago Arthur Etter, Game Commissioner in Saskatchewan, sent a somewhat laconic telegram down to the headquarters of the American Game Association in New York. The telegram read thus: "Dried out, blown out, burned out. Stop. No ducks." He told the truth, and your own department in this province has been urging for years on the American Game Conference which used to meet in Washington that it was going to be good economy for those men down there to spend their surplus money on this side of the line because on this side of the line 85% of the whole duck breeding area of the American continent existed and from that time there was some mighty clear thinking done by conservationists south of the International boundary. They recognized that to do an efficient job in protecting one of the greatest industries in the United States it was necessary to look

across the border and to do their work up here, and when the projects which they have under consideration in your province and my province and in the Province of Alberta are completed there will be many thousands of acres of fresh water available not only for ducks but for agriculture; for every form of migratory waterfowl and every variety of domestic and wild plant life as well. The name of the corporation does not adequately describe this work because every dollar that is invested in it by its sponsors in the United States, every cubic foot of earth that is raised, every acre foot of water that is retained, is bound to be productive not only in dividends in ducks but dividends in plant life and in improving the face of the country side. (Applause)

Canadian Corporations Must Chip In

And those American capitalists and this American corporation that are investing their moneys up here with us are setting one of the finest possible examples to Canadian corporations, and I am speaking now of Canadian corporations who make the very handsome profit of seventy-five odd millions of dollars a year that is spent in Canada in the pursuit of game, in ammunition, fishing tackle, boots, gasoline, tires, automobiles, railway fares, food, hotel accommodation and all the different ways in which a sportsman can spend his money, and I submit, Mr. Chairman, for your consideration that it is only reasonable to expect that the example as set by our neighbours to the south will stir and stimulate some of our Canadian corporations into action along similar lines,

Private Game Preserves Barred

Let me deal for the moment, Mr. Chairman, with some of the misguided interpretations which seem to be spreading around the country in regard to the performances and the objects of this corporation known as "Ducks Unlimited". May I say first and may I make it as definite and as clear as I possibly can that it is not the purpose of "Ducks Unlimited" to go up into this country and to create closed private game preserves for American owners or Canadian owners to enjoy to the exclusion of the public. We in western Canada opposed that idea. We believe in sanctuaries, every one of us believe in sanctuaries, but we also believe in this principle in the Dominion of Canada that what is sanctuary for the public must be sanctuary for the private individual as well, whether he is in the inner circle, whether he is rich or poor, whether he is resident or non-resident. I think that this Province of Manitoba and

the Province of Saskatchewan will stand for no other principle but that.

May I make this clear too, that the purpose behind this corporation is not selfishness but the whole purpose is based on this, on that theory of natural science which holds that a marsh without wild fowl and a forest without deer, elk, caribou, moose and a prairie without grouse and partridge and prairie chicken, the antelope and other forms of wild life are indicative of desolation and a disagreeable barrenness that should not be allowed to exist in this country in which we are living.

I realize that there have been prejudices between the two countries involved in the situation but let me tell you it is impossible to build a fence high enough that will keep ducks from flying north into Canada in the spring or to keep them in Canada in the winter time. It is only reasonable that our friends in the United States, when they see a duck shortage coming, when they see it getting worse, when they saw there was a possibility of our wild ducks going the same way as the passenger pigeon, that they wanted to come up here and help us to rectify the situation, and having done that I want to say we ought to welcome them and ought to do everything possible to co-operate with them.

Four Canadian Directors Appointed

Let me make this clear, too, that the control of the situation rests with four Canadian directors, Spencer Holden of Ottawa, James Richardson of Manitoba, Leigh Spencer of Calgary and myself in Saskatchewan. There are only eight directors and there are four of them Canadians, and that Board cannot do anything unless the four Canadian directors agree to it. These men with the four across the line will be responsible for the administration of the funds, they will be responsible for the expenditure of the money, they will be responsible for the future control of the works that are created, and speaking for myself—and I can only speak for myself—you may rest assured that all the rights of Canadians are going to be fully protected and above all that the rights and the privileges of Canadian sportsmen are not going to be unduly restricted any more than they have been in the past unless your Government says that they are going to.

Governments Approve of "Ducks Unlimited"

Now, this must be remembered too, that "Ducks Unlimited" is a non-profit Canadian organization, so much so that the Government at Ottawa are even remitting the ordinary incorporation fees that they would charge us on the filing of our application for a charter. May I make this clear too, that the title to any land we acquire will not be registered in the name of any American donor living south of the boundary line but those titles will be registered in the name of a Canadian corporation, "Ducks Unlimited" or the title will be handed over, perhaps, in some cases to the Crown in the right of the province where the work is being created. May I make that particular point of it clear: I know an instance now, one in particular, where the Dominion Government sent out its cheque to Saskatchewan to build a dam and when the engineers found on going around the area that they could get the consent of every farmer around that dam but one, they stopped and sent that cheque back to Ottawa. "Ducks Unlimited" can step into the picture there; they can go to that farmer and buy an easement on that land or get the title to that land and they can hand it over to the Prairie Farm Rehabilitation or to the Province that happens to be interested. That is why I say that control is in the hands of the Canadian corporation at all times, control is in the hands of the Canadian directors and I resent very much indeed some of the headlines that have appeared in our eastern papers about Yankees coming up here to buy a million acres of land in order to turn them into duck preserves because that is not what they are doing. Now, let me make this clear too, that every foot of water that you have got in the Province of Manitoba, that we have in the Province of Saskatchewan or Alberta is under the control of the Provincial Government. In Saskatchewan we cannot even dig a dugout unless we have got a license from the Government to do so; certainly we cannot build a dam across even a dry ravine unless we have a license to do so under the Water Rights Act and I am sure you have the same regulations in the Province of Manitoba. While my good friend and co-director, Mr. Richardson, may endeavour to control your transportation with his airplanes he cannot even go out and dig a dam that will hold a hundred barrels of water without a license from his government, so that there should be no alarm of any kind whatever that this corporation is going to come up here and tear up the whole country-side independently of the governments that are interested, because they cannot go one step in the way of raising a shovelful of earth in a dam unless they have got the consent of the minister in the Department of Natural Resources.

Governments Supreme Over Game Preserves

There are one or two more points I have got to cover here and one of them is the question of game preserves. I made some passing reference to it a little while ago. May I point out to you that the question of the creation of game preserves is absolutely in the hands of the provincial governments and no matter whether we buy a thousand acres or a million acres with funds of "Ducks Unlimited" we cannot make a game preserve there unless your government and my government or the Alberta government says it shall be a game preserve, and may I point this out too, so far as Manitoba is concerned and you are particularly interested in it because of your basic shooting areas. You have in this province the Netley-Libau marsh and the Delta marsh and Winnipegosis marsh, and those marshes are basic shooting areas, they are perpetual shooting grounds and "Ducks Unlimited" or you or anybody else is not permitted to buy those lands or to convert them into anything else than what they are now, namely, public shooting grounds for the benefit of everybody.

So far as I am concerned as a director of "Ducks Unlimited" I want to make this contention that if "Ducks Unlimited" goes out on the bare prairie and creates a lake or creates a water surface there where no water surface existed before, that we would have every justification in the world in going to the Minister of Mines or the Minister of Natural Resources in that Province and ask that that water be put into a game preserve, but I make this statement as well that where a lake has existed for many years as a free shooting ground for the public, though we may improve it to some extent, that we should not in that case go to the government and ask for those lakes to be turned into preserves.

Will Co-operate With Governments

I hope I have made that part clear, and I want to say this too, gentlemen, before I leave the subject, and that is that it is my hope, and I am sure that it is the hope of those who are my co-directors that this organization is going to work in the closest possible harmony with the Water Rights Department in each one of the prairie provinces and in the closest possible harmony with the Prairie Farm Rehabilitation Act. Your various water rights departments have been doing a noble work with a very little amount of money for the last six or seven years and the Prairie Farm Rehabilitation Act have been doing a lot of work.

They have made their surveys; they would have had their engineers from the road go and do five and six times the work they have done if they had the funds to do it, and I hope "Ducks Unlimited" is going to supply that money. Let me tell you something about this Prairie Farm Rehabilitation Act and what it has done. Since it was organized it has inspected 1,151 projects; it has built 419 dugouts, 567 stop dams, 165 irrigation dams; made 922 plans of work, 1,076 surveys. It has completed 695 projects 100% and 264 projects 50%. It has moved 1,200,000 cubic yards of dirt and 25,000 cubic yards of rip rap with a little more than a quarter of a million dollars. "Ducks Unlimited" must in its own interest work as closely as possible in co-operation with the officials of the Prairie Farm Rehabilitation Act and with the Water Rights Departments of the provincial governments because that is the way in which we can save the maximum amount of money for the maximum throwing up of earth works where they are necessary.

Summary of Objects of "Ducks Unlimited"

May I summarize now some of the objects of the formation of this institution; in close co-operation with the government its purposes are going to be these, one, to increase the permanent surface water supply of the prairie provinces, two, to provide adequate protection for wildlife from all predators. There is no use of us making large areas of water if we are going to let crows and other predators, some four-legged some of them two-legged and some with wings start to make their home on those waters. That would not be good business and we are going to see that is taken care of. The third object is to go into the business of propagation. There is no reason in the world why we cannot hatch one million ducks in a year. And then there is the matter of plant food propagation. There is no use creating a large surface of water if we have not food in it and if we can find by research a proper plant food that will grow in different localities and different kinds of soil, then we will be rendering a first-class service to the wildlife in the western Provinces.

Our next duty will be to investigate and check destructive diseases, and that is a serious matter. Thirty miles from where I live there are times that we lose half a million ducks a year with duck disease simply because the water in Lake Johnston is so low it is unfit for human consumption or any animal or bird consumption. Then our next job, and a whale of a big job it is, and this is the reason I am down in Winnipeg to-night, we have to alleviate prejudice not only in our states but along through the country and among agriculturists as well. We have got to provide the biggest of officers we can get to go around the country explaining our objects and doing the best they can to create good feeling all the way around. When they started with the Miami flood control problem a few years ago in the south, everybody recognized it was a necessity if their homes were going to be safe along that valley but it took them four or five years before they ever could get any where at all because some fellow had a farm or a few acres of hay land, some other fellow had a piece of ground, and one way and another they held up the project, and the biggest job we have to perform is to go around the prairie provinces selling our ideas clearly and as conscientiously as we can and with the hope it will meet with popular appeal for the whole of the western provinces.

Manitobans Must Take Advantage of Funds

I want to say this very frankly to-night and I say it in view of some of the letters that have appeared in the papers in Manitoba that some Manitoba people do not want this money, that one day James Richardson, and Leigh Spencer and myself are going to sit around the table and there is going to be three stacks of chips on that table and I say if you fellows in Manitoba are not behind James Richardson, I am going to take James Richardson's chips before I am through and Saskatchewan will be pretty glad to get the money if they do not want it in the Province of Manitoba.

In conclusion, Mr. Chairman, let me say this, that this question of conservation is not a local question; it is greater than a provincial question, it is greater than a national question; it is an international question and it is only by international action and international co-operation of the finest possible kind that we are going to succeed in dealing with that situation.

May I say again, Mr. Chairman, that it was a very, very great personal pleasure to be present at this wonderful gathering here to-night and I thank you for giving me the opportunity of being here. (Applause)

Appendix II

RADIO BROADCASTS — "REBUILDING THE WEST"

	Date	Subject	* Speaker
1938	24.5	International Cooperation in Sport and Conservation	E.S.R.
	31.5	International Cooperation in Sport and Conservation	T.C.M.
	7.6	Organized Cooperation	F.T.C.
	14.6	More Water — More Ducks for the West	D.M.S.
	28.6	Cooperation Unlimited in Sport and Conservation	E.S.R.
	6.7	The 1938 Wild Duck Census	B.W.C.
	13.7	Counting on 100 Million Ducks	E.S.R.
	20.7	Taking the Census of Duck Bills	B.W.C.
	27.7	Sky-writing of Ducks Unlimited	E.S.R.
	3.8	Changing the Face of Nature	E.S.R.
	10.8	The Challenge of Restoration	D.M.S.
	17.8	Bumper Harvest from Conservation	E.S.R.
	24.8	Publicity and Conservation	T.C.M.
	31.8	Ducks-eye View of our Northland	B.W.C.
	7.9	Bread on the Waters	B.W.C.
	14.9	Dirt and Water Farming	E.S.R.
	21.9	Future of our Prairie Ducks	F.T.C.
	28.9	The Earth for Our Life	W.G.R.
	5.10	Opportunity in Our Northland	T.C.M.
	12.10	Ten Thousand Farm Sanctuaries	E.S.R.
	19.10	Conservation — a National Issue	W.G.R.
	26.10	Waterfowl Win Lasting Friends	B.W.C.
	2.11	Ducks and Drakes	B.W.C.

	Date	Subject	* Speaker
	9.11	Rebuilding the West (E.S.R.)	Announcer
	16.11	A Crusade for Boys and Girls (E.S.R.)	T.C.M.
	23.11	Trial Balance of the Duck Count — 1938	E.S.R.
	30.11	Weeding out Crows and Magpies	
	7.12	Weeds to Waterfowl	G.R.F.
	14.12	Ducks Live Dangerously	B.W.C.
	21.12	Duck and Water Santa Claus	E.S.R.
	28.12	A New Year for Conservation	E.S.R.
1939	4.1	Along the Waterfowl Flyways	B.W.C.
	11.1	The Story of Wild Rice	B.W.C.
	16.1	Using Trees to Rebuild the West	E.S.R.
	23.1	The Key to Wildlife Restoration	E.S.R.
	20.1	Our Kee-Men Report	B.W.C.
	6.2	Where Ducks Go In the Winter Time	B.W.C.
	13.2	Saving Rare Birds	B.W.C.
	20.2	Migration of Birds	B.W.C.
	27.2	Ducks and Dugouts	B.W.C.
	6.3	Progress of Waterfowl Research	B.W.C.
	13.3	Where Ducks Nest	B.W.C.
	20.3	Wheat and Conservation — Prosperity	T.C.M.
	27.3	More About Bird Migration	B.W.C.
	3.4	This is Our Trust	G.R.F.
	10.4	Messages Through the Clouds	E.S.R.

* Note. Speakers are indicated as follows, in order of listing.

E.S.R. — E. S. Russenholt
T.C.M. — T. C. Main
F.T.C. — F. T. Clarke
D.M.S. — D. M. Stephens
B.W.C. — B. W. Cartwright
W.G.R. — W. G. Ross
G.R.F. — G. R. Fanset

DUCKS Unlimited (CANADA)

A Permanent Work in Sport and Conservation

NEWS FLIGHT Number 26   For Immediate Release

Opportunity—in Our Northland

Radio Broadcast by T. C. Main, A.M.E.I.C.,
General Manager, Ducks Unlimited (Canada)

HELLO! Western Canada, home of North America's wild ducks—and potential homeland of millions of permanently prosperous people.

In the name of thousands of Canadians who are working to rebuild our West upon the sure foundation of conservation, we thank this radio station for the opportunity to tell you about Ducks Unlimited —an essential part of the vast work of restoration.

Before oncoming winter ends the 1938 construction season, Ducks Unlimited (Canada), will have completed three major water conservation projects in our Farmland belt—one at Many Island Lake, in Alberta; a second at Waterhen Marsh, in Saskatchewan; and a third at Big Grass Marsh, in Manitoba.

A great deal of other work will be finished—and more will be underway—that will restore water; affect the welfare of waterfowl in Western Canada; and increase the duck population of North America. It is the intention of Ducks Unlimited to extend and carry on our restoration program in the Farmland belt as long as such work is necessary and beneficial; and to co-operate with every agency working along similar lines. Working together, we must take full advantage of every opportunity for practical conservation and fullest use of water over our entire Farmland area.

Opportunity also beckons from our Northland— that wedge of interesting territory that lies between the frontier of our Farmlands belt and the southwestern edge of the Precambrian Shield.

The Precambrian Shield yields great mineral wealth. Our Farmland belt produces abundant agricultural wealth. Both can be developed far beyond their great productiveness. The strip of Northland—between our Farmland and the rock country—is at present a "No Man's Land." From it we reap little wealth. This vast territory will become a veritable desert within a generation, if we persistently neglect it. On the other hand, if we take appropriate action now, this Northland can be made to produce vast wealth in timber, fish, water power, recreation, fur and waterfowl.

Less Rainfall in the Northland

Too few people realize that in our Northland, rainfall averages only about eleven inches a year; compared with fifteen in our Farmland belt.

Ducks Unlimited (Canada) is vitally interested in this area. So is every sportsman, nature lover and conservator on this continent; because here nest 70% of North America's ducks. Every Western Canadian is concerned in seeing this area developed

and made to produce its fullest quota of useful wealth.

During August, 1938, Ducks Unlimited personnel flew 7,500 miles over this Northland in a census survey of ducks and water. We saw six large areas, shown as lakes on the maps, now entirely dry; and 190 water areas, shrunk from 5% to 90%. Of course, the dry portion of the climatic cycle has effected our Northland, as well as our Farmland belt. Another factor, however, is the chief one in this "drying out" process in the Northland.

Beaver Killed—Water Lost

Fifty years ago, numberless beaver built thousands of dams in this Northland; and, behind them, stored the limited rainfall. The beaver have been killed; their dams ruined; and the water area impounded by them drained away. Now, each spring, streams flood; swollen torrents wash the streambeds lower; and down go the lake areas. Many streams then dwindle to mere trickles—or dry channels—due to lack of balancing reservoirs at their sources.

As water disappears, fires sweep our timber resources. Tinder-dry marshes burn—down to the underlying sand or glacial drift. Muskegs smolder continuously; and, from this source, new fires start —whenever conditions are favorable. The net results of these accumulative disasters are: tremendous loss of timber, soil fertility, potential water power, fur, and fish; scenic beauty changed to desolation; and waterfowl drastically depleted.

Help Northern Natives—and Waterfowl

While waterfowl are decreasing in the Northland, their predators multiply. There, men kill for food or fur. No one shoots crows or magpies. Indians and Half-breeds take heavy toll of wild ducks. Many live on eggs during the spring and summer; and on immature or flightless birds throughout the season.

There is little use demanding that the Dominion Government implement its treaty obligations to protect migratory birds on their nesting areas, by stopping Indians and Half-breeds poaching. This would be a difficult job. Even if it could be done, it would only aggravate the already serious Indian and Half-breed problem for Dominion and Provincial Governments.

Duck eggs and flightless birds have been a staple summer food of these people for generations. It would be cruel—impossible—to take this from them without providing something better.

No! Plans for the development of our Northland can not be superficial. They must be fundamental. **"Exploitation"** will ruin the entire area in short order—**Solution** for the many interwoven problems of this "No Man's Land" will pay big dividends in timber, water power, fish, recreation, fur and waterfowl.

"Opportunity—in Our Northland"

Haphazard Exploitation Takes Heavy Toll

Civilization pushes our Farmland frontier further north, year by year. There is grave danger of haphazard settlement in this hinterland.

We realize, now, our mistake in settling submarginal lands in the southern part of our prairie provinces. In that Farmland belt, during the past two years, the P.F.R.A. has taken over land unfit for successful farming; and has made a million acres of it into forty community pastures.

Thousands of potentially useful citizens have spent years of their lives on these submarginal lands. Now, after being a burden to the taxpayer for years, they are forced to give up the impossible fight—and leave. It is an unfortunate fact, also, that a man's morale and character are, to a great extent, decided by his environment. Hence, the so-called "poor white trash" of the submarginal regions in the Southern States. It would be a sad thing if we herded settlers into our Northland, indiscriminately, to become, in time, poor white trash.

A Plan for Northland Development

For the efficient development of our Northland, I suggest that blocks of this huge territory be set aside as game preserves and fur factories; and developed in this, their natural use. Such blocks will be particularly effective along the southern edge of our Northland. Water control structures, cabins, lookout towers, etc., should be built; and other improvements undertaken to bring these blocks to their full usefulness as water storage basins and production centres. Given proper conditions, muskrats (our leading fur producers) will multiply to the capacity of each block—and overflow into adjacent territory.

A few beaver should be planted—and protected —in each block. In time, these beaver would do most of the engineering work on these developed blocks; and throughout the Northland (just as they used to do).

Opportunity for Northland Natives

Our Indian wards should be kept on their reserves in the provinces; the Half-breeds on territory between the developed blocks (or on such areas as are now being provided for them by the governments of Alberta and Manitoba). During two months of the year (say from February 15 to April 15) both Half-breeds and Indians might be allowed to trap muskrat (and, eventually, beaver) under contract and supervision. Their whole catch would be handled by a Commission set up to administer the developed blocks. The Commission would invest a fraction of the proceeds in administration and maintenance; and pay out the balance to each individual trapper, or family—a few dollars per month.

The developed blocks might employ Indians and Half-breeds all year—as is being done by the Hudson's Bay Company on their beaver ranch, on James Bay. All this would give them an opportunity to establish themselves as producers, paying their own way; and earning an assured welfare.

A Northland Commission

Remembering that our Indians are wards of the Dominion (and Half-breeds of the provinces) a Commission should be set up in each province to administer game preserves, sanctuaries and developed blocks. The personnel of such a Commission should include representatives of the Dominion government, Provincial governments; and, if desired Ducks Unlimited. Our program, based upon water restoration and control, is a natural part of the whole development of the Northland.

The Dominion is responsible for both Indians and Half-breeds in the North-west Territories. A special sub-department might administer such activities in that large area. Again, Ducks Unlimited would co-operate, if desired.

Experimental Blocks Underway

Some progress is already being made toward shaping such a development. The muskrat ranch being developed, jointly, by Dominion and Manitoba governments, at Moose Lake, is almost exactly what I have in mind. A similar area has been set aside by Manitoba. Some private muskrat ranches have also been established. These produce fur and ducks —but, unfortunately, do not solve the native problem.

Ducks Unlimited is now negotiating with the three provincial governments to establish experimental blocks in Alberta, Saskatchewan and Manitoba—and to develop them as fur and duck factories along the lines suggested. Ducks Unlimited will manage the projects; but suggest a supervisory Commission, consisting of permanent provincial officials and representatives of Ducks Unlimited. Our books would be open to the Commission; and, each year, a report and program of work would be submitted for their approval. When a net revenue is available, this would be invested by the Commission to further develop each block—or similar projects elsewhere in the same province.

Tourists

Experience indicates that suitable highways into our Northland will attract increasing thousands of motorists—who want to see for themselves the scenic wonders of our Northland—its waters, waterfowl, and fish. All promising vast returns in revenues, understanding and goodwill.

This suggestion is outlined with the knowledge that it must be improved with future study; but with the conviction that **there is a natural and efficient use to be made of our Northland**—which will:

1. Conserve our water resources;
2. Save—and extend—our forests;
3. Maintain—and multiply—the yearly catch of fish;
4. Greatly increase annual fur crops;
5. Make our Indians and Half-breeds self-supporting and productive;
6. Develop a tremendous tourist industry; and,
7. Reap enormous dividends from waterfowl.

So—goodnight Western Canada. And let us remember that we can reap **good days** from the resources that are ours, by working together in conservation. Let us follow the ancient law—to protect our birds—"That it may be well with thee; and that thou mayest prolong thy days."

DUCKS Unlimited (CANADA)

A Permanent Work in Sport and Conservation

NEWS FLIGHT Number 31   For Immediate Release

"REBUILDING THE WEST"

A Series of Broadcasts by Ducks Unlimited (Canada) with the generous co-operation of Radio Stations across Western Canada, including;

CJRC, *Winnipeg*	CJRM, *Regina*
CJGX, *Yorkton*	CFAC, *Calgary*
CJOC, *Lethbridge*	CJCA, *Edmonton*
CFGP, *Grande Prairie*	

Rebuilding The West

HELLO, Western Canada, home of North America's wild ducks—and potential homeland of millions of permanently prosperous people.

In the name of thousands of Canadians who are working to rebuild our West upon a sure foundation of conservation, we thank this radio station for the opportunity to tell you about Ducks Unlimited—an essential part of the vast work of restoration.

These discussions on "Rebuilding the West" have consistently pointed out how all resources—all development—all activities—in this great land of ours, are linked together; how each affects the other; and how our resources of land, water, and people can yield fullest usefulness and permanent prosperity to all our people in a co-ordinated and planned development—on a comprehensive, long-time basis.

The development of each item of our resources vitally affects all development. In the same way any short-sighted and uneconomic exploitation and depletion of any resource, re-acts against efficient use of all other resources. Shortage of water, for instance, handicaps farm, ranch, forest, fisheries, mines, power, transportation and tourist travel—as well as wildlife. The fires that this summer have covered the West with smoke—from Winnipeg to Edmonton—have killed millions of trees. In addition to the direct loss in saw-timber, these fires have inflicted upon us a far greater loss by their destruction of mile after mile of forest cover—and thus, accelerating the drying-up of water, particularly in the Northland.

Conservation and Utilization of Resources

Recently T. C. Main, general manager of Ducks Unlimited (Canada), broadcast a plan for restoring our Northland waters—and developing the resources of that 319,000 square miles of "No Man's Land" wedged between our Farmland belt and the Pre-Cambrian rock country, beyond. This plan has aroused wide interest throughout the West. Many of the elements of this plan have been urged for years by far-seeing Government (and other) authorities. Mr. Main's plan is based upon the close and vital interlocking of all resources. He suggests a co-operative development—in which provincial departments, Dominion authorities, and Ducks Unlimited shall team-up to restore Northland Water Areas and make them more useful; putting beaver back on the job damming up streams, ponds, marshes, lakes (as in the old days); enlisting "Zeb Musquash", (the lowly muskrat) to pay for the entire project, offer Indians and half-breeds a livlihood and multiply fur production; promoting commercial and sport fishing; expanding tourist travel; creating reservoirs for power development; protecting timber; and, incidentally, multiplying the waterfowl crop from that vast area where wild ducks nest in millions.

Certainly it is true that all our resources are related—interdependent; and that, in their development, we must co-operate—in plan and in action. Each intimate interest can best be served in a balanced and progressive development of all resources from which all our people reap prosperity. In Ducks Unlimited, our immediate purpose is to multiply the wild duck population of North America. We can best do this (in fact we can only do this) by restoring our permanent water areas in Western Canada—and efficiently controlling and utilizing these permanent waters. Each and every one of us knows that restoring, controlling and utilizing permanent water areas is the imperative essential in Rebuilding the West. Prosperity of all our Western people has been, is, and shall always be, measured by the supply of water available—and the efficiency of it. Every pailful of water we can help restore in permanent water areas through our Ducks Unlimited work program, is a direct CASH benefit to every Canadian interested in farms or forests, or fisheries, or furs, or power, or transportation, or tourists, as well as wildlife—including waterfowl.

The Co-operation of the Lloydminster Gun and Crow Club

All over the West we meet a wonderful readiness to co-operate in this great restoration work. Organized sportsmen have worked closely with us in predator control campaigns; and have given every encouragement to our work. For instance, this letter from Lloydminster, Saskatchewan. "Dear Sirs: At the Annual Meeting of the Gun & Crow Club of Lloydminster, this club went on record in heartily supporting the splendid work that Ducks Unlimited had done throughout the United States and the Dominion; and we want you to feel that we would be only too willing to co-operate with you in any move to assist in the preservation of game birds, in which the sportsmen in this district are vitally interested. We only hope that the work which you have started will be carried on for years to come."

We thank the good sportsmen of Lloydminster for their assurance of continued co-operation. They have a active Club. We will be glad to help them along in any feasible project.

Improving Farm Ponds

Some of our recent broadcasts on "Rebuilding the West" have discussed making farm water ponds more useful by levelling banks, planting protecting trees, and giving sanctuary to birds. Copies of these broadcasts were mailed to five thousand farmers in Alberta, Manitoba and Saskatchewan who have built farm water ponds in co-operation with P.F.R.A. and their provincial government departments. Many are writing us about their plans to improve their farm ponds—and asking for further information. Mr. Alf Simpson, of Hodgeville, Saskatchewan, writes: "Thank you for the copies of radio addresses you sent me. I will do what I can to encourage birds. The best thing I know is to fence out stock—

from at least a part of dam; thus allowing natural cover to grow. **Pastures are always too closely grazed.**

"Willows seed themselves; and I am propagating white poplar to plant near water. I would like to know of other suitable trees or shrubs which would provide food for waterfowl. I will follow your broadcasts; and shall be glad for any hints on how to increase the numbers of waterfowl."

We are glad to hear from Mr. Simpson. He is quite correct about protecting part of the farm water pond from livestock. Many farmers also plant small patches of grain or sweet clover to provide cover and food for the birds.

Suggests Sanctuary at Red Deer River

Here's another interesting letter from S. E. Hay, Atlee, Alberta. "Received copies of your broadcasts, 21 and 22; and would like very much to get all of them. I am all in favor of the work you are doing. I live four miles south of the Red Deer River, and have often wondered why this river has not been made a sanctuary. Since the sloughs have dried up, this river is the only resting-place for migrating ducks and geese. When they are shot at there, they have no place left to go. I have a reservoir here, fed by a spring, and am going to do all I can to make it attractive to ducks and geese. We have some water in the sloughs in the spring-time, for about three months. Plenty of young ducks appear on these sloughs, but, as they gradually dry up in the summer, the coyotes wade out and catch the floppers. The reservoir will save some of them."

In answer to Mr. Hay's request we have added his name to our mailing list—to get copies of all broadcasts. We will be glad to do likewise for every other interested person in Western Canada.

From Wadena, Saskatchewan, Einar Erickson writes: "I have been listening to your broadcasts on the radio re waterfowl, and I certainly do enjoy them. **Something has to be done soon,** if we want any ducks left at all. I have been in this part of the country for 35 years and have always taken an interest in game birds and outdoor life. I remember when ducks were here by the thousands. Today, there are hardly any at all. So, if I can be of any help to you, please let me know and I'll give you all the information I've had in the last 35 years."

We thank Mr. Ericson for his good offer of co-operation. We will certainly enlist him in the work that must be done in every Western community next season.

Teaching Conservation in the Schools

An Alberta school divisional superintendent, interested in wildlife conservation, writes: "Your radio talks interest me. I am eager to help in any way I can. I cover the territory from Whitecourt to a few miles east of Onoway; south to nearly the gravel; and north—some 12 miles south of Barrhead. In our 87 rooms we have done something toward killing crows and magpies. I will be glad to redouble efforts. If you have any splendid prints of game, I could show these to scholars and give a little talk when I visit the schools, and we could make a drive next spring. Faithfully yours, J. D. Aikenhead."

We appreciate Mr. Aikenhead's letter; and assure him that supplying material to schools as the basis for lessons on wildlife and conservation is part of the work planned for this winter. Immediately material is available, we will be glad to send it out to any school teacher in Alberta, Manitoba or Saskatchewan who is interested.

Mr. Mickleborough of Eston, Sask. Offers Prize

Here is an intensely interesting letter from Mr. R. S. Mickleborough of Eston, Saskatchewan. "Greatly enjoyed your address of October 13th over the radio—advising farmers who have had work done by the P.F.R.A. on dug-outs to try and make these havens for wildfowl. This should meet with high approval and no doubt we will see the benefit of your talk.

"This summer I had a large dugout completed under the P.F.R.A.; with some brush to act as shade—plus some grass seed and a few oats sown for the young birds in the spring. Am hoping for a large hatch in the spring. I have about twenty-five birds as breeding stock. These include Canadas, Hutchins', Snows, Blues, American White Fronts and Egyptians. Ducks are easily raised. The farmer usually has screenings around; and these will winter any breeding stock he may decide to keep over. Our birds here are quite tame and know when it is feeding time. It is worthwhile to see eight or ten big honkers floating around the yard to settle down beside you.

"You mentioned the fact that you were giving a prize for the best dug-out that would draw wildfowl. I will donate a true mated pair of wild geese to the boy or girl who wins this prize. If there is anything I can do to further your work in Ducks Unlimited, I would be only too glad to assist."

We thank Mr. Mickleborough for his good letter —for his suggestions based upon actual experience; and for his offer to donate a mated pair of wild geese to interest boys and girls.

As we hinted in a recent broadcast, Ducks Unlimited plans a farm sanctuary program next summer. We hope to enlist hundreds of boys and girls (and men and women as well) in a contest for developing the best sanctuary for ducks and other birds on farm ponds.

Substantial prizes will be awarded to those who do good work. We will be glad to get suggestions for making this program most interesting and effective.

Crow Campaigns

During the past summer, Ducks Unlimited co-operated with the organized sportsmen, and Provincial authorities in Alberta, Manitoba, and Saskatchewan in campaigns to bring predators, such as crows and magpies under control. Ducks Unlimited provided $3,100.00 prize money for the hunters who took part. We will tell you about the chaps who won substantial prizes,—in a broadcast soon.

So, goodnight, Western Canada. And let us remember that we can reap **good days** from the resources that are ours, by working together in conservation. Let us follow the ancient law—to protect our birds—"That it may be well with thee; and that thou mayest prolong thy days."

DUCKS Unlimited (CANADA)

A Permanent Work in Sport and Conservation

NEWS FLIGHT Number 33   For Immediate Release

Adding up the Duck Account for 1938

HELLO, Western Canada, home of North America's wild ducks and potential homeland of millions of permanently prosperous people.

In the name of thousands of Canadians who are working to rebuild our West upon a sure foundation of conservation, we thank this radio station for the opportunity to tell you about Ducks Unlimited—an essential part of the vast work of restoration.

Our Western Co-operators

This vast work in which we are engaged, of restoring ducks and wildlife (as a vital part of developing all our resources to their utmost usefulness) brings us into contact with an army of stout crusaders in this great cause. On our voyaging across the West (from Lethbridge to The Pas; from Lake of the Woods to Great Slave Lake) we speak with hundreds of sportsmen, farmers, traders, officials who, each in his own way and community, are carrying on the good work of rebuilding the West— through Conservation. Hundreds more write to us telling of conditions in their own neighborhoods; and submitting suggestions and recommendations. Every item of information, every suggestion, every recommendation is welcome; and helps shape plans for further restoration work.

As a matter of fact, restoring the wild duck population of this continent depends upon the co-operation of our people of Western Canada; upon active observers, over the entire duck breeding grounds in our West, reporting facts, and making recommendations. This season, Ducks Unlimited has started 100,000 acres on the way to full development—which can produce crops of 100 ducks per acre per season; and has taken the first steps to launch development of vastly greater acreages next year. A great achievement in one short season. But—a more vital guarantee of success is that, when we invited workers to become Ducks Unlimited Kee-men, over 2,700 responded—and reported facts on water and duck conditions in their neighborhoods.

A Final Report on Ducks

Now, to complete the entries in this season's account, so to speak—and strike a trial balance—we ask all our Ducks Unlimited Kee-men to fill out and return a brief final report. Forms for this report go by mail to all our Kee-men. We will be glad to enlist in our Kee-men organization, every interested observer who will volunteer to advance the work of restoration—by returning this final report. We will mail each a report form; and reprints of these weekly broadcasts on Rebuilding the West.

┌─ "REBUILDING THE WEST" ─┐

A Series of Broadcasts by Ducks Unlimited (Canada) with the generous co-operation of Radio Stations across Western Canada, including;

CJRC, *Winnipeg*	CJRM, *Regina*
CJGX, *Yorkton*	CFAC, *Calgary*
CJOC, *Lethbridge*	CJCA, *Edmonton*
CFGP, *Grande Prairie*	

The True Definition of Conservation

Now, before we discuss the information needed about the last part of this wild duck season, let us agree on one point about conservation—the vital issue in our national life. In all our discussion about restoring ducks and getting the best use out of water (and all our resources) one thing is noticeable; that is: the variety of meanings which are given the term "Conservation." Around 1932 and '33, we met folks who pretended that conservation meant doing something to make more rain fall upon our semi-arid prairies. Down in old Ontario, "Conservation" means trees; and includes the great work townships and counties are doing with lands which have failed as farms—and come back through tax sale. The municipalities are making these lands useful and productive again, by planting them to tree crops. Some folks think of "Conservation" as building a 10-wire fence around some resource—and keeping everybody away from it. Once in a long while, some such idea creeps out in suggestions that ducks, for instance, should not be hunted; that all shooting be prohibited; that all the enjoyment and health of days in the open be denied to everyone; and that the ducks, in their turn, be left to perish in thousands on the muddy bottoms of ponds and marshes that dry up in early summer, killed in ten thousands by crows, magpies and other predators and fried in hundred thousands in marsh fires.

Now, all of these things may be included in "Conservation"—but "Conservation" includes far more than all of them. The Encyclopedia Britannica tells us: "The name 'Conservation' has been given to the movement for using and safeguarding the natural resources of any country for the greatest good of the greatest number for the longest time." That definition will bear repeating—"Conservation is using and safeguarding natural resources for the greatest good of the greatest number for the longest time." The Britannica goes on "It is a fundamental misconception to suppose that Conservation means nothing but husbanding of resources. The first principle of Conservation is use; but it refuses to recognize needless waste and destruction as normal processes in proper development and enjoyment of natural wealth."

Thus, Rebuilding the West through Conservation is: using and safeguarding all our natural resources for the greatest good of the greatest number for the longest time. And Ducks Unlimited—a vital part of the vast work of restoration—aims at using and safeguarding wild ducks for the greatest good of the greatest number for the longest time— through eliminating needless waste and destruction —and promoting proper development and full enjoyment—of this great wildlife resource.

From the very inception of the conservation movement 30 years ago, it has been recognized that the first step toward better use of resources is taking a complete and accurate inventory of all facts about resources and their development. The success of this program in which we are all working together to restore wild ducks (and other useful wildlife)

"Adding up the Duck Account for 1938

depends entirely upon getting all possible information from every corner of the wild duck range in our West. Hence, our Ducks Unlimited Kee-men (and the work they are doing in reporting on their own neighborhoods) are the foundation of our restoration work.

A Request for Information

That brings us back to the final brief report needed to complete our entries in the restoration account for 1938. The following letter goes to all our good Ducks Unlimited Kee-men: "Dear Kee-man: The reports sent in by Ducks Unlimited Kee-men have proven to be of outstanding value in the great work of restoration of water and waterfowl. Your help and interest has resulted in the most comprehensive collection of information on water-fowl and surface water conditions ever gathered together in one office. To round out the work of the season, will you kindly fill in carefully the enclosed questionnaire and return same in the within envelope, at your earliest convenience. Thanking you in advance for your co-operation. Yours for restoration, Ducks Unlimited (Canada).

The report form asks these 12 questions: "1. Compared with last year, did fall flight of ducks show increase or decrease? 2. Did fall flight of geese show increase or decrease? 3. Which species showed increase? 4. Which species showed decrease? 5. Did sloughs and potholes dry out before young ducks could fly? 6. What loss occurred through this cause—few? hundreds? thousands? 7. Were water levels in larger lakes in October higher or lower than last year at the same time? 8. Did duck disease cause loss in your district? 9. If so, when did the outbreak occur? 10. At what date did freeze-up occur: (a) on marshes, sloughs and potholes? (b) On larger lakes and rivers? 11. Did any of the following factors cause loss of ducks: (a) Shooting out of season? (b) Caught in fishing nets? (c) Caught in animal traps? (d) Forest fires? (e) Marsh fires? (f) Mowing machines? 12. Did ducks do any serious damage to crops in your district?"

The report form concludes: "Your report will be treated as confidential. Please use other side of this sheet for any suggestions and general remarks you care to make. We'll be glad to get them. Thank you."

During 1939 Ducks Unlimited will invest around half-a-million dollars in restoration work. The continued co-operation of our Kee-men will help us invest it wisely—to return the greatest good to the greatest number over the longest time. Many observers have begun to think that our ducks and geese are changing their flyways; that, in their flight south to their winter homes, they this fall swung away eastward. The truth (or otherwise) of such change in migration routes can be determined only by boiling down information, contributed by our good Ducks Unlimited Kee-men from over the entire breeding range.

A Message of Interest and Co-operation from Creelman, Saskatchewan

The number of reports completed will run into thousands. We base that estimate on the fact that every day more people tell us of their keen interest in wildlife—and wildlife conservation. For instance, here's a letter off the top of the pile that have come in recently. It is from Creelman, Saskatchewan. Our new friend writes:

"I received the other day some of your literature and would be glad to hear from you any time. I have been interested ever since I heard of the work you are trying to do in increasing our game population. I was brought up a sportsman but get very little time for shooting lately although I enjoy it very much. I have a dam and a large dugout just completed. There were 4 or 5 acres of water in the dam all summer; and there were a dozen families of ducks in it, some so late that they couldn't fly when the shooting season opened; and my friends from town (so-called sportsmen) had pretty well cleaned them out when I caught on and stopped them. I should have "No Shooting" signs up and was wondering if Ducks Unlimited have them. I have a good growth of trees at the dam and intend planting trees around the dugout; and around my farm I have the best windbreak of trees in the country. Every winter we have a bunch of Hungarian partridges and Prairie Chicken around. Last winter we had a dozen Prairie Chicken who seemed to live on the buds of the trees with what little wheat I gave them. We were afraid they might spoil the trees by eating all the buds, but they didn't seem to hurt them at all. This fall after the hunting season we counted a flock of 40 chicken just a mile east, the largest flock I ever saw so near home. You may count on me for every co-operation possible in the preservation of our game birds, both land and water. If any of the Ducks Unlimited people are in this district would be glad to have them call and talk things over."

We thank our friend at Creelman for his letter —and for his interest in wildlife restoration. Ducks Unlimited has not yet begun to supply "No Shooting" signs; but our plans for 1939 do include supplying these signs to all co-operators who take part in our program to develop dugouts and ponds as sanctuaries. Indications are that hundreds of farmers who have built dams and dugouts under the P.F.R.A. and provincial authorities—as well as clubs, schools and communities—will co-operate in this program to develop water areas to their full usefulness as bird sanctuaries. By dotting the map of our Western Farmlands with hundreds of ponds where birds may find sanctuary, these co-operators will help in the great work of restoring ducks and other useful wildlife—and, at the same time, benefit themselves and their communities. Ducks Unlimted will supply "No Shooting" signs; will help all co-operators improve their water areas to the utmost; and will award substantial cash prizes for the best sanctuaries developed. However, that is looking ahead to next season. Right now, we ask all interested to send us final reports on ducks in their neighborhood.

So, Good-night Western Canada. And let us remember that we can reap **good days** from the resources that are ours, by working together in conservation. Let us follow the ancient law—to protect our birds—"That it may be well with thee; and that thou mayest prolong thy days."

DUCKS Unlimited (CANADA)

A Permanent Work in Sport and Conservation

NEWS FLIGHT Number 36   For Immediate Release

Any part, or all, of this News Flight may be freely used by anyone sincerely interested in conservation.

Ducks Live Dangerously

By B. W. Cartwright

HELLO, Western Canada, home of North America's wild ducks and potential homeland of millions of permanently prosperous people.

In the name of thousands of Canadians who are working to rebuild our West upon a sure foundation of conservation, we thank this radio station for the opportunity to tell you about Ducks Unlimited—an essential part of the vast work of restoration.

With the co-operation of nearly three thousand Ducks Unlimited Kee-men throughout the three prairie provinces a final report on the waterfowl season of 1938 is now being prepared in our office.

Hundreds of reports are being received daily and the answers to the questions asked are being tabulated as rapidly as possible.

1938 Final Report

Our Kee-men have been asked the following questions:

1. Compared with last year did the fall flight of ducks show an increase or decrease?

2. Did the fall flight of geese show an increase or decrease?

3. Which species showed an increase and which a decrease?

4. Did sloughs and potholes dry out before young ducks could fly?

5. If so, what loss occurred through this cause? Few? Hundreds? Thousands?

6. Were water levels in larger lakes in October higher or lower than last year at the same time?

7. Did duck disease cause loss in your district?

8. If so, when did the outbreak occur?

9. At what date did freeze up occur? (a) On marshes, sloughs, and potholes? (b) On larger lakes and rivers.

10. Did any of the following factors cause loss of ducks? Shooting out of season; Caught in fishing nets; Caught in animal traps; Forest fires; Marsh fires, Mowing machines?

11. Did ducks do any serious damage to crops in your district?

In addition to answering these questions, the Kee-men were invited to send in suggestions and comments.

Non-Stop Flight this Fall

It will be some time before we can give you the results of the questions; but already it is apparent that the fall flight of ducks passed up large sections of Alberta and Saskatchewan. The fall was long and mild and when the onset of winter did come the ducks migrated through the southern sections non-stop.

The comments of our co-operators are of great interest. The great decrease in waterfowl in the last ten years has been due to loss of water areas. There seems to be general agreement on that. J. C. Stephens of Leader, Sask. puts the matter as concisely as anything I have seen. He writes: "Land, where big lakes and sloughs used to be, has been plowed and cultivated nearer and nearer to water each year, until lakes dried. Then they cultivated lake bottoms." Apart from the drought there is the story in a nutshell.

Our farmers delight in seeing living creatures on their land. Many letters reveal this feeling of loss to the beauty of the countryside in the disappearance of the waterfowl. For instance, J. M. Armstrong of Beaufield, Sask. writes: "There are no large lakes or rivers in this district but the P.F.R.A. dams are holding considerable water as are some of the larger sloughs. We are sure longing to see the ducks and geese back again in this district as in the old days."

Wildlife Must Have Water

And listen to John Urban—his name is Urban but he is truly rural. He writes from Osage, Sask. "The summer of 1937—the driest year we had—I was hauling water for stock 5 miles and when I left the water tank in the yard, prairie chickens, partridges and other birds were all around it trying to get water that was dripping out, so I set a shallow trough in the ground out in the pasture and I kept this filled for them. They got so tame and used to it that when they saw me coming with water they were all around the trough waiting for me."

Dr. M. L. Moore of Medicine Hat writes: "I have been interested in Fish and Game organizations for several years and I am more than pleased to co-op-

"Ducks Live Dangerously"

erate in such ways as I can with your organization. It is great to think that Many Island Lake may be filled again as it has always been considered one of the finest breeding areas in the prairies. Of course, you will make it a closed sanctuary." Dr. Moore refers to a project which Ducks Unlimited completed this year. It has been for many years a Bird Sanctuary. A dam was built which will ensure five feet of water over several hundred acres where in previous years the water spread out over 8,000 acres and evaporated leaving ducklings and goslings to perish miserably of thirst. In August this year Ducks Unlimited Kee-men, Sam White and Tom Hargrave organized the school children in a fine rescue of stranded ducklings, goslings, shorebirds and coots. In all, 780 birds were rounded up and transported to permanent water—some of them a distance of 60 miles.

The pathetic picture of several families of Canada Geese wandering hopelessly over the dry bed of Many Island Lake, looking for water has been made the subject of our staff Christmas Card this year. T. C. Main, General Manager of Ducks Unlimited, secured a fine photograph of one of these groups. It shows also the faithfulness of this grand bird; for the adults refused to desert their young even when human beings approached to within fifteen feet of them. 43 Canada Geese young were rescued.

To Fight Duck Sickness

To return to Dr. Moore's letter. He discusses another cause of depletion of waterfowl in the dread "duck sickness" or botulism which is said to have killed some 2 million ducks since 1930. He writes; "The duck sickness seems most prevalent in artificial lakes of irrigation areas and seems due to the sudden changes in water levels as more or less water is used for irrigation purposes. A survey of a chain of two or three lakes east of Vauxhall early in September showed an appalling condition. We walked the shore for several miles and counted the carcasses of dead ducks. They averaged 25 to 30 for every 100 feet. This matter has been reported and taken up with the Game Department at Edmonton through their Mr. T. Kyar and action next year has been promised. More power to your work," concludes Dr. Moore.

In respect to duck sickness, I am able to say that Ducks Unlimited plan to have specialists in the affected areas next summer and will take quick action to salvage sick ducks and transfer them to sweet water where they speedily recover.

Stop-Over on Migration

In mild falls such as Alberta has experienced this year, there is a tendency for many ducks to remain in northern waters. It appears that the urge to migrate gradually wanes and finally becomes dormant and then when winter weather sets in the bewildered birds are trapped and die of starvation. On December 5, G. A. Degroff of Bentley, Alberta, writes: "There are quite a few thousand ducks here yet. They were here yesterday, December 4. There are open places on the Blindman River and not frozen much anywhere. It may be that these ducks will have to be fed this winter. It has happened at

Sylvan Lake and may happen here if they don't go south soon."

Another Kee-man, G. L. Gould of Edmonton voices a similar alarm. He suggests that the duck problem at Buffalo Lake be followed carefully. "On November 17 there were several thousand feeding between Mirror and Bashaw and I understand that last week—his letter is dated December 5—there are still a large number in the district. Their condition at present is poor and some arrangements should be made for winter feeding and watering in order to conserve as many as possible."

We wired our Alberta manager yesterday as follows: Ducks Unlimited are prepared to help in any practical plan to save stranded waterfowl. Survey the situation and advise.

To Restore Whitewater Lake in Manitoba

Many are the letters we receive from that once famous duck breeding paradise—Whitewater Lake in south-western Manitoba. This 48,000-acre former lake has been bone dry from midsummer on for several years and thousands of ducklings perish there every year.

C. R. Zetterstrom of Whitewater writes: "Sure would like to see something done and would do anything I can to help."

M. S. Colquhoun of Deloraine, Man., writes: "You will save a good many thousands of young ducks when you throw that dyke around the southwest corner of Whitewater Lake. There is a large area of the lake which fills each spring sufficient to accommodate thousands of geese and ducks for a while. Then the geese go north and the ducks start raising families, but recently the marsh has been drying up before the young ones could fly."

And George Ross Sexton, of that grand old pioneer family at Regent, on the north shore of Whitewater Lake writes: "Would not a series of ditches in this lake solve our problem. Thousands of pintail and other species had nests in the rushes and naturally, all the young ducks died from want of water."

I can say this to the many people who have written of the heartbreaking conditions in Whitewater Lake: Ducks Unlimited engineers and naturalists made a preliminary investigation of the lake this fall and definite plans are afoot to alleviate the wildlife death toll of this lake next near. A survey party will be in there before Christmas.

We are sorry that our hands were so full with other projects that we could not get at Whitewater Lake this fall, but we shall be right there on the job next spring.

So—goodnight Western Canada, and let us remember that we can reap **good days** from the resources that are ours, by working together in conservation. Let us follow the ancient law—to protect our birds—"That it may be well with thee; and that thou mayest prolong thy days."

Appendix III
RADIO BROADCASTS 1950-1951

Five minute presentations. Staff or studio personnel were used in characterizations.

1. 1950 Waterfowl Conditions — G. R. Fanset
2. Post breeding waterfowl movements — B. W. Cartwright
3. Let's Play Ball with the Ducks — W. G. Leitch
* 4. Wildlife Art — Angus H. Shortt
5. Co-operation in Conservation — Haden Wilks
6. Hunting Safety — Jim Houlden
7. Land Negotiations — Dialogue — Robert McEwing, D.U. Landman and Farmer
8. Importance of Obeying Hunting Regulations — Dialogue Between Two Boys — Alton Cleland
9. Sustained Yield from Forests — Allen Beaven
10. The Farm Woodlot — Allen Beaven
11. Development and Conservation of Water Resources — E. E. Eisenhauer
*12. Training Young Hunters — Dialogue Between Old Timer and Boy in the Marsh — Alton Cleland
13. Use a Retriever — Dialogue Between Two Hunters — Alton Cleland
14. Ducks Unlimited Projects in Western Canada — Judge L. T. McKim
15. Attracting Small Birds — Judge L. T. McKim
16. Training Young Hunters — Dialogue Between Old Timer and Boy in a Marsh — Alton Cleland
17. Utilization of Barren Ground Caribou — John P. Kelsall
18. Indian Legend "Origin of the Wavey Goose" — Dialogue — Alton Cleland
19. Breeding Biology of the Coot — Peter Ward
20. Waterfowl Populations — A Look into the Future. — Dialogue — Alton Cleland
*21. Mallards and Pintails — Dialogue between Morty Mallard and Percy Pintail — Alton Cleland
22. Botulism — Dialogue between Judy, Mary, and Ducks Unlimited Biologist — Alton Cleland and W. G. Leitch
23. and 24. — missing
*25. Aerial Reconnaissance — Dialogue while airborne — Haden Wilks and W. G. Leitch
26. "Duck Factories" — Dialogue Between Two Hunters — Alton Cleland
27. Missing
28. Ranching and Ducks Unlimited Projects — Dialogue between Old Timers and Grandson — Alton Cleland
29. Ducks Unlimited Projects and Landowner Co-operation — Dialogue — Alton Cleland
30. National Wildlife Week — Family Dialogue — Alton Cleland
31. Waterfowl Habitat and Prospects for 1951 Season — Morty Mallard and Percy Pintail — Alton Cleland
32. Landowners Co-operation with Ducks Unlimited — Dialogue between Fieldman and Farmer — Alton Cleland
33. Waterfowl Projects and Farmers — Alton Cleland

DUCKS UNLIMITED
CONSERVATION SERIES
BROADCAST NO. 4
Angus Shortt

Do you know ducks and geese well enough to be able to create paintings or drawings in color of some of the various species? Some of you may consider such activity to be a rather oblique contribution in the nation-wide movement toward waterfowl conservation. Actually, the artistic study of waterfowl in the field is one of the most direct methods of acquainting oneself with the haunts, habits and status of our ducks and geese.

The primary requirement of a bird painter is accurate knowledge of the subject matter, a knowledge which must be gained through years of study in the field. It must be self-taught. Art schools can give the necessary training in the correct handling of pigments and develop the talents of the artist, but the form and color-accuracy of a finished painting will depend upon the amount of field observation accomplished beforehand.

Books and magazines featuring both popular and scientific information about ducks and geese are a definite aid to a fuller understanding of the subject. Those which contain color plates and descriptive material have a much greater general appeal.

Museum collections are a source of valuable material for use in the final coloring and pattern of the feathering. We are fortunate in having in our Manitoba museum a fine collection of study skins for this purpose.

Every species of bird has an individuality of its own, whether it be a Canvasback, a Redhead duck, a Bittern or a Marsh Wren. Rapid pencil sketching of birds as seen in the field is of first importance and the lifelike appearance of the birds in the finished picture is dependent on the accumulated knowledge derived from these pencil impressions.

The difference in coloring of the eyes, bill and feet of live birds is remarkable. They differ in almost every species and in many cases between male and female and immature birds. For instance, in the case of the Red-necked Grebe, a common resident of lake and marsh, the color of the eye changes with age. In the downy young, the iris is light brownish, in birds six weeks old, it is light yellow and in adults it is red.

The bills of many ducks exhibit strikingly bright colors during the breeding season. In the Mallard drake it will be a bright yellow; in the female a deep orange, much mottled and spotted with dark brown. In the drake Ruddy duck the bill is brilliant blue, while that of his mate is a dull gray.

As these colors fade soon after the bird dies, "on the spot" records must be made. These may consist of water-color or oil sketches of the bird's head and feet, the colors being painted in by direct comparison with the freshly collected specimen. Even the color of the eyelids and the gape, the fleshy portion at the base of the bill, should be matched. These latter items are prominent color characteristics in many of our gulls, terns and other species.

The artist also must be accurate in depicting habitat or surroundings of the various birds. A Blue-winged teal is at home against a background of prairie marsh, while a Merganser or fish duck looks best in a setting of a rockbound, deep water lake of the Pre-Cambrian country.

In summary, the bird artist must know the field marks and characteristics of the bird he is painting; be familiar with the habitat in which it is found and, equally important, know his working medium, whether it be oil paints or water colors. The finished product should be as faithful to nature as he can make it.

Taking art along on your field trips will not only provide you with a keener enjoyment of the outdoors, it will also make a better-informed conservationist who will be better equipped to deal with the problems inherent in conservation work.

DUCKS UNLIMITED
CONSERVATION SERIES
BROADCAST NO. 12

OLD/TIMER — "Billy, now that you're in a blind on a marsh for the first time, which would you sooner do; start shooting at the first ducks which come into range or, take a few pointers and learn how to identify at least some of the ducks?"

BOY — "Gee, Uncle Joe, it's great to be out here with you, even if we did have to take our places in the blind before daylight. I'll do whatever you say."

OLD/TIMER — "We can do a little shooting later in the day, but right now would be a good time for a few lessons. If you know what you're shooting at, your future days on the marsh will be more enjoyable and you will learn to be a sportsman, not a killer."

BOY — "Just what is there to learn, Uncle Joe? Aren't you just supposed to shoot until you have your limit?"

OLD/TIMER — "There's much to learn, Billy. First, there are over 20 species of ducks to be found on our western marshes and you may be lucky enough to bag several species in a single day's shoot."

BOY — "Tell me, Uncle Joe, is size the only difference in the various species?"

OLD/TIMER — "No, Billy, there are two classes — the surface feeders and the deep-water feeders. The first feed by tipping up in shallow water, while the latter dive for their food. They have been taken in fishermen's nets to a depth of 40 feet. Some of these deep-water ducks, especially the Mergansers, are fish-eaters and not fit for table use."

BOY (Excited) — "Oh, Boy! . . . Here comes a nice flock . . . What are they, Uncle Joe?"

OLD/TIMER — They're Mallards, the largest of our surface-feeders. . . . When I say go, you just shoot about two feet in front of the leading bird and if you don't bring him down, give him the second barrel."

BOY (impatient) — "Gee . . . Are they close enough now?"

OLD/TIMER — "Steady . . . SHOOT." . . . Good boy, Billy! . . . A clean kill and what a beauty — a full-plumaged drake Mallard. I'll bet he weighs over three pounds."

BOY — "Look! . . . Here comes another flock — gee, are they ever travelling!"

OLD/TIMER — "They're canvasbacks, Billy, our largest deep-water ducks. . . . Notice how they come straight through without flaring or swerving, and the faster wing-beat peculiar to the diving ducks. On a weight ratio, the divers have smaller wings than the surface-feeders."

BOY (eager) — "Do you think they'll come in range, Uncle Joe? Can I try my luck again? Boy . . . This really is fun!"

OLD/TIMER — "This is going to be tough, Billy. . . . They're coming straight at you. . . Throw up your gun, cover the bird, then jerk the gun upward until the bird is hidden — then, let drive."

SOUND — Gun fires twice, slightly spaced . . .

BOY — "Gee, I missed. . . . What was wrong, Uncle Joe?"

OLD/TIMER — "Even an experienced hunter could easily have missed that one. . . . You shot behind your bird, Billy, but cheer up. . . . A clean miss is far better than a partial hit which only wounds and leaves another cripple in the marsh."

BOY — "Here come three more. . . . I can tell they're divers, but what species are they, Uncle Joe?"

OLD/TIMER — "They're Lesser Scaup, a medium-sized diving duck. . . . Keep still now, they're sure to decoy. . . . When they are over the decoys, pick your bird and lead according to speed. . . . They almost stand still at times over the decoys. . . . (SOUND — Gun shot) . . . Good boy! Another clean kill."

BOY — "This is the most fun I have ever had, Uncle Joe. . . . Do you think I'll become a good shot? Will you take me out again soon?"

OLD/TIMER — "Yes, Billy. . . . I will take you out again, and soon. You have the makings of a good shot and, better still, a good sportsman."

DUCKS UNLIMITED
CONSERVATION SERIES
BROADCAST NO. 21

M.C. — "We have two very special guests with us today. . . . They flew in especially for this broadcast. Both gentlemen are from the deep south. . . . (low quacks) What's that? Oh, you're just wintering there! . . . However, may I introduce Morty Mallard (deep quack) . . . and Percy Pintail (shrill quack) . . . Members of two of our most prominent duck families. . . . The Mallards probably are more numerous than the Pintails. . . .

MORTY — "Probably," he says . . . The Mallards have more branches than a cottonwood. . . . If all the Mallards were laid end to end. . . .

PERCY (very loud) — "Who cares?"

M.C. — "Please, gentlemen! . . . Both families are noted for their sporting qualities. . . . But they can tell you about that. . . . Morty, how was the trip north?"

MORTY — "Rugged is the word. . . . Wings iced up twice. . . . Had to sit on chimneys to thaw out. . . Sure plenty hot over New Mexico. . . . We got inspected by fighter planes by day, searchlights at night. . . .

PERCY — "Atomic testing area. . . . Bet they'd suspect even a mosquito. . . . Never figured a duck would have to be given flight briefing, like I gave Morty when he wanted to fly low and peek at an atomic pile . . . Imagine!"

M.C. — "You really had excitement. . . . Morty, will you give us some family history?"

MORTY — "Sure. . . . I'll rattle off a few quotes from Kortright's fine book, "The Ducks, Geese and Swans of North America" . . .

PERCY (loudly) — "How'd the geese and swans get in here? . . . I thought this was a special program for ducks?"

M.C. — "Ducks Unlimited! Top billing for ducks!"

MORTY — "Kortright says, quote, 'Of all ducks, the one that is of the greatest importance to man is, unquestionably, the Mallard. For thousands of years the wild Mallard has furnished mankind with countless tons of food. . . ."

PERCY (scoffing) — "A super-market with web feet. . . ."

MORTY — ". . . 'No one country or even continent can claim the Mallard for its own' . . .

PERCY (mock amazement) — "It's here! . . . A duck without a country! . . ."

MORTY — ". . . 'It inhabits almost the whole of the Northern Hemisphere and among the ducks is probably the most abundant species! . . . Here's one of Kortright's notes which shows how democratic we Mallards really are . . . quote, 'The Mallard crosses freely with other species, especially its near-relative the Black Duck. It also crosses with the Gadwall, Pintail, Baldpate, Green-winged Teal and others. . . .'

PERCY — "What, no penguins?"

M.C. — "Alright, Percy. . . . How about some of your family history?"

PERCY — "Kortright was really on the beam when he got around to us . . . quote, 'On this continent the American Pintail has the widest breeding range of all ducks. As a result of this wide distribution, its abundance throughout its range and the strikingly handsome appearance of the drake, it is probably one of the best known of North American wild fowl' . . . Here's a gem . . . 'No duck is more readily recognized in flight than the trim, handsome Pintail drake. Its racy lines, as much as the rapidity of its flight, have earned it the name of greyhound among ducks'. . . ."

MORTY — "Greyhound? The Pintail? . . . Oh, Mr. Kortright . . . The Canvasback family will be furious!"

PERCY — "Okay, so Clem Canvasback is fastest. . . . But I never saw a Mallard I couldn't fly rings around. . . ."

M.C. — "Very interesting. . . . Now is there any final message you'd like to. . . ."

MORTY AND PERCY — "Message? You bet! . . . We're glad we came to give you facts, regarding ducks and why they quack, but now we're off to warmer clime and lucky, too — we're out of rhyme!"

SOUND — Loud quacking, fading, then crash of breaking glass. . . . .

M.C. — "Oh, well. . . . That window needed washing, anyway. . . ."

DUCKS UNLIMITED
CONSERVATION SERIES
BROADCAST NO. 25

SOUND — Aircraft engine operating at cruising speed. (2-place Stinson)

BIOLOGIST — "Smooth as silk up here today. . . . Visibility good. . . . Boy, what a day for reconnaissance!"

ENGINEER — "Nothing like 'hitting the ball' in the morning if you want smooth flying. . . . Say! That should be the area. . . . Better check the map."

BIOLOGIST — "That's it, alright. . . . There's the town about three miles to the south. . . . Let's swing high over the marsh and get the general picture for a starter. . . ."

ENGINEER — "That water certainly is low. . . . Won't last over two weeks."

BIOLOGIST — "A marsh like that, overgrown by emergent plants, tells its own story. . . A sure sign that it frequently goes dry. . . . Wonder what we can do about it . . . How about a dam across the outlet?"

ENGINEER — "I don't think that would be enough. . . The Reeve of the municipality told me there is a creek over to the west. . . . If we can divert the creek into this marsh, then put a dam on the outlet, I think we'll have it. . . Let's have a look."

BIOLOGIST — "There's the creek. . . . Looks pretty good, too. . . . Skirts along the marsh. . . . See, here it is on the map."

ENGINEER — "This looks good. . . . It won't take much of a cut to get the water over into the marsh. . . . We can put a small diversion dam on the creek, cut a canal over to the marsh, build a dam on the outlet. . . What! — the land location?"

233

BIOLOGIST — "That road runs along the township line and the schoolhouse is on section 11. . . . Which means that the marsh is on sections 10 and 15 and the creek at the proposed diversion is on 16."

ENGINEER — "Okay. . . . We'll give that dope to the survey party and send them right in here. . . . Seen everything you want to see?"

BIOLOGIST — "Just a minute. . . . I want to get a couple of pictures of the layout from up here. . . . Then we can go down on the deck and have a look at the vegetation. . . . (10-second pause) . . . Okay, . . . And you can omit the outside loop on the way down."

SOUND — Engine sound indicating a dive. . . .

BIOLOGIST — "Hey! That's close enough . . . I don't want to pick the bulrush. . . . This is going to be a dandy project. . . . Just needs more water for permanency, and open areas so food plants can develop."

ENGINEER — "Well, the engineering is simple enough. . . . Should get water over there without difficulty."

BIOLOGIST — "No haying or cultivation, so there should be no land complications. . . Gentle shoreline, good nesting cover, lots of grass and buckbrush. . . This almost looks like a biologist's dream."

ENGINEER — "Looks unusually easy from an engineering viewpoint, too."

BIOLOGIST — "Well, we'll get a report on the ground from the district project manager. . . Pour the coal to her, son. . . . Let's go upstairs."

ENGINEER — "Where to now?"

SOUND — Engine tempo changes, indicating climb. . . .

BIOLOGIST — "About 20 miles north-west. . . . A big marsh which a farmer reports as drying up most years. . . . May be worth a look."

ENGINEER — "If it's half as good as this one, the trip will be worthwhile. . . . Hold your hat. . . . I'm going to see how quick this crate can move. . . ."

SOUND — Engine tempo increases, gradually fades out . . . then fades in. . . .

BIOLOGIST — "There's an area which could be the right one. . . . Not much plant growth and it seems to be half dry. . . . How does it impress you?"

ENGINEER — "That's it, alright. . . . From here it looks as though the dam would have to be very long to assure permanency. . . . I'm afraid this one would cost far too much to be practical. . . . Not even sure a ground survey would be justified."

BIOLOGIST — "Oh, well . . . We can't expect to be lucky every time out. . . . Let's head back."

SOUND — Engine tempo steps up, gradually fades out. . . .

Appendix IV

DUCKS UNLIMITED (CANADA)
DIRECTORS, OFFICERS, AND COMMITTEES

1938
DIRECTORS
CANADIAN
Judge William G. Ross
O. Leigh Spencer
James A. Richardson
S. S. Holden

AMERICAN
Louis H. Barkhausen
Harold W. Story
Butler F. Greer
Arthur M. Bartley

OFFICERS
President — Judge William G. Ross
1st Vice-President — Louis H. Barkhausen
2nd Vice-President — O. Leigh Spencer
*Secretary — Edward B. Pitblado
Treasurer — Harold W. Story
*Asst. Treasurer — J. Gray Mundie

FINANCE COMMITTEE
Chairman — Harold W. Story
James A. Richardson
Butler F. Greer
S. S. Holden
Louis H. Barkhausen

EXECUTIVE COMMITTEE
Chairman — Judge William G. Ross
Louis H. Barkhausen
Harold Story
James A. Richardson
Arthur M. Bartley
*Non voting appointments
Date of Annual Meeting, 1 April 1938.
Place of Annual Meeting, Winnipeg, Manitoba.

1939
DIRECTORS
CANADIAN
Judge William G. Ross
O. Leigh Spencer
James A. Richardson
S. S. Holden

AMERICAN
Louis H. Barkhausen
Harold W. Story
Butler F. Greer
Arthur M. Bartley

OFFICERS
President — Judge William G. Ross
1st Vice-President — Louis H. Barkhausen
2nd Vice-President — O. Leigh Spencer
Secretary — Edward B. Pitblado
Treasurer — Harold W. Story
Asst. Treasurer — J. Gray Mundie

FINANCE COMMITTEE
Chairman — Harold W. Story
James A. Richardson

Butler F. Greer
S. S. Holden
Louis H. Barkhausen

EXECUTIVE COMMITTEE
Chairman — Judge William G. Ross
Louis H. Barkhausen
Harold W. Story
O. Leigh Spencer
Arthur M. Bartley
Directorate increased at 1939 meeting to 10.
Date of Annual Meeting, 14 April 1939.
Place of Annual Meeting, Winnipeg, Manitoba.

1940
DIRECTORS
CANADIAN
Honorable John Bracken
Judge W. G. Ross
O. Leigh Spencer
Austin C. Taylor
S. S. Holden

AMERICAN
L. H. Barkhausen
A. M. Bartley
M. W. Smith
B. F. Greer
H. W. Story

OFFICERS
Chairman of the Board — Judge William G. Ross
President — O. Leigh Spencer
1st Vice-President — Louis H. Barkhausen
2nd Vice-President — Vacant
Secretary — Edward B. Pitblado
Asst. Secretary — W. S. McEwen
Treasurer — Morton W. Smith
Asst. Treasurer — J. Gray Mundie

FINANCE COMMITTEE
Chairman — Morton W. Smith
The Hon. John Bracken
Austin C. Taylor

EXECUTIVE COMMITTEE
Chairman — O. Leigh Spencer
Louis H. Barkhausen
Judge William G. Ross
Morton W. Smith
Arthur M. Bartley
Date of Annual Meeting, 27 April 1940.
Place of Annual Meeting, Winnipeg, Manitoba.

1941
DIRECTORS
CANADIAN
Honorable John Bracken
W. G. Ross
O. Leigh Spencer
Austin C. Taylor
S. S. Holden
W. C. Fisher

AMERICAN
L. H. Barkhausen
A. M. Bartley
M. W. Smith
B. F. Greer
H. W. Story
Major Max Fleischmann

OFFICERS
Chairman of the Board — Judge William G. Ross
President — O. Leigh Spencer
1st Vice-President — Louis H. Barkhausen
2nd Vice-President — The Hon. John Bracken
Secretary — W. S. McEwen
Treasurer — Morton W. Smith

FINANCE COMMITTEE
Chairman — The Hon. John Bracken
Morton W. Smith
Austin C. Taylor
W. C. Fisher

EXECUTIVE COMMITTEE
Chairman — O. Leigh Spencer
Louis H. Barkhausen
Judge William G. Ross
Morton W. Smith
Arthur M. Bartley
Directorate increased to 12.
Date of Annual Meeting, 2 May 1941.
Place of Annual Meeting, Winnipeg, Manitoba.

1942
DIRECTORS
CANADIAN
Honorable John Bracken
Judge W. G. Ross
O. Leigh Spencer
Austin C. Taylor
S. S. Holden
W. C. Fisher

AMERICAN
L. H. Barkhausen
A. M. Bartley
M. W. Smith
B. F. Greer
H. W. Story
Major Max Fleischmann

OFFICERS
Chairman of the Board — Judge William G. Ross
President — O. Leigh Spencer
1st Vice-President — Louis H. Barkhausen
2nd Vice-President — Hon. John Bracken
Secretary — W. S. McEwen
Treasurer — Morton W. Smith

FINANCE COMMITTEE
Chairman — The Hon. John Bracken
Morton W. Smith
Austin C. Taylor

(Continued on next page)

W. C. Fisher
EXECUTIVE COMMITTEE
Chairman — O. Leigh Spencer
Judge William G. Ross
Louis H. Barkhausen
Morton W. Smith
Arthur M. Bartley
Date of Annual Meeting, 15 May 1942.
Place of Annual Meeting, Winnipeg, Manitoba.

1943

DIRECTORS
CANADIAN
O. Leigh Spencer
S. S. Holden
Hon. John Bracken
Judge W. G. Ross
A. C. Taylor
W. C. Fisher
AMERICAN
A. M. Bartley
L. H. Barkhausen
H. W. Story
M. W. Smith
Major Max Fleischmann
H. R. Basford

OFFICERS
Chairman of the Board — O. Leigh Spencer
President — William C. Fisher
1st Vice-President — Louis H. Barkhausen
2nd Vice-President — Judge William G. Ross
Secretary — W. S. McEwen
Treasurer — Morton W. Smith
Asst. Treasurer — J. Gray Mundie
FINANCE COMMITTEE
Chairman — H. R. Basford
Morton W. Smith
S. S. Holden
EXECUTIVE COMMITTEE
Chairman — W. C. Fisher
Louis H. Barkhausen
Judge William G. Ross
A. M. Bartley
O. Leigh Spencer
Morton W. Smith
Directorate increased to 18: 12 to be elected immediately, and 6 during the year.
Date of Annual Meeting, 28 May 1943.
Place of Annual Meeting, Calgary, Alberta.

1944

DIRECTORS
CANADIAN
W. C. Fisher
O. Leigh Spencer
Judge W. G. Ross
Chief Justice W. M. Martin
S. S. Holden
W. J. Dick
John B. Richardson
Gordon Konantz
S. F. Heard
AMERICAN
M. W. Smith

Will J. Reid
A. C. Glassell
Glenn L. Martin
H. R. Basford
L. H. Barkhausen
Major Max Fleischmann
A. M. Bartley
H. W. Story
OFFICERS
Chairman of the Board — O. Leigh Spencer
President — William C. Fisher
1st Vice-President — Louis H. Barkhausen
2nd Vice-President — Judge W. G. Ross
Secretary — W. S. McEwen
Treasurer — Morton W. Smith
Asst. Treasurer — J. Gray Mundie
FINANCE COMMITTEE
Chairman — H. R. Basford
Morton W. Smith
S. S. Holden
EXECUTIVE COMMITTEE
Chairman — W. J. Dick
Louis H. Barkhausen
A. M. Bartley
Directors decided to increase directorate to 30 but it was some years before all vacancies were filled.
Date of Annual Meeting, 7 October 1944.
Place of Annual Meeting, Calgary, Alberta.

1945

DIRECTORS
CANADIAN
W. J. Dick
W. C. Fisher
Col. W. F. W. Hancock
S. S. Holden
S. F. Heard
G. E. Konantz
Judge L. T. McKim
Chief Justice W. M. Martin
J. B. Richardson
O. Leigh Spencer
Judge W. G. Ross
Charles H. Wentz
AMERICAN
A. M. Bartley
L. H. Barkhausen
H. R. Basford
Major Max Fleischmann
A. C. Glassell
Glenn L. Martin
M. W. Smith
H. W. Story
Will J. Reid

OFFICERS
Chairman of the Board — W. C. Fisher
President — S. S. Holden
1st Vice-President — Louis H. Barkhausen
2nd Vice-President — Judge W. G. Ross
Secretary — W. S. McEwen
Treasurer — Morton W. Smith
Asst. Treasurer — Gordon Konantz

FINANCE COMMITTEE
Chairman — Morton W. Smith
H. R. Basford
Gordon Konantz
EXECUTIVE COMMITTEE
Chairman — S. S. Holden
Louis H. Barkhausen
Morton W. Smith
Arthur M. Bartley
Judge W. G. Ross
LEGAL COMMITTEE
Chief Justice W. M. Martin
Judge W. G. Ross
Judge L. T. McKim
Date of Annual Meeting, 28 September 1945.
Place of Annual Meeting, Saskatoon, Saskatchewan.

1946

DIRECTORS
CANADIAN
S. S. Holden
Judge W. G. Ross
W. C. Fisher
Judge Louis McKim
Col. W. F. W. Hancock
O. Leigh Spencer
Chief Justice W. M. Martin
W. J. Dick
C. H. Wentz
G. R. Konantz
AMERICAN
L. H. Barkhausen
M. W. Smith
A. M. Bartley
H. R. Basford
H. W. Story
Glenn L. Martin
A. C. Glassell
Major Max Fleischmann
Will J. Reid
OFFICERS
Chairman of the Board — W. C. Fisher
President — S. S. Holden
1st Vice-President — Louis H. Barkhausen
2nd Vice-President — Judge W. G. Ross
Secretary — Edward B. Pitblado
Treasurer — Morton W. Smith
Asst. Treasurer — Gordon Konantz
FINANCE COMMITTEE
Chairman — Morton W. Smith
H. R. Basford
Gordon Konantz
EXECUTIVE COMMITTEE
Chairman — S. S. Holden
Louis H. Barkhausen
Morton W. Smith .
Arthur M. Bartley
Judge W. G. Ross
LEGAL COMMITTEE
Chief Justice W. M. Martin
Judge W. G. Ross
Judge L. T. McKim
Date of Annual Meeting, 9 April 1946.
Place of Annual Meeting, Ottawa, Ontario.

1947

DIRECTORS

CANADIAN

Judge W. G. Ross
Col. W. F. W. Hancock
G. E. Konantz
Judge L. T. McKim
Chief Justice W. M. Martin
W. C. Fisher
W. J. Dick

AMERICAN

M. W. Smith
H. R. Basford
A. C. Glassell
A. M. Bartley
L. H. Barkhausen
H. W. Story
Major Max Fleischmann
Will J. Reid
Glenn L. Martin

OFFICERS

Chairman of the Board — W. C. Fisher
President — Judge W. G. Ross
1st Vice-President — Louis H. Barkhausen
2nd Vice-President — Gordon E. Konantz
Secretary — Edward B. Pitblado
Treasurer — Morton W. Smith

FINANCE COMMITTEE

Chairman — Morton W. Smith
H. R. Basford
Gordon E. Konantz

EXECUTIVE COMMITTEE

Chairman — Judge W. G. Ross
Louis H. Barkhausen
Morton W. Smith
Gordon E. Konantz
Arthur M. Bartley

Date of Annual Meeting, 30 May 1947.
Place of Annual Meeting, Regina, Saskatchewan.

1948

DIRECTORS

CANADIAN

W. C. Fisher
Chief Justice W. M. Martin
W. J. Dick
G. E. Konantz
Judge L. T. McKim
Col. W. F. W. Hancock
Senator N. M. Paterson
R. L. Hutchinson
Dr. Walter F. Tisdale
A/V/M Leigh F. Stevenson

AMERICAN

A. M. Bartley
L. H. Barkhausen
H. R. Basford
H. W. Story
M. W. Smith
Major Max Fleischmann
Will J. Reid
A. C. Glassell
Glenn L. Martin

OFFICERS

Chairman of the Board — Judge L. T. McKim
President — Dr. W. F. Tisdale
1st Vice-President — Louis H. Barkhausen
2nd Vice-President — Col. W. F. W. Hancock
Secretary — Edward B. Pitblado
Treasurer — Morton W. Smith

FINANCE COMMITTEE

Chairman — Morton W. Smith
H. R. Basford
Gordon E. Konantz

EXECUTIVE COMMITTEE

Chairman — Dr. W. F. Tisdale
Louis H. Barkhausen
Morton W. Smith
Col. W. F. W. Hancock
Arthur M. Bartley

Date of Annual Meeting, 7 April 1948.
Place of Annual Meeting, Winnipeg, Manitoba.

1949

DIRECTORS

CANADIAN

W. C. Fisher
Chief Justice W. M. Martin
Gordon Farrell
G. E. Konantz
Judge L. T. McKim
Col. W. F. W. Hancock
Senator N. M. Paterson
R. L. Hutchinson
Dr. W. M. Tisdale
A/V/M L. F. Stevenson

AMERICAN

A. M. Bartley
L. H. Barkhausen
H. R. Basford
H. W. Story
M. W. Smith
Major Max Fleischmann
Will J. Reid
A. C. Glassell
Edgar M. Queeny

OFFICERS

Chairman of the Board — Judge L. T. McKim
President — Dr. W. F. Tisdale
1st Vice-President — Louis H. Barkhausen
2nd Vice-President — Col. W. F. W. Hancock
Secretary — Edward B. Pitblado
Treasurer — Morton W. Smith

FINANCE COMMITTEE

Chairman — Morton W. Smith
Gordon E. Konantz
H. R. Basford

EXECUTIVE COMMITTEE

Chairman — Arthur M. Bartley
Dr. W. F. Tisdale
Morton W. Smith
Col. W. F. W. Hancock
Louis H. Barkhausen

Date of Annual Meeting, 26 March 1949
Place of Annual Meeting, Reno, Nevada

1950

DIRECTORS

CANADIAN

W. C. Fisher
Chief Justice W. M. Martin
Gordon Farrell
G. E. Konantz
Judge L. T. McKim
Col. W. F. W. Hancock
Senator N. M. Paterson
R. L. Hutchinson
Dr. W. M. Tisdale
A/V/M L. F. Stevenson

AMERICAN

A. M. Bartley
L. H. Barkhausen
H. R. Basford
H. W. Story
M. W. Smith
Major Max Fleischmann
Will J. Reid
A. C. Glassell
Edgar M. Queeny

OFFICERS

Chairman of the Board — Dr. W. F. Tisdale
President — Judge L. T. McKim
1st Vice-President — Louis H. Barkhausen
2nd Vice-President — Col. W. F. W. Hancock
Secretary — Edward B. Pitblado
Treasurer — Morton W. Smith

FINANCE COMMITTEE

Chairman — Morton W. Smith
Gordon E. Konantz
H. R. Basford

EXECUTIVE COMMITTEE

Chairman — Arthur M. Bartley
Judge L. T. McKim
Morton W. Smith
Col. W. F. W. Hancock
Louis H. Barkhausen

Date of Annual Meeting, 3 June 1950.
Place of Annual Meeting, Calgary, Alberta.

1951

DIRECTORS

CANADIAN

W. C. Fisher
Chief Justice W. M. Martin
Gordon Farrell
G. E. Konantz
Judge L. T. McKim
Col. W. F. W. Hancock
Senator N. M. Paterson
R. L. Hutchinson
Dr. W. M. Tisdale
A/V/M L. F. Stevenson

AMERICAN

A. M. Bartley
L. H. Barkhausen
H. R. Basford
H. W. Story
M. W. Smith

(Continued on next page)

(Continued on next page)

2nd Vice-President — Dr. W. F. Tisdale
Secretary — Edward B. Pitblado
Treasurer — Robert Winthrop
FINANCE COMMITTEE
Chairman — Robert Winthrop
R. Earle Harcourt
R. H. G. Bonnycastle
EXECUTIVE COMMITTEE
Chairman — Arthur M. Bartley
R. Earle Harcourt
R. M. Gaylord
Robert Winthrop
R. H. G. Bonnycastle
Date of Annual Meeting, 21 March 1959.
Place of Annual Meeting, Baton Rouge, Louisiana.

1960

DIRECTORS
CANADIAN
Hon. C. Wallace
R. L. Hutchinson
Col. W. F. W. Hancock
Gordon Farrell
George T. Richardson
Dr. W. F. Tisdale
R. H. G. Bonnycastle
R. Earle Harcourt
Fred Auger
R. A. Kramer
William Nolan
E. H. Moncrieff
J. N. Connacher
Dr. W. Kenneth Martin
AMERICAN
A. M. Bartley
L. H. Barkhausen
H. W. Story
M. W. Smith
C. A. Gross
E. M. Queeny
A. C. Glassell
R. M. Gaylord
Robert Winthrop
H. Bliss Rucker
Carsten Tiedeman
OFFICERS
Chairman of the Board — Col. W. F. W.
   Hancock
President — R. H. G. Bonnycastle
1st Vice-President — R. M. Gaylord
2nd Vice-President — Dr. W. F. Tisdale
Secretary — Edward B. Pitblado
Treasurer — Robert Winthrop
FINANCE COMMITTEE
Chairman — Robert Winthrop
R. Earle Harcourt
R. H. G. Bonnycastle
EXECUTIVE COMMITTEE
Chairman — R. H. G. Bonnycastle
R. Earle Harcourt
George T. Richardson
E. H. Moncrieff
R. M. Gaylord
Carsten Tiedeman

Robert Winthrop
Bliss Rucker
Arthur M. Bartley
Date of Annual Meeting, 7 May 1960.
Place of Annual Meeting, Detroit, Michigan.

1961

DIRECTORS
CANADIAN
Fred Auger
R. H. G. Bonnycastle
J. N. Connacher
Gordon Farrell
Col. W. F. W. Hancock
R. Earle Harcourt
R. L. Hutchinson
R. A. Kramer
Dr. W. Kenneth Martin
E. H. Moncrieff
William Nolan
George T. Richardson
Hon. C. Wallace
AMERICAN
Stirling S. Adams
A. M. Bartley
L. H. Barkhausen
William F. Elser
R. M. Gaylord
A. C. Glassell
E. M. Queeny
H. Bliss Rucker
Carsten Tiedeman
Mandt Torrison
Robert Winthrop
OFFICERS
Chairman of the Board — R. H. G. Bonnycastle
President — Fred Auger
1st Vice-President — R. M. Gaylord
2nd Vice-President — George T. Richardson
Secretary — Edward B. Pitblado
Treasurer — Robert Winthrop
FINANCE COMMITTEE
Chairman — Robert Winthrop
R. Earle Harcourt
R. H. G. Bonnycastle
EXECUTIVE COMMITTEE
Chairman — R. H. G. Bonnycastle
R. Earle Harcourt
George T. Richardson
E. H. Moncrieff
R. M. Gaylord
Carsten Tiedeman
Robert Winthrop
H. Bliss Rucker
Arthur M. Bartley
Date of Annual Meeting, 15 April 1961.
Place of Annual Meeting, Las Vegas, Nevada.

1962

DIRECTORS
CANADIAN
Fred Auger
R. H. G. Bonnycastle

J. N. Connacher
Gordon Farrell
Col. W. F. W. Hancock
R. Earle Harcourt
R. L. Hutchinson
R. A. Kramer
Dr. W. Kenneth Martin
George T. Richardson
E. H. Moncrieff
Hon. C. Wallace
William Nolan
F. S. Sharpe
Peter Bawden
AMERICAN
Stirling S. Adams
A. M. Bartley
William P. Elser
R. M. Gaylord
A. C. Glassell
H. Bliss Rucker
Carsten Tiedeman
Mandt Torrison
Robert Winthrop
Edgar M. Queeny
OFFICERS
Chairman of the Board — R. H. G. Bonnycastle
President — Fred Auger
1st Vice-President — R. M. Gaylord
2nd Vice-President — George T. Richardson
Secretary — Edward B. Pitblado
Treasurer — Robert Winthrop
FINANCE COMMITTEE
Chairman — Robert Winthrop
R. Earle Harcourt
R. H. G. Bonnycastle
EXECUTIVE COMMITTEE
Chairman — R. H. G. Bonnycastle
R. Earle Harcourt
George T. Richardson
E. H. Moncrieff
R. M. Gaylord
Carsten Tiedeman
Robert Winthrop
H. Bliss Rucker
Arthur M. Bartley
Date of Annual Meeting, 7 April 1962.
Place of Annual Meeting, New York, N.Y.

1963

DIRECTORS
CANADIAN
R. H. G. Bonnycastle
Gordon Farrell
R. Earle Harcourt
Hon. C. Wallace
R. A. Kramer
F. S. Sharpe
G. T. Richardson
Peter Bawden
Dr. W. Kenneth Martin
J. N. Connacher
Fred Auger

AMERICAN
Stirling S. Adams
A. M. Bartley
A. C. Glassell
Edgar M. Queeny
R. M. Gaylord
Robert Winthrop
H. Bliss Rucker
Carsten Tiedeman
Mandt Torrison
A. B. McKee, Jr.
W. P. Elser
OFFICERS
Chairman of the Board — Fred Auger
President — Dr. W. Kenneth Martin
1st Vice-President — R. M. Gaylord
2nd Vice-President — George T. Richardson
Secretary — Edward B. Pitblado
Treasurer — F. S. Sharpe
FINANCE COMMITTEE
Chairman — F. S. Sharpe
R. Earle Harcourt
Robert Winthrop
EXECUTIVE COMMITTEE
Chairman — R. H. G. Bonnycastle
R. Earle Harcourt
George T. Richardson
Dr. W. K. Martin
R. M. Gaylord
Carsten Tiedeman
F. S. Sharpe
J. N. Connacher
H. Bliss Rucker
Arthur M. Bartley
Fred Auger
MANAGEMENT SUB-COMMITTEE
OF EXECUTIVE
Chairman — R. H. G. Bonnycastle
George T. Richardson
F. S. Sharpe
Dr. W. K. Martin
J. N. Connacher
HONORARY ADVISORY COMMITTEE
Col. W. F. W. Hancock
R. L. Hutchinson
Chief Justice W. M. Martin
Date of Annual Meeting, 6 April 1963.
Place of Annual Meeting, Pasadena, California.

1964
DIRECTORS
CANADIAN
Gordon Farrell
Hon. C. Wallace
F. S. Sharpe
Peter Bawden
Dr. W. K. Martin
Fred Auger
R. Earle Harcourt
R. A. Kramer
R. H. G. Bonnycastle
J. N. Connacher
Dr. E. A. McCusker

AMERICAN
Stirling S. Adams
A. C. Glassell
R. M. Gaylord
H. Bliss Rucker
W. P. Elser
A. B. McKee, Jr.
A. M. Bartley
E. M. Queeny
Robert Winthrop
Carsten Tiedeman
Mandt Torrison
Robert D. Marcotte
OFFICERS
Chairman of the Board — Fred Auger
President — Dr. W. Kenneth Martin
1st Vice-President — R. M. Gaylord
2nd Vice-President — Robert A. Kramer
Secretary — Edward B. Pitblado
Treasurer — F. S. Sharpe
FINANCE COMMITTEE
Chairman — F. S. Sharpe
R. Earle Harcourt
Robert Winthrop
EXECUTIVE COMMITTEE
Chairman — R. H. G. Bonnycastle
R. Earle Harcourt
Dr. W. K. Martin
R. M. Gaylord
Carsten Tiedeman
F. S. Sharpe
J. N. Connacher
H. Bliss Rucker
Arthur M. Bartley
Fred Auger
Peter Bawden
MANAGEMENT SUB-COMMITTEE
OF EXECUTIVE
Chairman — R. H. G. Bonnycastle
F. S. Sharpe
Dr. W. K. Martin
J. N. Connacher
Peter Bawden
HONORARY ADVISORY COMMITTEE
Col. W. F. W. Hancock
R. L. Hutchinson
Chief Justice W. M. Martin
Date of Annual Meeting, 25 April 1964.
Place of Annual Meeting, Baltimore, Maryland.

1965
DIRECTORS
CANADIAN
Hon. C. Wallace
R. A. Kramer
F. S. Sharpe
R. H. G. Bonnycastle
Peter Bawden
Dr. W. K. Martin
J. N. Connacher
Fred Auger
Dr. E. A. McCusker
Max Trimble

A. O. Ackroyd
Gordon Farrell
R. Earle Harcourt
AMERICAN
Stirling S. Adams
A. M. Bartley
A. C. Glassell
E. M. Queeny
R. M. Gaylord
Robert Winthrop
H. Bliss Rucker
W. P. Elser
A. B. McKee, Jr.
R. D. Marcotte
Henry G. Schmidt
HONORARY LIFE MEMBERS
Chief Justice W. M. Martin
William Nolan
Col. W. F. W. Hancock
R. L. Hutchinson
OFFICERS
Chairman of the Board — Dr. W. K. Martin
President — Robert A. Kramer
1st Vice-President — R. M. Gaylord
2nd Vice-President — Peter Bawden
Secretary — Edward B. Pitblado
Treasurer — F. S. Sharpe
FINANCE COMMITTEE
Chairman — F. S. Sharpe
Robert Winthrop
R. Earle Harcourt
EXECUTIVE COMMITTEE
Chairman — R. H. G. Bonnycastle
R. Earle Harcourt
Dr. W. K. Martin
R. M. Gaylord
F. S. Sharpe
H. Bliss Rucker
Arthur M. Bartley
Fred Auger
Peter Bawden
Robert A. Kramer
J. N. Connacher
Henry G. Schmidt
MANAGEMENT SUB-COMMITTEE
OF EXECUTIVE
Chairman — R. H. G. Bonnycastle
F. S. Sharpe
Robert A. Kramer
Peter Bawden
J. N. Connacher
Date of Annual Meeting, 5 April 1965.
Place of Annual Meeting, New Orleans, Louisiana.

1966
DIRECTORS
CANADIAN
Hon. C. Wallace
R. A. Kramer
F. S. Sharpe
R. H. G. Bonnycastle
Peter Bawden

(Continued on next page)

Dr. W. K. Martin
J. N. Connacher
Fred Auger
Dr. E. A. McCusker
Max Trimble
A. O. Ackroyd
Gordon Farrell
AMERICAN
Stirling S. Adams
A. M. Bartley
A. C. Glassell
E. M. Queeny
R. M. Gaylord
Robert Winthrop
H. Bliss Rucker
W. P. Elser
A. B. McKee, Jr.
R. D. Marcotte
Henry G. Schmidt

On April 22, 1966, at a Special Directors' Meeting, the following Canadians were also appointed to the board subject to their acceptance.

Robert A. White
George L. Crawford
Thomas H. McLeod
James T. Miller
S. Price Rattray
Elswood Bole
Richard K. Moore
John Lecky
Walter Staheli
T. E. Percival
Lorne M. Cameron
H. G. H. Moody
W. C. Harris

HONORARY LIFE MEMBERS
Chief Justice W. M. Martin
Col. W. F. W. Hancock
William Nolan
R. L. Hutchinson

OFFICERS
Chairman of the Board — Dr. W. K. Martin
President — *Robert A. Kramer
1st Vice-President — R. M. Gaylord
2nd Vice-President — Peter Bawden
Secretary — Edward B. Pitblado
Treasurer — F. S. Sharpe

FINANCE COMMITTEE
Chairman — F. S. Sharpe
Robert Winthrop

EXECUTIVE COMMITTEE
Chairman — R. H. G. Bonnycastle
Dr. W. K. Martin
R. M. Gaylord
F. S. Sharpe
H. Bliss Rucker
Arthur M. Bartley
F. S. Auger
Peter Bawden
J. N. Connacher
Henry G. Schmidt
*R. A. Kramer

MANAGEMENT SUB-COMMITTEE OF EXECUTIVE
Chairman — R. H. G. Bonnycastle
F. S. Sharpe
Peter Bawden
J. N. Connacher
Fred Auger (added April 22/66)
Dr. W. K. Martin (added April 22/66)
*R. A. Kramer

*Resigned as President April 22/66. Replaced by Peter Bawden for remainder of term. Sharpe became 2nd Vice-President and Treasurer (Directors' Meeting April 22/66). Bawden was unable to accept presidency and Dr. W. K. Martin acted in both capacities of President and Chairman during the year.

Date of Annual Meeting, 5 March 1966.
Place of Annual Meeting, San Diego, California.

1967

DIRECTORS
CANADIAN
Hon. C. Wallace
F. S. Sharpe
Dr. W. K. Martin
A. O. Ackroyd
R. A. Kramer
Elswood Bole
H. H. G. Moody
Robert A. White
Walter Staheli
T. E. Percival
George L. Crawford
Richard K. Moore
Peter Bawden
R. H. G. Bonnycastle
Fred Auger
Gordon Farrell
Max Trimble
James T. Miller
Lorne M. Cameron
S. Price Rattray
W. C. Harris
John Lecky
Edward B. Pitblado
J. N. Connacher
T. H. McLeod
AMERICAN
Robert Winthrop
W. P. Elser
Henry G. Schmidt
Stirling S. Adams
Charles B. Allen
Dale Whitesell
H. Bliss Rucker
R. M. Gaylord
R. D. Marcotte
Albert B. McKee, Jr.
Wyndham Hasler

HONORARY LIFE MEMBERS
The Hon. W. M. Martin
Col. W. F. W. Hancock
Edgar M. Queeny

William Nolan
R. L. Hutchinson
Arthur M. Bartley
OFFICERS
Chairman of the Board — Dr. W. K. Martin
President — F. S. Sharpe
1st Vice-President — R. M. Gaylord
2nd Vice-President — John Lecky
Secretary — Edward B. Pitblado
Treasurer — Lorne M. Cameron
FINANCE COMMITTEE
Chairman — Lorne M. Cameron
Wyndham Hasler
EXECUTIVE COMMITTEE
Chairman — R. H. G. Bonnycastle
Dr. W. K. Martin
R. M. Gaylord
F. S. Sharpe
Chas. B. Allen
Dale Whitesell
John Lecky
Walter Staheli
Lorne M. Cameron
J. N. Connacher
Henry G. Schmidt
H. H. G. Moody
Elswood Bole
S. Price Rattray
Edward B. Pitblado

Date of Annual Meeting, 8 April 1967.
Place of Annual Meeting, Richmond, Virginia.

1968

DIRECTORS
CANADIAN
A. O. Ackroyd
Fred Auger
Peter Bawden
Elswood Bole
R. H. G. Bonnycastle
Lorne M. Cameron
**J. N. Connacher
George L. Crawford
Gordon Farrell
W. C. Harris
R. A. Kramer
John Lecky
G. W. Malaher
Dr. W. K. Martin
Dr. E. A. McCusker
Thomas H. McLeod
James T. Miller
**H. G. Moody
Richard K. Moore
T. E. Percival
E. B. Pitblado
S. Price Rattray
Walter Staheli
Max Trimble
Hon. C. Wallace
Robert A. White
AMERICAN
Stirling S. Adams

Charles B. Allen
Chester F. Dolley
Gaylord Donnelley
W. K. duPont
W. P. Elser
R. M. Gaylord
W. Hasler
R. D. Marcotte
Albert B. McKee, Jr.
H. Bliss Rucker
Henry G. Schmidt
Dale E. Whitesell
HONORARY LIFE MEMBERS
A. M. Bartley
Col. W. F. W. Hancock
R. L. Hutchinson
Hon. W. M. Martin
Wm. Nolan
Edgar M. Queeny
OFFICERS
Chairman of the Board — Dr. W. K. Martin
President — Dr. W. K. Martin
1st Vice-President — R. M. Gaylord
2nd Vice-President — John Lecky
Secretary — E. B. Pitblado
Treasurer — Lorne M. Cameron
FINANCE COMMITTEE
Chairman — Lorne M. Cameron
Wyndham Hasler
EXECUTIVE COMMITTEE
Chairman — *R. H. G. Bonnycastle
Dr. W. K. Martin
R. M. Gaylord
W. G. Malaher
Chas. B. Allen
Dale Whitesell
John Lecky
Walter Staheli
Lorne M. Cameron
Henry G. Schmidt
Elswood Bole
S. Price Rattray
E. B. Pitblado
**H. G. Moody
**J. N. Connacher
*Martin likely replaced Bonnycastle after his death.
**Resigned September, 1968.
December 16, 1968 — Winnipeg — Special
Directors' Meeting. Following directors appointed
for balance of term of the director each replaced.
Rod McIsaac
G. Fitzpatrick Dunn
Norval Hellofs
Date of Annual Meeting, 27 April 1968.
Place of Annual Meeting, Milwaukee, Wisconsin.

1969
DIRECTORS

CANADIAN
A. O. Ackroyd
Fred Auger
Peter Bawden
Elswood Bole

Lorne M. Cameron
G. L. Crawford
G. Fitzpatrick Dunn
Norval Hellofs
R. A. Kramer
John Lecky
G. W. Malaher
Dr. W. K. Martin
Dr. E. A. McCusker
T. H. McLeod
J. T. Miller
Richard K. Moore
T. E. Percival
E. B. Pitblado
S. Price Rattray
Walter Staheli
Max Trimble
Robert A. White
R. W. Burns
AMERICAN
Stirling S. Adams
Charles B. Allen
Chester F. Dolley
Gaylord Donnelley
W. K. duPont
W. P. Elser
R. M. Gaylord
Wyndham Hasler
R. D. Marcotte
Albert B. McKee, Jr.
H. Bliss Rucker
Henry G. Schmidt
Dale E. Whitesell
HONORARY DIRECTORS
Gordon Farrell
Col. W. F. W. Hancock
Hon. W. M. Martin
William Nolan
Hon. Clarence Wallace
A. M. Bartley
OFFICERS
Chairman of the Board — Fred Auger
President — Lorne M. Cameron
1st Vice-President — R. M. Gaylord
2nd Vice-President — John Lecky
Secretary — E. B. Pitblado
Treasurer — G. W. Malaher
FINANCE COMMITTEE
Chairman — G. W. Malaher
Wyndham Hasler
EXECUTIVE COMMITTEE
Chairman — Dr. W. K. Martin
Elswood Bole
Lorne M. Cameron
Norval Hellofs
John Lecky
G. W. Malaher
E. B. Pitblado
S. Price Rattray
Walter Staheli
Chas. B. Allen
Wm. Elser
R. M. Gaylord

Henry G. Schmidt
Dale E. Whitesell
Date of Annual Meeting, 28 March 1969.
Place of Annual Meeting, Victoria, British Columbia.

1970
DIRECTORS
CANADIAN
A. O. Ackroyd
Fred Auger
Peter Bawden
Robert W. Burns
Lorne M. Cameron
J. A. Cranstoun
G. Fitzpatrick Dunn
Norval Hellofs
R. O. A. Hunter
D. M. Jessiman
A. MacGregor Kennedy
R. A. Kramer
John Lecky
G. W. Malaher
Dr. W. K. Martin
Richard K. Moore
James T. Miller
Dr. E. A. McCusker
Thomas H. McLeod
E. B. Pitblado
T. E. Percival
S. Price Rattray
Walter Staheli
Max Trimble
Robert A. White
AMERICAN
Stirling S. Adams
Charles B. Allen
Chester F. Dolley
Gaylord Donnelley
W. K. duPont
Wm. Elser
R. M. Gaylord
Wyndham Hasler
R. D. Marcotte
Albert B. McKee, Jr.
H. Bliss Rucker
Henry G. Schmidt
Dale E. Whitesell

HONORARY DIRECTORS
Hon. Chief Justice W. M. Martin
Col. W. F. W. Hancock
William Nolan
Arthur M. Bartley
Gordon Farrell
R. L. Hutchinson
Hon. Clarence Wallace
OFFICERS
Chairman of the Board — Dr. W. K. Martin
President — Lorne M. Cameron
1st Vice-President — R. M. Gaylord
2nd Vice-President — Robert A. White
Secretary — E. B. Pitblado
Treasurer — J. A. Cranstoun
(Continued on next page)

243

EXECUTIVE COMMITTEE
Chairman — Lorne M. Cameron
Norval Hellofs
Gerald W. Malaher
E. B. Pitblado
S. Price Rattray
Walter Staheli
Dale E. Whitesell
J. A. Cranstoun
R. O. A. Hunter
D. M. Jessiman
Robert A. White
Charles B. Allen
Wm. Elser
R. M. Gaylord
Henry G. Schmidt
Date of Annual Meeting, March 20, 1970.
Place of Annual Meeting, Winnipeg, Manitoba.

1971

DIRECTORS
CANADIAN
F. S. Auger
A. O. Ackroyd
P. Bawden
R. W. Burns
L. M. Cameron
J. A. Cranstoun
G. F. Dunn
D. C. Groff
N. Hellofs
R. O. A. Hunter
D. M. Jessiman
M. Kennedy
R. A. Kramer
J. Lecky
Dr. W. K. Martin
T. H. McLeod
Dr. E. A. McCusker
G. Malaher
G. L. Molgat
J. T. Miller
R. K. Moore
T. E. Percival
E. B. Pitblado
I. G. Purves
S. P. Rattray
W. Staheli
M. Trimble
R. A. White
AMERICAN
C. B. Allen
G. Donnelley
W. P. Elser
R. D. Marcotte
N. H. Ott
H. Taylor, Jr.
H. B. Rucker
C. F. Dolley
W. K. duPont
R. M. Gaylord
A. B. McKee, Jr.
H. G. Schmidt
D. E. Whitesell

HONORARY DIRECTORS
William Nolan
Col. W. F. W. Hancock
Gordon Farrell
Hon. Clarence Wallace
A. M. Bartley
OFFICERS
Chairman of the Board — Lorne M. Cameron
President — Robert A. White
1st Vice-President — R. M. Gaylord
2nd Vice-President — R. O. A. Hunter
Secretary — E. B. Pitblado
Treasurer — J. A. Cranstoun
Asst. Treasurer — D. M. Jessiman (From Nov. 30/71)
EXECUTIVE COMMITTEE
Chairman — Lorne M. Cameron
R. A. White
R. M. Gaylord
R. O. A. Hunter
J. A. Cranstoun
E. B. Pitblado
C. B. Allen
R. W. Burns
W. Elser
D. C. Groff
N. Hellofs
D. M. Jessiman
T. H. McLeod
G. W. Malaher
G. L. Molgat
I. G. Purves
S. P. Rattray
H. G. Schmidt
D. E. Whitesell
Date of Annual Meeting, 27 March 1971.
Place of Annual Meeting: Vancouver, British
Columbia

1972

DIRECTORS
CANADIAN
J. Norman Hyland
John Lecky
Robert A. White
G. Fitzpatrick Dunn
Peter Bawden
Robert W. Burns
Walter Staheli
Robert A. Kramer
Dr. E. A. McCusker
Thomas H. McLeod
Dr. W. K. Martin
Thomas E. Percival
Dr. Herb H. Cowburn
Lorne M. Cameron
Douglas C. Groff
R. O. A. Hunter
D. M. Jessiman
S. R. Lyon
G. W. Malaher
Senator Gil L. Molgat
E. B. Pitblado
Ian G. Purves
S. Price Rattray

Norval Hellofs
MacGregor Kennedy
Richard K. Moore
Hugh H. Mackay
Hugh D. Fairn
AMERICAN
Charles B. Allen
Chester F. Dolley
Gaylord Donnelley
William K. duPont
William P. Elser
F. Rudy Etchen
R. M. Gaylord
Lee C. Howley
R. D. Marcotte
S. Prosser Mellon
Norman H. Ott
Henry G. Schmidt
Herman Taylor, Jr.
Dale E. Whitesell
HONORARY DIRECTORS
Fred Auger (added)
OFFICERS
Chairman of the Board — Lorne M. Cameron
President — Robert A. White
1st Vice-President — R. M. Gaylord
2nd Vice-President — R. O. A. Hunter
Secretary — E. B. Pitblado
Treasurer — D. M. Jessiman
EXECUTIVE COMMITTEE
Chairman — Lorne M. Cameron
R. A. White
R. M. Gaylord
R. O. A. Hunter
D. M. Jessiman
E. B. Pitblado
R. W. Burns
G. F. Dunn
W. K. duPont
W. P. Elser
D. C. Groff
L. C. Howley
S. R. Lyon
T. H. McLeod
H. H. Mackay
Senator G. L. Molgat
R. K. Moore
I. G. Purves
S. P. Rattray
H. G. Schmidt
H. Taylor, Jr.
D. E. Whitesell
G. W. Malaher
Date of Annual Meeting, 25 March 1972.
Place of Annual Meeting, Regina, Saskatchewan.

1973

DIRECTORS
CANADIAN
J. Norman Hyland
John Lecky
Robert A. White
G. Fitzpatrick Dunn

(Continued on next page)

L. C. Howley
R. O. A. Hunter
J. Lecky
S. R. Lyon
H. H. Mackay
Hon. W. J. McKeag
G. W. Malaher
J. D. McDiarmid
Senator G. L. Molgat
E. H. Moncrieff
R. K. Moore
I. G. Purves
S. P. Rattray
H. Taylor, Jr.
R. A. White

FINANCE COMMITTEE
Chairman — J. D. McDiarmid
J. N. Hyland
G. F. Dunn
I. G. Purves

LONG RANGE PLANNING COMMITTEE
Chairman — D. C. Groff
E. H. Moncrieff
J. D. McDiarmid
S. R. Lyon
G. W. Malaher
I. G. Purves
H. H. Mackay
J. C. Greer
R. B. Trethewey

PERSONNEL COMMITTEE
Chairman — I. G. Purves
S. R. Lyon
Senator G. L. Molgat
R. O. A. Hunter

PREMISES COMMITTEE
Chairman — L. M. Cameron
J. D. McDiarmid
E. H. Moncrieff
S. P. Rattray

1978 DU, INC. CONVENTION COMMITTEE
Chairman — D. C. Groff
I. G. Purves
R. O. A. Hunter
D. M. Jessiman
S. R. Lyon
G. W. Malaher
J. D. McDiarmid
Hon. W. J. McKeag
Senator G. L. Molgat
E. H. Moncrieff
S. P. Rattray
E. B. Pitblado

Date of Annual Meeting, 6 March 1976.
Place of Annual Meeting, Winnipeg, Manitoba.

1977

DIRECTORS
CANADIAN
Roger B. Baikie
Lorne E. Johnston
Frank H. Logan
G. F. Dunn

J. N. Hyland
R. B. Trethewey
R. A. White
R. W. Burns
J. C. Greer
R. F. Jennings
Hon. Mr. Justice Michael O'Byrne
Dr. H. H. Cowburn
R. A. Kramer
Dr. W. K. Martin
T. E. Percival
L. M. Cameron
D. C. Groff
R. O. A. Hunter
D. M. Jessiman
S. R. Lyon
G. W. Malaher
J. D. McDiarmid
Hon. W. J. McKeag
Senator G. L. Molgat
E. H. Moncrieff
I. G. Purves
S. P. Rattray
N. H. Hellofs
R. K. Moore
H. D. Fairn
Arthur L. Irving
H. H. Mackay
**Richard A. N. Bonnycastle
**D. Steele Curry
***Peter M. Ramsay

AMERICAN
N. I. Dunn
John E. Spence, Sr.
J. C. Bailey
C. F. Dolley
G. Donnelley
W. K. duPont
L. C. Howley
R. D. Marcotte
H. P. McIntosh, IV
S. P. Mellon
K. Russell
H. Taylor, Jr.
S. P. Williams
Dr. Jerre R. White
*Henry J. Nave

MEXICAN
A. G. Laguera

OFFICERS
Chairman of the Board — D. M. Jessiman
President — H. H. Mackay
1st Vice-President — J. D. McDiarmid
2nd Vice-President — G. Donnelley
Secretary — D. C. Groff
Honorary Secretary — E. B. Pitblado
Treasurer — G. F. Dunn

*Elected to the Board of Directors and the Executive
Committee May 25, 1977
**Appointed to the Board of Directors June 26, 1977.
***Appointed to the Board of Directors and the Executive Committee June 26, 1977.

EXECUTIVE COMMITTEE
Chairman — H. H. Mackay
D. M. Jessiman
J. D. McDiarmid
G. Donnelley
G. F. Dunn
D. C. Groff
R. W. Burns
L. M. Cameron
Dr. H. H. Cowburn
W. K. duPont
L. C. Howley
R. O. A. Hunter
A. L. Irving
S. R. Lyon
Hon. W. J. McKeag
G. W. Malaher
Senator G. L. Molgat
E. H. Moncrieff
R. K. Moore
H. J. Nave
I. G. Purves
P. M. Ramsay
S. P. Rattray
H. Taylor, Jr.
R. B. Trethewey
R. A. White

FINANCE COMMITTEE
Chairman — G. F. Dunn
D. C. Groff
A. L. Irving
E. H. Moncrieff
R. K. Moore

PERSONNEL COMMITTEE
Chairman — J. D. McDiarmid
R. O. A. Hunter
S. R. Lyon
R. A. White

HEAD OFFICE CAPITAL APPEAL COMMITTEE
Chairman — L. M. Cameron
Dr. H. H. Cowburn
R. O. A. Hunter
A. L. Irving
R. F. Jennings
R. A. Kramer
R. K. Moore
R. A. White

BIOLOGICAL AND PROJECT EVALUATION
COMMITTEE
Chairman — E. H. Moncrieff
G. W. Malaher
R. B. Trethewey

LONG RANGE PLANNING COMMITTEE
Chairman — D. M. Jessiman
D. C. Groff
S. R. Lyon
J. D. McDiarmid
Hon. W. J. McKeag
G. W. Malaher
E. H. Moncrieff
I. G. Purves
R. B. Trethewey

(Continued on next page)

NOMINATING COMMITTEE
    Chairman — D. M. Jessiman
    G. Donnelley
    R. O. A. Hunter

1978 DU, INC. CONVENTION COMMITTEE
    Chairman — D. C. Groff
    Vice-Chairman — I. G. Purves

R. O. A. Hunter
D. M. Jessiman
S. R. Lyon
G. W. Malaher
J. D. McDiarmid
Hon. W. J. McKeag
Senator G. L. Molgat
E. H. Moncrieff

S. P. Rattray
Peter M. Ramsay
Edward B. Pitblado

HEAD OFFICE BUILDING COMMITTEE
    S. P. Rattray
    Date of Annual Meeting, 5 March 1977.
    Place of Annual Meeting, Regina, Saskatchewan.

Appendix V

FRONT PAGE FORMAT OF DUCKOLOGICAL

A Permanent Work in Sport and Conservation

THE DUCKOLOGICAL

| No. 2, Volume 18 | Winnipeg, Manitoba | June 3, 1955. |

NESTING SEASON PROGRESSES FAVORABLY

The waterfowl breeding season is developing favorably in all parts of the range in the prairie provinces. The first Pintail broods were seen on May 18-22 in southwestern Saskatchewan and were common by May 27th; in southern Alberta on May 28th; and Mallards (11) in eastern Saskatchewan on May 25th; Pintail (9), Blue-winged teal (10) in Manitoba May 31.

Surface water conditions are generally high - too high in some parts of Saskatchewan and Manitoba but little or no flooding loss is reported as the waters were high when the birds returned and they are nesting on high ground. Heavy precipitation in southern Alberta in May eliminated an incipient drought threat in that area except for a small area in the southeast from Hanna south to the Bow River and east to the Saskatchewan border. Searle Precipitation Report #3 states "Growing season rains from April 1 to May 17 now stands at 132 percent of normal in the case of Alberta; 213 percent of normal in the case of Saskatchewan and 112 percent of normal in the case of Manitoba, giving a weighted average for the three prairie provinces of 184 percent of normal."

Normal June rains will be required to keep the sloughs and potholes in good shape in parts of Alberta and Manitoba

The rains in all three provinces have delayed agricultural activities and as the birds are nesting one to two weeks earlier than last year, indications are that a large percentage of the stubble nesting Mallards and Pintails will have their broods off before farming operations destroy the nests. For the same reason impassable roads have delayed completion of the ground transects in the more northern portions of the agricultural belt and parklands but enough have been run in the southern areas to indicate a reduction in breeding pairs per square mile as compared with last year. This reduction is apparently slight in Alberta and Saskatchewan but more severe in Manitoba.

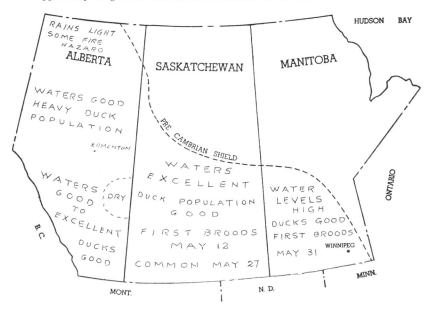

Appendix VI

SUMMARY OF WATERFOWL BREEDING SEASONS 1939-1977

Condensed from Duckologicals

First report on record titled "Ducks and Water Conditions in the Canadian West" dated June 30, 1939. Name changed to "Ducks and Duck Waters in the Canadian West", and then to "Duckological" in July, 1940. First water and duck situation map appeared May 31, 1940.

1939

Spring water conditions excellent in Alberta, good in Saskatchewan, and poor in Manitoba. Increase in ducks nesting on prairies. Dry July but timely rains saved situation. Ducks estimated to have increased by 20% over 1938. Migration long drawn out, some ducks remaining into December.

1940

West of 106th meridian which bisects Saskatchewan, spring water conditions excellent, east very poor. Marshes at south end of lakes Manitoba and Winnipeg lower than "oldtimers ever remember". Increase in nesting ducks. Good June rains. Hot summer but good August rains. Fall population estimated to have increased 18% over 1939, principally in Alberta. Main migration first days of November.

1941

Spring water conditions improved over 1940 but still only classed as fair. Greatest improvement in Manitoba where 1940 was the worst in history. Increased breeding population. Fall flight reduced by drought in central and Saskatchewan "northland", but overall prairie production well above 1940. Heavy fall rains delayed harvest and improved water conditions for 1942 on prairies but "on the 2 million-acre delta of the Saskatchewan River, waters fell to lowest known level". Major migration last days of October and beginning of November.

1942

"Spring water conditions fair in extreme western prairies, bad in the central half, and over the eastern third the best for many long years." Northern areas still relatively low. Increased breeding population. Good summer rains maintained surface water. Greatest fall population of ducks on the prairies since 1928. Best carryover of water since DU began. Major migration October 24 and first week in November.

1943

Great increase in breeding ducks; biggest population in last 20 years. Water conditions better than for many years. Sufficient rain to maintain water through summer. Duck crop estimated to be 25% above 1942. Great increase in Manitoba "phenomenal duck numbers everywhere" in the province. "Mallards in countless numbers." Major migration November 7, 8, and 9th.

1944

Fall and winter precipitation 60% of normal. Runoff below normal in Saskatchewan and Manitoba, light in Alberta. Thirty percent more ducks returned to Canadian West than in 1943 but bigger percentage than in recent years "trekked onward, into the big waters and marshes of the Northland". Widespread heavy June rains resulted in good water condition which lasted through summer. Fall duck population estimated to be 10% above 1943. Output "good average" in Alberta; "heavy" in Saskatchewan; and, "very heavy" in Manitoba. More ducks on prairies than for 30 years, "flights begin to look like 'oldtimes' ". Heavy fall rains, harvest delayed. First recorded big fall migration of blue geese, but went right out. Ducks still abundant November 1 — mass migration on the 26th.

1945

Spring water conditions good in Manitoba, fair to poor in Saskatchewan and Alberta where many migrants continued on north. Migration earliest on record (heavy in third week of March), 10 to 20% more ducks and geese than 1944. Spring drought in prairie Alberta and Saskatchewan and heavy late frosts. June rains failed to relieve the situation — dry through the summer in Saskatchewan and Alberta but excellent conditions in Manitoba. Although a small increase was forecast in the fall flight, 1945 was said to be an unfavorable nesting season. Good fall rains. Major migration first week in November, all gone by the 5th.

1946

Migration early. Return of breeding stock reduced from 1945. Runoff disappointing in many areas in Alberta and Saskatchewan; Manitoba in excellent condition. June rains greatly improved situation in Alberta and Saskatchewan. Fall population "down moderately" compared to 1945. Good fall rains saturated soil. Mass migration November 13-15.

1947

More surface water over a greater area than for many years in the prairie provinces, conditions generally good. Migration late on eastern prairies (April 26-27). Breeding population similar to 1946. Heat and mid-summer drought reduced production and resulted in a fall population similar to 1946. Mass exodus of waterfowl November 5, 6, and 7.

1948

Late spring, major thaw did not occur until April 17. Waterfowl migration three weeks late. Very heavy runoff, greater than anything known in last 50 years, and flooding all across prairies. Small increase in nesting ducks on prairies. Early drought was replaced by heavy July rains removing any threat of drought loss. Fall population increased over 1947 particularly in Alberta. Final migration began November 6 and spectacular evening flights continued through November 10.

1949

Good runoff in Manitoba, poor in Saskatchewan and practically nil in Alberta south of Edmonton. "Great areas which produced waterfowl abundantly in 1948 are dry". Migration at normal dates and about the same numbers as last year. Decrease in prairie breeding populations and increase in northern parklands. Good June and July rains improved prairie prospects. Fall populations estimated to have increased because much of breeding population overflew the drought-stricken prairies to well watered parklands where they nested successfully. Major migrations took place October 22, 23, and also the 27th and 28th.

1950

Runoff poor in Alberta, fair to good in Saskatchewan and Manitoba and habitat conditions similar. Migration two to three weeks late, delayed even further in the north. Breeding population similar to 1949. Good June rains maintained water levels which were critical in southern Alberta. Abnormally late renesting attempt successful due to good fall weather. The fall population estimated to be unchanged from 1949. Mass migration occurred November 8-10.

1951

Spring surface water conditions excellent on the prairies and parklands. Breeding population about the same as 1950. Migration somewhat delayed. June rains maintained satisfactory water levels. "Overall picture indicated a substantial increase in the fall duck population with the southern prairies coming through with its best production in many years." Best surface water and waterfowl numbers since Ducks Unlimited began. Mass migration took place October 15-21 and again on the 24th and 25th, and finally on 29th and 30th.

1952

Spring surface water throughout the prairies and parklands excellent, followed by a dry abnormally hot spring. Increased breeding stock. "Copious rains" in June completely eliminated any drought threat. Cartwright says, (of the June Duckological). "This is probably the most optimistic report it has been my privilege to sign". A bumper duck crop already in sight. Excellent conditions continued through summer. Saskatchewan production described as phenomenal. "Western Canada is sending south a duck crop which many oldtimers say is the greatest in memory". A warm open fall. Final migration November 19 to 23.

1953

Good spring water conditions due to carryover and March and April precipitation but less ideal than last year. Spring migration late March to April 5 exceeded even that of 1952. Season two weeks late due to mid-May snowstorm. Heavy June rains removed any danger of drought losses and delayed summer-fallowing. Some losses anticipated from flooding. Fall population estimated to be down 25% from 1952 due to limited success of mallards and pintails resulting from late spring snowstorms and flooding of renesting attempts. Major migration began October 29 and continued through November 4.

1954

Prairie bare until mid-March. Good runoff in parkland but little on prairies, however a good carryover from last year. Extremely cold spring extending into July. April coldest on record. Only 8°F. at Saskatoon April 27. Ducks and geese did not arrive until April 9-11. Heavy June rains removed all danger of prairie drought, some loss due flooding. Hatch two weeks late due to adverse spring, but good. Summer rains kept streams running and ponds and sloughs at near full supply. Fall population maintained at the high level of 1953. A major migration took place from Manitoba and eastern Saskatchewan on November 1, but the final exodus all across the west took place November 22-27.

A remarkable reverse migration into the Delta Marshes involving thousands of birds was reported on November 22 by Albert H. Hochbaum, Director of the Delta Waterfowl Research Station, who checked with the Lower Souris Refuge and found they had also seen the northern movement. Had only mallards been involved, this would not have been such an exceptional event but wigeon, lesser scaup, redheads, canvasback, and even some blue-winged teal were included. Most of the birds left on the 24th but several thousand were still present the following day when large numbers of wigeon and a few blue-winged teal were observed with the mallards.

1955

Spring water conditions excellent prairie wide, the nesting season near normal, a good two weeks ahead of the last two years. Breeding population estimated to be somewhat reduced from last year. Heavy spring rains delayed agricultural activities and impassable roads prevented completion of population surveys. In July, Saskatchewan had the best water conditions in living memory, no danger of water shortage anywhere on prairies except a small area in southwestern Alberta. Cartwright says, "Saskatchewan is turning out a humdinger of a duck crop. . . . The season should surpass that of 1952 — heretofore the most successful year in our experience. It is amazing how these prairies can kick through when conditions are right. Generally an excellent production season. Everything points to one of the most satisfying flights of waterfowl in many years. 1955 should stack up as one for the book". Mass migration October 29-31 and November 1.

1956

Little or no runoff in extreme southern Alberta and southwestern Saskatchewan. Spring water conditions good elsewhere. Migration normal, delayed by cold in Manitoba. Substantial increase in breeding waterfowl, nesting delayed by winter "hanging on into May". Heavy June rains eliminated drought hazard in southern Alberta and southwestern Saskatchewan. Fall duck population estimated to even exceed that of "phenomenal output" of 1955. "Summing up, we would say that the 1956 waterfowl breeding season in western Canada is establishing a new record of abundance. Looking back over the season it is now clear that the highly satisfactory production was due to outstanding success of renesting and late nesting birds. This was in marked contrast to 1955 when favorable weather enabled the early nesting mallards and pintails to bring off a bumper crop." Mass migration from the prairies took place October 28-29.

1957

Spring runoff light except for Manitoba and eastern Saskatchewan. Generous rains needed to keep the prairie sloughs and potholes functioning. Major migra-tion April 22, earlier in southern Alberta. Numbers equal to last year or somewhat better, pronounced shift to northern parklands. Good first hatch but renesting below 1956 due to deteriorating water conditions. Overall production expected to equal 1956. Manitoba one of best production years for sometime. Mass migration October 21-27, final flight November 16-17.

1958

Spring opened with a rush first two weeks in April and extended well into the north. Migration also came with a rush at the same time. Slight increase in breeding birds with a shift to better watered parklands. Nesting about two weeks early compared to recent years. Little or no runoff on prairies. Early nesters safe, but heavy rains urgently needed for renesters and late nesters. Water conditions deteriorated, serious in early summer, and then were stabilized by mid-July rains but August was dry and water conditions rapidly deteriorated. It was estimated the fall flight would not be much below 1957, with the exception of Saskatchewan, and remained at a high plateau. Mass migration took place November 15-18.

1959

Good return of breeding ducks but prairie water conditions very poor, northern parklands good. Reduction in breeding pairs in agricultural area, increase in northern parklands. Reports of concentrations of mallards and pintails on larger waterbodies showing no signs of dispersing to nest. Possibility they may not breed. Good rains in early July but too late to change the situation. In August, Cartwright reports an explosion of broods, particularly of late nesting species but including surprising numbers of mallards and pintail. "The latest hatch on record." This failed to compensate for earlier failures and non-breeding and the conclusion was that there was a moderate decline (15%-25%) in the fall population. A major freeze and snowstorm caused 75% of the ducks to migrate October 9-10. The remainder left November 2-4.

1960

Prairie spring water conditions greatly improved over 1959 but still well below exceptional years of the mid-1950's. Drought area in central plains of Saskatchewan and Alberta. Manitoba excellent. Early migration third week in March in the west and first week of April in Manitoba. Overall breeding population about the same as 1959. Disruptive snowstorms in mid-April. Good June rains in Saskatchewan but southern Alberta continued to deteriorate. July dry and hot. Improved production over 1959 in Manitoba and Saskatchewan. Southern Alberta poor due to drought but good in parklands. No comment on relative size of fall population. Major migration October 19-20 and finally November 1-7. One of the least spectacular migrations in recent years.

1961

Prairie water conditions poor and condition extends well into the parklands in Saskatchewan. Manitoba somewhat better. Waterfowl returned to prairies early — March 16 and 17 — in good numbers. Reports of large flocks overflying prairies and piling up at edge of ice in the northern parklands. Some reports of non-breeding birds. Hot, dry weather persisted through the spring and summer. Only the deepest sloughs and reservoirs survived. Prairie duck production greatly decreased from previous years. Good production in northern parklands but unable to compensate for failure on the prairies. Major exodus October 19-23, remainder forced out November 1 and 2.

1962

Water conditions poor on prairies, improved over 1961 in the parklands. Waterfowl returned to the western prairies March 20 but were almost a month later in eastern Saskatchewan and Manitoba. Breeding population reduced. Good spring and summer rains maintained water areas at spring levels. Drought loss minimal and good late hatch. Production improved over 1961 but well below the good years of the mid-fifties. Warmest October and November in 10 years, ducks just slowly drifted south. Large marshes in Manitoba froze November 10. Major movement out of Saskatchewan November 12-17 and from Alberta 16-18.

1963

Prairie water conditions still rated only fair to poor though improved over 1962. Parklands and Manitoba good. Waterfowl returned early in increased numbers — an early nesting season. Above normal rainfall from early April through the summer improved water situation. Waterfowl production, particularly dabblers rated excellent, exceptionally successful early hatch. Best production season since 1957 — estimated at 30% over 1962. A long warm fall, a major migration November 11, and final movement November 16-18.

1964

Poor runoff across prairies and even into parklands. Only bright spot southwestern Manitoba and southeastern Saskatchewan. Breeding population increased in this area but unchanged elsewhere. Migration about a week late. Essential good spring and summer rains failed to appear on the western prairies and drought worsened. Production good in parklands but poor from prairies where considerable drought loss occurred. First major movement October 26 and 27 and final migration November 12-17.

1965

Best runoff in Western Canada since 1960. Good water conditions all across prairies and parklands. Break-up did not occur until mid-April and migration and nesting correspondingly delayed. Decrease in breeding population. Heavy spring and summer rains improved water conditions even further but late May snowstorms appeared to have adverse effect on mallards and pintails. Late nesters did exceptionally well. Fall population considered to be about equal to 1964. Exceptionally cold September in Manitoba, coldest since records kept. A major migration all across west September 22-24. There was a further movement October 26 and 27 and the final exodus November 3-6.

1966

Substantial carryover and a good runoff resulted in good water conditions across the prairies and parklands. Waterfowl returned to the prairies on schedule the third week in March in significantly increased numbers. Heavy spring and summer rains maintained habitat in good condition. Production best in the last decade. Fall concentrations reminiscent of 1950's. Major migration last days of October, last ducks pushed out of southern Alberta November 5 and 6.

1967

Spring water conditions good to excellent prairie-wide and through the parklands. Cold and snow persisted through to mid-May. Spring approached a record for lateness. Breeding population increased over 1966. The summer was hot and dry but the water survived exceptionally well except for central Alberta. In southeastern Saskatchewan and adjacent Manitoba some drought loss occurred. Overall production was rated as good. Final migration began October 27 and had been completed by November 3.

1968

Water conditions fair to good through parklands but poor across the prairie due to an open winter with little snow. Most of what runoff there was took place in late February. Very early migration — geese arrived in Manitoba March 7 — as early as anyone could remember. Main duck migration into prairies April 11-13 and 19-22. Prairie breeding population reduced, evidence of a substantial shift to large marshes and lakes, and to the north. Although there were good July rains these were insufficient to maintain water levels and considerable reproductive effort was lost particularly in Saskatchewan. Situation reminiscent of 1959 and 1961. Cool, rainy August helped brood survival. Reduction in fall flight from 1967 forecast. Slow fall freeze-up. Major migration over by November 15.

1969

Water conditions excellent all across the prairies and parklands due to heavy fall rains and a late but quick spring. Great increase in ducks nesting on the prairie. Main migration in mid-April. Early hatch outstandingly successful and from a brood production standpoint, one of the earliest on record. Broods numerous by early June. Cool, rainy July maintained water levels. Season may well have been the most productive on record. More ducks than in any year since the 1950's, but below that period due to smaller breeding population. First major movement took place last two weeks of October. Final departure November 9-12.

1970

Spring water conditions excellent across prairies and parklands except for southern Alberta. Spring delayed and major migration first week in April. Breeding population increased substantially in Saskatchewan, unchanged in Alberta, and decreased in Manitoba. Cold and snow of April and a cool May delayed nest initiation, and season about two weeks late. Broods slow in appearing compared with 1969. Good spring and summer rains maintained habitat in excellent condition. Good late hatch. Considered a good production year. Fall population equal to 1969. British Columbia better than usual and Maritimes had an excellent year, particularly for black ducks. First major migration October 25-27. Final exodus in mid-November.

1971

Water conditions good to excellent through prairies and parklands except for southeastern Saskatchewan, southwestern Manitoba and southern Alberta, where conditions only fair and rain needed. Improved conditions expected in British Columbia and situation good in Maritimes. Migration to prairies delayed to first week in April. Small increase in breeding population on prairies now estimated at about the average of the 1950's. Spring and summer rains maintained water levels and even improved the situation in some areas. Season late but good in British Columbia and normal and good in the Maritimes. Another fine production year on the prairies. A quick early freeze-up moved all the ducks off the prairies between October 25 and 27.

1972

Spring water conditions good on northern prairies and parklands only fair in the south. First ducks returned in mid-March a good ten days early but main flight arrived mid-April. Spring late in Maritimes and nesting delayed. Season also two weeks late in British Columbia but habitat good. Prairie waterfowl breeding population somewhat below 1971 and shifted to northern prairie and parklands. Cool, showery July weather maintained water levels in northern area but some production was lost on southern prairies in a hot, dry August. An average nesting season with mediocre production on the prairies compensated for by northern prairies and parkland. In the Maritimes, black duck production down somewhat, other species produced well. Good production from British Columbia. Cold in north brought migrants to prairies early. Severe cold triggered a major migration October 16 and the remainder October 26 and 27. Ducks moved out of central British Columbia on about the same dates while migration into the Maritimes was late and at the end of November the major migration still had not taken place.

1973

Spring water conditions poorest of last four years on prairies. Good in parklands. Early spring and waterfowl returned to prairies in numbers in mid-March. Breeding population about the same as 1972, pronounced shift to parklands. Habitat conditions good in British Columbia, less flooding in river valleys. Waterfowl returned early to Maritimes but extreme floods destroyed many nests. Good summer rains on northern prairies and parklands and good production. Light rains until late August on southern prairie with no better than fair production. Manitoba particularly poor. Compared to the past four years a poor production year across the west.

Production good in British Columbia and also in the Maritimes particularly for black ducks. Waterfowl swept completely from the prairies by abnormal cold November 1-3.

1974

One of heaviest runoffs in history on prairies. Spring water conditions excellent except for southern Alberta. Waterfowl return delayed to mid-April but nesting early due to good weather. Breeding populations about equal to 1973. Spring late in British Columbia and extensive flooding expected. Early spring in Maritimes but later cold adversely affecting nesting. A dry early summer on prairies but wet August. Water conditions good for what was a protracted nesting season. Production considered to be almost almost equal to 1969 due to exceptionally successful late hatch. Production below normal in Maritimes. In British Columbia a very satisfactory production season for all species. Major migration from the prairies November 10 and 11.

1975

Little winter snow but heavy April precipitation resulted in good to excellent water conditions all across the prairies and parklands. Main duck migration April 24 — very late, concentrated and spectacular. A small increase in breeding population. Spring migration most retarded in recent years in British Columbia. Water conditions good. Very cold spring in the Maritimes and a late nesting season. Prairie hatch very late, one of latest on record, but exceptionally good for a late hatch. Water abundant to mature broods. A good production year, at least as good as 1974 and probably better. Hatch also late in Maritimes but production good, better than 1974. Adequate water in Ontario and good production. In British Columbia, good habitat conditions and another satisfactory production year. Major migration from the prairies October 18 and 19. Remainder of waterfowl departed gradually in the period November 12-21.

1976

Runoff light but spring water conditions good through prairies and parklands, except for southern Alberta, due to carryover from 1975. Main migration early — last week of March. Small increase in breeding population, evidence of considerable overflight of pintails due to dry conditions in southern Alberta. A late season in British Columbia but water conditions good. Water conditions good in Ontario. Some flooding in Quebec; cold, and migration delayed. Rain and snow in Maritimes but black ducks in above average numbers nesting successfully. Spring warm and dry on prairies, water rapidly deteriorated and nesting early. More early broods than for past several years. Heavy June rains and July showers put the prairie and parkland habitat in good condition for the remainder of the season. Best early hatch in several years and strong renesting effort resulted in a good production year from the prairies and parklands. In British Columbia, water conditions excellent and production good. A wet summer in both Ontario and Quebec, water conditions and production good in both provinces. Also a good production year in Maritimes, particularly for black ducks. Major migration from prairies October 23 to 27, remainder left beginning November 10.

1977

Spring water conditions on prairies only fair to poor. Particularly poor in southern Alberta, southwest Saskatchewan and southern Manitoba. Fair to good through the parklands. Significant reduction in prairie breeding population and a considerable overflight of ducks, normally prairie breeders, particularly pintails, into the north. Spring water conditions good in British Columbia, little flooding of river associated marshes. Breeding population about the same as 1976. Ontario and Quebec an early dry spring with considerable loss of water. Good early nesting effort. Cold spring delayed nesting in the Maritimes. Heavy spring and summer rains across the prairies and parklands greatly improved water conditions. Production as much as three weeks late. Poor in extreme south, fair to average through remainder. Drought continued in Ontario but was relieved by good rains in Quebec and in late August in Ontario. Good production from both provinces. Cold, wet weather continuing in the Maritimes was not conducive to a good breeding season but production was average to good. Production good in British Columbia. Flight on a par with 1976 or perhaps better. Major migration from the prairies began November 9.

Appendix VII

ACTIVE KEE-MEN AS OF DECEMBER 31, 1977

By publishing this list of active Kee-Men — Ducks Unlimited seeks to honor all those Kee-Men (there were once over 3,000) who served faithfully but whose names have now disappeared from the record.

ALBERTA

Helge S. Abrahamson, Sylvan Lake
R. R. Adam, Vulcan
Earl C. Adams, Barrhead
Gary J. Algot, Derwent
Vernon Arnold, Foremost
Frank Bacon, Alberta Beach
F. F. Balderson, Magrath
Wayne L. Ballinger, Endiang
Jack G. Barkley, Three Hills
W. L. Barritt, Mirror
Fred Baxandall, Barrhead
Ray Bouchard, Lac La Biche
Reg A. Breen, Three Hills
Aron P. Brown, Winfield
Adolf Brusky, Coronation
P. H. Bureyko, Drayton Valley
Murray A. Busch, Bonnyville
Alex Chaba, Redwater
Richard N. Charlton, Czar
I. L. Chase, Milk River
James L. Chevraux, Killam
Russ Cotterill, Wetaskiwin
Gavin Craig, Wembley
H. R. Donovan, Oyen
Elmer W. Driver, Fort Macleod
Barney Eymundson, Flatbush
M. C. Fahner, Irma
Clifford A. Fletcher, Nanton
John Grant Fredericks, Bruce
George H. Gates, Innisfail
W. D. Geldert, Coaldale
J. M. Goodall, Chauvin
John Guglick, Ranfurly
Charles R. Hale, Bow Island
Ernest A. Hanson, Viking
Don O. Harding, Taber
George Hart, Drayton Valley
Ken W. Harvey, Vermilion
Herman Hennig, Bruderheim
Melvin Herron, New Brigden
H. O. Johnson, Rochester
Roger S. Johnson, Provost
Donald Johnston, Bowden
Edward G. Jones, Evansburg
George Kestner, Veteran
Walter Kolisniak, Two Hills
William Kureluk, Vilna
W. B. Kyca, Andrew
Roger Laplante, Vimy
C. D. Laughlin, Youngstown
Silas M. Lawrence, Red Deer
Geoffrey Lickiss, Vauxhall
Patrick E. Long, Grande Prairie
J. W. Luker, Warner

Don MacDonald, Beaverlodge
D. C. MacRae, Thorsby
M. A. Matwichuk, Andrew
Walter McCaughan, Islay
H. McCormick, Lac La Biche
T. B. McKirdy, Morinville
Gordon D. Melary, Big Valley
H. W. Meyer, Gwynne
Ralph D. Michelson, Lethbridge
J. H. Mosher, Lethbridge
Garry Nanninga, Caroline
Kenneth C. Nelson, Eaglesham
Jacob P. Nett, Castor
Oscar Nock, High Prairie
Proctor Paulsen, Ponoka
George E. Perrenoud, Cochrane
Syl A. Pompu, Vermilion
Donald G. Rankin, Calgary
T. H. Rayson, Paradise Valley
Clarence E. Rinker, Buffalo
Blair Rippin, St. Paul
L. J. Robertson, Huxley
L. C. Ronalds, Thorsby
Andy Russell, Waterton Lakes Park
William Sandul, Rycroft
Don Scheideman, Stony Plain
August Schlender, New Sarepta
Perce Sibbald, Munson
Ernest V. Smith, Camrose
Lloyd T. Smith, Delburne
James Spencer, Three Hills
Wayne Stefanyk, Hilliard
Orest Stefiszyn, North Cooking Lake
Ed Steinley, Jr., Empress
Vic Sturm, Bindloss
Ralph F. Tate, Donalda
I. W. Tchir, Spedden
Bill Thorburn, Claresholm
L. B. Trick, Carstairs
Garth Turner, Sherwood Park
F. P. Wackenhut, Rochfort Bridge
Frank Walker, Stettler
Larry A. Warawa, St. Paul
Les Wheaton, Oyen
Bruce L. Whelen, McLennan
Peter Willis, Galahad
W. E. Willows, Valleyview
W. Art Wright, Mannville
Wayne Yoder, Camrose
Irvine Zemrau, Ardrossan

SASKATCHEWAN

Joe Abel, Lake Lenore
Ken Arn, Kinistino
Chris Arndt, Golden Prairie
Frank W. Arnie, Preeceville

D. R. Arnott, Ceylon
Melvin Bauck, Chaplin
John M. Bell, Wilkie
Harry Benjamin, Willowbunch
Steve Bonyoi, Lestock
Mickey Bos, Cabri
Ernie Bowman, Oxbow
Jim K. Boxall, Tisdale
James E. Bradley, Milestone
Barry Braun, Paynton
Charlie S. Brooks, Mistatim
Ronald A. Brown, Outlook
John Brunner, Jr., Burstall
Cliff Burseth, Invermay
Oscar Carlson, Fosston
Earl Carson, Whitewood
Reg Carter, Saskatoon
J. David Chandler, Val Marie
L. G. Chase, Regina
Bradshaw Clark, Ardath
John T. Collins, Debden
Hector DeCloedt, Kamsack
Eric A. Dieno, Young
Walter H. Donnelly, Stoughton
Jake Epp, Major
Del Erickson, Saskatoon
Ed W. Erickson, Wynyard
Wes Esche, Swift Current
W. Frank Fansher, Govan
R. G. Finley, Luseland
Adam F. Folk, Hudson Bay
Glenn Foss, Creelman
Doug Francis, Broadview
Clifford H. Fysh, Crestwynd
John B. Gaillard, St. Brieux
Jack Gerein, Vibank
John W. Glover, Windthorst
Grant Gould, Big River
Gordon H. Graves, Biggar
R. G. Hammond, Elrose
Carl Hanson, Eston
Ed S. Harriman, Meacham
C. E. Hedegard, Estevan
Steve J. Helfrick, Jr., Francis
George H. Herber, Duval
W. H. Hewitt, Carlyle
G. M. Hewson, Langbank
Garry Higginson, Abbey
Willard Hill, Manor
Edgar Holderness, Quill Lake
James Von Holwede, Paradise Hill
Douglas B. Hooker, La Fleche
Art Howland, Outlook
Ralph Hynne, Handel
J. R. Illingworth, Atwater

Rex Jennings, Melfort
Keith Johnston, D'Arcy
John P. Kelly, Pilger
Milton Kilborn, Naicam
Joey Kimoff, Blaine Lake
John Koenning, Cudworth
Edward Krushen, Ituna
Tom Kwitkoski, Wadena
Gerald Lacerte, Meota
Stuart R. Laing, Bethune
E. F. Lamb, Outlook
N. A. Lamont, Lanigan
Stuart Langley, Speers
G. S. Larson, Hudson Bay
Mrs. Marilynn Lazorko, Bankend
George Lerminiaux, Montmartre
James W. Luthi, Punnichy
Harry Lyle, Melfort
J. D. MacFarlane, Nipawin
George D. Maloney, Meadow Lake
Tony Mann, Unity
J. M. Martin, Maymont
Doug McGregor, Central Butte
Earl K. McKenzie, Aylsham
M. V. McLean, Regina
Glen McVeigh, Kenaston
Roy Memory, Outram
Ken Meyer, Swift Current
R. S. Mickleborough, Eston
J. Archie Miller, Lloydminster
Joseph Miller, Regina
Gordon Millward, Kyle
Gordon Mitchell, Regina
Louis Molnar, Rose Valley
Ralph P. Mueller, Humboldt
Harry Nightingale, Okla
Gunnar W. Olson, Assiniboia
Philip Pajot, Carlton
W. A. Palmer, Fort Qu'Appelle
L. A. Peltier, Moose Jaw
Henry Penz, Waldheim
Herman Persson, Eastend
Miss Christine Pike, Waseca
John Poberznek, Insinger
D. L. Pollock, Sturgis
Fred Porter, Kinistino
Nick Postnikoff, Blaine Lake
Rob Potruff, Brownlee
John Pound, Swift Current
George J. Predy, Canora
Sam Quiring, Dalmeny
Frank Raab, St. Gregor
Leslie A. Ray, Creelman
Bill Reed, Shell Lake
O. C. Rindero, North Battleford

Don H. Robertson, Avonlea
Emil P. Rolsted, Baldwinton
Don Ruep, St. Benedict
A. H. Saip, Lang
S. J. Sapchuk, Mayfair
John Sautner, Flaxcombe
James T. Scott, Raymore
Miss Colleen Scrimbit, Kayville
Stan Simpson, Shellbrook
Walter L. Smith, Cupar
Richard Steele, Hazlet
D. G. Stott, Radisson
S. W. Stout, Wakaw
Ralph P. Stueck, Abernethy
Phillip D. Sweeting, Gull Lake
Eddie Tadie, Rosthern
Terry A. Taylor, Riceton
Ed Tetreault, Choiceland
Arlen Third, Regina
Norman Thompson, Langenburg
James Trafananko, Wroxton
Art Unsworth, Maple Creek
Leon Uytterhagen, Minton
Dave Van Patten, Wadena
Carl Veikle, Cut Knife
Cliff Watkins, Aylesbury

Louis Wendel, Jr., Neudorf
Clinton and Colin Westgard, Cando
W. Whitfield, Kindersley
Norman Wig, Watrous
Norman Wilde, Cudworth
Walter Winkler, Fox Valley
W. Yanchinski, Naicam
Mr. and Mrs. Mack Zibin, Quill Lake

MANITOBA

R. H. Amey, Deloraine
Owen Anderson, Cypress River
Robert E. Armit, Alonsa
Allan Bailey, Gimli
E. L. Barnard, Swan River
Jack A. Barrie, Stonewall
James F. Bartley, Selkirk
Norman Beddome, Minnedosa
Charles Brade, Roblin
C. E. Browning, Gladstone
O. W. Bulloch, Ninette
Stan Burdett, Lundar
Ken Burtle, Napinka
Adam Chaytor, Angusville
Arnold Collins, Pilot Mound
Art Dowsett, Eriksdale

D. A. Doyle, Carman
Johnson Drewry, Mather
Jacob Dyck, Winnipegosis
Otto Elvers, Rossburn
Raymond Fetterman, Winnipeg
George R. Fowler, Baldur
Bill and Sam Gee, Lake Francis
Allan Good, Minto
Ed Gosskie, Riding Mountain
Gilbert G. Graham, Roland
Robert J. Grant, Teulon
Lloyd Hatch, Oak Lake
Emil Hoffman, Virden
Jack Hogg, Lenswood
Michael N. Hryhorczuk, Ethelbert
John Hyrchuk, Gilbert Plains
Hugh Keffen, Killarney
Lawrence King, Clarkleigh
W. L. Leppert, Neepawa
A. E. Macklin, Pilot Mound
S. Macks, Plumas
Felix Magne, St. Claude
Al McDonald, Shoal Lake
J. R. McMurachy, Elphinstone
John S. Milliken, Reston
William F. North, Elma

Raymond O'Connor, Langruth
A. C. Orchard, Miami
Harry Otto, Ashern
Tim Penner, Virden
George Pettapiece, Rapid City
Daniel Petznick, Libau
Leo Pittet, Somerset
David Pizzey, Binscarth
Donald S. Porter, Dauphin
James Rice, Wawanesa
Bob Sear, Carberry
L. G. Sheridan, Hamiota
W. R. Sibbald, Alexander
Hugh Sinclair, Brandon
F. Skertchly, Souris
F. R. Smart, Waskada
D. T. Watson, Newdale
William C. Watson, Neepawa
Percy Watt, Miniota
Clinton Welch, Roland
Edward Wenzoski, Tyndall

ONTARIO

E. W. Strain, Kenora
Alan Ward, Orillia

Appendix VIII

CO-OPERATING LANDOWNERS

Ducks Unlimited (Canada) celebrates "40 years of Co-operation in Conservation" during 1978. The success of the corporation's waterfowl habitat conservation program over the past 4 decades has depended entirely on the outstanding co-operation of landowners in Canada, both Crown and private.

The comprehensive list following is the result of an extensive investigation of our files and those in Municipal offices to determine the names of all the original and current landowners involved with Ducks Unlimited projects to the end of 1977. The lack of available data for interim landowners, that is those who may have owned the land between the first and present landowner, prevented those individuals from also being included in this list. Their support is herewith acknowledged.

The company recognizes the inherent danger of compiling this list, whereby due to the nature of historical records, some landowners will unintentionally be omitted. Apologies are extended to any of these individuals, who are asked to advise Ducks Unlimited (Canada) of this omission.

Ducks Unlimited (Canada) wishes to formally recognize the Government of Canada for its co-operation and assistance during the past 40 years. In addition, the support of the company's conservation objectives by each of the Provincial governments, local and municipal bodies, and Irrigation Districts, has immeasurably assisted Ducks Unlimited's objectives of preserving our waterfowl heritage for future generations.

Thanks to all.

BRITISH COLUMBIA LANDOWNERS
*Original Landowners
Bergenham, John and Caroline
*British Columbia Waterfowl Society
Canadian Forest Products
Canadian Wildlife Service
Cornwall, Hugh
Creston Valley Wildlife Management Area
Delkatlah Wildlife Sanctuary
Durrell, Jack
*Gang Ranch
Hook, Roger
Jennings, K.
Klassen, June M.
Lower Kootenay Indian Band
*Newsome, R.F.J.
108 Mile Ranch
Onward House Mission Ranch
Pitt Polder Ltd.
Province of British Columbia
Riske Creek Ranching Ltd
River Ranch
Second Century Fund

ALBERTA LANDOWNERS
*Original Landowners
A.J.B. Holdings Ltd.
Aanestad, Edwin
*Aanestad, Rangvalt
*Abrogast, James M.
Adams, John and Olga
Adolf, Benjamin
*Adolf, Heinrich
Ahlstrom, Charles E.
*Akkerman, John
Albert, Charles E.
Albert, George H.
*Albert, Harvey
Alberta Agricultural Development Corporation
Alberta Concrete Products Co. Ltd.
Alberta Eastern Gas Ltd.
Alberta Gas Trunk Line Co. Ltd.
*Alberta State of Zion
*Anderson, Andrew
*Anderson, Anton C.
*Anderson, D. S
Anderson, Edwin A.
Anderson, Gordon E.

*Original Landowners

Anderson, Ken
Anderson, Kenneth and Lillian
Anderson, Lawrence E.
*Anderson, Louis
*Anderson, Oscar C.
Anderson, William and Dorothy
Anderson, William R.
Andrech, Mike
Andriowski, William
*Archer, Edward H.
Armstrong, Arthur H.
Arthur A. Voice Construction Co. Ltd.
Athley, P.A. and Phyllis
Atkinson, Allan R.
*Atkinson, Roy
Audley Farms Ltd.
Ausenhus, Noralf
Austin, Richard E.
Babych, Edward P.
Babych, Steve
Bach, Neils and Irene
Baergen, G. John and Mary
Bahler, Sam
Baik, Stanley
*Bailey, Stuart G.
Bailie, Carson H., Carson T. and Geo. A.
*Bailie, Robert
*Bakstad, M. C.
Ball, Lloyd G.
Ballachey, John M.
Bantel, Arthur
Bantel, Erna
Bar O.W. Ranches Ltd.
Bar 3 Cattle Co. Ltd.
Barker, Alexander and Helen
*Barker, F.
Barlow, Lawrence
Barnett, James T.
Barnett, William and Sandra
*Baron, Louie H.
Barr, Charles
Barr, James D. and Stewart C.
*Barrack, William C.
*Bartman Brothers
*Bartman, Russell S.
Bartel, Henry
*Bassano Grazing Association
Bates, Donald B.
Batke, Everet F.
Batke, Lee G.
Batke, Louis

*Baugh, Percy Levi
Baxandall, Janet
Bazant, Francis
Bazant, Joseph T.
Bazant, Teresa
Beaver, Ollie Lenora
*Beck, Ben C.
*Beck, Irwin C.
*Beck, J. E. and B. C.
Belcher, Gladys
Bell, Agnes A.
Bennett, Ralph and Iris
Bennett, Winslow W.
Berger, Jacob and Gunhild
*Berger, Trond
Berry, Adrian D. and Muriel D.
Berry, Hugh Wallace
Berry, Dr. Lynn
Besuyen, Henry and Margaretha
Bickel, Otto
Bidlock, Theodore
Bienert, Norman
Bienert, Reuben and Gary
Bietelspacher, Edward
Biggar, Evelyn M.
Biggs, Thomas K.
Bilsborrow, Donald
Bilsborrow, Maurice
*Bisborrow, Edward B.
Bishop, Leo D.
Bjur, Fritz O.
Blackwell, James A.
Blackwell, William T.
Blades, John R.
Blades, Katie
Blair, James C.
Blair, John K.
*Blair, T. K.
Blake, Derrick Granville
Bliesner, Chris A.
Blood Reserve
Boadway, James H.
Boden, John
Boden, Ted
*Bog, Mike
Bogi, Mike
Boida, Alexander
Bollen, Nicholas A
Bonnyville Regional School District No. 4
*Boreen, H. D.

Borgedahl, Wendell H.
Bossert, Ervin E.
Bowie, Lloyd G.
*Bowlen, Lt. Governor J.
*Bowlin, Gus
Boy Scouts Association — Property Society of Alberta
Bracha, Emily and Chester
*Bracha, J.
Bracha, Stanley
*Bradbury, William H.
Bradley, John A.
Bradshaw, Evans C.
Braim, Bryan
*Brainard, Dora
Branting, Clifford
Brehens, Martin
Briam, Keith M.
*Brimstin, W.
British American Oil Co. Ltd.
*Brix, Pedar
Brockhoff, Herman W.
Brooks, Leonci D.
*Brosten Bros.
Brothen, Arne and Grace
Brown, Burton and Judith
Brown, Clarence
Brown, Clifford and Kathy
Brown, Donald P.
*Brown, E. G.
Brown, Edwin H.
Brown, John A.
Brown, Leo A.
Brown, Norman A.
*Buchards, C. L.
Buckland, Edward C.
*Buehler, Wilf J.
Bunbury, Cyril
*Burke, Roy
*Burkinshaw, O. V. and O. H.
Burnco Industries Ltd.
Burns, Wilfred Marlow
*Burstad, P.
*Burrell, Arthur
*Burrell, Martha
*Burrell, Willis
Busmann, Dale S. and K.
Busmann, Paul E.
Busness, Selmar E.
*Bye, Gilbert
*Bye, John

Byers, Ralph G.
C. O. Johnson & Sons Ranches Ltd.
Caldwell, Maxwell
Calgary & Edmonton Railway Co.
Calgary Exhibition & Stampede Ltd.
Calgary Power Ltd.
Callaghan, Donald
Calvary Lutheran Church
Camco Agricultural Investments Ltd.
*Campbell, Dagmar and Richard
*Campbell, J. W.
Canadian National Railways
Canadian Northern Railway Co.
Canadian National Realties Ltd.
Canadian Pacific Oil & Gas Limited
Canadian Pacific Railway
Canadian Pacific Limited
Can-Tex Drilling & Exploration Ltd.
*Carmichael, William R.
*Carpenter, Bryer C.
Carrell, Frances G.
*Caspell, Murray C.
Caugler, Beatrice and William
Cermak, Robert and Phyllis
Chaba, Alex
Challenger, Gordon
*Chamberlain, Thomas
Chapple, Leonard R.
Chapple, John S.
Charles, Kenneth S. and Betty J.
Checkel, Philip
Checkel, Tony
*Christensen, Myron J.
*Christensen, O. Russell
*Christiansen, Aage
Christiansen, Clifford
*Christianson, Chris
Christianson, Gene N.
*Christianson, Ralph
*Chrystian, Paul
Chupka, W.
*Clark, Ronald John
Clark, Thomas C. and Lavinia M.
Cleveland, Louis R. and Marilyn I.
Cliffe, Darrell
Cline, James H. and Arnold J.
*Clyne, A. E.
Clyne, W. S.
*Cohen, Emanuel
Colbert, Malcolm M.
Coldwell, J. W.
Cole, Arthur
*Collins, Fanny E.
Colpoys, Victor W.
*Colquhoun, Malcolm
*Comrie Grazing Association
Conley, Darrell L.
Connel, Harold A. and Sandra R.
*Conrad, H. G.
*Conrad, M. W.
Conrad, Victoria
Conray Construction Co. Ltd.
Coon, Albert W.
Core-Mix Concrete Ltd.
Cottle, Frank
Countess Grazing Association
County of Camrose No. 22
County of Grande Prairie No. 1
*County of Mountainview
County of Ponoka No. 3

County of St. Paul No. 19
County of Smoky Lake No. 13
County of Two Hills No. 21
County of Wetaskiwin No. 7
County of Wetaskiwin No. 10
Cowles, Harriet M.
Cowling, Clara A.
Cowling, Stanley J.
Crandall, George
*Crory, H. C.
*Cross Bar Ranch Ltd.
Cruden, Dolores
Cruikshank, Gordon F.
Cruikshank, Gordon P.
*Cruikshank, Howard
Cruikshank, James M.
*Cruikshank, R. G.
*Cruikshank, William N.
Cumberland Community Club
*Cumming, W. R.
Currah, John E.
Currier, Allen T.
*Curtis, William R.
Curtis, William R.
Cuthbertson, Henry and Daphne
Dadensky, Paul
Dagnone, Dominic
Dahl, Katherine
Dahl, Leonard J.
Dallaire, Ernest and Sybil
*Dambrowski, L. A.
Damen, Alberta and Hubert
Damen, Hubert J.
*Damsguard, J. F.
Dankwerth, Alvin C.
Davis, Olive May
Dawkins, F. C. and M. L.
*Dawkins, W. J.
*Day, Percy
Day, William T.
Dearing, Victor P. and Emma J.
Debock, Glen
Dederer, R.
Degenstein, Blain J.
Denman, Jeanette
Department of Veterans Affairs
Derooy, John, Isabella and Willyan
Dersch, Allan Edward
Detert, Frederick
*Dick, Hazel
Dingman, Agnes
Dingman, Harold E.
Dingman, Stanley B.
Dirks, Eric
*Disgard, C.
*Divitt, N. C.
Doan, Lynn and Donna
Doenz, Leo R.
Doenz Ranches Ltd.
Doerksen, Clarence and Martha
Dofka, Frederick
Dolzlaf, Julius and Olga
Domet, Jack G.
Donaldson, Lulu E.
*Doncaster, Frank
Don-Del Investments Ltd.
Doneff, George
Doneff, Mary
Donnan Family Farm
Donnan, Martin, William, James,

and Sandra
Donnan, Peter and William
*Doondale Ranching Co.
Dorin, Emil
*Dornan, L. J.
Dorrow, Nedra M. B.
Dougherty, John and Patricia
Douglas, Clarence W.
Douglas, Frederick W.
*Douglas, L. V.
Douglas, Lillian
Dovichak, Victoria
*Downey, A. I.
Draganiuk, Marshall
Drake, Terrence J.
Drysdale, S.
Duke, Albert E.
Duncan, George
Duncan, Richard H.
*Durand, Lawrence F.
Durnin, Patrick
Dyck, Peter
Dyck, William C.
Dyke, Anthony and Margaret
Eagleson, Arthur R.
East and West Ranching Co. Ltd.
Eastern Irrigation District
Eastman, Roland R.
Eden, Ernest J. and Allison C.
*Edge, Harry A.
Edwards, Walter G.
*Edwardson, Thomas A.
Egeland, Olai
Eklund, Dale M. and Virginia C.
*Elgersmer, Andrew
Eliuk, Mike A. and Victoria
Elkow, Nick
Ellis, Betty M.
Ellis, Bruce and Betty
*Ellis, Chris
Englberger, Franz and Mathilde
English, George A.
English, James and Reginald
English, Samuel Rene
Englund, E.
Enmas, Hannah M.
Enstrom, Robert and Marilyn
Erickson, Carl
Erickson, Erick and Reginald
Etty, Roy
*Evans, George W.
Evans, Frederick M.
Evans, Frederick Michael
*Evans, N.
*Evans, R. A.
Ewen, Archie
*Ewing, F. J.
Eyehill Farms Ltd.
Faechner, Herbert P.
Fair, E. M. Lynne
*Fairburne Ranch Ltd.
Farkas, Joseph A.
Farthing, James Milton
Farthing, Nellie M.
*Faubion, J. R.
Faupel, Calvin L.
Faupel, Wayne E.
*Fecho, Fred
Fedick, Andrew H.
Feil, Arthur

Fenske, Clarence
Fenske, Harold F.
*Ferguson, Robert
Field, Harvey and Hilda
*Fijell, A. E.
Filard, Elwood and Jessie M.
Finlay, James C. and Audrey
*Fischer, C. M.
*Fischer, Douglas
Fischer, John
*Fischer Ranching Ltd.
Fischert, James A.
Fischert, Paul
*Fisher, Cornelius
Fisher, Dennis
Fitterer, Fred
Fitzpatrick, Desmond O'Dell
5K Cattle Co. Ltd.
Fix, Frank
*Fix, Frank
Fix, John Leo
*Flemmer, Clarence and Mildred
Fletcher, Earl
*Flett, L. A. and O. C.
Flinn, Dale B.
Flying Circle Cattle Co. Ltd.
Forbes, John L. and Naudya M.
*Forgren, N. R.
Forseth, Howard Gilmour
*Fortems, Lucien
Forth, Henry A.
Four Mile Stock Improvement Assoc.
Franca Oil & Gas Ltd.
Franklin, Isaac C.
Fraser, Claire
Fraser, Douglas
*Freeman, John Henry
Freeman, John W. and Linda
Frere, Maurice J.
Friedel, Bernard
Friedenberg, Bernice
Friesen, Henry
Friesen, John
*Gade, Chris
Gaehring, Garvin
*Gaetz, G. F.
*Galdue, Peter
*Galliford, Albert
Gallinger, Dorothy
*Galorneau, E. A.
Garden Plains Grazing Group
Garner, Lyman R.
*Garstad, J. A.
Garstin, Valerie
Gattey, Frank A.
Gauske, Awald and Ida
Gazdarica, Marie
Geier, Floyd E.
Geier, J. W.
Geier, Martin
*Gem Grazing Association
George Healey & Son
George, James C.
*German, Albert B.
*German, Christopher
*German, John
Gerth, Gustave
*Gibletz, Wilfred
Gibson, Losure T.
Gibson, Nannie M.

Gibson, Orville
Gilbert, Lois A.
*Gillbie, Elizabeth
*Gillespie, D.
Gilmour, Janette
*Gilmour, T.
Glasier, Dwayne E.
*Gleddie Brothers
Glenister School District No. 8890
Gogowich, John and Mary
Gold, William J.
Gooseberry Lake School District
   No. 2519
Gordon, Clarence and Sheila
Gordychuk, Mike N.
Gore, Mildred L.
Gorgichuk, Andrew
*Gormley, Grace
*Gottlieb, Theo and Jess
*Gouchee, Ernest Cleo
*Grainger, Dewey W.
Grambart, Werner and Inga
Grand Trunk Pacific Railway Co.
Granigan, Darrell and Carmen
Grasiuk, Fred
Grasiuk, Peter
Graumann, Ivan
*Gray, Alexander
*Gray, David
Gray, David S.
*Gray, Leonard
*Greenslade, Lloyd
Greenwood, Harvey N.
*Greenwood, N.
Greig, William A.
Grettum, Raymond F.
*Griffith, Glen R.
Grindi, Willie F.
Gronberg, William and Philomena
Groves, John R.
Gudmundson, Howard Clive
Guenther, Alexander
Gunderson, Clarence
Gunderson, Guy H.
Guttormson, Ed
Haag, Henry
Haeberle, Beulah
Haessel, Friedel and Irene
Hagen, Alvin B.
Hagen, David A.
Hagen, Larry Alan
Hagen, Lloyd D.
Hagen, Ole
Hagen, Palmer T.
*Hagenson, George
Haggblad, Nick
Hainsworth, Arthur and Verna
Hallett, Greta M.
Hallett, John
Hallick, Harold T.
*Hallock, Darrell
Hallowes, Arthur B.
*Hallowes, Gary
*Hallowes, Irene
*Hallowes, Richard B.
*Halverson, Selmar
Halwa, Theodore
Hampton, B. W.
Hannah, Lorne C.
Hannas, Nicholas

Hansen, Carl
*Hansen, Hans G.
*Hansen, Myrtle F.
*Hanson, Anna L.
Hanson, Arthur W.
Hanson, Leslie
*Hanson, N. C.
Hanson, Roald M.
Hanson, William James
Harasiewich, Andrew and Mary
*Harbison, John
Harbison Ranch
*Hardcastle, Leonard
*Harding, H. B.
*Harding, Harry
*Harris, C. E.
Harris, Raymond E.
*Harris, W. L.
Harsch, Edith A.
Hart, Edwin and Barbara
Hartell, Alexander G.
Harwood, Joseph and Garry
Hauck, G.
*Hauer, Pedro
*Hausch, G.
Hauser, Morris and James
Hawk, Alton L.
*Hawken, W. F.
*Hawrelko, Michael
*Hayden, Arthur H. P.
Hayden, Howard and Helen
*Hayden, Mabel H.
Hayes, Leonard
*Hayes, Robert and Leroy
*Hays, A. E.
*Heatherington, G. E.
*Heatherington, V. G.
Heck, Vincent H.
*Heck, William
*Heggen, Clarence
Heidebrecht, Abraham and Elizabeth
Heidecker, Ronald
Heidinger, Laverne and Shirley
Heighinton, Elizabeth M.
Heinz, Norman Reinhold
Heise, Benno and Herta
Helfrich, Eugene and Ellen
Helm, Lawrence M.
Helm, Lillian D.
Henderson, A. Douglas
*Henderson, Ernest E.
*Hendrickson, Harvey
Herder, Robert W.
*Hertz, R.
Hesson, Edith
*Hettler, P. P.
Hickey, David and Verna
*Hickle, R. E.
Hiller, Charles and William
Hills Ranching Co. Ltd.
*Hiltbrand, Emil
*Hinds, T.
Hines, George T.
Hines, Lyle V.
Hironaka, Kaisuke and Tsuyoshy
Hirsche, Arvin S.
Illavoy, Steven
Hobberstad, Hans
*Hockley, G.
Hoelscher, Erwin

Hoelscher, Otto
Hofer, Jacob E.
Hoff Agriculture
*Hogarth Brothers
Hogberg, James W.
*Hok, Peter
Holland, Sandra M.
Hollinger, Francis and Lois
Holloway, Thomas and Frederick
*Holt, I.
*Honens, W. H.
Horrell, John D.
Hotton, Lyndel E.
Hougham, Kenneth and Joanna
Houle, Emanuel
*Howe, Orval
Howrish, Edward Mike
Hryniw, Harry H.
Hudeck, Cecelia M.
*Hudecek, Frank
*Hudson's Bay Company
*Hudyma, Effie
Hughes, Darrell and Isobel
Hughes, Gary and Diane
Hughson, James and Arnie
Humbke, Leonard
Hunchak, William J.
Hunka, Anna
*Hutchison, R. D.
Hutchison, Ray G.
Hutterian Brethern Church of Bassano
Hutterian Brethern Church of Fort
   MacLeod
*Hutterian Brethren Church of Handhill
Hutterian Brethern Church of King's
   Lake
Hutterian Brethern Church of Newell
Hutterian Brethern Church of Sandhill
Hutterian Brethern Church of Springvale
Hutterian Brethern Church of Tschetter
Hutterian Brethern Church of Veteran
*Hutton, A.
*Hutton, A. A.
Hutton, Albert E.
*Hyler, Lewis
Ingram, Duncan and Berna P.
Isom, Charles B.
Isom, D. and C. R.
J. T. W. Holdings Ltd.
Jack, Gordon M.
Jackson, M. C. and D. M.
Jacobs, Eva M.
Jacobs, Mervyn and Truda
*Jacobsen, M. K.
Jacobson, Elmer E.
Jacobson, Orval W.
Jacula, Steve
Jaeck, Lionel W.
Jager, Donald C.
Jager, John and Pearl
James Guy Jacobs & Sons Ranches Ltd.
*James, S. W.
*Jamieson, Claude B.
Janke, Godfried and Marine
Janzen, John D.
Jenkins, Charles T.
*Jenkins, Edwin A.
Jenkins, Irwin W.
Jenkins, Lloyd and Marcella
Jenkins, Robert C.

Jenkins, Stephen W.
*Jenkins, Waller Thomas
Jesperson, Lorrie Arthur
Jesperson, Roland
*Jess, Theodore
*Joaseff, Archbishop
Johnson, Brian and Janette
Johnson, C. H.
*Johnson, G.
Johnson, Gladys
*Johnson, Iner
*Johnson, William
*Johnston, Albert A.
Johnston, Allan R. and Florence H.
*Johnstone, Mary E.
*Jones, Alex
Jones, Donald W.
*Jones, Ernest A.
Jones, R. G.
Jorgensen, Solphus
*Jorgenson, A. Bert
Jorgenson, Harry
Joss, Elma D.
*Juhan, George D.
K & B Motors Ltd.
*Kaempf, Otto
Kaiser, Fred J.
Kalbhen, William A.
Kalinski, John and Rose
*Kallal, Charles F.
Kallal Hereford Ranch Ltd.
*Kaprowski, Nellie
Karaki, Gordon W.
*Karasevich, Michael
*Kary, Bennie
Kaserman, Alfred
Kask, John
*Kaster, W. W.
Kauffman, Elton L. and Esther
Kaut, Robert
*Keck, Florian
Keeler, Frederick E.
Keith, E. V.
Kelly, Charles E.
*Kelm, Arthur
*Kent, L. R.
Kent, Leslie R. and Eileen M.
*Kent, William Howard
Kenwynn Farms Ltd.
*Kerner, William
Kerr, Dyde and Becker
Kiist, Rudolf and Herbert
*Killick, Gordon H.
*Kimura, James T. and Chizuko
King, Bessie Blanche
Kinnaird, John S. and Vera B.
Kip Coulee Ranching Ltd.
*Klassen, Ernest
*Kleinschroth, George
*Klem, David
Klumph, Samuel G.
Knight, Jack Bryant
*Knight, R. M.
Knopp, Melvin and Maureen
Knutson, Clarence L.
*Kok, Peter
*Kondo, F. A.
Kondo, James and Margaret
*Konopelka, Jean
Konopelka, William

Kosik, Albert
Kostrub, Walter and Hazel
Kotash, Peter R.
Kotelko, Jack
Kotowich, Marshall and John
Kowalchuk, Annie
*Koziar, Phyllis
Koziar, Walter
Kraft, John M. and James M.
*Krause, Jakob P.
Krause, John F. and Edward Henry
*Kroeker, Henry
*Kroker, Henry
Kronholm, Helmer
Kronholm, Nels J. H.
*Krpan, Frank
Kubbernus, F. G.
Kuczmak, John and Mary
Kuhlik, Albert
Kuhn, August F.
*Kunish, R.
L.K. Ranches Ltd.
La Corporation Episcopal Catholique
  Romaine De Grouard
Laing, David C.
Laisnez, John
Lakusta, Dan
*Lamb, Edgar G.
*Lambert, Melvin C.
*Landis, George
Landry Acres Ltd.
Langan, Andrew S. and Sheryl F.
Lanuke Cemetery Company
Lapointe, Andre
Larson, Aslaug and Sharol
Larson, August and Doris
Larson, Sigrid
Laschowski, John
Lasek, John
Lasek, John
Laskowski, Waldeman and Gladys
Latimer, James Thomas
*Latimer, Norman
Latimer, Russell
*Laughlin, Clarence D.
Laughlin, Marvin W.
Laumback, George D.
La Verne, M. E.
Lavigne, Henry
Lawes, James W. and W.
Lawes, Leonard L.
Lawes, Bud J. W.
*Laycock Bros.
Lea Park Cattle Association
Leavens, Elmer
Leduc Alfalfa Products Ltd.
Lee, Brian
*Lee, Ralph
Lefebure, Paul R. and Jeanne R.
*Lefetork, Paul
*Lefsrud, Helge
Lefsrud, Milton
Leggatt, Harold J.
Lehman, Otto
Leidl Enterprises Ltd.
Leitheiser, Edward and Ruth
Lepp, Aron
Leroux, Jules and Rosetta
*Lessard, Ed
*Letiak, James

*Letniak, Andrew G.
*Letniak, John
*Lewin, Elmer
Lewis, Frank C.
*Ley, William K.
Liland, Brynjulf
Liland, Donald
Lindberg, Eileen
Lindman, John A.
Lintick, Elizabeth E.
*Locke, Emma C.
Lockhart, Wyman C.
*Lomond Grazing Association
*Lone Butte Grazing Association
*Loree, Catherine and Gerald
Loree Farms Ltd.
*Losing, Christian
Lowis, Samuel T. and Gladys T.
Luciak, Annie
Ludlow, Sylvia B.
*Lufers, H.
Luft, Richard J.
Luka, Walter
*Lusk, James E.
Luz, Walter
Lyall, Emanda S.
*Lybbert, Carl Weston
Lydia Public School District No. 2372
*Lynn, Bob E.
Lynn, Robert W.
Lyons, Ellwood H.
MacDonald, Hugh J.
MacGregor, Grant and Carmen
Mackay, Donald A.
*MacKenzie, Murdo
*MacKey, Christine
MacKenzie Ranching Co. Ltd.
Mackey, Thelbert
*MacLaren, J. I. and W. R.
Maclean, Pete
Madge, George R.
Madge, Phillip J.
Madison Development Corporation Ltd.
*Maetche, George M.
Mailer, William and Viola
Malaka, Mathew A.
Maleson, Albert
Maleson, Carlo
Maleson, Franc
Malinowski, Leonard
Mansfield, John J.
Marathon Realty Co. Ltd.
Marchand, Homer
*Marchinski, E.
Marlow, Arnold A.
*Marr, T. L.
Marshall, Arthur T.
*Martin, Andrew G.
Martin, Martin and Elizabeth
*Martin, S. J.
Martin, Vernie
Mason, Alfred John
Masse, Armand and Delphine
*Matheson, W. D.
Matties, M.
*Mattis, D. A.
Mattis, Emilie
Maunsell-Wybrants, Mark
Mayer, Florian
*Mayer, John

*McArthur, Edward
*McBean, Lloyd G.
*McBride, Leslie
McCarty, Thomas M.
McClain, Donald
McClain, Neil J.
*McCloskey, W.
McDonagh, Charles A.
McDonald, George W.
*McDonald, James
*McDonald, Sylvia
McIvor, Clifford, Jerry and Lillian
McKay, Terrence W. and Susan H.
*McKay, William A.
McKeeman, Kathleen
McKeeman, Thomas
McKenzie, Dale and Irma
McKinney, Edward D.
*McKinnon, Don
*McKnight, K.
McKnight, Lora Mary
*McLachlan, Frank
*McLaren, C. C.
McLauchlin, Douglas
McLauchlin, Kenneth A.
McLauchlin, Leonard A.
McLennan, Daisy and Wilfred
McLeod, Robert
*McMeckan, W. N.
McMann, Roy J.
McNary, James and Evelyn
McNaughton, Alice
McNeight, Vernon J.
McRae, Alastair A.
McSporran, Alec
Melnychyn, Peter J.
Melnyk, John
Melnyk, William
Melton, Doreen
Menzies, Alexander and Donald
Menzies, Archibald
*Mercer, A.
Mercer, Charles and Lucille
*Merchant, R. L.
Metheral, John and Clark
Metzger Farms Ltd.
Michielsen, Johanna
Miciak, Irvin
Midbo, Harold A.
*Middlestead, E. H.
*Midyette, William
Mikalson, William D.
Miklos, Emil and Lillian
*Miller, Harold M.
*Miller, James A.
Minor, Perry Arthur
Mitchell, Frank D.
*Mitchell, Frederick and Pearl
*Mitchell, Floyd E.
*Mitchell, J. (Estate)
Mix, Walter and Adelgunde
Moberg, Arthur Emil
Moe, Stanley Allister
*Moerman, John
*Mohler, R. C. A. and A. D.
*Mohrmann, Edward P.
*Mohrmann, Gladys F.
*Molzan, Mathilde
Mooney, Mary H.
*Moore, Paul

Morgan, F.
Morrison, Philip D.
Morton, Thomas A.
Motkoski, Steven J.
Motley, Arnold L.
Motz, Otto
Municipal District of Bonneyville,
  No. 87
Municipal District of Cardston No. 6
Municipal District of Foothills No. 31
Municipal District of Highwood No. 31
Municipal District of Rocky View
  No. 44
Municipal District of Rosenheim
  No. 361
*Munro, Jack
Murchie, Alexander H.
Muriel Ranch Ltd.
Murray Cattle Co. Ltd.
Murray, Donald E.
Murray, Ervin K.
*Murray Ranching Co.
Murray, Robert and Lorraine
Muskoday Farms Ltd.
*Musselman, Jessie
Musselman, Menno
Musselman, Roy G.
*Mychaluk, Alexander
Mychaluk, Morley W.
Myshak, Frank
Nadeau, Lucien
Nahorney, Lowell and Bernice
*Narder, W. R.
National Trust Company
Negrych, Anna
*Neibauer, Robert
Neilson, Neils
Nelson, Daniel and Evelyn
Nelson, Harry G.
Nelson, Tepora R.
Nemeth, Edward J.
Ness, James H. and Lawrence D.
Newell, Raymond J.
Nickel, Rudolf
Nicklom, Rudolph
*Nicoud, F. A.
Nielsen, Betty E.
Nikoforuk, Harry
Nikoforuk, Victor
*Nixon, W. G.
Nordin, Allan H. and Margaret A.
Nordstrom, Ralph and Wilma
Normandale School District No. 2578
Northern Alberta Dairy Pool
  Limited
Northern Alberta Railways
Northwest Farms & Ranches Ltd.
Oakes, Walter and Dorothy
Obermeyer, Gary I. and Irvin A.
Odland, Bernard
Odland, Bert
Odland, Eider
Odland, John
O'Donovan, P. and E.
Olah, Julius and Ruby
*Olsen, Harold
Olson, Gordon E.
Olson, Hjalmer C.
Olstad, Nora
Orcutt, Floyd

Orlowski, Edward and Marianne
Ornburn, Elsworth A.
Orsten, John W.
Orr, Arthur W.
Orr, Neil John
Orsten, Dennis M.
Osowetski, Peter
Oswald, Bernice
Oustinow, Vitaly
*Page, Herbert
Pahl, Dick
*Pahl, Otto F.
Pahl, Packy E.
Pakarno, Gilbert J.
Palmer, Morris N.
*Pals, Cornelius F.
Pals, Francis M.
Paradis, Richard
*Parker, B.
Parker, Donald C. and Gwyneth
Parlee, Everett N.
*Parson, Allan B.
*Parson, Stanley E.
*Paschetag, Fred
*Pask, Bernard W.
Patricia Bar 4T Ranch Ltd.
Patrick, Donald A.
*Patterson, Charles E.
Patterson, John Glen
*Patzer, Arthur I.
*Patzer, Harry
*Patzer, J.
Paulgaard, Oscar M.
Paync, Ransome L.
Paziuk, Richard and Constance
Peace River Bible Institute
*Peake, Richard W.
*Pearce, James M.
Pearce, Orlin G.
Pearson, Gerald E.
Pearson, Harold C.
Pentecostal Assemblies of Canada
*Percy, Leslie and Mary
Perra, Frank F.
Peters, Stanley Jon
Peterson, Arnold H.
*Peterson, George E.
*Peterson, Hans M.
Peterson, Milton
Peterson, Verner
Petryshen, Carl
Pfahl, Herbert
Philips, Victor
Phillips, Leland and Dianne
Pickett Ranching Ltd.
*Pickett, Thomas
Pilling, Melvin and Belva
*Pincombe, Arthur
Pinowar, Antoni
Pipke, Jack A.
*Place, George E.
*Poffenroth, A.
*Poffenroth, J. P.
Poffenroth, Murray L.
Poffenroth, Walter
Polasek, Michael and Margery
*Pollock, Ida M.
Polnau, Willie
Pope, William J. I.
Porter, Dale and Alfred

Poulin, Alphonse
Power Farms Ltd.
*Pratt, Blake and Fred
Pratt, Eveline
Prentiss, Mack
Prentiss, Mary
*Preston, Joseph
Preston, Richard A.
Price, Bruce Calvin
*Price, John T.
Price, Lee
*Price, M. J.
*Price, Milver J.
Price, Ralph H.
*Pringle, James
Proctor, Sheila M.
Province of Alberta
Pruden, John A.
*Prymo, C.
Prymo, Peter
"Q" Ranch
Quast, Donald
*Quast, John
*Quast, Oscar and John C.
Quiring, Anna
*Quiring, George
Rabulsky, William
*Rall, Arthur
Ramsay, Thomas
Randle, Craig G.
Randle, Gerald
Rankine, R. P. and E.
*Ravenisk, Matthew
Readibuilt Homes Ltd.
*Readner, A.
*Reasbeck, James A.
Reasbeck, Mary
*Reaume, James F.
*Reece, R. G.
*Regner, D.
Reid, Alma
Reidford, Nathaniel
Rejo Ranches Ltd.
Reynar, Violet I.
*Rickett, Robert M.
*Rickett, T. M.
Riddelvale School District
No. 2700
*Ries, William
River Valley Ranch Ltd.
*Robertson, E. C.
Robertson, George
*Robinson, J.
Robinson, Joseph
*Robbs, Lyle
Rochefort Investments Ltd.
Rockarts, Maurice D.
Rode, Edward
*Roder, John R.
Roder, Robert
Roder, Robert J.
Roen Farms Ltd.
*Roen, Lawrence
Rogers, Gerald W. and
Colleen S.
Rogers, Gerald W.
Rokosh, Stanley and Doris
Rolling Hills Grazing Association
Rolls, Alice M.
Roman, William and Ella

Romanchuk, Alexander
Romaniuk, Mike W.
Rondeau, Jules
Rooke, Bradley E.
*Rooke, L. E.
Roseglen Cementery Company
*Rosemary Community Pasture
Rosemary Grazing Association
Rosenau, Charles W.
Ross, David G.
*Ross, Herman L.
*Rossler, Millie
Rosychuk, Ernie
*Row, Lorne
Rowley, Denis
Rubusky, William
Rudko, Fred and Anne
*Ruff, D. W. E.
*Rumohr, Edith B.
Rumohr, George W.
*Rural Municipality of Westbourne
Russell, Charles W. and Marie E.
*Rutledge, Gordon and Willis
Rutledge Ranching Co. Ltd.
*Ryan, E.
*Sadler, Annie E.
Sadler, Ian W.
*Sadlowsky, Alex
Sadlowsky, Kay
St. Arnaud, Richard and Lucien
St. George School District No. 3226
*Saito, Fuku (Estate)
Sakaluk, John
Samuelson, Glen A.
*Sanborn, J. B.
*Sands, D.
Sarafinchan, Mary
*Sarsons, P. E.
*Sayers, F.
*Schacker, James A.
*Schafer, M. and B.
*Schell, Ida May
Schiebner, A. B.
Schmaltz, Balthasar
Schmaus, Victor J.
Schmidt, Ewald
Schmitke, Emmanuel
Schneider, James H.
*Schoch, Lydia
Schoen, Joseph P.
*Scholl, R. B.
Schonknecht, Otto
Schopman, John
*Schritt, George
Schwengler, Murray
Schwenk, Walter
Schultz, Harold C.
Schultz, Roger and Elmer
Scott, Allan Gerald
*Scott, Sidney
Scott, Thomas A.
*Scoville, H.
Seifert, James and Opal
Seitz, Arthur
Seitz, Fred J.
Seitz, Kenneth and Bonnie
Semak, Peter
*Sempa, H. and W.
Seney, Robert and Donald
Seney, Theodore C.

Serna, Victor and Lily
7L7 Ranches Ltd.
Severtson, Milton
Sewell, Dorothea
Shaw, Carol Lee
*Shaw, D. B.
Shaw, George W. A. and Anne
Shennan, Alexander H.
Sherman, Lydia
Shorter, Katherine
Showalter, G.
Shura, James and Mary
Shute, Lois
Schwed, Andrew
Siegel, Donald W.
Sinclair, John Henry
62 Bar Ranch Ltd.
*Skarlicki, Frank
Skibster, Willard C.
Skilnick, Jack
*Skinner, A.
Skipworth, Bryan D.
*Skladon, Anna
Skretting, Arnold
Skretting, Edwin T.
Skretting, G. G.
*Slocum, C. H.
*Slorstad, Sverre and Jean
Sloville, Conrad W.
Slowe, Robert G.
Small, Majorie and William
Smith, Albert
*Smith, Arthur E.
*Smith, Albert (Estate)
Smith, Allan
*Smith, Harold A.
*Smith, Howard W.
*Smith, J.
Smith, John C. and Ruby
Smith, Norah M.
Smith Ranches Ltd.
Smith, Swayne V.
Smith, Violet
*Smith, Wesley Walter
*Smith, William
Smolanski, John and Helen
Smyth, A. Ross
Smyth, Robert R.
Smyth, W. Ross and Clara I.
Smyth, William B.
*Sneath, G. W.
Sneath, Walter
Snider, Stewart S.
*Snow, J. G.
Soderquist, Harold E.
*Soderquist, J.
Soderquist, Richard A.
*Solberg, K. V.
Soldan, Thomas
Sorensen, Carl D.
Sorochan, Emil F.
Sparks, H. Donald
Sparrow Developments Ltd.
*Sparshu, Gustav
Spondin School District No. 3375
Sporran, D. M.
*Squire, Irven S.
Sroka, Charles and Robert
Stadnyk, Anthony and Sharon
Stadnyk, William and Josephine

*Staples, Rowland
*Starchenko, M.
*Starko, Frank
Starzko, John
*Steer, Ralph J.
*Steeves, George
Steeves, George H.
*Steeves, L.
Stegmeier, Jacob
Stein, Irene E.
Stein, Phillip
Steinbach Ranching Co. Ltd.
*Steinbech, Bernard (Estate)
Steinke, Thomas L.
Stenger, Lorenz and Aline
Stern, Henry
Stevenson, Mark and Mary
Stewart, Lawrence
Stewart, Loren J.
*Stewart, M.
Stewart, Robert A.
Stewarts Cattle Co.
Stickel, Fred
*Stickney, Andrew
Stifle, John C.
Stimson, George, Dale and James
Stobart Farms Ltd.
*Storch, Colin A.
Storch Farms Ltd.
Stouffer, Clayton P.
Strathmore Golf Club
Stringam, George
Stringer, Cecil and Mary
Stringer Ranches Ltd.
Stringham, Bryce
*Stringham, Woodrow
Stroman, Chester
Stuber, Otto
Stroman, Chester
*Stuber, Otto
*Suchy, Gordon
Suddaby, Foster W.
Suhan, George Donald
*Suitor, Andrew J.
Suitor, Merlyn A.
Sukkel, Elizabeth
Sulz, David
Sunderland, Thomas F.
Suntjens, Elizabeth
*Suntjens, Gilbert J.
Suntjens, Ian L.
*Suntjens, Siebert
Suntjens, Walter
Swanson, Edwin and Rose
Swanson, Roy E.
Sweere, Antonius A.
T & G Cattle Co. Ltd.
Tabler, J.
Tabler, Joseph and Cecille
*Tangeb, B.
*Taransky, Godfred
Tateson, Scott
Taubert, Arthur
*Taylor, Ella M.
Tenbrink, Ralph and Anna
Teske, Roy and Gladys
Tetz, Walter
Tetzlaff, Max H.
*Thiessen, Abe
Thiessen Farms Ltd.

Thiessen, George
Thiessen, Henry
*Thiessen, J. P.
Thiessen, Jake
Thiessen, John and Fred
*Thiessen, P.
*Thomas, Lionel H.
*Thomas, N. H.
*Thompson, Albert
*Thompson, George H.
Thompson, Gertrude R.
Thompson, Kenneth H.
Thompson, Leslie
Thompson, Stanley
*Thomsen, A.
Thornton, Douglas G. and Jean K.
Thornton, Harold and Dolores
Three Walking Sticks Ranch Ltd.
*Tide Land Grazing Association
*Tilley Rolling Hills Grazing
  Association
*Toews, Aron
Toews, Earl Harvey
Toews, Harvey and Elda
Tolefson, Neil F. and Sharon A.
Tolway, Tislaw E.
Tomlinson, Henry J.
*Torie, Addle
Toronto General Trusts Corporation
Tovell, Arthur Lawrence
Tovell, Lloyd A.
Town of Barrhead
*Town of Bonneyville
Town of Camrose
Town of Fairview
Town of Leduc
Town of Strathmore
Town of Two Hills
*Treacy Ranches Ltd.
Trick, Lloyd B.
Tschetter, John and Mike
*Tschritter, Emil
*Tubiary, Anthony
Tuckey, Ken C.
Turner, E. G. and A. W.
Twomey, Alice
*Uffelman, Harvey
Unrau, John
Upton, Harry and Elizabeth
Urwin, William Richard
*Usher, Thomas
Valee, Jules E.
Valentine, Margaret J.
Valshel Holdings Ltd.
Van Immerzeel, Gerald and Linda
Van Patten, Dennis
Van Patten, Norman
Van Petten, Stewart
Van Verdegem, George and Mary
*Van Wezel, J.
Vegara, Eugene M.
Vegara, Nick M.
*Vend, K. C.
*Veno, Cecil E.
Verchomin, Emma
*Veterans' Land Act
*Viener, Harry
Vigen, John
Village of Edberg
*Virden Valley Ranching Co. Ltd.

Virostek, Wayne W.
Visscher, Hendrika and Henry
Visscher, John
Voice, Arthur A.
Voth, Henry H.
Voth, Theodore
Voutier, R. P.
*Waddell, R. S.
Wagner, Albert O.
Walburger, Thomas Theodore
Walcoth, Wilfred E. and Elizabeth H.
Walker, Michael W.
Walrath, Charles E.
Walter, Max
Walters, Muriel and Richard
*Walters, Raymond C.
Walters, Worden A.
Wanchuko, John
Warburton, William
Ward, George F.
Ward, Jack, Milton and Myrtle
*Ward, M. A. and Walter J.
Watson, George V.
Watts, Thomas G. and Karen L.
Wearmouth, Thomas Richard
*Weaver, Bertren L.
Webster, Bruce M.
Webster, Harry L.
Webster, Lloyd
Webster, William J.
*Weder, A. Roy
Weder, Albert C.
Weich, Glen and Ben
*Weisse, F. A.
*Weller, Edwin W.
Wells Ranching Co. Ltd.
*Welsh, Erman
Welsh Farms Ltd.
West, Francis D.
West, Norris J.
Western Irrigation District
Westmount Industrial Development Ltd.
Wetenkamp, A. H.
Wetthuhn, Earl
Weyga Farming Ltd.
Whaley, Charlie
*White, Geoffrey and Helen
*Wickham, S. J.
*Widner, F.
Wiesse, Richard H. and Norma L.
*Wildig, A. J.
*Wiley, E. L. and M. E.
Wiley, Euart and Elizabeth
Wiley, Samuel
Wilkie, Donald
Wilkie, William H.
*Wilkinson, George
*William, R. C.
*Williamson, A. C.
Williamson, Douglas and Joan
Willows, Ronald R.
*Wilson, Gordon L.
Wilson, Jeannie
*Wilson, Robert S.
Winkler, Max and Julia
Winsnes, Dale D.
Wise, Letra
*Witherbe, Beth
Witschen, Edward F.
Wold, K. E. and S. E. L.

*Wolfe, Leo
*Wolfert, Fred
*Wolfert, Herbert W.
*Wolfson, Phillip
Wolters, Arthur and Marjorie
*Wood, Peter L.
*Woodrow, M. Harold
Woodruff, Henry V.
*Woods, Ralph and C. B.
Worobo Farm Ltd.
*Wozney, Mike
Wright, Orpha G.
Wutzke, Ferdinand
Wynder, Cecil Duane
Yelenik, Lawrence
*Young, K. E.
*Young, L. C.
Young, Robert
Yuskow, Walter
Zambau, Irvine
Zavisha, Richard
Zaychuk, M.
Zelinski, Joseph P.
Ziegler, Arthur
*Ziemer, Albert
Zurborg, Frances
*Zylinski, Waslaw

SASKATCHEWAN LANDOWNERS
*Original Landowners
Abele, Alfred
Afseth, Jack W. and Donald
Akins, Mary
Albert, Lawrence
Alexander, Ronald B.
Alger, Gordon
Alger, Hans
*Alger, Ken
Algrove Farm Co-operative Association
  Ltd.
Allan, Kenneth R.
Allin, Alfred
Amundrud, Cletus E.
Anders, John F.
Anderson, Arni
Anderson, Carl
Anderson Farms Ltd.
*Anderson, Herluf
*Anderson, Herman
Anderson, Mary E.
Anderson, Orval
Androsoff, William I.
Angott, E.
Angrimson, J. M. and N. S.
*Archibald, David L.
Arendt, Louis
Armbruster, V. E.
Armistead, G. W. and C. T.
Armstrong, F. C.
Arnason, Thor S.
Arngrimson, B. S. and J. M.
Arnott, Jean
Artland Grazing Co-operative Ltd.
Asgeirson, Thor
Atkinson, Charles
Attridge, C. H. and G. E.
Austfjord, Einard
Azure, Clarice
Badley, Desmond L.
*Badley, James L. (Estate)
Badley, James M.

Baines, D. C. F.
Baker, Rose E.
Bakke, Olaf Alexander
Bakken, Leonard
Baldwin, Douglas G.
Baldwin, Grant G.
Bamford, Albert G.
Barclay, George
Barclay, R. A.
Barnett, Allan V.
Barnett, Edward
Barnett, Leo
Barsness, Louis
Bartch, Nick
Bartley, George
Bath, Richard S.
Battle Creek Ranch Ltd.
Baumberger, J. (Estate)
Beach, J. P.
Beach, Paul W.
Beaudry, Millie
Beckett, Clifford
Beckstead, E. B.
Beckstead, Edith Mary
Beeler, Ralph Edward
Bell, F. S.
Bell, George
Bell, Herbert
Bell, Ralph
Bell, Robert
Bellanger, Celine M.
Belza, Carl
Bendig, William
Benjamin, George
Berlinic, John
Berry, Raymond N.
*Bexson, H. A.
Bezmutko, John
Bezmutko, Tony
Bisson, K. I.
*Bjorklund, August (Estate)
Bjorklund, Elmer L.
*Black, John
Block, Adolph
Bloom, Evert and Ejnar
Blundell, John T.
Blyth, Donald and Kenneth
Bodie, Ben
Bodnar, Alex
Body, Thomas
Body, Arden
Boehm, Jacob
Bogdanski, Nick
Bohun, John
Bonderud, Allan N.
Bonnett, Orval L.
Borzel, Fred
Boser, Paul
Bourne, Victor F.
Boyle, James C.
Brackton, Fred
Bradford, Edmund R.
Braitenbach, T.
Breton, Louis J.
Brick, Eldon J.
Brick, Roy
Bridgeman, Beatrice M.
Brock, Warren M.
Brockelsby, Anne
Bronson Grazing Co-operative Ltd.

Brooks, A. J.
Brooks, Ben
Brooks, Chester
*Brown, Clifton
Brown, Ernest and Evaline
Brown, Harry P.
Brown, Lorne W.
Buck, Fred
*Buck, Otto
*Bugg, Lila
Buist, James W.
Burgess, G. A., R. E., and L. L.
Bushnell, Harold
Buzila, John
*Cairns, Elsie
Cairns, Owen Robert
Campbell, Bruce I.
Campbell, John N.
Canadian Wildlife Service
Cappelle, Cyril
*Carleton, Ralph R.
Carnahan, Rose
Carr, Thomas
Carter, Edward
Carter, J. R. H.
Caton Cattle Company
*Caton, John W.
Cattanach, George
Central Lands Limited
Cey, William A.
Chesney, Donald E.
Chesney, Henry J.
Chomicki, Myron
Christian, Robert L.
Chritenia, Anna
Chritenia, Stanley
Clark, Fred M.
Clark, Margaret
Clark, Orval
Claydon Grazing Co-operative
   Association
Claypool, Harvey
Claypool, Morris
Cochrum, L. E.
Colby, Catherine
*Cole, R. A.
Cole, Walter
Collins, W.
Cook, Alexander
Cooke, John T.
Colwell, M. F.
*Colwill, R.
Corker, Cyril L.
Corkis, Dorothy E.
Corsuch, Amy
Cowan, Myrtle M.
Coward, J. K.
Craigs Ranching Company Ltd.
Credit Foncier Franco Canadian
Crist, Minnie L.
Culbertson, William and Willima
Cull, Frank
Cull, Leonard
Cull, William H.
Culp, James D.
Curtis, H. F. and W. G.
Curtis, W. F.
*Cuthbert, Spencer L.
Cutts, William F.
*Cyba, Fred

Cyba, Jaroslaw
Cyba, Syl
Czerwonka, Joseph
Czerwonka, Stanley
Czerwonka, Veronica
Daelick, A. B.
Dahl, Magnus
Dale, R. M.
Danyluk, Fredrick N.
*Darby, L.
Davidson, Glen
Davies, Alfred
*Davis, Alfred W.
Davis, Charles B.
Davison, George
Davison, Henry A.
Dedick, William
DeGraaf, Peter H.
Dennis, Gilbert
Dennis, Russell
Deroo, A. A., M. and D. F.
Deslauriers, E. R.
Deslauriers, Fay
Devine, J. R.
Dibacy, Bert
Dieno, Eric A.
Dillabough, Fred E.
*Dillabough, John H.
*Dillabough, William A.
Dimmock, D. M. and E. B.
Dimmock, Stanley
Dittmer, Clarence J.
Dittmer, Reuben
Doane, Stuart L.
Dobmeier, Mathew
Doidge, Alfred Edward
Doidge, John Edward
Donald, Peter
Donison, George D.
Donison, Nick
Dotschkat, Adolf
Douglas, Gordon
*Dowkes, David J.
Downey Lake Grazing Co-operative
Drackett, Stanley
Drury, H. R.
Dubielew, Frank
Duncan, Lucy May
*Duncan, Ross F.
Durell, Ronald D.
Dusyk, Tytus J.
Dutkewich, Mike
Dyck, Elmer G.
Dyck, Henry
Dyck, Peter J.
Eaglehill Pasture Association
Earl, Clarence
Earl, Ernest
Earl, E. Robert
Eberl, C.
Ediger, Ronald and Marie
Edwards, John
Eischen, G.
Elder, Alfred
Elke, Robert
Elliott, A. A. and Terry
Ellis, Wesley
Emde, George
Emde, Henry F.
Emde, Roy

Enerson, C. T.
Epp, Cornelius
Epp, Victor A.
Erickson, Albin
Evans, J. L. and J. S.
Evans, John
Evans, T. P.
Ewaschuk, Metro
Facca, Lewis
Facca, Gardiner
Fansher, W. F. and P.
Fansley, L. H.
Faulkner, Joseph E.
Fawcett, John E.
Fedderson, Max
Federspiel, Elmer
Fedeyko, Konstantine B.
Fenner, Leonard
Fenske, Mary
Ference, Wasyl
Fialkowski, Carl
Filion, Gary
*Filion, Julius
Filion, Mabel
*Fillion, Charles E.
Fillion, Clarence
Fillion, Leonard M.
Finnson, John
Finnson, S. F.
*Fisher, Edward
Fisher, O. E. and W. E.
*Flack, Ross
Flahr, Frank
Flowers, Matthew
Forbes, George and Margaret
*Forbes, Hugh
Forrest, Robert W.
Forsyth, Keith A.
Foster, E. J. and B.
Foster, Mary Winnifred
Francis, J. P. and T. E.
Frank, Eugene
Frank, Phillip
Frey, Alfred B
Frey, George
*Frier, Lorne
Friesen, John K.
Friesen, P.
Fritz, Andrew P.
Fritz, John A.
Froats, William H.
Frolick, William
*Fry, T. R.
Fry, W. R. and A. F.
Funk, Cornelius P.
Fusick, Martin
Fusick, Paul
Fusick, Stanley
Gafencu, Mary
Gamble, D. J. and O. W.
Gandy, Evelyn
*Gartner, Peter J.
Gates, Harold I.
*Gatzke, Victor John
Gaudreau, Armand
Gehl, Mary J.
Geib, Nick
Gerard, Edmund J.
Gerbrandt, Jacob H.
Getz, John

Getz, Solomon
Giblin, Patrick
Giles, Nelson and Clarence
Gilmour, Matthew and Thomas
Gislason, Karl
Glass, Everett L.
Glass, Lillian F.
Glass, Lloyd
Glen, James
Glover, Ronald E.
Golling, Carl
Gomersell, William G.
Gordon, Bruce
Gordon, James B.
*Gordon, S. A.
*Gosling, Robert
Gosling, Thomas R.
*Graham, A. M.
Graham, C. G.
Graham, Dorothy
Graham, L. D.
Grant, John P.
Greenfield, Leland
*Greenwald, Sebastian
Greenwold, Jacob
Greff, Joseph
Gregg, Evelyn M.
Gregg, George R.
Groenewoud, L. S.
Grzenkowicz, Steve
Gudmundson, Einar
Gudmundson, Gudmundur F.
Gudnason, Carl
Guenther, M. B. and M. F.
*Gunderson, Henry
Guse, Dennis G.
Haarsma, Ronald J.
Hagel, Ernest F.
Hagel, Henry G.
Hagen, Oscar A.
Hainstock, Janet
Halarewich, John
Halarewich, Tytus
Halbgewachs, Alvey J.
Haldron, Vilborg
Haliuk, Orest and Iris
Halliday, Walter
Halverson, Ogel C.
Hamilton, Robert
Hand, Percy
Hansen, Clarence
Hanson, H. and J. O.
Harder, Henry
Harder, Nick
Hards, Leslie G.
Harmel, Albert
Harriott, J. H. and Norma
Harris, N. B.
Hartell, Nelson
Harvey, Charles
Harvey, Percy W.
Harwood, Kenneth W.
Harwood, Leslie A.
Hassett, Dean
Hauk, Philip
Haus, Herbert and Bernice
*Hawkins, Robert
Hawreluik, Nick
Hawryluk, Steve
Hawrysh, Julian

Hayman, Arnold W.
Hayne, Earl
Hayward, Rolland L.
*Heaver, Fred
Heaver, Richard
Heintz, Emil
Helgason, Sigmundur
Helgason, T.
Helgeson, Clifford
Hemmingson, Philip
Henderson, C. B. (Estate)
Hennan, Bramwell B.
Henry, George
*Herman, Edward
Herman, John H.
Herman, Walter
Hesla, Henry E.
Hewson, Robin and Thomas
Hicke, Henry
Hicks, Albert and Martha
Hillaby, Arthur
Himmelsbach, Paul and Gerhardt
Himour, Abdou and Jean
Hingten, Vernon
Hoath, E. M.
Hodel, John J.
Hodel, Walter
Hoffarth, Roy
Hoffer, Ernest
Hoffer, Jonathon B.
Hoffman, Charles
Hoffman, Frank
Hoffman, J. C.
Hoffman, Otto
Hogberg, Agnor J.
Holfeld, G. and A.
Holfeld, Reinhold B.
Holfeld, Henry
Holliday, Ernest S.
Holtby, Donald
Horan, Teras
Horchynski, Myron
Hoseasson, Bjorgven
Hoseasson, Joseph
Hounsell, Jennie
*Howe, Oswald R.
Howe, Ronald S.
Hrycak, John
Hubbard, R. H.
Huber, Eric
*Huber, Frederick J.
Huber, Hugh L.
Hunt, James N.
Huss, Theodore
Hutterian Brethern of Dundurn
Hutterian Brethern of Hillcrest
Hutterian Brethern of Kyle
Hutterian Brethern of Sand Lake
Hyme, Martha
Illes, Joseph
Ingold, Paul R.
Ireland, Joseph A.
Irwin, J. B.
Ismond, Charles A.
Ismond, Ronald M.
Iwanchuk, N. (Estate)
Jackson, Harvey
Jacobsen, Carrie
Jacobson, Leonard
*Jahnke, Elmer and Peter

Jahnke Ranches Ltd.
James, O. B.
Jancy Holdings Ltd.
Jansen, B.
Jensen, Harry C.
Jesmer, Carl T.
Johannesson, H.
Johnson, Frank
Johnson, Ingar
Johnson, John
*Johnson, John R.
Johnson, Malla
Johnson, Martin
Johnson, W. C.
Johnston, Earl G.
Jones, Alfred
Jones, Kenneth C.
Joorisity, Don V.
Josephson, Johann B.
Josephson, Sigurros
Kachmarski, Joseph A.
Kalheim, Ralph
Kallichuk, Louis
Kardash, Peter O.
Karst, Pauline and Edward
Kaufman, Harry (Estate)
Kaufmann, Keith and Garth
Kelso Grazing Co-operative Ltd.
Kemmer, Ruben
Kemp, G. E.
Kemper, Herman L.
Kereluik, Allan
Kerpan, Robert
Kessler, Karl
Kihn, Walter
Kimott, Alexander A.
Kinch, Lester
King, Russell
King, Thomas
Kingsley, Alan
Kirkwall Moor Ranch
Kistner, Leonard
Klatt, P.
Klatt, R.
Klause, John
Klein, Fred
Knapp, John J. and William A.
Knight, Cyril and Leah
Knolly's Grazing Co-operative Ltd.
Kohut, Raymond
Kohut, Tekla
Koivula, Larry E.
Kolodziejak, Felix
*Kopp, Magnus
Kopp, Raymond
Korolewich, Frank F.
Kostichuk, John and Morris
Kostichuk, Maurice
Kowalchuk, Henry
Kozicki Farms Ltd.
Kramer, Steve
Kratchmer, Nick J.
Krause, Dan
Kreick, Theodore
Kroeger, Abram and Peter
Kroeger, Henry and Agnes
Kronberg, Henry
Krueger, Roy T.
Krywy, Steve A.
Kucheran, William

*Kucik, John
Kucik, Michael
Kuzmicz, F. J.
Kwasnik, Walter
Labuik, Mike
Lafrenierre, Lloyd J.
Lakness, Walter O.
Landry, Joseph
Last, Harold
Lang, John
Lang, Lawrence
Lario, Errold R.
Larrivee, Willie
Larson, J. J.
Laursen, Lloyd
Lathan, Roman
Lazarescu, Andrew
Lazorko, Lorne
Lazorowich, Nick H.
Lee, Lorne E.
Leffler, Philip A.
Leslie, James F.
*Leslie, John
Levesque, Marcel
L'Heureux, George
L'Heureux, Henry
Libke, James
Libke, Lily
Lidfors, Olaf
Lisoway, Jim
Little, Thomas
Loeffler, John H.
Loney, Elsie
Long, Kenneth F.
Lorge, Edwin II
Lucas, Roy
Luchsinger, Phillip W.
Ludwig, George
Lundago, Edward J.
Mackie, Arnold G.
Mackie, James
Maddaford, C. H.
Mair, R. Gordon
Mann, Harvey
*Marchewka, John
Marchewka, Peter
Marshall, Charles
Marshall, William
Martens, Gordon K.
Martindale, Percy
Masse, Andrew
Massie, Charles W.
Massier, Lloyd W.
Matador Community Pasture
Mathieson, A.
Matkowski, Stanley
Matthews, Fred W.
Mayert, Sam
McCaw, H. E.
McColl, John A.
McCorriston, John (Estate)
McCurrach, Georgina
*McDonald, C. R. and J. R.
McFayden, D. I.
McGough, Stanley
McGown, F. A.
McGrath, Mervin and Norbert
McGrath, Roy
McGrath, Thomas and Mervin
McIntosh, James S.

McIntyre, Alex
McIntyre, Robert C.
McKeith, Stewart
*McLatchie, Andrew
McMillan, D. D., D. R. and R. D.
McMillan, Roy and Percy
McPhee, Maude and Ed
McPhee, William E.
McRae, D. A.
McVicar Stock Farms Limited
McWilliams, C. E.
Meili, Walter and Werner
Meilicke, Arthur E.
Meinhart, Donald
Meinhart, Shirley
Melenchuk, Edward and Shirley
Melle, Kasmir J.
Melrose, J. B. (Estate)
Merrison, Percy and William
Merrison, William H.
Metzgar, Andrew
Michayluk, Slawko
Mickey, H. L.
Mielke, William
Millar, George
Miller, Eldon C.
Mills, Charles
Mills, Charles
Minke, Henry
Mitchell, Leo
Moat, L. T.
Moffat, J. C. (Estate)
Moir, Norman B.
Mooney, Floyd A.
Moorhead, John (Estate)
Morgan, David G.
Morgan, John
Morhart, Rudolph
Morhart, Thomas J.
Morin, William
Moritz, Ronald
Morrow, Orville
Moser, Art
Moxness, Walter
Moynes, James
Muir, William
Mulvena, Roy E.
Munns, Howard
*Munns, Hugh W.
Murray, Charles
Murray, Gratton S.
Murray, William
Muryn, Charles
Muryn, Sam
Myers, Harriet
Nagy, Helen
Natske, Edmund
*Natske, Jacob
Neithercut, Barry D.
Nelson, John E.
Nelson, Marcus
Nelubowich, Andrew H.
*Nelubowich, Joseph
Neuhalfen, M.
Nevdoff, Walter
Newlove, Walter
Newton Farms Ltd.
Nicol, Albert
Nixdorf, Emil
Noble, Harold S.

North Lumber & Supply
Northern Trusts Company
Nyholt, Henry
Ogden, Cliff
Ogden, Howard K.
Ogle, Arthur J.
Olafson, B. J., Carl, and J. M.
*Olfert, Abraham A.
Olfert, Abram
Oliver, Robert W.
Olson, Maurice R.
Olynick, Mike
Onion Lake Indian Reserve
Orheim, Peter S.
Orr, T. H. L.
*Osterhold, C. F.
Osterhold, E. and H.
Ostlund, Louie L.
*Ostlund, Lovi L.
Owen, Emma and Frank
Owen, Leo and Isobel
Pahlke, Jacob and James
Paley, Pauline
Palmer, Cecil S.
Palmer, Henry M.
Palmer, J. S.
Pander, Alois
Parker, Harry
Parker, R. L.
Parsons, James R.
Paton, Lorne
Paton, W.
Patterson, Charles
Patychuk, George
Pearson, Helmer and Emil
Pederson, Abram
Peecock, F. O. and I.
*Peecock, H. C. J.
Pelletier, Elizabeth
Pengert, W. A.
Penner, Henry W.
Penner, Jacob W.
Penner, John J.
Pepper, W. L.
Perdue Ranching Co-operative
Perras, Frank
Perrin, Peter J.
Perrin Ranching Co. Ltd.
Peru, Emille
Peters, Henry
Peterson, Frank
Peyton, F. A.
Picklyk, John
Picklyk, Philip A.
Piggott, Albert C.
*Piggott, Emily E.
Pillar, Frank A.
Pillar, George
Pilotti, Charles
*Piot, Frank X.
Plaksey, John
Pliska, John and Henry
Podjan, Fred
Polichuk, Taras D.
Polichuk, Walter
Pool & Sons Farm
Porten, Archie M.
Porten, C. F.
Porterfield, Cecil J.
Prairie Farm Rehabilitation
Administration
*Proctor, Arthur
Prokop, Katherine
Prokop, Mike
Province of Saskatchewan
Pruden, James
Pryor, Alice A.
Prystupa, Frank D.
Prystupa, Joseph
Prystupa, Renie
Purdy, John B.
Qualman, Elmer O.
Qualman, Kenneth
Qualman, Lawrence
Quellette, Frank
Radies, Ernest
Radies, Hugo
Raiche, Goldie Mae
Raiche, Lewis P.
Raine, Stan
Rainville, Emile
Rath, Theodore
Rayner, John A.
Read, R. G.
Reimer, Mary
Rennick, Joseph
Rewega, John
Reynolds, William
Richardson, R. A.
*Riddell, Leonard
Robertson, James
Rodger, Dan
Rodger, Thomas R.
Rodgers, Russell
Rogoza, Fred
*Rogoza, Joseph
Romaniuk, William
Romaniw, John
Ronald, Donald B.
Ronald, Glen
Rosenmeyer, Levi L.
Roskiewicz, Czeslaw
Ross, Albert
*Ross, William W.
Rowan, Edward R.
Rowland, Cecil
Rubletz, George and Antonia
Running, A. C.
Rural Municipality of Big Quill
    No. 308
Rural Municipality of Caron No. 162
Rural Municipality of Hazeldell No. 335
Rural Municipality of Kindersley
    No. 290
Rural Municipality of Morris No. 312
Rush, Grace
Rydzik, Sigmund
Saccucci, P. E.
*Salmon, N. A.
Sandbeck, Florence
Sanders, K. W., S. J., and H. N.
*Sanders, Svein G.
Sapergia, Gligor
Sapergia, John
Sapergia, Paul
Sapergia, Robert, Alex and Vernon
Saskatchewan Fish & Game League
Saskatchewan Water Supply Board
*Saunders, John
Sautner, John

Sawatsky, John
Sawatsky, Pete
Sawchuk, Carl and Hazel
Sawchuk, William
Schaan, Nick P.
Schafer, Edward
Schedel, Robert A.
Schellenberg, J. J.
Scheller, Annie
Schick, C. W.
Schick, George A.
Schleibinger, Frank and Willie
Schlunegger, Alfred
Schmidt, W. R. and E.
*Schneck, Alfred
Schneider, Albert F.
Schneider, John A.
Schotts, Russell
Schroeder, Otto
Schumacker, Fritz T.
Schwartz, Otto
Scotsguard Grazing Co-operative
Sekal, Joe
Sells, Alma
Senger, Anna
Senger, Anthony (Estate)
Senger, Mike
Senger, Otto C.
Senger, Paul R.
Senger, Pius A.
Senger, Wendlin A.
Senholt, Lawrence
Setrakov, Eugene
Sharber, Michael
Sharrock, Bill
Sharrock, H. M.
Shaw, William J.
Shea, W. V.
Shields, John
Shields, Robert E.
*Shields, Thomas W.
Shiels, William
Shier, W. E.
Showers, Elmo
Sibley, Nelson
Siewert, A. and E.
Siewert, Ed
Siewert, Emanuel
Sigstad, Raymond
Silvius, Agnes V.
Skafel, Magnus J.
Skalney, Nick
Slotzer, Russel J.
Smart, Murray
*Smith, Catherine T.
Smith, Douglas
Smith, Douglas J.
Smith, Edward J.
Smith, G. M.
Smith, Larry J.
*Smith, R.
Smith, Walter
Sokochoff, William
Solyma, Jerry D.
Sorrell, William
Spreacker, H. M.
Sperle, Balzar
Sperling, Paul
Sproule, George H.
Stack, Leroy L.

Stahl, August and Mary
Stanford, Walter
*Steele, Rupert
Steppan, Leonard
Sterling, D. T.
Stevenson, Charles
Stevenson, James and Florence
Stewart, Peter H.
Stewart, William
Street, William G.
Strom, Erling O.
Struck, M. J.
Suderman, S. and D. D.
Suderman, S. D. and A. H.
Sunderland, John A.
Sunderland, Donald
Sunderland, Kenneth
Sundquist, Harold A.
*Sundquist, P. A.
Sutor, Ross
*Sutter, J. A.
Sutter, Joseph G.
Sveinbjornson, S.
Swanson, Denton
Sweeney, E. L.
Sweeney, Lloyd
Swingley, G.
Symchych, Peter
Symens, Lionel A.
Symes, David J.
Symes, Douglas
Symes, Lionel
Tangen, Peter
Taylor, Alex and Jean
Taylor, James A.
Tederoff, Peter
Tenncy, Wilber
Ternes, Bernard
Tharp, R. J.
Thibault, Orval
Thiele, Henry J.
Thierman, John A.
Thiessen, Menno D.
Thingvold, Carl A.
Thompson, A. E.
Thompson, Gilbert F.
Thompson, Vivian
Tiessen, Peter
Todd, Clifford
*Todd, David
Toner, Theodore
Torgerson, Mary
Torguson, Clarence and Jens
Torguson, I. J.
Torguson, Ingval J.
Toth, Frank W.
Toth, Mike
Tottle, W. B.
Tracey, Mary
Treen, Lewis
Tremblay, Joseph H.
Tremblay, Wilbrod
Tress, Frank
Turuk, Sam and Olga
Unger, John H.
Unruh, Carl
Usselmann, Anton
Valentine, John Carson
Vanstaveren, Peter, Nick and Jasper
Varjassy, Alexander J.

Viden, Erick
Village of Waldeck
Voisey, James
Vokes, Edith
Vopin, Gudjon
Vopni, Laurence
Waimark, John A.
Walby, John
Wallace, Henry E.
Wallace, William
Wallis, Herb
Wasyluk, William S.
Waterhen Lake Indian Reserve
Watkins, Frank E.
Watson, John F.
Watson, L. E.
Weatherall, Cecil and Rose
*Weber, Jacob K.
Weber, Richard R.
Weinberger, W. J.
Weinheimer, George
*Weiss, Emanuel
Weiss, John C.
Weiss, Laverne
Welke, George
*Wellock, John
Wells, John M. and Peter
Wells, Laura
Wensley, Thomas H.
Weppler, J.
West, John O.
Wheatley, Gertrude
Whitley, Olive
Wickenheiser, Ralph
Wigness, John B.
Wildeman, Ewald E.
Wiley, Russell
*Wilhelm, Lloyd and Fern
Wilhelm, Ronald and Donna
Willhoft, Henry C.
Williams, G. Everett
Williams, Norman W.
Williams, Stella
Williams, W. J. and A. H.
Willis, Roy R.
Willows, J. Wilfred
Wilson, A. C.
Wilson, Earl H.
Wilson Land & Cattle Company Ltd.
Wilson, Russell and Gwendoline
Wilson, Sidney
Wilton, W. A.
Winguist, Carl B.
Winquist, C. B.
Wittal, Adam
Wittal, Philip
Wlasichuk, George
Worotniak, Wawara
Worrall, Roald
Woytuik, Pete
Wright, Raymond
Yager, H. L.
Yalte, Peter
Yaremowich, J.
Yoerger, James K.
Young, Donald C.
Zacharias, Adam
Zacharias Brothers
Zacharias, Henry
Zagozeskie, Walter

Zazula, Peter H.
Zelinski, Joseph
Zeller, Joe
Zentner, Frank
Zucht, Manuel

MANITOBA LANDOWNERS
*Original Landowners
A.L.E. Farms Ltd.
*Adderson, James R.
Anderson, A. A.
Anderson, L. W.
Anderson, Lawrence and Beryl
Anderson, Vern C.
Andrew, Cecil H.
Andries, C.
Angus, James Alexander
*Arason, O. S.
*Archibald, E. J.
Armstrong, Robert
*Arnason, John
*B & L Land & Livestock Ltd.
*Bain, Donald H.
Ballatine, John Ralph
*Ballantine, W. N.
Banman, Cornelius W.
*Bardarson, E. V.
*Bardarson, John
Bardarson, Loreen J.
Barre, Maurice A.
Barrett, Louis W.
*Barron, George
Baskerville, Charles R. and Lyla L.
Bartley, Lorne J.
Batho, Everett Herbert
Battersby, Herman W.
Beattie, Roland G.
Beaupre, Henry R. J.
*Beck, M.
Beckwith, Harold Dean
Beckwith, Harold Dean
Bell Holdings Inc.
*Berney, Albert
*Bertrand, Rev. J.
*Bertholet, Frank
Bertholet, William J.
Besant, Gordon E.
Best, Clarence H.
Bigelow, Dan R. and Wilfred G.
Bigelow, James Gordon
Bigelow, Dr. Wilfred G.
Bjornson, Beryl
Bjornson, Kari
Boake, Ralph B.
*Bollman, Franklin and Robert
Bonner, Robert W.
*Bothe, Chris
Boulet, Aime
Boulet, Felicien and Eveline
*Boulet, Joseph and Orise
Boulet, Leonide
*Boulet, Norbert
*Bouvier, A. A.
*Bouvier, Armand A.
Bouvier, Robert A.
*Boyd, Burton J.
Bradford, Wilbur (Estate)
Bradley, Thomas Earl
Bray, Ronald Ivan
Breidal, Kristjan
*Bridgett, F. W.
Brinkworth, Melvin A.

Brown, C. W.
Brown, Donald R. and Margaret W.
Bryant, Jack and Irene
Budd, John Henry
*Buhr, E. C.
*Burch, Samuel E.
Burch, William Harold
Burns, James O.
*Byers, John
*Canadian National Railways Real Estate
Cameron, Robert A.
Campbell, Alexander G.
*Canty, William G.
Capon, Albert R.
*Carr, Darryl
*Carr, Delbert
Carr, Jane V.
Carr, Robert L.
Cassan, E. R. R. and Lois
Caswell, Donald A.
Catellier, Severe
*Caul, Steve
*Chapman, John M.
Chase, Stanley
Chatel, Raymond
Chegwin, Mary (Estate)
*Chegwin, William
Christiansen, Lorne
Christopherson, J. B.
*Christopherson, S. H.
City of Winnipeg
Clare, A. Agnes
*Clark, Walter E.
Clarke, John
Clearwater, Charlie W.
Clements, Willard M.
Coleman, William J.
*Cooper, John H.
Cooper, Nelson H.
Copeland, M. Aileen (Estate)
Coppens, Madeleine M.
Corbey, Victor F. M.
Corlett, Raymond J.
*Cote, Harry
Coveney, Beverley Ann
Coveney, Ronald L.
Cramer, Barry James
Cramer, James Edward
*Cramer, Wilfred
Crawford, Donald M.
*Crawford, E. R.
Creith, Lois Jean
*Crisp, Jack
Crompton, Norman W.
Cuff, Peter W. W.
Culbertson, Glenson and LaVern
Curry, Constance N.
*Curry, Larry
Curtis, Mervin James
Cuthbert, Emily Louise
*Cuthbert, J. W.
Dalman, Kristjan
Davidson, Orville L.
*Davies, David
*Dawson, M. W.
De Ceuleneer, Marcel
*DeGalley, Eucher
De Jaegher, Aime Arthur
De Jaegher, Victor
Deschambault, Marjorie and Joseph

Deschambault, Venance
Devlin, Benjamin
Devlin, Joseph
Devloo, Jules
*Dionne, Andrew
Dix, Peres A.
*Dixon, James F.
Dobbelaere, Albert
Dobranski, Albert
Dodds, Robert L.
*Dodman, H. A.
*Draper, Albert L.
Draper, Douglas and Molly
Drewry, Robert Mack
Dry Creek Farms Ltd.
Dryden, D. O.
*Dryden, W. M.
*Du Bedat, Trevor
Duncan, Raymond G.
*Dyck, Sarah
Eastley, Ernest H.
*Elgar Bros.
Elgar, Charles H.
Elgar, George E.
Elgar, George Empy
Elgar, James H. (Estate)
Elgar, William Nelson
*English, Oliver
Erlendson, David J.
Erlendson, Marlind L.
Esler, Charles E.
Esler, Jennie May
Esler, John Kenneth
Esler, Roy Elmer
Esler, William Keith
Esler, Winston Murray
Etsell, Marjorie E.
*Etsell, Thomas E.
Fairholm Holding Co.
Falk, Arthur P. and Erma
Falk, Henry Peter
*Fallis, Albert A.
Fallis, Milton A.
Fallis, Wesley J.
Fast, Eric J. and Donna M.
Fast, John
*Fennell, Arthur H. G.
*Fenton, Harry E.
*Fey, Eugene
Fey, John E. and Donna M.
*Flack, Barbara A.
Fleming, Allan J. D. and Deborah
Fleming, David
*Fletcher, Charles W.
Fouillard Holdings Ltd.
Fouillard, L. J., A. B. and E. R.
*Fraser, G. H.
Fraser, Ken A.
Freeman, Asmundun G.
*Freeman, Harvey W.
*Freeman, Thomas H. (Estate)
Fulton, Ernest Victor
Fulton, Harvey
Garabed, Harry
Gardiner, Leonard J.
Gardner, Treverne H.
Gemmill, David George
Geras, George
Gibb Farms Ltd.
*Gibb, James

Giesbrecht, William and Adena
Gillis, Harold E. A.
Ginter, John and Irma
Gittoes, Harold F.
Goerzen, Henry W.
Gompf, W. Lorne and Jean Verna
Good, Robert W.
Goodman, Arthur K. and Irene V.
*Goodman, Vilborg and Thori
*Gourlay, A. J.
*Gourlay, Andrew
Gourlay, Catherine McLeod
Grandin, C. L.
*Grass River Holding Co.
Greig, Douglas W.
*Grift, Gerald
*Grift, John and Gerald
*Gullett, John
Gurr, Donald C.
Gurr, Lewis A.
*Habok, Fred
Habok, John and Fred
*Hagborg, Andrew
Haines, W. W. and Judith K.
Halldorson, O. Keith
Hallson, Robert and Elsie
Hallson, S. Hamilton, Harold D.
Hamilton, Harold D.
*Hamilton, Herbert
*Hammond, E. T.
*Harbottle, Alexander
Harburn, Albert J.
Hardy, Clair
Hardy, Edgar G. A.
Hardy, Francis K.
Harms, David
*Harms, John
*Harrison, A. C.
*Harrison, H.
Harrison, Robert
Harrison, Ronald A.
Harrison, Williard J.
Hatch, Henry W.
Hatch, Honor
Hatch, Lloyd M.
Heapy, Ivy
Heapy, Wilfred D.
Heintz, Frank C.
Helgason, Chris
*Henderson, Alexander
Henderson, Mabel
Henderson, William A. and John H.
Henowitch, Joseph
Henuset, Roland J.
*Hill, Edgar Edwin
*Hinch, Florence
Hinch, Howard R. and Sophia E.
Hinch, Ross Elliott
Homefield Holding Co.
Horvath, John
*Howard, Edward W.
Howey, Richard J.
Hovorka, Frank
Hrytsak, John
Hunter, Gordon C. and Kenneth L.
*Hunter, Grace
Hunter, Robert B. and Glen C.
Hutchison, David G
Hutchison, Frank A. and Jose
*Hutlet, Celestin

Hutterian Brethren Colony of Fairholm
Hutterian Brethren of Holmfield
Hutton, Roy B.
*Hyndman, William E.
*Irving, Gerald A.
*Iverson, Lloyd
Jago, Cecil A.
James, Kenneth O.
Jiggens, Edith Emily
Jiggens, Edward Ernest
Jiggens, James W.
Johnson, Allan Skuli
Johnson, Frank G.
Johnson, Norvall Everett
*Johnston, John L.
Johnston, Robert Barry
*Jones, Alva D.
Jones, Alva David
Jones, Ross Herbert
*Josephson, Oscar
Juskowiak, G.
*Juskowiak, Gerhardt and Wanda
Juskowiak, Hans G. and Darlene A.
Kaasgaard, Kristen M.
*Keating, Grant J.
*Keen, Walter
Kehler, Arthur
Kehler, August
*Kelly, James Frank
Kelly, Morley G.
Kelly, William Wallace and Erma M.
Kemp, John W. and Edward S.
*Kemp, S.
Kennell, Roland
Kernested, Gordon
*Kerr, Alexander
Kerr, John C.
Kester, William Raeburn and Alice M.
King, Dwight K. and Marilyn W.
Kirbyson, Charles H.
Kirbyson, Robert C. and Faye M.
*Klassen, Dan D.
Kostuik, Mike
Kress, George
Krueger, Henry D.
*Kruger, Evert
Krysowaty, Joseph
Krysowaty, Stephen
*Kuzenko, Harry
Kynock, James
*Lafournaise, Joseph
Lamb, Arthur W.
Lang, Katherine M.
Lawrence, Bertram K.
Law, Harold W.
Lawson, Charles I. and Lillian J.
Leafloor, Arthur E.
Leafloor, Ken
Lebeau, Bertrand and Hilda
*Lebau, Albert
Lee, Levi Rafie
*Lee, Theodore
Leech, Joe
Lees, David W. and Marilyn H.
Le Strat, August
Liban, F. Ranch
*Liban, Hortal
*Liffman, Arthur
Lindell, John A.
*Lindsay, A. W.

Lindsay, Stanley G.
Local Government District of Alonsa
Locke, Harold S.
Logeot, Victor C.
*Lowe, Audrey L.
*Ludman, Lorne
Lukianchuk, John and Helen
Lussier, Charles
Lyall, Roy Edwin
Mack, Norman Egbert
*Maes, Alfonse
Mailman, Gilbert H.
Manitoba Agriculture Credit
  Corporation
Manitoba Hydro
Manuliak, Leonard P.
Markle, Lydia I.
*Massin, Frank
*Masson, Adelard
Masson, Joseph A. and Emma
Masson, Robert A. J.
*Masson, Wilfred
Mathison Farms Ltd.
Matiowsky, Frank
*Maxwell, Charles C.
May, Wilbert Larry
*Mazur, William
*McCannell, Donald C.
McCannell, Ross F. and Eunice
McCauley, Lorne Oliver
*McCausland, A. J.
McCoy, Roy Alexander
McCullagh, James A.
McDiarmid, Dr. R. O.
*McDonald, Cecil
*McDonald, Kenneth and Melville
McDonald, Morley H. and Annie
McDougall, Delbert J.
McGregor, Morris
McKay, Arthur and A.
McKay, Walter
*McKenzie, George
*McKenzie, Robert C.
McKenzie, Wayne G. and Wanda R.
McKinnon, Norman K.
McKitrick, Harold W.
McLaren, Alice E.
*McLaren, William
*McLean, George A.
McLean, Lewis A.
McLenehan, Donald O.
*McLeod, Albert J.
McLeod, Daniel Edwin
McLeod, Donald N. and Joyce P.
*McLeod, Edward
McLeod, Horace J.
McTavish, Floyd Walter
*McTavish, Herbert
*McWhirter, George
Meighen, Charles O.
Meighen, F. O.
Melechko, Mykola A.
*Meyer, Henry and June
*Miles, Frank
Mitchell, R. H.
*Mitchell, V.
Moffatt, Mervin L. and Doreen E.
*Moffatt, Percy H.
Moore, Albert F.
*Moore, Orville A.

266

Morningstar, William Roy
Mosiuk, John
*Mowat, Benjamin A.
*Mowez, Michael J.
*Mowez, Nickoli
Muenchow, Otto R. and Ursula B.
*Muir, James (Estate)
Munro, Edwin Harle
Munro, Roy
Murphy, Robert E.
*Murphy, William
*Murray, Donald
Murray, Ian G. and William C.
Mutch, F. L.
*Mutch, George
Mutch, J. N.
Mutch, Robert Lind
Muzylowski, John
*Muzylowski, Nick
*Nadin, Richard
*Nankivell, W. E.
Nelson, Andrew S.
*Neufeld, Frank
*Nevraumont, Felix and Jeanne
Nichols, A. E.
Nicholson, Donald
*Nicholson, John
Nicholson, Kenneth
Nicholson, Murdoch
*Norton, Russell J.
Nykoliation, A. M.
*Oak Lake Farming and Ranching
    Association
O'Callaghan, Margaret
O'Callaghan, W. T.
Olive, J W. A.
Olynyk, John S.
*Olynyk, Peter B.
Paddock, Walter S.
Paramor, Edwin E. and Ardyth N.
Partridge, Edmund A.
Patterson, James T.
*Pavlick, Frank
Pearn, Viola
Penner, Cornelius
*Penner, David D.
*Penner, Henry
*Perrin, John D.
Peterson, Larry and Ruth
Peterson, Leo
*Phillips, B.
*Phillips, Frank
Phillips, John
Phillips, S. H. and Freda
Pierce, Charles
*Pigg, Charles H.
*Plaisier, Rene A. and Mary E.
Plett, John K. and Ellen
Plum Lake Shooting Club
Podlaski, Joseph
Prairie Farm Rehabilitation
    Administration Community
    Pasture
Pringle, Stuart C.
Province of Manitoba
Puhach, N.
*Quintaine, Peter
Rahnefeld, Gunther W. and Patricia A.
*Ralston, R. H.
Rasmussen, Ralph N.

Redpath, Eric P.
Redpath, William E.
*Reekie, John R.
*Reid, John J.
*Reid, T. W.
Reimer, Cornelius and Nettie
Reykdal, David
Reykdal, Steven W.
Reynolds, John
Reynolds, Kenneth
Rice, Garry B. and Corinne M.
*Riehl, Annie M.
Riehl, William John
Riley, Conrad S.
Robertson, Beverley P.
Robertson, Douglas R.
Robertson, Judith Ann
*Robertson, Leonard S.
Robertson, Patricia
*Robinson, J. B.
Robinson, William M.
*Robson, Alonza W.
Rogers, George F.
Rolston, R. H.
Rolston, W. A.
Romand Catholic Archpiscopal
*Roper, Benjamin
Rousson, Cleophus
Routledge, Elgin Roy
Routledge, Glen M.
Rowland, Percy R. and Elma J.
Rural Municipality of Ellice
Rural Municipality of Lakeview
Rural Municipality of Lansdowne
Rural Municipality of Lorne
Rural Municipality of Louise
Rural Municipality of Sifton
Rural Municipality of Siglunes
Rural Municipality of Silver Creek
Rural Municipality of Thompson
Rural Municipality of Wallace
Rural Municipality of Westbourne
Ryan, Carman
*Sadler, Leonard A.
St. Germain, Maurice and Carol
Sander, G. A. C.
Sawatzky, Peter
Sawatsky, Ronald V.
Sayer, James David
Scheer, Forrest W. and Virginia M.
Scheirlinck, George and Margaret
*Scheppner, Hans
*Schott, Albert
*Schroedter, Ernest and Mathile
Schroedter, Peter and Linda
Schultz, Henry P.
*Schultz, Peter P.
Seven Sisters Falls Wildlife
    Association Inc.
Shatford, Ralph W.
*Shaw, Edmund G.
Shaw, George L. V.
Shingfield, Evelyn
Short, Gerald L.
Shwaluk, William John
Siemens, Albert
Sigfusson, Gisli J.
Sigurdson, Gudjon M.
Sigurdson, John
*Skanderbeg, John S.

Skardal, Norman S.
*Skelton, David D.
Skelton, Ethel S.
Skinner, John Wendell
Skinner, Margaret A.
*Skinner, R. L.
Smith, Albert Alex
*Smith, Aubrey
*Smith, Colin
Smith, Kenneth
*Somerfield, T.
Sopchuk, William
South Central Development Ltd.
Southam, Ewart L.
Speelman, George Leroy
Spence, Allan C.
Spence, Conrad
Spence, Edward
Spraggs, William John
Stefanishyn, Jackie
Stefanishyn, Peter
Stefanyshen, William and Julia
Stobbe, Eldon A.
Stone, Keith
Stott, John Henry
Stowe, R. T.
Stowe, George A.
Stowe, J. E. and Alma
Stowe, Mabel
*Strachan, Thomas
Strachan, Garth M.
Strain, Ivan E. J. and Roberta G.
Studer, Henry W.
Studer, Melbourne S.
Sturrock, James Neil
Suski, Arnold and Treasure
*Taylor, Cecil J.
*Tegelberg, F.
Templeton, Harvey E. and Muriel I.
*Thomson, Dougal
*Thomson, M. J.
*Todd, George L.
*Tokaryk, George
Tokaryk, John and Teenie
Tokaryk, Milton
Toronto General Trust Corp.
Torry, Alex
Town of Selkirk
*Townsend, John O.
Tschetter, John
Turnbull, Sam F.
Van Damme, Lawrence G. J.
Van Damme, Maurice
*Van De Walle, J.
Van De Walle, Robert V.
Voden, Albert J.
Vodon, Hubert
Wakaluk, Frederick (Estate)
*Wakaluk, Tekla
*Walker, Charles
Walker, Leonard
Wallace, Roberta
Wallace, William
Wallace, William
Waller, Dorothy I.
*Waller, G. E.
*Wanlin, Emil
Ward, Hugh
Wasurchak, Michael and Elizabeth
Watson, William and Annie (Estate)

Watt, Hugh
Watters, Francis J.
*Weddall, Charles
Westwood, Kathleen A.
*Westwood, Malcolm A.
*Wheeler, H.
*Whiteside, Allan J.
Whiteside, Frank A.
Whiteside, James
*Whiteside, Robert J.
*Whiteside, William
*Whiting, Robert R. (Estate)
Whitmore, Glen Alvin and Marion
Widdall, Hugh B.
Wiebe, Bernhard
Wiebe, Jacob
*Wightman, Reginald
Wildblood, Robert T.
Wilkinson, Douglas A.
*Williams, Charles G.
*Williams, Earl K.
Williamson, Leslie H.
Wilson, Cecil R.
*Wilson, G.
Wilton, Sidney
Wolaniuk, William
*Wolstenholme, Gilbert
Wood, James Edward
Woods, F. C.
*Woolner, Fred
Wray, Eugene C.
Wright, Herbert C.
Wright, Herbert C.
Wright, Wm. John and Karen Isabella
Young, Mary
Zastre, Andre and Ferne
Zatylny, J. L.
Zatylny, Raymond A.
Zieroth, Arnold

ONTARIO LANDOWNERS
Baker, Glenn
Brant, Chief William J.
Connor, Alan
deBac, E.
DeSoer, Carol and Bernard
Dodds, Don
Gimmer, David
Goldsack, Ron
Good, Peter
Henderson, Gil
Keenan, P. J.
King Haven Farms Ltd.
Lang, Ted
Leslie, Don
Macfarlane, David A.
McCloskey, Terry
McCormick, Don and Doris
McLeod, J.
Metro Toronto Region Conservation
    Authority
Niagara Peninsula Conservation
    Authority
North Grey Region Conservation
    Authority
Northcott, John
Paterson, J. W.
Pletzer, A.
Province of Ontario
Robertson, Peter M.
Scott, John

Scott, Paul
South Lake Simcoe Conservation
  Authority
Spring, James
Steele, W.
Symmes, S. L.
Taylor, Norm
Upper Thames River Conservation
  Authority
Vanderburg, Bryan
Verbeek, Hilda

QUEBEC LANDOWNERS
Audy, Rene
City of Granby
Clement, Marcel
Dionne, Alain
Ferland, Joseph
Harnois, Roland
Le Domaine de L'Isle Aux Oyes Inc.
Letendre, Real
Province of Quebec
Quebec Hydro
Simard, Adolphe
Trottier, Maurice

NEW BRUNSWICK LANDOWNERS
Blacklock, Bruce
Bunker, Art
Bunker, Wendell
Hanson, Robin
Horsley, Percy
Mersereau, Keith
Mersereau, Oscar and Roland
Noble, Frances
Pierce, Fred

Province of New Brunswick
Smith, Gordon Owen
Smith, Lillian C.
Smith, Owen M.
Stennick, Viva
Thulium Farms Ltd.
von Kuntzel, Hugo
Waugh, Fraser E.
Wood, Lee

NOVA SCOTIA LANDOWNERS
Avon Foods Ltd.
Baker, Wylie
Bonnyman & Byers Ltd.
Brownell, Edward
Canard Poultry Ltd.
Davidson, Douglas and Arthur
Eaton, Alfred
Eaton, Gerald
Ells, E. S.
Graves, James
Haliburton, Richard
Hicks, E. C.
Huntley, Carrie
Hurley, Gardner P.
Kerr, Greg
Lamy, A. R.
Langille, Donald
Lees, John G.
Lynds, Harold E.
MacKay, James A.
MacKay, J. Albert
Manning, Albert
Muller, Dieter

Murphy, John
Murray, C. Vernon
Oostrum, Peter Van
Pace, Eldon
Patriquin, Otis
Patterson, Dennis
Peel, R. T.
Pierce, Fred
Province of Nova Scotia
Robbins, Clyde
Rodgers, George
Schroeder, Dietrich
Scott Farms Ltd.
Scott Paper Company
Smith, J. A.
Smith, Leon
Smith, Wendall
Snell, Norman
Taylor, Alberta
Trenholm, Ron
Ward, Bernard

PRINCE EDWARD ISLAND LANDOWNERS
Beagan, Alvin
Beagan, Ernest
Beagan, Michael
Brazel, Lewis
Brazel, Melvin
Buell, Alvin
Cann, J. Horace
Carmody, Earl
Caseley, Joseph
Corcoran, Allan

Corcoran, Thomas
Curran, Frank
Docherty, Cyrus
Douglas, Howard
Douglas, Wallace
Doyle, Richard
Driscoll, Fred
Freehan, Lyle
Gill, Gerrard
Gill, Herman
Granger, Laura
Gunn, Sheldon
Gunn, Sterling
Johnson, Allison
Johnston, Lester
L. G. Lawton, Inc.
MacDonald, Wilson
MacLeod, Vernon
McIsaac, Leo
Mallett, Walter
Myers, Arthur
Ployer, George A. and John A.
Power, Charles
Power, Frank
Province of Prince Edward Island
Simmons, Georgia
Smith, A.
Stavert, Donald
Stewart, Norman F.
Trainor, Elmer
Weavers, Margaret
Wood, David
Wood, Wallace

PRINTED IN CANADA